OF THE CITY OF
GEORGIA 1871
ALEXANDER ST
HARRIS
ALABAMA ST
FRASER
TERRY
MARTIN ST
McDONOUGH
E N CALHOUN
BUTLER ST
FILLMORE
HILL ST
FOSTER
JENKINS
D1564750
DRAWN & PUBLISHED BY A. RUGER, ST LOUIS
I Air Line
K Planning Mills
L Foundries
M Rolling Mill, Iron Work
N Grist Mills, Flouring Mills
O Brewery
CHURCHES.
11 3d Baptist
12 Christian
13 Episcopal
14 1st Methodist South
15 2d Methodist
16 Methodist
17 Paynes Chapel
18 Evans Chapel
19 1st Presbyterian 20 Central
21 R.Catholic 22 Col Baptist
23 Col Methodist
Division of Maps
FEB 28 1941

#  *Strangers Within the Gate City* 

*Assemble the people, the men and women and the little ones, and the stranger that is within thy gates . . .* DEUTERONOMY 31:12

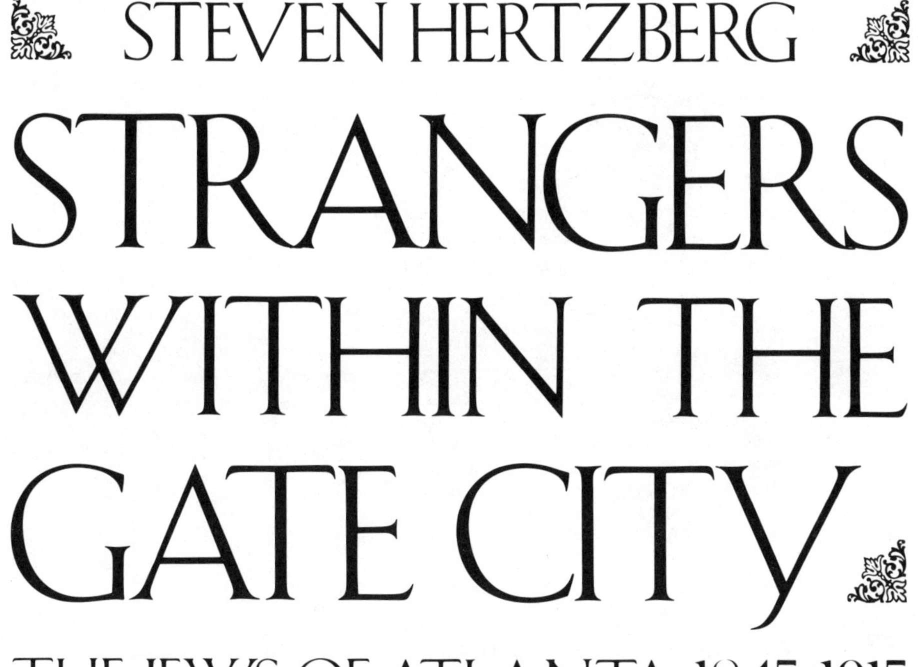


THE JEWS OF ATLANTA · 1845-1915

*The Jewish Publication Society of America*

*Philadelphia 5738–1978*

*ISBN 0-8276-0102-6*
*Library of Congress catalog card number 78-1167*
*Manufactured in the United States of America*

*Designed by Adrianne Onderdonk Dudden*

*Photographs reproduced courtesy of*
*the Atlanta Historical Society*

*To my parents*
*and to the memory of my grandparents*

# *Contents*

# *Figures*

FIGURE

# Tables

TABLE

# *Strangers Within the Gate City*

# Introduction

This study describes and analyzes the Jewish experience in a major American city during the seven decades prior to the outbreak of World War I and the disruption of mass immigration. Belonging to the genre of local Jewish history, it differs from most other works of its kind in subject, conceptualization, and methodology.

No section of the United States has received less attention from students of American Jewry than the South, and the reason is not difficult to fathom. Southern Jews have always been small in numbers, scattered, and usually distant from the major centers of American Jewish life. Consequently, they have remained on the fringe of the collective Jewish consciousness. Although approximately half of the 2,700 Jews in the United States in 1820 lived below the Mason-Dixon line, this proportion declined markedly in the face of changing patterns of immigration, settlement, and economic development. Only 14 percent of American Jews resided in the South in 1878, 5 percent in 1907, and 7 percent in 1968. And while the number of southern Jews increased during these nine decades from 32,000 to 394,000, their proportion of the region's population rose from only 0.2 to 0.7 percent.[1] They were, as one writer recently observed, "the provincials, the Jews of the periphery . . . out there on the rim where it didn't count—for the great Jewish drama in America was being played elsewhere."[2]

If their small numbers and distance from the major Jewish population centers account for southern Jewry's having been neglected by historians, this does not make their experience any less dramatic or interesting. Merchants in a region dominated by an agrarian ideal, religious dissenters in a Christ-haunted land, venerators of learning in a society plagued by illiteracy, victims of violence and religious prejudice who took sanctuary in a section characterized by a militant spirit and racial oppression, and foreigners in a hotbed of xenophobia, they lived the drama of isolation, accommodation, and mobility. Understanding this experience is an essential prerequisite for a comprehensive historical synthesis of Jewish life in America.

Ideally, local history should provide the specifics from which we can generalize national tendencies and also furnish the basis for comparing patterns of demography, institutional life, civic involvement, economic achievement, social structure, migration, religio-ethnic identity, and intergroup relations. However, American Jewish local history has rarely been written with these purposes in mind. Much of the responsibility for this shortcoming may be attributed to the legacy of the men who founded the American Jewish Historical Society in 1892. Like their Irish and black contemporaries, the concerned rabbis and lay leaders who first advocated the exploration of the American Jewish past did so in reaction to the growing body of historical and popular literature which stressed the Anglo-Saxon roots of American civilization and the implicit foreignness of Jews and other "lesser breeds." Accordingly, the well-intentioned amateurs who organized the AJHS regarded history as a weapon for self-respect and social advancement. They believed that the investigator's job was to document the respectability of American Jewry by demonstrating its ancient origins and manifold contributions and thereby strengthen the Jewish claim to full enjoyment of American citizenship. Fortunately, in the three decades since the end of World War II, the decline of anti-Semitism, the coming of age of a third generation secure in its dual heritage, the entrance of unparalleled numbers of Jews into academia, and, more recently, the growing interest in ethnicity have resulted in the professionalization of American Jewish historiography.[3]

While the quality of local history benefited from this professionalization, on the whole, the genre has not kept pace with accomplishments in the areas of American Jewish cultural, intellectual, and political history. Like the earlier studies most local histories continue to be poorly researched and written by dedicated amateur enthusiasts—usually with deep local commitments—who are intent upon building a good case for their communities. With several noteworthy exceptions, the prevailing approach remains filio-pietistic, biographical, impressionistic, antiquarian, and anecdotal with a tendency to include as many names as possible and ignore the unseemly aspects of communal life and the shady sides of individuals. Frequently written under local sponsorship, very few of the professionally authored volumes are characterized by the objectivity, not to mention the analytical rigor and scope, of Josef Barton's examination of Cleveland's Italians, Rumanians, and Slovaks, Kenneth Kusmer's work on that city's blacks, or Oscar Handlin's classic study of Boston's immigrants.[4] Reflecting the nature of the narrative sources and the backgrounds of their authors, even the better local histories concentrate unduly on institutional—especially congregational—development and on the activities of the communal elite.[5] Because the sources and methodology of the "new social history" have yet to make a serious impact, we still know very little about the Jewish socioeconomic structure, the parameters of mobility, and the ways in which Jews differed from and interacted with their gentile neighbors.[6]

The preceding observations apply even more strongly to research on southern communities. Although the period prior to 1865 has been accorded relatively ample treatment, and a few studies have investigated developments since 1950, the nine decades between the downfall of the Confederacy and the onset of the desegregation crisis remain virtually untouched. While this may reflect the peculiarly southern emphasis on the time "befo' de war" and the consequent desire of Jews to link themselves with this more romantic epoch, the omission is unfortunate since it was not until the postwar period of mass immigration that large numbers of Jews first settled in the South.[7]

The first studies of Jewish life in the South were published during the years between the founding of the AJHS and the outbreak of World War II. Biographical in orientation, apologetic in tone, and written primarily by amateurs, these works focused largely on the period before Appomattox and, though crammed with data, lacked organization and analysis.[8] The preference for the hoary past was retained during the next three decades, but the quality of historical scholarship improved markedly and was complemented by a growing sociological literature.[9]

The publication in 1968 of Leonard Dinnerstein's trenchant analysis of the Leo Frank case signaled the coming of age for southern Jewish historiography. Dinnerstein followed this case study with two insightful articles exploring the ambivalent position of the Jew in southern society and with a valuable collection of readings. Meanwhile, histories of Mobile, New Orleans, Birmingham, and Baltimore Jewry made their appearance.[10] Since 1973 an entire issue of the *American Jewish Historical Quarterly* and a well-attended national conference have been devoted to the history of Southern Jewry, and we have seen a best-selling "personal history" of Jews in the South, an anecdotal account of the region's influential Jews, and two well-received novels.[11] The elevation of Jimmy Carter to the presidency is certain to focus still greater attention on the subject.

Despite the recent growth of interest, much remains to be written before the Jewish experience in the South can be adequately understood. This history of Atlanta Jewry is intended as a contribution toward that end. While such traditional concerns as communal origins, individual accomplishments, institutional developments, and internal dynamics are discussed in detail, an equal emphasis is placed on exploring matters which have received little or no attention in even the better local histories: the parameters of economic and geographic mobility, the socioeconomic and demographic structure, relations between Jews and blacks, and the manner in which Jews were perceived and treated by native white Gentiles.

The investigation of these topics is made possible in part through utilization of sources and techniques which have yet to gain wide acceptance among students of the American Jewish past. In addition to using such traditional sources as the local press, institutional records, and personal papers, other materials such as tax digests, census schedules, death certificates, city directories, interment records, and naturalization documents were carefully mined to extract information on nearly every Jew who resided in Atlanta in 1870, 1880, and 1896 (1,934 persons), plus hundreds of those who arrived between 1896 and 1915.* This data was then fed into a computer to facilitate analysis. Consequently, this history not only focuses on previously neglected issues and on the inarticulate masses as well as the elite, but also presents many of its findings in quantitative terms that will permit comparison with those of future studies.

Finally, a few words concerning my choice of subject and chronological limits. Because the greatest dearth of literature on southern

*This compiled data is not cited in footnotes. For a discussion of the sources and techniques used to identify Jews and their characteristics, see appendix 1, page 225.

Jewry is for the half century between Lee's surrender at Appomattox and the outbreak of the First World War, I decided to focus primarily on this period. Atlanta is an excellent setting for such a study. Incorporated in 1843, Atlanta was devastated by the Civil War only to be resurrected in 1865 and rapidly emerge as a major regional center and embodiment of the New South Creed. Although Jews had first settled there in 1845, not until after the war did they arrive in large numbers, and by 1915 the Gate City contained one of the three largest Jewish communities in the South.[12]

Moreover, Atlanta provides an interesting case study for the changing status of southern Jews. The half century following the Civil War began with Jewish newcomers being hailed as harbingers of commercial progress and opportunity, and ended with the Leo Frank case—a virulent outbreak of anti-Semitism culminating in the lynching of a Jewish factory superintendent who had been wrongfully convicted of murdering a gentile girl.

My interest in the Jews of Atlanta began with a research paper for John Hope Franklin's New South seminar, and later blossomed into a doctoral dissertation directed by Neil Harris. Both men influenced my thinking in more ways than they will recognize.

Except for six frenetic months "on the road," this study was researched and written at the University of Chicago, approximately eight hundred miles from Atlanta's rolling hills and bountiful archives. To the extent that the problems of distance and the hardships of "the life of the mind" were overcome, I owe a special debt of thanks to the staff of the university's Regenstein Library. I also gratefully acknowledge the assistance of M. C. Gettinger of the Atlanta Jewish Welfare Federation, who provided hospitality and useful advice in large measure; Franklin M. Garrett and Richard T. Eltzroth of the Atlanta Historical Society, who generously shared their extensive knowledge of a city I too have come to love; Richard Hopkins of Ohio State University, who patiently guided me through some of the muddy waters of quantitative analysis; the late Rabbi Philip Alstat of the Jewish Theological Seminary in New York City, who kindly translated two Yiddish memoirs into English; and the staffs of the American Jewish Historical Society, the American Jewish Archives, the Georgia Department of Archives and History, and the Federal Records Center at East Point, Georgia. Parts of chapter six previously appeared in the *YIVO Annual of Jewish Social Science* and the *American Jewish Historical Quarterly* and are used here with permission of the publishers.

Finally, I wish to thank my parents, whose support, insight, and encouragement have been invaluable in so many ways beyond the writing of this book.

# 1

## *The Pioneers*

Founded in an area poor in natural resources and distant from the nearest navigable waterway, Atlanta was a creation of the railroads, an incidental by-product of Georgia's search for an inexpensive means to import the foodstuffs of the West and transport to market cotton produced in the interior. As early as 1826, plans were made to establish a statewide transportation network. However, the inauguration of the system was delayed by the occupation of northwest Georgia until 1838 by the Cherokee Nation, the discovery of a series of ridges which made a projected canal infeasible, and bitter commercial rivalry between both the interior market towns of Macon and Augusta and the seaports of Savannah, Brunswick, and Darian.[1]

In 1833 the Central Railroad of Georgia, the Georgia Railroad, and the Monroe Railroad were chartered. Controlled respectively by Savannah, Augusta, and Macon, these rival roads were intended to bring cotton from the interior to the urban markets and thereby enrich their parent communities. While they would have alleviated one of the state's transportation problems, they could not fulfill the more pressing need for cheap western foodstuffs. Only the incorporation a year later of two out-of-state railroads whose operation would have effectively cut off Georgia's seacoast from western commerce convinced the three Georgia railroads that they should cooperate. They agreed in 1836 that if the State of Georgia were to tap the western trade by constructing at its own expense a railroad from Ross's Landing (the present site of Chattanooga) on the Tennessee River to some point on the south bank of the Chattahoochee River in De Kalb County, the Monroe and the Georgia railroads would extend branches to the southern terminus of the state road. The Georgia General Assembly promptly accepted the offer and chartered the Western and Atlantic Railroad. It was soon determined that the terrain on the south bank of the Chattahoochee was unsuitable for the construction of branch roads and, with legislative authorization, the projected terminus was moved six miles to the southeast where a confluence of ridges offered unobstructed paths to the northwest, southwest, and the east.[2]

The future site of Atlanta was virgin wilderness in 1836. One farmer eked out a meager living nearby and a tavern was located two and a half miles to the southwest, but the nearest incorporated spot was the town of Decatur, six miles to the east. Almost immediately after the Western and Atlantic was chartered, several people moved to the terminus hoping to reap real estate and commercial benefits. But the nationwide depression which began in 1837 slowed the progress of the railroad builders, and during the next few years the population of the settlement fluctuated markedly. The Georgia Railroad, which originated in Augusta, finally reached the terminus in 1845. The following year the Macon and Western (previously, the Monroe Railroad) arrived providing connections with Macon and Savannah, and in 1850 the first train ran on the Western and Atlantic tracks from the terminus to Chattanooga. One final antebellum line, the Atlanta and West Point Railroad, was completed in 1854 and extended as far as the Alabama border.[3] (See fig. 1.)

In 1843 the terminus was incorporated as the town of Marthasville and in 1845 was renamed Atlanta, partly because railroad agents had difficulty fitting "Marthasville" on one ticket. Eight years later Atlanta became the seat of newly created Fulton County. As Atlanta grew from a railroad terminus to a railroad junction to a railroad center, her population increased from approximately 20 families in 1845, to 300 to 500 persons in 1847, 2,572 in 1850, 6,025 in 1854, and 9,554 in 1860. The increase in trade was equally dramatic as the value of goods sold by local merchants rose from $200,000 in 1849 to over $1,000,000 in 1851 and to approximately $3,000,000 in 1859. Where there were but a handful of stores in 1845, there were 57—"exclusive of drinking saloons"—in 1854 and nearly 200 in 1860. Despite this remarkable growth, probably only the most confirmed city booster might have guessed that fifty years and ten railroads later Atlanta would have a population of 150,000 and be the third largest city in the South.[4]

The railroad builders also failed to anticipate Atlanta's growth for the era of great interior cities was just beginning in the 1840s. Indeed, the Western and Atlantic's chief engineer predicted in 1837 that the "terminus will be a good place for one tavern, a blacksmith shop, a grocery store; and nothing else." The early policies of the railroads toward the new town reflected their expectations of its future. The location of the terminus had not been chosen for its suitability as a town site, and the heavily wooded hilly terrain made clearing and street grading difficult. The tracks of the entering railroads divided the town at its center into three sections, and the railroad companies resisted the construction of viaducts and the extension of streets. More significantly, because Atlanta was distant from any water route which might have offered competition to the railroads, she was subjected to freight discrimination, a serious problem since the low agricultural productivity of the surrounding countryside made her heavily dependent upon western trade. Furthermore, passenger trains mostly passed through the city at night, and few stopped long enough to give their riders time to patronize local emporiums. Savannah, Macon, and Augusta had each hoped to be the major beneficiary of the improved railroad network, and they were unwilling to brook competition from an upstart rival. Therefore, while Atlanta's location as the "Gate City" on the border of two diverse agricultural regions and at the vortex of a vast railroad system made her the main distributing point for foodstuffs throughout the eastern cotton belt and gave her an important share of the east-west transportation of cotton and manufactured goods, the city's future remained uncertain.[5]

Local promoters responded to the challenge with boundless optimism, shameless self-advertisement, and aggressive trading practices—what became known as the "Atlanta Spirit." In 1847 and again in 1854 they brashly attempted to wrest the state capital from Milledgeville. Blessed with low rent and cheap clerical help, but lacking sufficient capital to extend credit, her fledgling merchants sold on a strictly cash basis which fortuitously enabled them to offer goods at lower prices than could be obtained in more established cities where credit tended to drive up costs. The merchants also cemented a trade alliance with the small farmers in the mountainous and Piedmont areas of Georgia and neighboring states who transported their produce to Atlanta by wagon and availed themselves of the town's low-priced stores, public market, and recreational facilities. In 1850 the annual fairs of the Southern Central Agricultural Society were transferred to Atlanta and thereafter promoted

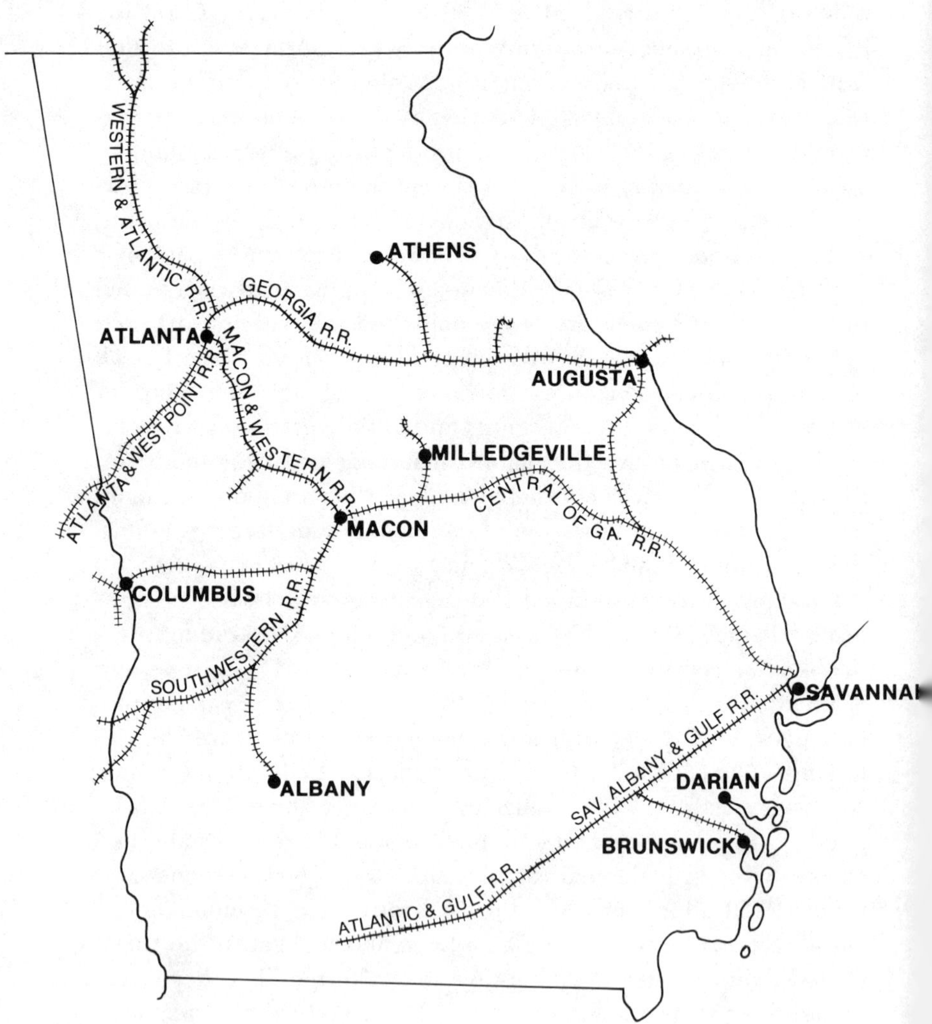


FIGURE 1. *The Railroads of Georgia, 1861.*

both the resources of northwest Georgia and the town's reputation as a trading center. Finally, to combat freight discrimination and widen markets, local boosters campaigned for two new railroads that would be more responsive to local interests and persuaded the city council to purchase $300,000 worth of stock.[6]

While the point can easily be overstated, Atlanta's growth during the antebellum period and the spirit of enterprise which nurtured it were closely related to the character of her population. Native southerners, drawn in large part from the upper Piedmont and mountainous areas of Georgia and the Carolinas, accounted for 92 percent of the white population in 1850. Most were ambitious men of humble origin whose prospects for success as farmers had been circumscribed by the plantation economy. Confronted with the opportunities created by the railroads, they approached the task of city building with what one early resident likened to "the fire and enthusiasm . . . of those who . . . turned their faces toward the California wilds in search of gold."[7]

The debilitating institution of Negro slavery had a relatively minor effect upon the town's commercial life. Slaves never accounted for more than 20 percent of the antebellum population, which led one observer from New York to remark approvingly that "white men black their own shoes, and dust their own clothes, as independently as in the north." Slightly less than 4 percent of the white residents in 1850 were from the free states, but several of these and other northerners who arrived during the next decade assumed prominent positions in the town's economic life. Foreigners, mostly former Irish railroad laborers and a sprinkling of German merchants and mechanics, constituted 4 percent of the white population in 1850 and perhaps as much as 8 percent in 1860. Finally, as early as the 1840s Atlanta contained an additional element which was destined to contribute significantly to her development: Jews.[8]

Although it is likely that many Atlantans had never seen a Jew prior to settling in the community, Jews had resided in the South since the seventeenth century, and a party of 42 Jews landed at Savannah in July 1733, just five months after the arrival of Georgia's first colonists. At the time of the first federal census in 1790, nearly half of the approximately 1,300 to 1,500 Jews in the United States lived below the Mason-Dixon line, and Charleston, with an estimated 200

Jewish inhabitants, sheltered the second largest Jewish community in the country.[9]

The Jewish population of the South soon exceeded that of the North. In 1820, of the 2,650 to 2,750 Jews in the United States, 2,150 lived in six cities. Charleston led the nation with 700 Jews, followed by New York, 550; Philadelphia, 450; Richmond, 200; Baltimore, 150; and Savannah, 100. Significantly, while Jews constituted only 0.5 percent of New York's white population and 0.4 percent of Philadelphia's, they accounted for 5 percent of Charleston's, 3 percent of Richmond's, and 3 percent of Savannah's. Nationally, somewhat more than half of the Jewish heads of families were foreign-born although nearly all had lived in the United States for several decades. England, Germany, and Holland had supplied most of the Jewish immigrants, and Ashkenazim—Jews of Central European descent—had for nearly a century outnumbered Sephardim, those of Iberian descent. Regardless of their origin, nearly all of the Jewish immigrants who settled in America prior to the 1820s had come as individuals or as isolated families whose decision to emigrate had been based on personal rather than communal considerations. The era of mass immigration which was about to begin would radically alter the characteristics of the American Jewish community.[10]

Between the mid-1820s and the start of the American Civil War, more than 100,000 Jews emigrated to the United States, almost all of them from the German-speaking lands of Central Europe. The reasons for this mass emigration were primarily economic. Mostly petty merchants and traders, Jews found it increasingly difficult to earn a livelihood, as the peasants with whom they customarily dealt abandoned or were ejected from their ancestral lands. As the Industrial Revolution rendered obsolete previously remunerative handicrafts, Jewish artisans found themselves in similar straits. Furthermore, the effects of overpopulation plagued Jew and Gentile alike.[11]

Aggravating the effects of these economic vicissitudes was the growth of political reaction after the signing of the Treaty of Vienna in 1815. Anti-Jewish riots in Wurzburg, Bamberg, Frankfurt, and the Hanseatic cities, the rise of exclusivistic brands of German and Slavic nationalism, and the imposition of discriminatory taxes in several German principalities deepened the insecurity of an impoverished Jewish population. Conditions were especially severe in economically depressed Bavaria. There, members of the Diet demanded that the Jews be banished to America, and because Bavarian law restricted the number of Jews in each district, a young Jewish man had little hope of marrying within his district or becoming a permanent resident.[12]

Meanwhile, the influence of the Enlightenment and the short-lived Emancipation under Napoleonic rule generated a desire for improvement and, by weakening the bonds of communal authority, made it easier for Jews to detach themselves from the towns and villages of their birth. Especially after the abortive Revolutions of 1848 disappointed those who hoped for a democratic Germany and an early lifting of anti-Jewish disabilities, tens of thousands of Jews succumbed to the lure of America.[13]

As a consequence of this emigration, the estimated Jewish population of America increased from less than 3,000 in 1820, to 15,000 in 1840, 50,000 in 1850, and 150,000 in 1860.[14] The newcomers arrived in the United States during a period of great economic and territorial growth. Generally lacking both capital and marketable skills, most of them became peddlers—a familiar vocation for many—and in this capacity followed the routes of continental expansion. With hard work and good fortune the basket, trunk, or pack peddler might acquire the means to purchase a wagon and team and could look forward to settling down and opening a store.[15]

For coincidental, economic, and temperamental reasons, the northern and midwestern states attracted more Jewish immigrants than did those in the South. The large majority landed at northern ports from which the principal routes of land and canal transportation extended westward. The North and West also contained sizeable numbers of German settlers with whom the newly arrived Jew could easily communicate and trade. Furthermore, accustomed for centuries to the fellowship and institutional sustenance provided by town and village life, a Jewish peddler seeking a place to settle was less apt to choose the overwhelmingly rural South. The prevalence of slavery in the South may have also affected Jewish settlement patterns. The spread of free soil and abolitionist doctrines, the emancipation of the slaves in the North and in the British Empire, and the growth of liberal thought in Germany, all made the South's "peculiar institution" appear increasingly peculiar after 1830 and no doubt influenced Jewish perceptions of the region. Besides, free men rather than slaves were more likely to provide a better market for his dry goods and "Yankee notions," and as sectional tensions increased, the itinerant foreigner was apt to be mistaken for an abolitionist agent.[16]

However, many Jews did land at southern ports, were unperturbed by the existence of slavery, willingly risked the hardships of isolation, and assessed favorably the region's commercial potentiality. The opening of the Southwest to cotton and sugar cultivation created new business opportunities for those willing to service the scattered population, and even in the more settled areas agrarian biases limited the size of the native merchant class. Into this inviting vacuum stepped the Jewish peddler and storekeeper.[17]

Although the available estimates are crude, in 1860 perhaps a quarter of the 150,000 American Jews resided in the slave states.[18] In 1820 Richmond, Charleston, and Savannah were the only southern cities with synagogues. By the eve of the Civil War Jewish congregations had been founded in twenty-four additional southern communities: Mobile and Montgomery, Alabama; Augusta, Columbus, and Macon, Georgia; Louisville, Kentucky; New Orleans, Shreveport, and Plaquemine, Louisiana; Baltimore and Cumberland, Maryland; Jackson, Port Gibson, Vicksburg, and Natchez, Mississippi; St. Louis and St. Joseph, Missouri; Columbia, South Carolina; Memphis, Nashville, and Knoxville, Tennessee; Houston, Texas; and Norfolk and Petersburg, Virginia. Isolated Jewish storekeepers were scattered in hundreds of other southern communities, and at least nine synagogueless towns had Jewish cemeteries or benevolent associations. One of these towns was Atlanta.[19]

The Jews who settled in Atlanta during the 1840s were ambitious and independent men who shared the restlessness that characterized their age. Jacob Haas and Henry Levi were the town's first Jews. Born in Hamn, Hessendarmstadt in 1803, Haas and his wife Jeanetta came to America in 1842. After peddling for three years in and around Philadelphia, he and Henry Levi, a twenty-three-year-old bachelor from Frankfurt am Main, decided to go south and open a store. Early in 1845 they established a dry-goods business in Decatur, six miles east of Marthasville and, encouraged by the completion of the Georgia Railroad, moved to the new town later that year. Their general merchandise business prospered, but in 1850 Levi was stricken with gold fever, withdrew from the partnership, and departed for California. The following year Haas left his business in the hands of another Jew and retired to Philadelphia where he died in 1855.[20]

Herman Haas, two years younger than his brother Jacob, emigrated to America in 1845 and peddled for two years in Pennsylvania and Ohio before he raised enough money to send for his wife Wilhelmina and their four children. He found rooms for them in Philadelphia and returned to the road, sometimes traveling as far west as Indiana. In 1848 he brought his family to Indiana and a year later moved to Atlanta, where a partnership had been arranged for him with Henry Levi's younger brother Herman. The journey south by covered wagon was made in the company of relatives who planned to settle in Marietta, twenty-two miles north of Atlanta. During their four weeks on the road they slept under a roof only once and rested only two days; the first time because of a sick horse, and the second to observe Yom Kippur. "The cholera was prevailling [*sic*]," recalled Haas's son Aaron, and "we passed many deserted houses, especially in Kentucky." The partnership with Herman Levi was short lived. Levi followed his brother to California in 1850, and Haas departed for Newnan, forty miles to the southeast, which he felt offered better opportunities than Atlanta. After seven years in the small Georgia town he moved to Philadelphia, but returned to Newnan on the eve of the war and to Atlanta at the war's end.[21]

Aaron Alexander was the only native-born Jew among Atlanta's male antebellum pioneers. Born in Charleston in 1812, the grandson of a Revolutionary War officer and lay rabbi of Sephardic descent, Alexander married Sarah Moses in 1836 and settled first in Vicksburg, Mississippi and then in Athens, Georgia before he came to Atlanta in 1848. After a short while as a railroad engineer he opened the town's first drugstore. In 1859 Alexander moved to Philadelphia where he failed in business and was briefly imprisoned for debt. Upon his release he settled in Columbus, Georgia, where he spent the war years and returned to Atlanta in 1865.[22]

Moses Sternberger, Simon Frankfort, and Adolph J. Brady also settled in Atlanta during the 1840s. Sternberger, who arrived with his wife in 1846 or 1847, operated a large general store until he left for unknown parts sometime before 1850. Frankfort and his wife were both born in England in 1814 and settled in Atlanta in 1847 or 1848. He owned two clothing and dry goods stores before he moved to New York in 1857 to engage in the commission business. Brady was born in Hamburg in 1818 or 1821 and came to the United States in 1842. He went south almost immediately and resided first in Charleston, where he married Alexander's sister-in-law, and then in Athens where he remained until coming to Atlanta in 1849. Brady established a hardware store but moved to New York in 1858 to better supply his business. Like Aaron Alexander and Herman Haas, he returned to Atlanta after the war.[23]

Of the sixteen Jewish adults who settled in Atlanta prior to 1850, only David Mayer and his wife Eliza remained in 1860. Born in Bavaria in 1815 and trained as a dentist, at the age of twenty-four Mayer sailed for New York. Advised upon his arrival that he could earn a good livelihood in the South, Mayer settled first in Tennessee and then in Washington, Georgia. After eight years of pulling teeth, he purchased a stock of goods and set out for Atlanta where he intended to open a store. Despite its two completed railroads, Atlanta in 1847 was an unimpressive sight, and Mayer quickly disposed of his merchandise. However, a year later he returned with a larger stock of goods and a wife newly brought from Germany, and except for a brief absence occasioned by the war, he remained in Atlanta until his death in 1890.[24]

In 1850 Atlanta's 26 Jews made up only 1 percent of the town's 2,572 inhabitants and 17 percent of its foreign-born population. Like the rest of the community, the Jews were relatively young, their average age being seventeen years. While Atlanta's population expanded by 270 percent during the next decade, the number of Jews merely doubled. Like those who preceded them, nearly all of the newcomers were of German descent.[25]

With few exceptions, the Jews engaged in trade and in 1850 owned more than 10 percent of the town's stores. Most of the Jewish merchants—Jacob Haas and Henry Levi, Herman Haas and Herman Levi, Simon Frankfort, David Mayer, and later in the decade, Bernard Brown, Morris Lazaron, Marks Greenbaum, Isaac Greenbaum, and M. Oppenheimer—specialized in clothing and dry goods. M. Wittgenstein was a dealer and importer of wines and liquors. Aaron Alexander's drugstore at the "Sign of the Negro and the Mortar" carried a wide assortment of medical and dental supplies, paints, oils, brushes, window glass, wines, liquors, and perfume. "Here," observed a visitor in 1854, "country merchants and physicians can replenish their stocks at New York prices." Alexander also brought the first carload of ice to Atlanta and opened the town's first soda fountain. The hardware firm of Adolph J. Brady and Solomon Solomon sold paints, oils, carriage trimmings, mill irons, mechanic's tools, agricultural implements, and groceries, and was also the local agency for the Bank of the State of Georgia. Only one Jewish woman, "fashionable milliner" Mrs. A. Isaacs, was employed outside the home. In addition to bonnets, embroideries, corsets, hosiery, and cosmetics, she sold "T. A. Wright's Celebrated Hair Tonic, an infallible preventive for the loss of Hair and a certain restorative . . . in cases of baldness." Like other Jewish merchants, she sold both wholesale and retail.[26]

Most of Atlanta's stores, including those owned by Jews, were located on Whitehall Street between Mitchell Street and the railroad. Like other Atlanta merchants, the Jews usually made periodic buying trips to New York, Philadelphia, and Baltimore since they preferred to deal directly with northern suppliers rather than patronize expensive middlemen in Charleston and Savannah. To obviate the necessity for such trips and to supply their Atlanta partners better, the Greenbaums and Brady moved north during the fifties. While some Jewish businessmen may have failed, others were remarkably successful, for in 1862 David Mayer's local assets were valued at $59,150, M. Saloshin's at $33,000, M. Wittgenstein's at $25,750, and A. Hirshberg's at $13,000.[27]

In contrast to the high degree of residential clustering that would characterize the postwar Jewish community, no such tendency was evident during the 1850s. At the beginning of the decade the Haas brothers resided next to each other, probably above or near their Whitehall Street stores. In another part of town, only a few houses separated Mayer and Frankfort, and on Peachtree Street, between Cain and Harris streets, Alexander and Brady occupied adjoining dwellings. The neighbors of Alexander, Brady, Mayer, and Frankfort were mostly fellow merchants, while those of the Haases were mainly skilled and semiskilled workers. Because living space was at a premium during the early years and wages were low, gentile clerks boarded in the homes of their Jewish employers. Ten years later, only the Mayer, Brown, and Lazaron families had their own homes: Mayer probably near his Whitehall Street store, and Brown and Lazaron northeast of the passenger terminal. The other five Jewish families roomed in as many hotels and boarding houses north and south of the terminal.[28] (See fig. 2.)

Despite the absence of free public education for all but the indigent, most of the Jewish boys between the ages of six and sixteen were enrolled in the town's private academies. In 1847 a local schoolmaster observed: "I get along fine with my scholars. . . . Herman Levi, a little German Jew is one, and I am teaching him English by giving him a German fable to translate into American words. I shall be improved in my German by this practice also." Herman was somewhat more worldly than his fellow pupils; while they brought their teacher apples, he gave cigars. Aaron Alexander and Herman Haas both sent their sons north to complete their education, but other Jews apparently did not.[29]

In the absence of sufficient empirical evidence, it is difficult to ascertain how the early Jewish pioneers were regarded by the general community. The nativist American Party had many followers in Georgia, and in nearby Cassville, a Know-Nothing minister verbally assaulted banker August Belmont and diplomat Pierre Soulé, "who not alone are Foreigners but foreign circumcised not-shaving and rag-trading Jews."[30] In 1857 Benjamin Hill, the party's candidate for governor, allegedly charged that unrestricted immigration would jeopardize slavery, desecrate the Sabbath, lead to godlessness and eventually make the Jew as good as the Gentile—even better if he had plenty of money.[31] That same year the Southern Mutual Insurance Company in Athens instructed its agents not to issue policies to persons of "bad or doubtful reputation," specifically, "Jews without real estate property." Though similar expressions of Judaeophobia may have manifested themselves in Atlanta, it is reasonable to assume that the tiny, unobtrusive, orderly, and enterprising Jewish population was welcomed by community leaders who recognized the contribution it could make to city building. In any case, the religious bigotry of the southern Know-Nothings was directed almost entirely against Catholicism, and the Southern Mutual Insurance Company's Atlanta agent, Adolph J. Brady, was probably disinclined to discriminate against his fellow Jews.[32]

A more direct indication of the acceptance of Jews by Gentiles was their active participation in local Masonry. Fraternal affiliation was taken seriously in antebellum Atlanta, and its importance was magnified by the limited availability of socially sanctioned recreational alternatives. In 1857 David Mayer and Simon Frankfort became founding members of Atlanta's second Masonic lodge, Fulton Lodge No. 216. Luther J. Glenn, who was elected mayor of Atlanta the following year, was the lodge's first worshipful master; Mayer and Frankfort held the second and third highest offices. In 1859 Mayer, one of only two Jews in the fifty-member lodge, was elected to the first of five consecutive terms as worshipful master and was primarily responsible for the construction of the Masonic Hall.[33]

With few exceptions, Jews played no role in the antebellum town's civic and cultural life: David Mayer and Sol Frank were active in Democratic politics; M. Oppenheimer was a member of the Atlanta Amateurs, a theatrical society; Simon Frankfort was a charter

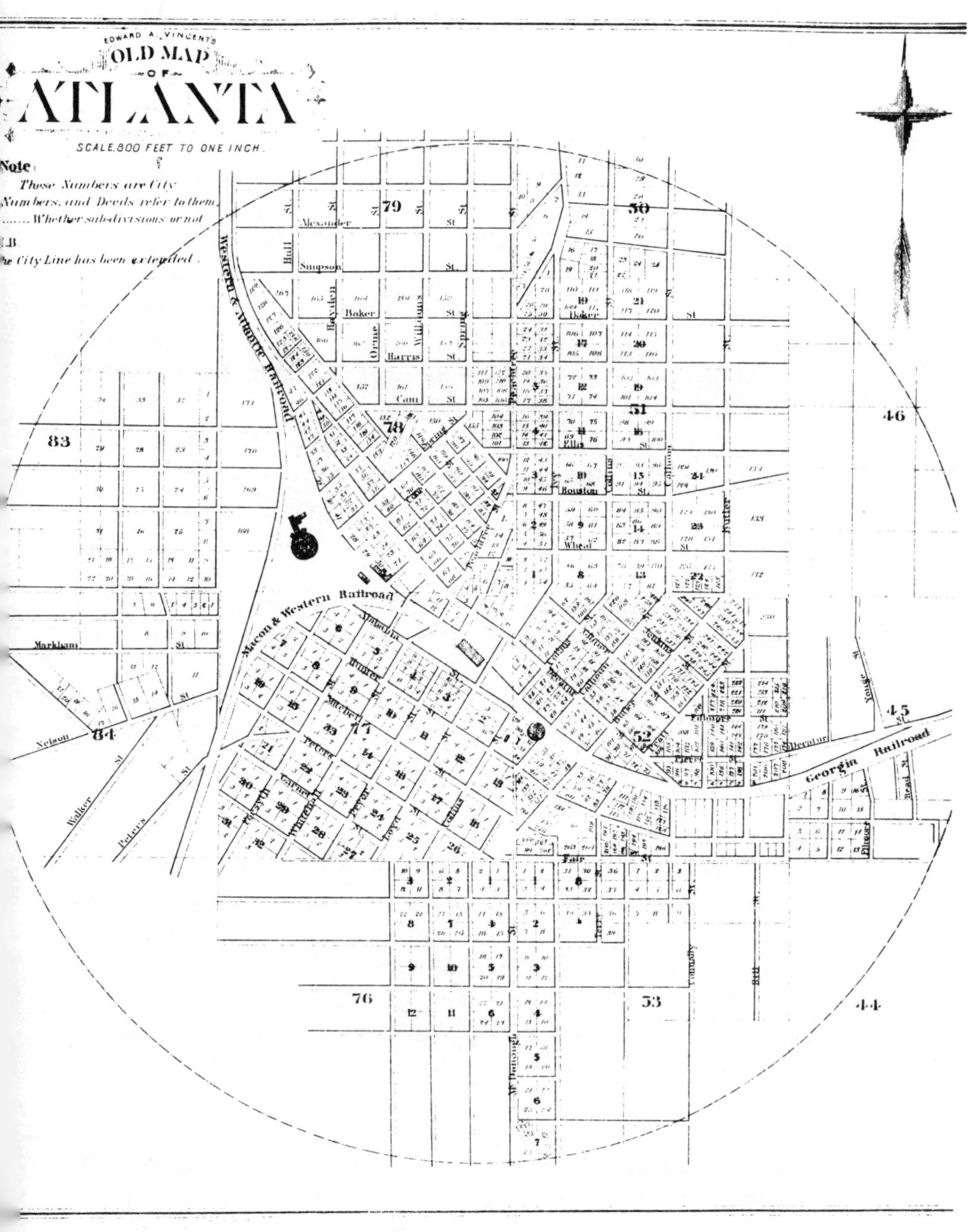


FIGURE 2. *Atlanta in 1853.*

member of Atlanta Fire Company No. 1 and persuaded the city council to dig wells to meet the danger of fire.[34]

Slavery probably exerted a selective influence on Jewish settlement in the South, for those who were squeamish about human bondage were apt to avoid the region or did not remain long. The institution also furthered the Jew's social acceptance. By providing a class of defenseless victims, slavery acted as an escape valve for frustrations which might otherwise have been expressed more frequently as anti-Jewish sentiment and, by ordaining race as the all-pervasive distinction in society, even made the poor immigrant Jew a member of the master class. Because of their small numbers, relative isolation, and dependence as merchants upon the goodwill of their customers, the attitudes of Jews toward slavery were likely to be strongly influenced by conversations with their gentile neighbors. While suspicion engendered by their foreign birth and alien religion may have induced some Jews to conform outwardly to regional values as a means of protective coloration, most willingly embraced southern attitudes because they had a consuming desire to succeed in their new home.[35]

In Atlanta, 4 of the 6 Jewish households in 1850 contained a total of 7 female slaves—a sizable showing in a town with only 493 slaves and 149 slaveowners. Ten years later, Adolph Brady was the only Jewish slaveowner. In 1862 David Mayer owned 6 slaves worth approximately $5,000; that same year he entered the auction and commission business with slaves among his merchandise. Levi Cohen, who settled in Atlanta in 1862 and later became president of the synagogue and the community's first *mohel* (ritual circumciser), purchased slaves in several Georgia counties during the Civil War. He may have been in the employ of Solomon Cohen, a large-scale dealer with offices in both Atlanta and Augusta, who offered 75 Negroes for sale in September 1862.[36]

The small size, rapid turnover, and materialistic orientation of the Jewish population inhibited the growth of Jewish institutional life. Probably not until 1860 did ten Jewish males over the age of thirteen—the minimum number required for the establishment of a congregation—reside in Atlanta at the same time. Furthermore, while they were sufficiently conscious of their identity to contribute money for the relief of Jews in distant China and Morocco, Judaism was not a dominant influence in their lives.[37]

Occasional religious instruction for the young was provided by the wives of Aaron Alexander and Simon Frankfort, and when visiting Jews from other towns and local religious interest made a *minyan* (quorum) possible, services were held. Rev. Isaac Leeser of Philadelphia, the editor of the monthly Anglo-Jewish *Occident* as well as a leading spokesman for traditional Judaism, passed through Atlanta in January 1852 and conducted services in Adolph Brady's home. Leeser unsuccessfully urged the worshipers to join with other Jews from Griffin, Newnan, Athens, and Marietta and form a "congregational union" or at least share the services of a *shohet* (ritual slaughterer) and pray together on the holidays. "A little exertion," he suggested, "would render the execution of this project much easier than is generally considered possible." Two years later the ravages of a yellow fever epidemic led many Jews from Charleston, Savannah, and Augusta to assemble for the High Holy Days in the more salubrious atmosphere of Atlanta. "[W]e hope," Leeser chided, "that the resident Israelites will not suffer the present to be the last occasion for the public imploring of our Father."[38]

Leeser continued to urge Atlanta's Jews to form a congregation, but no progress was made until 1860 when the Hebrew Benevolent Society was organized, and at the request of David Mayer received from the city council six 15-by-30-foot lots in the municipal cemetery. As the Jewish population increased after the outbreak of war, the society assumed congregational functions. In September 1862 the Hebrew Benevolent Congregation was organized by thirty families, several of whom resided in neighboring communities. The new congregation worshiped in the Masonic Hall, and $2,000 was subscribed toward the erection of a synagogue. The High Holy Days, noted the *Daily Intelligencer,* were "observed with imposing religious ceremonies as prescribed in the 'Laws of Moses,' by all the faithful of that most ancient denomination of people."[39]

The Civil War was a watershed in the evolution of Atlanta and her Jewish community. It stimulated manufacturing, doubled the population within four years, and resulted in the city's destruction and subsequent rebirth as a major regional center. The Jewish community, which accounted for only 0.5 percent of Atlanta's population in 1860, grew substantially during the war years and in the period that followed became an increasingly integral part of the general society.

Unionist sentiment was strong in Atlanta during the 1850s for the city's economy was heavily dependent upon western trade, and her merchants, who had strong commercial ties with northern suppliers, had come to regard the aspirations of other southern cities with deep suspicion. The Unionist tickets headed by Stephen Douglas and John Bell received 63 percent of Atlanta's presidential votes in 1860, but the election of Abraham Lincoln convinced two-thirds of the voters subsequently to endorse secessionist delegates to the state convention.[40]

Because of her railroads, rolling mill, foundries, and seemingly secure inland location, Atlanta became one of the Confederacy's major hospitalization, relief, supply, and ordnance manufacturing centers. In 1862 an arsenal was established making the city a military post subject to martial law. From the arsenal, rolling mill, foundries, and several quickly established government and private works flowed a profusion of pistols, pikes, cannons, canteens, swords, saddles, armor plate, ammunition, tents, knives, rails, and railroad cars to sustain the Confederacy's war effort.[41]

Under the impact of the war, Atlanta's population rose to over 20,000, and among the newcomers were a sizable number of Jews. Some were refugees from areas of the South that had fallen under Federal control, while others, like the Einsteins from Savannah and the Moses and Cohen families from Charleston, preferred the inland security of Atlanta to the exposed position of their seaport homes. Atlanta's most distinguished wartime Jewish resident was Charleston journalist and economist Jacob N. Cardozo, who wrote on financial matters for the local *Southern Confederacy.* However, most were apparently merchants from Newnan, Madison, La Grange, Columbus, and Marietta who were attracted by expanded opportunities for trade.[42]

Pockets of Unionist sentiment persisted in Atlanta during the war, and resistance to conscription was widespread throughout Georgia.[43] Like their gentile neighbors, the Jews of Atlanta were divided in their response to the conflict. Several actively participated in the fight for southern independence; others, because of age, principle, disinterest, or opportunism, did not.[44]

In January 1860 David Mayer was one of a minority of local merchants who called upon Georgia storekeepers to withdraw their patronage from "black Republican and Abolition" wholesale houses in the North. Nine months later he, Sol Frank, and Solomon Solomon joined the Minute Men Association of Fulton County, which vowed to second any attempt by Georgia to withdraw from the Union. Mayer, who was forty-one years old at the outbreak of the war, became a supply officer on the staff of Governor Joseph E. Brown, and Solomon established a foundry which produced buttons, spurs, bridles, and buckles for the army. At least five Jews—M. Wittgenstein, M. Friedenthal, Isaac Frank, Sol Frank, and Bernard Brown—enlisted as privates in local infantry companies. Wittgenstein died from exposure and starvation in Virginia in December 1861. Herman Haas's son Aaron moved to Atlanta in 1861 and participated in several blockade-running voyages to England, where he negotiated for the sale of southern cotton. Although the Hebrew Benevolent Society never explicitly endorsed secession, early in the war it contributed fifty dollars to the Georgia Hospital Fund "with the heartfelt prayer, that the amount though small, may go far towards alleviating the wants and pains of our suffering fellow citizens."[45]

After the Confederate Congress passed a law in April 1862 which authorized the conscription of all white males including resident aliens between the ages of eighteen and thirty-five, several Jews left the city and drifted north. Among them were David Mayer's native-born clerk, Leo Cahn, and two recent immigrants from Bavaria, the brothers Jacob and David Steinheimer. Several other Jews of conscriptable age remained in Atlanta and may have hired substitutes to serve in their stead—a permissible though unpatriotic alternative to military service.[46] At least one Jew was lambasted by the press for "having contributed to his country's service one of the largest and oldest and most influential substitutes in the army."[47]

Far less typical than the patriotic Jewish enlistee or the civilian slacker, but more frequently noted by the press, was the speculator and the land blockade runner. Only a tiny minority of Jews were speculators, and only a small percentage of speculators were Jews. However, the war unleashed heretofore dormant prejudices, and the Jew provided a convenient and popular scapegoat for much of the South's anger, fear, insecurity, guilt, and frustration. Jews were denounced as disloyal extortionists in Talbotton, Thomasville, Milledgeville, and other Georgia towns, and several Confederate congressmen held them responsible for the shortage of goods and the rise of prices.[48]

In reality, speculation was a result rather than a cause of the South's economic woes. Among the true causes were the Federal blockade, which cut off the South from its traditional markets and sources of supply, the divergence of industrial potential into the production of ordnance, the banking system's inability to control the currency, the breakdown of the railroad system, the impressment of rolling stock, and the Confederate government's interference with commerce and trade. Everyone who produced, sold, or purchased goods was involved in the inflationary spiral. In Atlanta the shortages were further aggravated by the imposition of martial law and the confiscation of foodstuffs by soldiers.[49] One resident of a nearby town observed that Atlanta was a veritable

> Sodom and Gemorrah [*sic*] of extortion, engrossing and speculation, whose maw Ne're knew satiety, nor conscience law—where high prices begin and radiate to all parts of the country—where merchants and traders rush frenzied through the streets in their eagerness to by [*sic*] for a dollar and sell for two, who, when a customer takes an article of [*sic*] them at their own price, are mad with themselves because they did not ask more.[50]

Heyman Herzberg was one of many blockade runners who made his headquarters in Atlanta. Formerly a resident of Cartersville, Georgia, Herzberg served in the Confederate Army for several months, and then secured his discharge by hiring a sixty-year-old substitute and giving his first lieutenant a handsome gold watch "as a souvenir." He moved to Atlanta and made several trips to New York and Philadelphia to purchase goods which he then brought south to sell at "fabulous prices." Arrested several times by both Union and Confederate troops, Herzberg either bribed his captors or convinced them—on his honor as a Mason—that he was not a blockade runner.[51]

Much more successful and more despised than Herzberg was salt speculator Lazarus Bendigo. Prior to the war, most of the South's salt had been imported from Europe and the West Indies, and the imposition of the blockade drove the price of this necessary commodity to fantastic heights. By speculating in salt and other goods, Bendigo allegedly accumulated an enormous fortune and acquired ownership of several blocks of buildings. When Bendigo was robbed early in 1864, a local journalist recounted the incident, purportedly in the speculator's own words:

> Vell, you see I vas go to Memphis to make a leetle beezelas, and I vas pye de cavelry poots and tings for de poys; vell I am coming town te road mit te vaggon, ven some citizens on hoarses, mit guns on dare

> packs rides up, and dey says "stop you jeetle tyvel." Den I stops mine mules and dey breaks open de poxes and dakes all mine goods, and de kaptain lukes at mine peestal and say, "geeve me dat or I shoot you dead." And I gives him it and it makes me feel so weak. Dey call themselves gureelers, but I tink dey acts more lik roppers.[52]

The activities of men like Herzberg and Bendigo led to a grand jury investigation which concluded that while the consequences of scarcity and inflation were unfortunate, "no class of the community is more responsible for the evil than the other."[53] Among the Jewish merchants who resisted speculation were Henry Hirsch and David Mayer.

Henry Hirsch was Herman Haas's brother-in-law and in 1849 had accompanied the Haas family south as far as Marietta. In September 1862 Hirsch sold several slaves to a Virginia salt company and in exchange received a large shipment of salt at $40 per sack. A gentile speculator from Atlanta heard about the deal and offered Hirsch $65 per sack for the entire shipment, knowing that the salt could soon be resold at $75. Hirsch rejected the speculator's offer and informed him that the salt was for sale at $50 per sack but only to the people in the surrounding countryside. When asked to justify his odd behavior, the Jewish merchant articulated a credo to which his three nephews, who settled in Atlanta after the war, would come to subscribe:

> I have always tried to deal fairly with the people. They seemed to have confidence in me, and gave me a good share of their patronage. . . . With my own industry and economy, they have made me what I am; and I will not withhold my salt from them at a fair profit on what it cost me. Most of the dry goods on my shelves they can do without; they are not absolutely necessaries [*sic*]. If they buy them they must pay the current prices; but salt they cannot do without. That is an absolute necessary [*sic*] of life, and they shall have it. Speculators shall not have it even at a much higher price.[54]

Because Hirsch was a Jew, a member of "that dispised yet most industrious and frugal class of citizens," one of his gentile neighbors brought the incident to public notice. "[W]hen men come to 'be judged according to the deeds done in the body,' " he asked, "which will stand the ordeal best, the Marietta Jew, or the Atlanta christian [*sic*] speculator?"[55]

David Mayer donated 3 tierces of rice to the city council in July 1862 and an additional 2 tierces the following April (a total of about

2,500 pounds) "to relieve, in some small part, at least, the sorrows of our poor sufferers."[56] After Atlanta's surrender to Federal troops, Mayer reputedly refused a $100,000 inducement to enter into a cotton speculation with several Union officers.[57]

Atlanta's importance as a major Confederate industrial and supply center made it a key objective for the Union armies under the command of Major-General William Tecumseh Sherman. After a four-month campaign in which an estimated 67,000 soldiers perished, Atlanta was finally taken on September 2, 1864. Because the city was to be converted into a military installation, the Union general ordered the immediate evacuation of the civilian population. Sherman was determined to render Atlanta useless as a future base for Confederate military operations, and in the middle of November, before he embarked on his March to the Sea, he ordered the destruction of the city's warehouses, public buildings, factories, and railroad facilities. However, the zealousness of the soldiers and the unpredictability of the flames reduced more than two-thirds of the city to rubble.[58] One Union officer who witnessed the conflagration wrote his wife that "all the pictures and verbal descriptions of hell I have ever seen never gave me half so vivid an idea of it as did this flame-wrapped city tonight. Gate City of the South, farewell."[59]

# 2

## *The Reborn City*

The first thing that returning citizens noticed as they approached Atlanta early in December was the putrid stench of nearly three-thousand dead horses and mules that lay unburied within the city limits, providing food for the packs of wild dogs that roamed the streets. For miles around hardly a tree was left standing, the heavily wooded countryside having been denuded to provide shelter, fuel, and a clear field of fire for eighty thousand Union troops. The painfully constructed railroad network was in ruins, the rails bent into "Sherman's neckties," the crossties burned, and the car shed, depots, and machine shops reduced to charred piles of rubble. All of the factories, most of the stores, and about four thousand residences had been destroyed. Much of what had survived the bombardment, the demolitions of the retreating Confederates, and the depredations of the occupying Federals was looted by desperate men who had descended upon the deserted city from fifty miles around. In an effort to comprehend the magnitude of the devastation the returning exiles likened their city to Moscow, Babylon, and Palmyra. Nevertheless, all were confident that recovery would be swift.[1]

Although Atlanta had suffered greatly, unlike the older cities of the cotton belt, her economic base was not severely affected by the disruption of the plantation system. Between April 1865 and March 1867 the shops, depots, and tracks of all four railroads were restored, and the subsequent resumption of western trade generated a business boom that attracted scores of merchants from neighboring states and the North. The need to restore the town's economic vitality led the mercantile community to take firm control of the city government. Under their influence municipal services were apportioned to serve primarily entrepreneurial goals; public market facilities were expanded to revive the wagon trade; local businessmen were dispatched to western commercial conventions to enhance Atlanta's status as a trading center; and bonds were issued to purchase and equip grounds for the annual fairs of the State Agricultural Society.[2]

Once again Atlanta experienced flush times. In 1865, 150 stores were operating; 250 in 1867; and 875 in 1869. Nearly $35,000,000 worth of goods were sold in 1872, compared with $10,000,000 in 1869, $4,500,000 in 1866, and $3,000,000 in 1859. Within a year after the war, real estate had regained its 1859 value and by 1869 tripled to $8,792,000. Newly founded country stores provided additional markets for local wholesalers, and by 1872 ten banks had been established, enabling merchants to obtain necessary commercial loans. After several unsuccessful attempts, in 1868 Atlanta finally became the capital of Georgia and by 1870 boasted a population of 21,789, a 128 percent increase over 1860.[3]

Northern journalists who visited Atlanta in 1865 and 1866 differed little in their appraisal of the city. All remarked about the ankle-deep mud in the unpaved streets, the omnipresent evidence of destruction, and the "cheap and squalid look" of the new "frail and fire-tempting buildings." "Everywhere were ruins and rubbish, mud and mortar and misery," wrote J. T. Trowbridge. Hundreds of inhabitants lived in wretched hovels which made the suburbs resemble "a fantastic encampment of gypsies or Indians." "The city is hardly less pleasing to the eye than the people," observed John R. Dennett of *The Nation.* "A great many rough-looking fellows hang about the numerous shops and shanties where liquor is sold, and a knot of them cluster at each street corner."[4]

But what impressed the visitors most was the energy and activity of those who were "bringing a city out of this desert of shattered brick—raising warehouses from ruins, and hastily establishing stores in houses half-finished and unroofed. . . ." "Chicago in her busiest days could scarcely show such a sight," reported Sidney Andrews. "Rents," observed Andrews, "are so high that they would seem fabulous even on Lake Street, and yet there is the most urgent cry for store-room and office-room." "The one sole idea in every man's mind is to make money," he continued. "That this apparent prosperity is real no outsider can believe. That business is planted on sure foundations no merchant pretends."[5]

In her hectic pace of life, aggressive trading practices, and tolerant social outlook, Atlanta was perceptibly different from other postwar southern cities. A New York businessman in 1868 found his local counterparts to be "more like NY merchants than any he had met outside the metropolis." "It is true," admitted the *Atlanta Constitution,* that local merchants "are somewhat deficient in pedigree and have no family motto handed down from a Norman nobleman, but they fight under one banner. 'Quick sales and small profits. . . .' " An English visitor during the 1870s was disappointed to find that Atlanta was a physically unattractive community, very inferior in amenities to all the other southern towns he had seen. Lodging at the elegant Kimball House, he "realized for the first time what American spitting is. It really requires some nerve to walk across the hall." Another Englishman remarked that Atlanta comported herself in an arrogant, swaggering, high-handed manner as though she were saying, "see what a burnt-up city can do; look at my hotels and my banks, my colleges and libraries, my dry goods stores and my First Methodist Churches, and then talk of a crippled and impoverished South, if you dare."[6]

But the South was impoverished. In 1870 the total assessed property evaluation of the former Confederate States was less than half its 1860 value. Newly emancipated Negroes proved less willing to tolerate the old plantation discipline. Dissatisfied with economic and social conditions in the rural areas and not entirely certain about the meaning of freedom, hundreds of thousands flocked to the cities and emigrated to the Southwest, causing planters to express concern about the quantity and quality of their labor supply. Whites, too, were leaving the war-ravaged South—412,000 from Georgia alone between 1865 and 1900—and the loss of population threatened to weaken southern influence in Congress. "Political power in a republic means sectional legislation," warned a concerned Georgian. "Sectional legislation means sectional wealth; and unless we awaken to the fact that population alone will give us the power to influence legislation, the south will remain the commercial vassal of the north." Advocates of economic restoration and diversification recognized the need not only for "well regulated and reliable" agricultural labor but also for persons to purchase abandoned farmlands, and for skilled artisans, and investors who could develop the South's natural resources. Although the antebellum agitation over slavery had united southern whites in a general dislike of outsiders and the bitter experience of the Civil War and Reconstruction aggravated this prejudice, between 1865 and 1907 planters, speculators, railroad companies, industrialists, and the governments of every southern state endeavored to attract immigrants from Europe and the North.[7]

In Georgia the General Assembly was inundated with memorials to replace free Negro labor with "the Systematic, well directed and persevering industry of the old World, or even [that of] the heretofore free States of the Union." In October 1865 several prominent Savannah businessmen chartered the Georgia Land and Immigration Company to supply white laborers to Georgia planters, and the following year a similar venture was organized in Augusta. After the completion of the Union Pacific Railroad, there was even talk of importing Chinese coolies. In 1866 the state legislature authorized a private land lottery, ostensibly to encourage immigration, and three years later funds were appropriated for two immigration commissioners: George N. Lester, who was to publicize Georgia's advantages in the North, and Samuel Weil, a German-born Atlanta Jew, who was to do the same abroad.[8] The Immigration Society of the State of Georgia was created in 1871, and the following year the members of the Atlanta German Association attempted to influence their fellow countrymen to settle in Georgia. During the next few decades thousands of promotional tracts were produced and distributed at state expense, cheap land was offered on easy terms, and the railroads charged immigrants lower fares.[9] Nevertheless, few immigrants came. The number of foreign-born whites in Georgia actually decreased between 1860 and 1880, and although there were 3,400 more foreigners in the state in 1910 than there had been fifty years earlier, their proportion of the total population declined from 1.1 to 0.6 percent. Finally, most of the newcomers settled in the cities rather than in the countryside, where the demand for labor was most acute.[10] (See table 1.)

The primary reason for this condition was that most Georgians, fearful that their pure blood and way of life would be defiled, never reconciled themselves to immigration; and their legislative representatives refused to appropriate enough money to mount an effective campaign. Unfavorable publicity in the northern and foreign press informed potential immigrants that Georgia was an oppressively hot, fever-ridden, lawless land in which life and property were inadequately protected, manual labor was considered demeaning for white men, schools and churches were inferior, and outsiders were unwelcome. German agents who traveled through the South after the war reported home that opportunities were better in the agricultural belt of the Northwest, and in Europe and the northeastern ports agents of the western states and of railroad and land companies offered free land and transportation to prospective settlers, inducements which Georgia could not match. Finally there were no direct steamship connections between European and Georgian ports.[11]

Although Georgia failed to entice many immigrant laborers, farmers and artisans, she did attract sizable numbers of Jews, so that during the postwar period Atlanta emerged as a major center of Jewish settlement in the South. Jews were not influenced by reports of unfavorable agricultural conditions; their interests lay elsewhere. The ravaged and bankrupt South desperately needed goods and capital which Jewish merchants from the North were willing to supply. In addition, the millions of newly emancipated Negroes provided a lucrative market for less affluent Jews who actively solicited their trade, willingly bargained over prices, and did not eschew calling them "Mister" and "Mrs."[12]

The Jewish "invasion" of the South which began immediately after the war did not go unobserved by visiting journalists like John Dennett, who noticed aboard his southbound ship "a party of German Jews, ill-mannered and dirty, who fraternized closely with each other, and were profuse of attentions to the German nurses and waiting maids." "[A]in't they a 'penny-ante' lot," remarked a young Connecticut businessman to Dennett, "But they'll make more money in the Southern country in this year than you or I will."[13]

The postwar influx of Jews can best be measured indirectly. In the forty years prior to the Civil War synagogues had been founded in twenty southern communities (not including two each in Maryland and Missouri), while in the five years after Appomattox, Jewish congregations were established in seventeen additional cities: Eufaula and Selma, Alabama; Camden, Little Rock, Helena, and Pine Bluff, Arkansas; Jacksonville, Florida; Owensboro, Kentucky; Monroe and Morgan City, Louisiana; Meridian, Mississippi; Raleigh and Wilmington, North Carolina; Chattanooga and Knoxville, Tennessee; Galveston, Texas; and Harrisonburg, Virginia. Claims of "invasion" to the contrary, the number of southern Jews remained small, and because of more attractive economic prospects in the North and West, their proportion of the total American Jewish population actually declined since 1860. By 1878 an estimated 32,000 of the approximately 230,000 Jews in the United States (14 percent) lived in the South, more than half of them in a dozen cities with the remainder scattered in hundreds of other communities. Although they constituted an appreciable minority of the inhabitants of Knoxville, Shreveport, Little Rock, Galveston, and Nashville, only 1 out of every 500 Southerners was Jewish. Indeed, New York City (not including Brooklyn) contained twice as many Jews as the entire South, and San Francisco, half as many.[14] (See table 2.)

Although suspicion of Jews as religious and cultural aliens persisted after the war, they were increasingly respected for their "renowned business capacity" and were welcomed by New South advocates of commercial growth. "Where there are no Jews there is no money to be made," exclaimed the *Richmond Whig* in 1866.

> Where there are no rice-fields there are no rice-birds; where there is no wild celery there are no canvass back ducks; where there is no trade there are no Jews. We hail their presence in the Southern States as an auspicious sign. Instead of diminishing here they have probably increased. . . . and [a] more industrious and law abiding class of the population does not exist. They interfere with no one, mind their own business, observe their religious ceremonies, and pursue their peculiar enjoyments and indulgences. We hope they may never leave us. When they do, we shall begin to fear that we are giving over to ruin. . . . If there is to be a Jerusalem, let Richmond be the place.[15]

A similar view of the Jew as a symbol of economic progress, but without the connotations of parasitism, was expressed by the *Atlanta Daily Herald:*

> We congratulate ourselves because nothing is so indicative of a city's progress as to see an influx of Jews who come with the intention of living with you and especially as they buy property and build among you because they are a thrifty and progressive people who never fail to build up a town they settle in; and again because they make good citizens, pay their obligations promptly, never refuse to pay their taxes and are law-abiding.[16]

Jews and Gentiles were drawn to Atlanta for the same reasons. Atlanta was a boom-town; her railroads—five by 1873—funneled a vast amount of trade into the city and like a magnet attracted the restless and the ambitious. The sanguine prediction in 1866 that by 1900 Atlanta would have a population of 60,000 seemed quite plausible. "But this is not more strange," suggested a local booster, "than that a flourishing city should be built in the marshes of the Neva, and another on the banks of the Tiber, or a third on a pretty island, once the rendezvous for piratical cruisers. The whole secret is that Atlanta, like New York, St. Petersburg and Rome, is one of the predestined capitals of the world."[17]

In their quest for material success, local entrepreneurs discarded many traditional southern values and fostered a tolerant social climate. "Hang the old customs," demanded the *Daily New Era* in 1867. "They are rags and tatters, and as such are sloughed off with each generation." Despite the still-visible scars of sectional strife, a proposal to erect a memorial to Abraham Lincoln was seriously considered by the city council, and northern and foreign immigrants were encouraged to settle in the community. "Here the lamb and the lion lie down together," boasted the compiler of the 1870 city directory, "and if the lamb is a little frightened the first night, he's all right when the day breaks. . . . Come, then, whatever be your political and religious creed; visit us, live with us, *mind your own business,* and have no fear of G.A.R.'s, K.K.'s or anything else."[18]

Largely as a consequence of immigration, the population of Atlanta rose from 21,789 in 1870 to 154,837 in 1910. Blacks registered an impressive increase during the sixties, but despite continued growth during the next four decades, their proportion of the total population dropped from 45.6 to 33.5 percent. The number of foreign-born whites—mostly Germans, Irish, and British until the mass influx of Russian Jews during the nineties—quadrupled during the same period though their proportion of the total population declined from 5.0 to 2.8 percent. The growth of the Jewish population was especially dramatic: from just 50 on the eve of the Civil War to 4,000 half a century later, an increase of from 0.5 to 2.6 percent of the total population.[19] (See tables 3 and 4.)

Most of the adult Jews who settled in Atlanta during the two postwar decades were young males of Central European descent who engaged in trade, resided in family groups, and tended to cluster in the neighborhoods just south of the business district.

Approximately three hundred to four hundred Jews lived in the city in 1870, and six hundred in 1880.[20]

Like other American Jewish communities during the period, the Jewish community of Atlanta consisted mostly of Central European immigrants and their native-born children. Eighty-nine percent of the Jews in 1870 and 74 percent of those in 1880 had two foreign-born parents, and 96 percent in 1870 and 94 percent in 1880 had at least one. Because of the large number of children, nearly all of whom had been born in the United States, more than half of the Jews in 1870 and two-thirds in 1880 were native-born Americans. Germans—mostly from Bavaria, Hesse, Prussia, and Wurttemburg—constituted the largest foreign-born group, accounting for more than a third of the total Jewish population in 1870 and a fourth in 1880, or about three-fourths of the immigrant population in both years. Hungarians also arrived in substantial numbers and, together with a sprinkling of Bohemian, Russian, French, Dutch, and British Jews, accounted for the remainder of the foreign-born.[21] (See tables 5 and 6.)

Because Atlanta was distant from the nearest seaport through which immigrants might enter and offered few opportunities for the "greenhorn" without capital and marketable skills, most of the Jews who settled in Atlanta after the war had previously resided in other American communities where they had learned English, acquired knowledge of American ways, and in some cases accumulated sufficient capital to enter business. Illustrative of this tendency were the four Rich brothers, originally from Kaschau, Hungary. Morris and William Rich (ages twelve and sixteen) emigrated to America in 1859 and were followed three years later by brothers Daniel and Emanuel (ages seventeen and fourteen). Settling first in Cincinnati where they had kinsmen, the brothers clerked for local retailers, then peddled household goods in Ohio and Indiana and, after the war, in the South. William, who had made the most money, moved to Atlanta in 1865 and opened the first of three clothing and dry goods stores, while Daniel and Emanuel established a thriving business in the south Georgia town of Albany. Morris clerked for several months in Chattanooga, then peddled for a year and a half through Georgia, and in 1867 moved to Atlanta, where he borrowed five hundred dollars from William and started a modest dry goods business which Daniel and Emanuel subsequently entered. Here the typical becomes the extraordinary: M. Rich Dry Goods became within thirty years the second largest retail emporium in the city and eventually one of the largest stores in the Southeast.[22]

Of the 53 Jewish males (out of 112) ages 18 and over in 1870 whose whereabouts in 1861 could be determined, 33 had resided in the Confederacy, 16 in the Union, and only 4 abroad. Although there was a perceptible migration northward during the war, many of the future Atlantans who had resided in the South in 1861—such as Samuel Weil of Canton, Henry Hirsch of Marietta, and Solomon Dewald of Covington, Georgia—bore arms for the Confederacy. Those who had resided in the North—like Max Franklin and Joseph T. Eichberg—fought for the Union.[23]

Like the city in which they resided, Atlanta's Jews were young, their average age being 21.4 years in 1870 and 21.6 in 1880. Children under the age of 10 constituted nearly a third of the Jewish community in both years, while those ages 50 and above totaled only 4 percent in 1870 and 6.8 percent in 1880. Males consistently outnumbered females, especially in the early years like 1870 when the sex ratio was 147, and for the marriageable 20- to 39-year-old group, 211. But by 1880, as young married couples entered the community, unattached male drifters departed, local marriages increased, and female births exceeded male, the sex ratio declined to a more normal 108, and 122 for the 20- to 39-year old category. (See table 7.) Even so, this was substantially higher than the city's sex ratio of 90.[24]

Marital patterns were naturally affected by the community's unfavorable sex ratio as well as by its age and economic structure, the three factors resulting in the postponement of marriage for many males, intra-family unions, and a perceptible level of intermarriage.

Forty-nine percent of the Jewish males ages 18 and over in 1870, and 64 percent of those in 1880 were married; in the 18- to 29-year-old category, only 20 percent in 1870 and 13 percent in 1880 were married; while among those ages 30 and over, the proportions of married men were 78 percent and 85 percent respectively. (See table 8.) Most significantly, single Jewish men outnumbered single Jewish women 5 to 1 in 1870 and 2 to 1 in 1880. (See table 8.)

The high correlation between increasing age and marriage was more directly a function of occupational status and wealth. With few exceptions, younger males were either white-collar workers eager to rise to proprietary positions or recent achievers of proprietary status struggling to maintain and expand their businesses in a town overcrowded with traders and traumatized, between 1873 and 1877, by economic depression. Capital accumulation was vital to such men, only 20 percent of whom in 1870 and 15 percent in 1880 reported taxable assets, and the financial encumberances of marriage were apt to interfere with this goal. The consequent postponement of marriage resulted in a sizable age differential between husbands and wives: an average of 6.8 years in 1870 (No.=40 couples) and 8.8 in 1880 (No.=94 couples). In the latter year, 17 of the couples registered differences of more than 15 years and in one case, 27.

Although demographic logic should have indicated otherwise, only a handful of Jews appear to have married out of the faith.[25] But the limited availability of eligible Jewish women was a problem. In the scramble for brides, sets of brothers occasionally wed sets of sisters, as when Joseph, Morris and Henry Hirsch led Rebecca, Amelia, and Rosalie Hustler to the *huppah* (marriage canopy). Nor was the marriage of first cousins like Daniel Rich and Julia Teitlebaum unusual. Isolated Jewish families in the surrounding towns, dependent upon Atlanta for their religious needs, were another source of potential brides, and in 1878 future merchant prince Morris Rich married an eighteen-year-old girl from nearby Madison. Visits between Atlanta and other cities by Jews of marriagable age were encouraged by an increasingly intricate network of family and business alliances. Various Jewish social and cultural societies incidentally provided a meeting place for young men and women, and when two dozen young Jews from Macon journeyed to Atlanta to root for their local baseball team, the community arranged a reception at which the Jewish youth of the neighboring cities could get acquainted.[26]

The Jewish immigration from Central Europe was made up primarily of young couples and unattached men, and the economic factors which attracted ambitious single males to Atlanta did not hold true for single females. Consequently, 83 percent of the single adult males but none of the single adult females in 1870 were foreign-born, and the overwhelming majority of the marriages which occurred during the next decade, like those of the Hirsch brothers and the Hustler sisters, involved foreign-born men and younger native-born women of foreign parentage.

The industrial profile of the Atlanta Jewish community differed considerably from that of the city as a whole. Most notable was the prevalence of Jews in trade: 89 percent in 1870 and 71 percent in 1880 of the employed male Jews ages 18 and over, compared with only 25 percent of all employed male Atlantans ages 16 to 59 in 1880. Only 2 percent of the Jews in 1870 and 3 percent in 1880 performed personal or domestic services, whereas 27 percent of Atlantans were so employed. Manufacturing and the mechanical arts engaged 3 percent of the Jews in 1870 and 15 percent in 1880, compared with 29 percent of Atlantans in the latter year. Agriculture and transportation, which engaged 2 percent and 11 percent respectively of Atlantans in 1880, included no Jews.[27] (See table 9.)

Although a detailed occupational breakdown of employed Atlantans is not available, Jews clearly enjoyed a higher occupational status than most of their fellow citizens. Sixty-six percent of the Jews in 1870 and 60 percent in 1880 were proprietors or managers, and within this category retailers were most numerous. Although Jews included only 1 percent of the town's gainfully employed males in 1880, they accounted for 6 percent of the traders and dealers. Thirty percent of the Jews in both 1870 and 1880 were white-collar workers: mostly store clerks, commercial travelers, and bookkeepers. Only a handful, 3 percent each year, were in the professions or in the manual trades, 1 percent in 1870 and 6 percent in 1880. (See table 10.)

As noted above, most Jewish proprietors were retail merchants (75 percent in 1870 and 50 percent in 1880), and while dry goods and clothing dealers predominated, Jewish retailers also sold tobacco products, foodstuffs, alcoholic beverages, hardware, jewelry, and lumber. Their businesses varied considerably in size. At one extreme was the hardware firm of Julius M. and Jacob C. Alexander, which had been founded in 1865 and by "uniform courtesy and attention" increased its annual sales from about $40,000 the first year to nearly $200,000 in 1871. Much more modest was Gustave Saloshin's secondhand clothing store, patronized largely by blacks and the poorer class of whites, whose stock was assessed at only $50 in 1880. Most Jewish-owned retail establishments fell between these two extremes.[28]

Between 1870 and 1880 the proportion of Jewish wholesalers increased from 6 to 12 percent of the work force, or 10 to 21 percent of the proprietary category. Like the retailers, most of the wholesalers sold clothing, millinery and dry goods, alcoholic beverages, and tobacco products, although a few ventured into paper, notions, and spices. Most of these firms, like the millinery business of Julius Regenstein and Max Kutz which was assessed at $23,000 in 1880, were substantial enterprises. In a few cases, for example, clothiers

Henry, Morris, and Joseph Hirsch, the wholesalers of 1880 had been jobbers for more than ten years. But most, like Meyer Wellhouse and Max Franklin, had entered the field only after successful experience as retailers, or, like tobacco merchants Simon and Morris Benjamin, had settled in Atlanta during the seventies with sufficient capital to launch themselves immediately as jobbers.

The number of Jewish manufacturers increased between 1870 and 1880 from 2 to 9 percent, or from 3 to 9 percent of the proprietary class. In the former year there were only two manufacturers, hoopskirt maker William Teitlebaum and tin stove maker Herman Franklin; in the latter, there were thirteen.

The two largest Jewish-owned factories in 1880 were the Haiman Plow Works and Elsas, May and Co. Elias Haiman, a native of Prussia, had manufactured swords for the Confederacy and after the war applied the biblical injunction literally. In 1880 his factory was capitalized at $100,000, employed a work force of 75 men and 25 women and children, and manufactured $25,000 worth of cultivators and $35,000 worth of plows. Elsas, May and Co. produced $140,000 worth of paper bags in 1880 with a capital investment of $75,000 and a labor force of 100. The prime mover behind the company was Jacob Elsas, a native of Wurttemburg who had settled in Cincinnati during the fifties and went South after the war—first to Nashville, then to Cartersville, Georgia, and in 1869 to Atlanta. Elsas established several wholesale and retail concerns before he and partners Morris Adler, Julius Dreyfus, and Isaac May became manufacturers. In 1881 Elsas, May and Co. purchased a charter which had originally been granted to carpetbagger H. I. Kimball, and established the Fulton Cotton Spinning Company (after 1889, the Fulton Bag and Cotton Mill), destined to become one of the largest enterprises of its kind in the South.[29]

Other Jewish manufacturers in 1880 included Morris Wiseberg and the brothers Sigmond, Jonas, and Jacob Selig. Wiseberg, a native of Russia, settled in Arkansas before the war, came to Atlanta in 1865, and entered the wholesale millinery trade. His sunbonnet factory was capitalized at $6,000, employed 72 hands, and produced $25,000 worth of goods. The Selig brothers followed Wiseberg into the straw goods business. Natives of Bavaria who had settled in Atlanta during the seventies, they employed 94 to 130 hands and produced $50,000 worth of bonnets with a capitalization of $15,000.[30]

More modest enterprises were the leather-trunk factory of David

Kaufman and Leon Lieberman (15 to 20 hands, $7,000 capital, and $13,000 output), Herman Franklin's tin stove factory (12 to 16 hands, $2,500 capital, and $13,000 output) and Henry Rosenbaum's cigar factory (3 to 6 hands and $1,500 output). The two wholesale clothing houses, Hirsch Brothers, and Cohen and Selig, also engaged in production as an ancillary part of their business.[31]

White-collar workers constituted 30 percent of the employed Jewish males in 1870 and 1880. The most distinguishing characteristic of these bookkeepers, clerks, and commercial travelers, was their age. Eighty-one percent of the white-collar workers in 1870 and 51 percent of those in 1880 were between the ages of 18 and 30, although only 50 percent of the employed males in 1870 and 28 percent of those in 1880 were in this age category. Some young white-collar workers, like future manufacturers David Kaufman and Leon Lieberman, came to Atlanta independently and with the expectation of rising to higher things; but most, like Isaac Hirschberg, were the sons or younger relatives of established proprietors. For both types, as will be demonstrated in a subsequent chapter, clerkships and related occupations served as apprenticeships for future proprietors.

At a time when commerce appeared to be the surest avenue to status and riches, few Atlanta Jews entered the professions. Although 5 percent of Atlanta's employed males in 1880 were professionals (or semiprofessionals), only 3 percent of the Jews were so employed. Of the seven Jewish professionals in 1870 and 1880, two were rabbis of the synagogue and a third was about to succeed to the pulpit after a brief tenure as principal of a private school. The only Jewish physician during the period was Henry Bak, Hungarian-born and Vienna-trained, who settled in Atlanta in 1878 and remained for most of the next forty years. Albert Eichberg, the native-born son of prosperous Prussian-born hardware merchant Joseph T. Eichberg, established himself as an architect of local repute but eventually drifted into trade. Samuel Weil opened his law practice in Atlanta shortly after the war and remained a prominent member of the local bar for three decades. Undoubtedly the most prominent of Atlanta's early Jewish professionals was attorney Raphael J. Moses, probably the best known Jew in the state. A native Charlestonian of Sephardic descent, Moses achieved the rank of major during the war, executed the Confederacy's last written order, became one of Georgia's most popular orators, represented Muscogee

County in the legislature, and moved to Atlanta after losing in his bid for Congress in 1878.[32]

Like professionals, the proportion of Jewish manual workers was small—only 1 percent in 1870 and 6 percent in 1880—although their numbers increased appreciably during the next two decades as a consequence of Russian immigration. Among those with trades, tailors were most numerous. Those without skilled trades, such as beer bottler George Kleinart and courthouse janitor Jacob Morris, were former businessmen who had come upon hard times.

Not only did the occupational structure of the Jewish community differ from that of the city as a whole, but the Jews also constituted an economy within the economy. Although Jewish proprietors were principally engaged in providing goods and services for gentile consumption, few Jews—none in 1870 and 1880—had gentile partners. Indeed, most partnerships were family affairs involving either fathers and sons (as in the wholesale liquor house of D. Mayer and Son), of brothers (such as Hirsch Brothers and Selig Brothers and Co.), or brothers-in-law (like Regenstein and Kutz). Similarly, while Jewish proprietors primarily employed non-Jewish help, nearly all Jewish white-collar and manual workers were in the employ of other Jews, usually relatives. This apparent tendency toward economic separateness was due in part to a sense of insecurity that had been imported from Europe and not entirely dispelled in the New World. More significantly, however, was the need for partners and employees whom one could trust, the traditional injunction to care for one's own people, the relatively greater experience of Jews in trade, and also language and cultural barriers.

Although the property assessments of all Atlantans in 1870 and 1880 have not been systematically examined, the Jews, as their high occupational status would suggest, were clearly more affluent than most of their fellow citizens.[33] In 1868, when Jews constituted only about 1 percent of Atlanta's population, at least 13 were among the 358 Atlantans (3.6 percent) who reported annual earnings of more than $1,000. Eight years later, when Jews constituted 1.5 percent of the population, at least 10 Jews and Jewish-owned businesses were among the 300 (3.3 percent) who paid taxes on $10,000 or more in property.[34]

But not all Jews were wealthy. Of the 73 (out of 107) Jewish males ages 18 and over in 1870 for whom assessment data is available, only 27 (37 percent) reported property worth over $50 and only 13 (18 percent) owned real estate.[35] Perhaps significantly, of the 8 Jews who reported assets of $10,000 or more, 7 had spent the war years in the South.[36] On the basis of the more complete data available for 1880 (156 of the 160 Jewish males ages 18 and over), the prosperity of the Jewish community had increased appreciably. Twenty-seven percent now owned realty, 54 percent reported taxable assets over $50, and 57 percent of these had assets worth over $3,000.[37] (See table 11.)

Understandably, wealth was closely related to occupational status, age, and sex. Of those males ages 18 to 29 in 1870 (No.=34) and 1880 (No.=46) for whom assessment data is available, only 20 percent in the former year and 15 percent in the latter reported assets exceeding $50, compared with 57 percent of those in 1870 and 71 percent of those in 1880 who were ages 30 and over. None of the males under 30 in either year possessed real estate. Similarly, while 60 percent of the proprietors and professionals in 1870 and 78 percent of those in 1880 owned property worth over $50, none of the white- and blue-collar workers in the former year and only 19 percent of those in the latter were so endowed. Those white- and blue-collar workers who did own substantial amounts of property were in almost every case either former proprietors or men of mature years for whom the accumulation of property had been a function of age. Although for purposes of analysis the property holdings of women are included with those of their husbands, it is worth noting that 13 women in 1880 owned property and 7 of these had assets valued at over $3,000. Ten of the women were married and the other three were widowed. None were gainfully employed, and it is likely that their property—like Caroline (Mrs. Jacob) Haas's $10,000 worth of real estate—was the result of inheritance.[38]

The residential patterns of Atlanta's Jews were influenced by individual affluence, the availability of adequate housing, accessibility to places of employment, and the desire to live near other Jews. The men and women who cast their lot with the reborn city during the sixties were confronted with a tight housing market. The war had resulted in the destruction of most of Atlanta's residences, and in the postwar scramble for profit and economic advantage, the construction of stores was accorded preference over the erection of homes. Consequently, Jews, like other Atlantans, settled wherever reasonably suitable quarters could be found.[39]

In a pattern reminiscent of an earlier decade, several merchants, like Ephraim Block, William Silverberg, and Gustave Saloshin, lived above their stores, respectively on Peachtree, Whitehall, and Decatur streets. Others, like A. Beerman and Abraham Landsberg, took rooms in the hotels and boardinghouses that dotted the business district. However, most soon accumulated the means to rent—or less typically, purchase—houses in the residential districts. By 1870 Jews were scattered throughout the central section of town. Sixty percent lived in a small area bounded by the railroad tracks on the north and west, South Butler and McDonough streets on the east, and Fair Street on the south (areas A and B of figs. 3 and 4). The largest cluster of Jews within this area was at the intersection of Whitehall and Garnett streets. Sixteen percent of the Jews resided south of Fair Street (area D), 22 percent north of the railroad tracks (areas F and G), and only 2 percent west of the tracks (area C). Although a few Jews lived as far south as McDaniel Street and as far north as Merritts Avenue, most lived within walking distance of the business district and each other. The areas of the city in which they resided were not characterized by either racial or economic homogeneity; blacks and whites and families headed by merchants and laborers lived in close proximity to one another.[40] (See figs. 3 and 4; table 12.)

During the next decade, the construction of new dwellings and the increased rents in the central part of town resulted in economic segregation, driving blacks and poorer whites toward the outskirts or—especially in the case of blacks—into alleys, rear lots, and lower, poorly drained sections of the city.[41]

The erection in 1875 of the first permanent synagogue at the

FIGURE 3. *Atlanta in 1882.*

*Legend:*

The large rectangular area outlined in black corresponds to the section of the city depicted in figures 4 and 5, pages 46 and 47. The smaller areas represent the following sections of the city:

- A bounded by the tracks of the Macon and Western and the Georgia railroads, Peters, Fair, and South Butler streets
- B bounded by the Macon and Western Railroad, Peters and Fair streets
- C north and west of the Macon and Western and the Western and Atlantic railroads tracks
- D south of Fair Street and the Macon and Western tracks and west of McDonough Street (Capital Avenue)
- E south of the Georgia Railroad tracks and east of South Butler and McDonough streets (Capital Avenue)
- F bounded by Foster (Edgewood Avenue), Ivy, Decatur, Pratt, and College streets
- G east of the Western and Atlantic and north of the Georgia railroads tracks

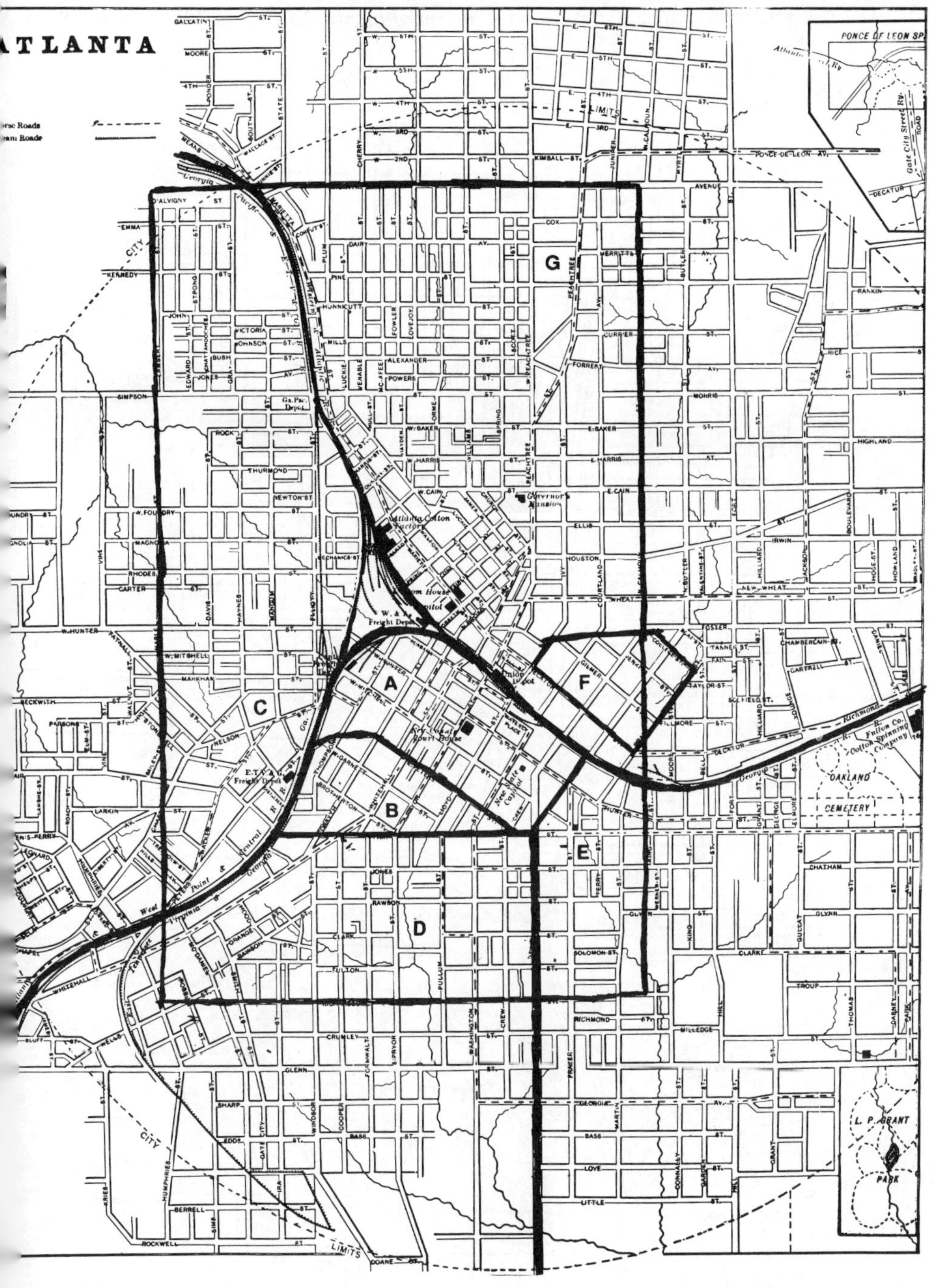


FIGURE 3. *Atlanta in 1882.*

FIGURES 4 and 5. *Residential Patterns of Identifiable Jewish Males (Ages 18 and over) by country of Birth, 1870 and 1880.*

*Legend:*

A Hebrew Benevolent Congregation

B Concordia Hall

■ Austria-Hungary (1)

● Germany (1)

○ Great Britain, Holland, or France (1)

✪ Russia (1)

★ United States (1)

✱ Unknown (1)

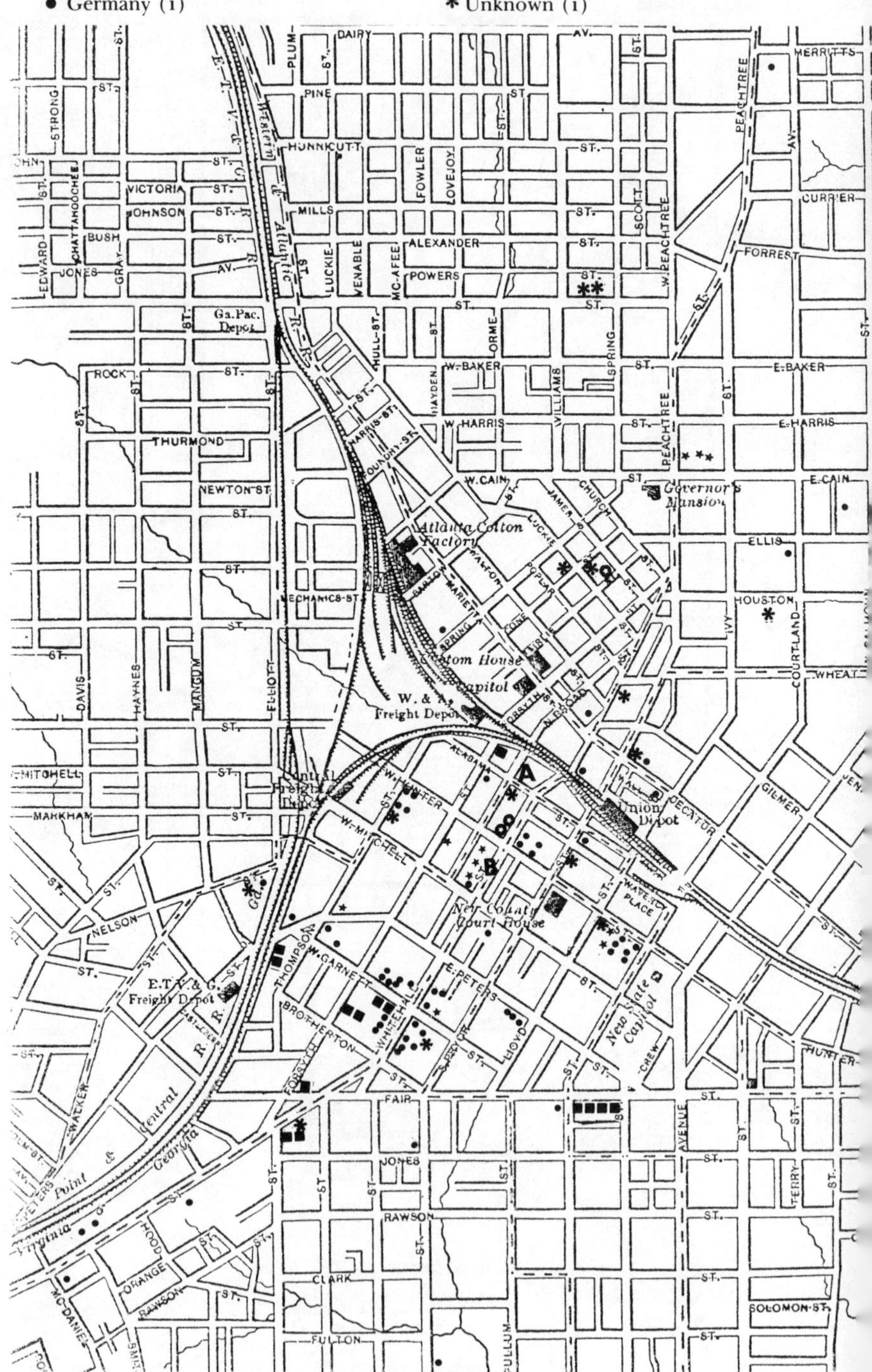


FIGURE 4.

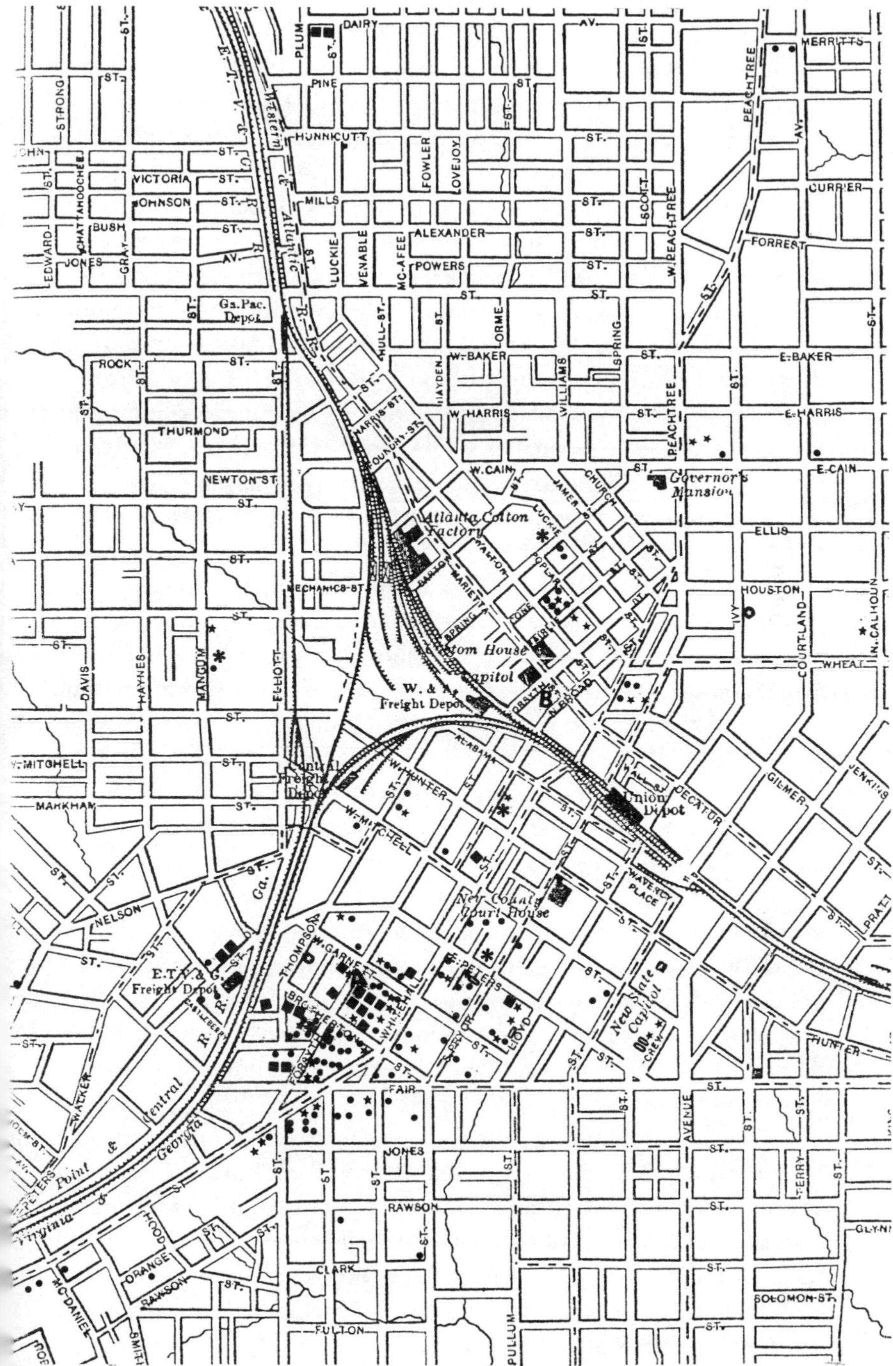

FIGURE 5.

intersection of Garnett and Forsyth streets acted as a magnet and encouraged Jews to settle in its vicinity. By 1880 half of Atlanta's Jews lived in a compact triangular area bounded by Peters Street on the north, Fair Street on the south, and the tracks of the Macon and Western Railroad on the west (area B); and nearly a quarter lived just south of Fair along Whitehall, Windsor, Cooper, and Formwalt streets (area D). Whitehall and Forsyth streets, from their junction just south of Fair until the intersection of Garnett Street, were almost solidly Jewish. Most of the wealthier members of the community—like Mayer, the Hirsch brothers, and the Haases—lived along these two thoroughfares and also on West Garnett and South Pryor streets among native-born white Gentiles of similar economic status. Less affluent Jews such as bookkeeper Monte Hustler and commercial traveler David Barwald were scattered along Thompson, Castleberry, Fair, Magnum, Mitchell, and Rawson streets, which were populated largely by gentile white-collar and skilled workers. Differences of nativity had only a slight effect on Jewish residential patterns. While German and Hungarian families lived next door to each other, several "minority" families like the Russian-born (but English-educated) Wisebergs and the native-born Alexanders and Magnuses lived on the northside, about a mile from the synagogue and the bulk of the Jewish community. Except for Hungarian-born Alex Dittler, whose grocery and residence on the corner of Fort and Houston streets was in the midst of a black neighborhood, nearly all the blacks who resided in the vicinity of Jews were servants who lived (with their families) in or adjacent to the homes of their white employers.[42] (See figs. 3 and 5; table 12.)

Like most of the homes in Atlanta, those occupied by Jews were generally detached, wooden, one- or two-story structures. David Mayer was one of the few Atlantans who owned a brick house. Although a few unmarried Jews like Louis Sondheimer lived in boardinghouses and hotels, by 1880 most Jews resided in private households. Single and often young married adults generally boarded with their parents, other relatives, or business partners, and most Jewish households included one or two in-laws or unmarried siblings. Because of this pattern, Jewish households were large by local standards: an average of 6.3 persons (5.8 if Negro servants and a few white gentile boarders are not included), compared with 4.8 for the city as a whole.[43]

Their residential patterns suggest that most of Atlanta's Jews preferred to live near one another, but because of their small numbers and desire for acceptance, they were neither able nor willing to create a homogeneous Jewish district. Even in the most heavily Jewish section of town (areas A and B), they made up only between 3 and 7 percent of the residents.[44] Consequently, while Jewish associational ties were strengthened, the close proximity of Jew and Gentile hastened the Jew's acculturation.

The synagogue was the most important Jewish institution in the city. With the passing of time and the consequent growth of secularism, and of organizational, economic, and ethnic diversity, its authority was eroded and to some extent superceded by other agencies.

The war had undermined the flimsy foundations of congregational life, and during the next two years Jew and Gentile alike were preoccupied with the task of economic reconstruction. Once again it was Rev. Isaac Leeser who prodded the religiously lethargic community into action. Visiting Atlanta for the third and last time in the winter of 1866–67, the Philadelphia cantor-editor officiated at the New Year's Day wedding of Abram Rosenfeld and Emily Baer and then pursuaded the assembled Jews to reestablish the Hebrew Benevolent Congregation.[45]

During the next few weeks a charter was procured from the state, Torahs were borrowed from congregations in Savannah and Augusta, and on February 15 a rented hall was dedicated as a temporary place of worship. During the next few years the congregation occupied several second-story halls on the south side of town while plans were made to erect a permanent synagogue. In 1871 a lot was purchased on Hunter Street near Lloyd, but construction was never begun. Four years later another lot was purchased, this time on the southeast corner of Garnett and Forsyth streets in the midst of what was already becoming a focal point of Jewish settlement. Here the congregation erected its handsome brick and stone synagogue, designed by a local architect in the Moorish style that characterized many postwar Jewish houses of worship. The cornerstone-laying ceremony in May 1875 was an elaborate affair in which the mayor, city council, police escort, and a brass band accompanied a procession of Masons, Odd Fellows, and B'nai B'riths up Broad Street to Alabama, across to Whitehall, down Whitehall to Garnett, and then west to Forsyth Street. The opening prayer was delivered by a Protestant minister. The congregation occupied the basement of the uncompleted building several months later and worshiped there until the synagogue was dedicated in August 1877. Twenty-five years later, in response to an increased membership and the changing character of the neighborhood, the congregation sold the synagogue and erected an imposing edifice on the southwest corner of Pryor and Richardson streets, about half a mile south. Here the congregation remained for three decades until, responding to the migration of its members to the northside, it constructed a new temple of neoclassical design on Peachtree Street.[46] The spiritual odyssey of the Hebrew Benevolent Congregation will be treated in the next chapter.

The synagogue soon became only one of several local Jewish organizations. The Hebrew Benevolent Society, which had been organized about 1860, was revived after the war, and in 1871 a Hebrew Ladies Aid Society was established. Local lodges of several national Jewish fraternal organizations were installed during the seventies. The first and most influential of these was Gate City Lodge No. 144 of Independent Order B'nai B'rith, founded in May 1870. In 1877 Atlanta Lodge No. 85 of the Free Sons of Israel made its appearance; two years later the Touro Lodge of Order Kesher Shal Barzel was born. The lodges differed only slightly in their rituals, sickness and death benefits, charitable activities, and fraternal objectives, while exercising both a supportive and a subversive influence on Jewish life. By means of their national connections and emphasis upon uniting all Jews by bonds of institutionalized brotherhood, the lodges strengthened Jewish ties and alleviated the sense of isolation and drabness. However, by offering more tangible benefits and by fostering camaraderie on a more discriminating and less demanding basis than did the synagogue, the lodges provided substitutes for formal synagogal affiliation.[47]

More prestigious and potentially more subversive than the lodges was the Concordia Association, founded in June 1866 and antedating the reestablishment of the Hebrew Benevolent Congregation by half a year. The Concordia was postwar Atlanta's second organization devoted strictly to recreation. Its early members, like the adult community as a whole, were mostly successful—but not necessarily wealthy—men in their twenties and thirties who had been born in Germany or Hungary and wished to foster the *gemütlichkeit* and cultural heritage of their fatherlands. The club's activities centered on German forms of sociability: dramatic performances, literary and musical soirées, debates, balls, and card playing. Its amateur theatricals were popular among Jew and Gentile alike and were favorably received by local critics. As late as the 1880s Atlanta had only one opera house, and the Concordia was gratefully recognized as a "powerful influence in preventing the absortion [*sic*] of the mind in business pursuits to the detriment of other matters."[48]

Like the synagogue, the Concordia led an itinerant existence during its first decade. However, in 1877 it settled into the third floor of the Grant Building on North Forsyth and Marietta streets and remained there for sixteen years. Among the building's other tenants were Civil War hero and U.S. Senator John B. Gordon and a fledgling lawyer destined for greater things: Woodrow Wilson. The Concordians outfitted their headquarters with a large banquet hall, a parlor and library, a bar, card and reading rooms, and a combination ballroom and theater. In 1893 the club erected its own building on the corner of South Forsyth and Mitchell streets, rented out the first floor, and used the upper two floors for the "largest, finest, best appointed clubhouse in Atlanta." The inaugural dinner, attended by many prominent Christians, was termed "one of the most notable social triumphs of the descendents of the ancient Hebrew fathers." Despite the ornate trappings, however, the club soon experienced financial difficulties. Younger American-born Jews were not attracted by its Old World atmosphere, and burdened by increasing debts and declining membership, the Concordia Association passed into receivership in 1901.[49]

Although a visiting rabbi from Cincinnati observed in 1874 that clubs like the Concordia "somewhat and somehow keep us together," the club, even more than the lodge, undermined the authority of the synagogue. Unlike the lodge with its ritual and at least nominal commitment to Jewish ideals, the Concordia Association had no specifically Jewish programs aside from annual Hanukkah and Purim balls and an occasional benefit for the synagogue. Nor was membership restricted solely to Jews. Prominent Lutherans like Charles Beerman were frequent officeholders, and until the mid-seventies the organization was commonly described as a German association with a largely "Israelitish" membership.[50]

The evolution of the Concordia from an ostensibly German into an almost exclusively Jewish organization reflected developments that occurred in many American cities. The attitude of Atlanta's German Gentiles toward Jews was ambivalent. On the one hand, Old World prejudices remained; but on the other, a common language and cultural tradition plus the financial support that Jews could provide led many Gentiles to recognize the Jew as a cobuilder of German culture. For their part, the Jews not only esteemed the legacy of Heine, Schiller, and Goethe, but also recognized the high regard that native-born Americans had for German culture and sought to utilize this advantage in their quest for recognition and social status.[51]

Just as Gentiles were members of the largely Jewish Concordia, Jews participated in and occasionally provided leadership for several largely gentile German organizations. The English-German-Hebrew Academy was founded in 1869 by David Burgheim, the Hebrew Benevolent Congregation's first rabbi, and was continued under the leadership of his successor, Rabbi Benjamin A. Bonnheim, until the public school system was inaugurated in 1872. The academy, located above Jacob Elsas and Company's warehouse at Hunter and Pryor streets, was modeled after the Prussian schools. Pupils of both sexes were taught reading and writing in both English and German, and also history, geography, the natural sciences, and mathematics. Not only did many of Atlanta's German Gentiles send their children to the rabbi's school, but so did Germans from neighboring states. Jacob Haas and Joseph T. Eichberg were among the presidents of the Germania Building and Loan Association which was founded in 1870. During the next three decades the association supplied part of the funds for the houses of many of Atlanta's Germans as well as for the synagogue. David Mayer and Samuel Weil were among the seven vice-presidents in 1871 of the largely German Organization of Foreign-born Citizens. The following year William Teitlebaum, Moses Frank, and Mayer were among the organizers of the Atlanta German Association. Schiller Lodge No. 71 of the Independent Order of Odd Fellows was founded by Jewish and gentile Germans in 1872 and conducted its meetings in German for the next two decades. In 1873 Aaron Haas was one of the five charter members of the Atlanta Turnverein, and other Jews subsequently served as officers.[52]

That relations between Jewish and gentile Germans were not always cordial is evident from a series of incidents which occurred in 1871. In September and October, Otto Palmer, the publisher and editor of the *Atlanta Deutsche Zeitung,* wrote several articles critical of conditions in the South and advised against further German immigration to the region. On October 17 a mass meeting of Germans in Concordia Hall presided over by former immigration commissioner Samuel Weil unanimously repudiated Palmer's claims. While acknowledging that some improvements were necessary, most of the speakers maintained that German immigrants had nothing to fear in the South and that the "life and property of those who do not meddle too much in politics" were as secure as anywhere else in the country. "Whitehall Street," declared Weil, "demonstrates that no discrimination is made against German merchants," and insisted that "a man has no right to abuse the country he lives in." In rebuttal, Palmer spoke disparagingly of the "quasi-German" meeting in Concordia Hall and alleged that it had been composed almost entirely of Jews, "and as the Jews . . . care but little for German immigration and the German element, it is considered an assumption [sic] that this Jew meeting should pass resolutions in the name of the Germans of Atlanta." The editor further maintained, perhaps correctly, that the Jews desired "to make political capital amongst the native population in relation to immigration." Finally, he charged that the Jews had "impeded the progress of the German element, the establishment of German churches and societies" and were engaged in a conspiracy against the German community and its journalistic organ. Palmer's views regarding immigration were endorsed by a meeting of thirty-nine German Gentiles on November 4, but two days later another German meeting of at least twenty-six Gentiles and an undisclosed number of Jews at the city hall insisted that the Concordia meeting had consisted of "solid representatives of the German element" and had expressed the sentiments of 80 percent of Atlanta's German citizens. The participants in the city hall meeting condemned Palmer's "call on religious prejudices and old social abuses . . . to escape the censure of fellow citizens," and were partially responsible for the editor's subsequent removal from the city.[53]

A similar example of a German Gentile seeking to dissociate himself from the Jews occurred a year later when a local Republican aspirant to the Georgia House allegedly exclaimed: "I know nutting bout Abraham, Isaac or Yacob being kin to me or my farder. . . . I know some tings about Pismark; he is der fellow me and my farder claims kin wid him and his farder."[54]

Incidents of this sort, while mirroring the Judaeophobia of some German Gentiles, were only partially responsible for the declining Jewish participation in German societies after 1880. More important were changes in the composition and orientation of the two groups. Although large numbers of Gentiles continued to emigrate from Germany during the eighties and nineties, the emigration of Jews declined sharply after 1870 following their complete emancipation and rapid integration into German society. Not only did the proportion of Jews among Atlanta's Germans drop from 34 percent in 1880 to 30 percent in 1896, but more significantly the proportion of the German-born among Jewish males ages 18 and over fell from 60 to 22 percent. Without an appreciable influx of young immigrants from Germany, the German Jews grew increasingly older and more americanized. They had little in common with the young, mostly working-class newcomers from Germany, many of whom had been influenced by the resurgent anti-Semitism that blossomed in the fatherland after 1877. Moreover, the creation of new Jewish organizations and the improvement of old ones satisfied their associational needs to a fuller extent than could the German clubs.[55]

With few exceptions, by the mid-eighties the Jews of Atlanta had ceased to think of themselves as Germans and were endeavoring to reconcile their Jewish and American identities.

# 3

## *From Traditionalism to Classical Reform: The Odyssey of the Hebrew Benevolent Congregation*

The character of American Judaism was transformed during the nineteenth century under the impact of secularism, voluntarism, and immigration. The pattern of "dignified orthodoxy" which had evolved during the preceding century was challenged during the 1840s by newly arrived rabbis from Central Europe who were imbued with the nascent ideals of Reform Judaism. Beginning in the eighties, a mass influx of Orthodox Jews from Eastern Europe overwhelmed the emerging Reform majority.

Judaism as practiced in Germany at the dawn of the nineteenth century differed little in form or content from that in neighboring Poland. It viewed every commandment of the Pentateuch and the Talmud as equally binding and thereby placed the ceremonial law on an equal plane with the ethical and moral commandments. The dress, diet, work habits, and even sexual conduct of the observant Jew were all carefully regulated by 613 *mitzvoth* (commandments) that had been codified during the sixteenth century. While observance of the *mitzvoth* made the Jew a cultural alien in the land in which he dwelt, it provided the inner strength and discipline that enabled Judaism to survive for centuries in a hostile society which granted Jews equality only at the price of conversion. However, under the impact of the Enlightenment and the subsequent gradual lifting of legal barriers to Jewish advancement, the authority and utility of many of the *mitzvoth* were called into question. It was in this milieu that Reform Judaism was born.[1]

The early reforms were conscious attempts to break with the ghetto, achieve complete political equality, acquire esteem in the eyes of the gentile community, and retain the loyalty of an increasingly irreligious younger generation. Such essentially aesthetic and opportunistic innovations like an abbreviated liturgy, sermons and supplementary prayers in the vernacular, family pews, and mixed choral singing with instrumental accompaniment drew hostile fire from traditionalists and, in turn, called forth far more subversive theoretical justifications. The Reform theoreticians distinguished between what they claimed were laws and customs rooted in historical circumstances and what they deemed to be the universal precepts of religion and morality that were to be found in Mosaic monotheism and prophetic idealism. While defining Judaism as a universal faith which emphasized the ethical tradition as its basic dimension, they argued that to fulfill its destiny, Judaism must be free to adjust to changing circumstances without being bound by the historic evolution and continuity of Jewish tradition.[2]

Opposed by the powerful and conservative central communal bodies which appointed rabbis in the community synagogues and were recognized by the state, Reform Judaism never triumphed in Germany. In America, however, Reform achieved its greatest victories and articulated its most radical manifesto. "Progress" and "reform" were popular slogans in the fluid, expanding society of mid-nineteenth century America. Furthermore, the voluntaristic character of American life, a tradition of congregational autonomy, the separation of church and state together with the absence of recognized sources of Jewish communal authority or strong communal leadership, and the fact that the Reform rabbis who began to arrive in the 1840s were the first ordained Jewish clergymen to appear in the United States, provided fertile soil for the seeds of Reform.[3]

American Jewry during the forties and fifties was still traditionally oriented. The established members of the old Sephardic congregations remained true to their heritage, while the newer German immigrants frequently went to extraordinary lengths to observe *kashruth* (dietary laws), circumcision, and the Sabbath. Most of these early immigrants had come from small towns in southern Germany and Posen which had not been affected by the theological arguments of the Reformers. Even where observance was lax, as on the expanding frontier, the traditional conception of Judaism remained. The leading spokesmen for this generation were Isaac Leeser and Samuel M. Isaacs, laymen who had received solid Jewish training in Europe and became *hazanim* (cantors) and editors of Anglo-Jewish periodicals in Philadelphia and New York respectively. They firmly believed that Judaism had to adapt itself to post-Emancipation and Enlightenment realities, but insisted that this could only be done according to biblical and talmudic teachings and in the light of the historical Jewish tradition.[4]

The initial progress of the Reformers was slow, but time was on their side. As the traditionalists grew older and more removed from their Orthodox roots, as their native-born children grew to maturity without adequate Jewish training, and as Reform-minded immigrants from Germany began to arrive in increasing numbers, the character of Jewish observance began to change. The desire to be integrated into American society and the vicissitudes of economic competition resulted in a further sloughing off of traditional practices, and Reform Judaism both accelerated and lent sanction to these developments.[5]

The Reform rabbis were divided into two camps. The moderates, led by Isaac Mayer Wise of Cincinnati, were primarily concerned with the modernization of the service and the institutionalization of American Judaism. Like many other Americans, they were largely indifferent to theoretical formulations. The radicals, led by David Einhorn of Baltimore and later of New York, sought to provide the movement with a sound theoretical foundation, even at the risk of preventing the organizational unity of American Jewry. Under the influence of Einhorn's followers the main tenets of American Reform Judaism were finally articulated. The Pittsburgh Platform of 1885 declared Judaism to be a "progressive religion, ever striving to be in accord with the postulates of reason" and dedicated to social justice. It rejected all Mosaic laws "not adapted to the views and habits of modern civilization," repudiated the national components of Judaism rooted in the concepts of Exile and Return, and denied the validity of bodily resurrection, heaven, and hell.[6]

For the first few years of its existence, the Hebrew Benevolent Congregation adhered to the traditional ritual. Men and women sat separately, the service was chanted entirely in Hebrew by knowledgeable members like Jacob Steinheimer, L. L. Levy, and William Silverberg, and there was no instrumental accompaniment. The situation changed after the death in 1868 of Isaac Leeser, who had guided the religious instincts of Atlanta's Jews since the 1850s. Almost immediately the congregation fell under the influence of

Isaac Mayer Wise, and a year later the Cincinnati Reformer journeyed to Atlanta and lectured on "Judaism" at the Concordia.[7]

Perhaps on Wise's recommendation, in 1869 David Burgheim was elected Atlanta's first rabbi. Born in Prussian Posen in 1830, Burgheim had come to the United States in 1867 and had served an Orthodox and a Reform congregation in Nashville before accepting the call to Atlanta. Like most of his colleagues in the American rabbinate, he had never received *semikhah* (ordination). Furthermore, despite the flexibility he had apparently demonstrated in Nashville, the new rabbi was determined to move his congregation in the direction of Reform. "Atlanta," observed Wise, "is a growing congregation and Mr. Burgheim can do a great deal for them, if they adhere to the side of reform which we expect they will."[8]

Within less than a year, Burgheim introduced four Reform innovations: a melodeon, mixed choirs, weekly sermons in German, and Wise's prayerbook, *Minhag America.* A like-minded member reported to Wise that

> the coreligionists living here at present [are] working so harmoniously together, having the cause of true religion at heart, not minding the dogmas and forms but the principles of religion, acting their part up to it. . . . formed the present congregation upon the moderate reform system, gradually taking in the *Minhag America* to such an extent that ere long it will be entirely so.[9]

The *Atlanta Constitution* observed a similar tendency:

> The Israelites of Atlanta have never divided upon the question of orthodoxy and reformation. They are extremists on neither side. While many of the prayers and customs . . . not applicable to the present age and the present conditions of the descendants of Jacob are omited [*sic*] . . . they do not go so far in ignoring ancient traditional usages as do the extreme reformers in other places. Moderation and toleration in regard to questions of mere form seem to characterize the Israelites of our city. . . .[10]

Whether Burgheim endeavored to push his congregation further toward Reform than it was willing to go, or because his dour and methodical disposition proved unappealing, his one-year contract was not renewed. Burgheim returned to Nashville in 1870 and during the next seventeen years served congregations in at least eight other cities, none for periods longer than three years.[11]

Unwittingly, Burgheim supplied his own successor in the person of Benjamin A. Bonnheim whom he had engaged as principal of his English-German-Hebrew Academy. The son of a rabbi, Bonnheim was born in Prussia in 1841, attended college at Marburg, and then taught in a government school for eight years. Arriving in New York in 1866, he supported himself for a year by giving private lessons, was then called to the pulpit of a Columbus, Georgia congregation, and remained three years. Bonnheim wore better than his predecessor and was twice reelected. He also occasionally preached in English. The *Constitution* remarked that the "pastor" was "a young man of far more than mediocre abilities and learning" and that he had become "deservedly popular, not only with his congregation, but with all classes."[12] Such tributes were frequently overdone:

> In the Jewish Synagogue, Rabbi Bonheim [*sic*] blows the silver trump of jubilee, and by his able expositions of the Law, the Prophets, and the Psalms, he is leading on the hosts of Israel to the goodly land flowing with milk and honey. Those who are not attracted and impressed by his immense diversity of gifts care nothing about the good things of the house of God, and have no excuse for their sins.[13]

Although Bonnheim devoted most of his time to teaching, he continued Burgheim's advocacy of Reform. The practice of confirmation on Shevuoth was introduced in 1873, but it did not replace the bar mitzvah ceremony as many Reformers had urged. After his reelection in July 1873, Bonnheim advised the membership not to follow the "so called ultra-orthodox Israelites [who] believe any myth, fable, the knowledge of angels, demons, the mystic arts, and all the great absurdities that the human mind [can devise], and put them on the same paralell [*sic*] of holiness as God's own word."[14]

The following month Isaac Mayer Wise visited Atlanta for a second time, and after lecturing under the auspices of the nonsectarian Young Men's Library Association, convinced the congregation to reduce the observance of Rosh Hashanah to one day. "Formerly two days were kept," noted the *Constitution,* "and this is the practice of the more orthodox."[15]

Changes in the ritual did not go so far as some members desired and were much too radical for others. "We can not boast," wrote the local correspondent of Wise's *American Israelite,* "that all these [reforms] have passed without any differences of opinion; of course such matters always rouse party feelings . . . [and] even give rise to personal injustice among members of the congregation." "It is sincerely desired," he added, "that all useless talking . . . should desist . . . since . . . any further contention can sooner harm the cause of our congregation in general, than bring about the repeal of either of the assumed measures."[16]

Benjamin Bonnheim may have been a victim of the controversy he helped engender, for in 1874 he returned to Columbus and during the remaining thirty-five years of his life occupied pulpits in at least half a dozen other communities.[17]

For its next rabbi the congregation chose a brilliant and controversial young man named Henry Gersoni. Born in Vilna, Russia, in 1844, Gersoni attended the Vilna Rabbinical Seminary but soon developed an interest in secular literature, and when he enrolled in the University of St. Petersburg against his parents wishes, was disinherited. During his two years at the university, Gersoni supported himself by writing Yiddish poetry and tutoring the son of a Russian count. Meanwhile, out of conviction or opportunism, he converted to Russian Orthodoxy, but soon regretted his decision and in 1866 fled to England in order to live again as a Jew. Arriving friendless and penniless, Gersoni drifted into a Protestant mission run by Jewish apostates and remained ten months. Repentant once more, he moved to Paris, penned a public confession, and reaffirmed his loyalty to Judaism. In 1869 he settled in New York, taught in the Temple Emanu-El Sabbath School, and during the next four years wrote articles for several journals, published a Hebrew translation of Longfellow's *Excelsior,* and authored *Sketches of Jewish Life and History.*[18]

How much the Jews of Atlanta knew of Gersoni's checkered past at the time of his election is uncertain, but they were undoubtedly impressed by his scholarly credentials, linguistic ability, and literary reputation. Even so, his unworldliness struck many of his materialistic and acquisitively oriented congregants as queer. "He is much more liberal with the congregation than they are with him," remarked a member. "But then this is no great praise, it only shows that he is not practical and knows not the value of money. Give him books and plenty of gas-light to burn the whole night and he is happy. Tastes will differ."[19]

Gersoni was highly regarded by the local press and at least during his first term proved to be a popular rabbi. "In the short time of his ministration," observed a member, "Rev. Mr. Gersoni has brought back to the flock several stray sheep of Israel. . . . This gentleman who came to us pretending to be 'no chazen at all' proves to be a great attraction to lovers of sonorous and harmonious voice."[20] His lengthy and tightly reasoned sermons were often published in their entirety by the *Atlanta Constitution* and the *American Israelite.*[21]

Despite his Orthodox upbringing, Gersoni was a confirmed Reformer and could be scathing in his criticism of tradition-minded members.

> We have no argument for those, who having nothing on God's earth to do, having spent their best years in adornation of self, and who in their old age embrace the cause of orthodoxy, ignorant of its meaning and false to its principles, they do so only for the purpose of having something to say, in order to palm themselves off as men of importance. . . .
> Keep Mr. Karo's code [the *Shulhan Arukh*], my orthodox friends, cling with nervous tenacity to the old landmarks. Your Reform brethren has a nobler duty to perform. He will teach the young, he will bring back to the fold those whom your intolerance has thrown out of the synagogue, he will show the magnificence of the Law of God in a light which is not obscure, and in forms which are not outworn with age. . . .[22]

However, the rabbi was equally critical of Reform's radical wing.

> If our apostles of reform would follow the routine of consciencious [*sic*] progress, and doing away carefully with the old customs and habits, they would substitute new exercises more befitting our progressive age in their stead—*A la bonheur:* this is the thing we require; but reform, as it has its aspect now, is tearing down edifices which have sustained our race for ages without providing anything to shelter us for a day.[23]

At the synagogue's cornerstone-laying ceremony in 1875, Gersoni refused to wear his rabbinical robe, declaring that "such paraphernalia may be necessary for a religion of the senses, but they are quite unnecessary—even objectionable—to a religion of the intellect and of the heart."[24] And in presenting himself for reelection to a second term, he stipulated that he would remain only if the triennial cycle of Torah reading (as opposed to the traditional annual cycle) was introduced and the observance of the second days of major holidays abolished. When warned by several Orthodox members that such forcible introduction of Reform would split the congregation, the rabbi withdrew his petition, was reelected, canvassed for the changes, and saw them enacted.[25]

Other changes introduced by Gersoni were the omission of the *kiddush* and the substitution of silent devotion for the first *Shemona Esreh.* Far more significant in terms of Reform was the transformation of Tisha B'Av, traditionally a day of fasting and mourning over the destruction of the Temple, into a day of rejoicing. In a lecture entitled "The Fall of Gods, The Triumph of Religion," Gersoni explained that without the destruction of the Temple and the consequent dispersion, the Jews could not fulfill their mission to diffuse the knowledge of God among men.[26]

Gersoni's association with the Hebrew Benevolent Congregation ended early in 1877, apparently under less than cordial circumstances. He then moved to Chicago, where he edited the weekly *Jewish Advance* and served a local Reform congregation until forced to leave "under a cloud of apostasy." Gersoni returned to New York in 1883 and supported himself by his pen until his death in 1897.[27]

If the Jews of Atlanta wished to avoid controversy, they could have done better than elect Edward Benjamin Morris Browne—nicknamed, because of his initials and academic credentials, "Alphabet" Browne. Born in Kaschau, Hungary, in 1844, Browne received a university education and mastered several languages before he emigrated to the United States shortly after the Civil War. After serving briefly on the faculty of the Savannah Hebrew Collegiate Institute, Browne went to Cincinnati where he studied for the rabbinate under Isaac Mayer Wise and earned an M.D. from the University of Cincinnati in 1869. Upon Wise's recommendation, Browne was chosen rabbi of a Montgomery, Alabama, congregation but was dismissed less than a year later. He was next elected rabbi of Milwaukee's Temple Emanu-El but was fired after five months and termed "incapable" of executing his duties "to the satisfaction of any part of . . . [the] congregation. . . ." However, the unsuccessful rabbi did manage to receive an LL.B. from the University of Wisconsin in 1871. With medical and legal degrees but apparently no practical experience, Browne convinced the Evansville (Indiana) College of Medicine to appoint him Professor of Medical Jurisprudence and Diseases of the Mind. Browne also served as rabbi of the local temple and edited the *Jewish Independent,* but he left Evansville in 1873 for unexplained reasons. During the next three years he occupied a pulpit in Peoria and translated a medieval midrashic text into English which he then published as "the lost book of the Bible."[28]

Wise took Browne to task for his protégé's shortcomings as a rabbi: ". . . if I had four places in five years, or so, and come away quarreling from cities, beyond a doubt I would have come to the conclusion that the fault is in me. . . . Can you not see the failures you have made?" Wise advised Browne not to answer his critics in print, to deliver "good sermons without sensation or humbug" and to diligently study the Jewish sources which he had forgotten. Above all, he urged the young rabbi to pay careful attention "to conduct in society, where prudence, forbearance, and moderation are as necessary as good moral character," concluding:

> The world is cold. Now do what you please; I have done my duty as a friend. If you want to remain in the ministry you must build up a reputation not only as a scholar and orator but also as a quiet, earnest and peaceable man who manages well. This will take time, resolution, and self-government.[29]

Browne failed to cultivate the talents his mentor had suggested, and to pay the bills during periodic bouts of unemployment he became a professional lecturer. It was as an itinerant spellbinder that Browne was first invited to Atlanta in 1875 to lecture on "The Talmud: Its Ethics and Literary Beauties." When the pulpit was declared vacant two years later, "Alphabet" Browne was offered the position. Like his predecessors, Browne began his career in Atlanta with the support of both the congregation and the local press. "Dr. Browne," observed the *Constitution,* "is a gentleman of fine culture, of vigorous mental constitution, and of blameless character. He will prove to be a proper head of a large and influential Jewish population in this city."[30]

The new rabbi immersed himself in a myriad of activities. In 1877 he founded, and for the next three and a half years edited, the *Jewish South,* the first Jewish periodical in the region.[31] Less successful was Browne's attempt to found a private boarding school The Southern Educational Institute for Jewish Boys. To supplement his meager salary and to raise funds for charity, Browne returned to the lecture circuit, speaking not only about the Talmud, but also on "The Crucifiction [*sic*] and the Jews; or Did the Jews Actually Crucify Jesus of Nazareth" and "The Jews and Temperance; or How the Chosen People Keep Sober." Between these various activities the rabbi found time to represent Georgia at the World Congress of Science in Stockholm and to audit the sermons of his Protestant colleagues. "[T]here are Jewish ministers," observed Browne, "who will 'play flunky' around some Christian preachers to be called 'nice men' rather than defend our cause. Let the Jewish minister be bold and outspoken and we shall not be belied in public."[32]

Browne could never be accused of failing to speak out, and therein lay much of his trouble. A contentious man with an exaggerated sense of his own importance, he was constantly embroiled in journalistic quarrels which, together with his frequent lecture-related absences from the city and several lengthy illnesses, caused him to neglect his congregational duties. In January 1881 the congregation decided not to renew the rabbi's contract. Publicly it was alleged that Browne had failed to teach the children and that the congregation had not made any progress under his leadership. Privately it was whispered that the rabbi had embezzled funds from a business enterprise with which he was connected and had offended in some unstated way two of the congregation's wealthiest members. Browne threatened legal action against any newspaper which carried "the libel." He subsequently moved to New York where he continued his erratic career.[33] "Few people who ever knew the learned rabbi will ever forget him," remarked the *Constitution* several years later. "He possesses a marked individuality and a capacity for making himself conspicuous wherever he goes. Perhaps his most striking characteristic is his capacity for getting into trouble."[34]

While in some respects Browne was sui generis, his tenure problems and those of his predecessors were by no means unique. Few qualified European rabbis were tempted to cross the Atlantic, and in the absence of nationally recognized agencies of certification, the American rabbinate attracted more than its fair share of incompetents and frauds who adversely affected the status of the profession. At a time of heated theological debate, rabbis were understandably the initiators and often the victims of party strife. Independent-minded rabbis confronted a strong tradition of lay leadership, and inflated, sensitive egos were to be found on both sides of the pulpit. Offering niggardly remuneration to men frequently ill equipped for the task, small, isolated congregations like Atlanta's expected their rabbis to be not only preachers and counselors but also teachers, *hazanim, shohetim,* and ambassadors of goodwill to the gentile community. A "Jewish rabbi, to be orthodox or reform, must be very circumspect," cautioned the *American Israelite,* "particularly in an age and in a country where rabbis are looked upon as ice-cream only."[35]

No significant changes in the ritual were made during Browne's three-and-a-half-year tenure. The synagogue he helped dedicate in 1877 had family pews and was generally referred to as the Temple, but mixed seating and the Reform nomenclature were probably not new. An organ was installed, but instrumental accompaniment had been part of the service since 1870. Like Gersoni, Browne did not believe in the messianic restoration of the Jewish people to Palestine, and "unreasonable" prayers to that end may have been deleted from the service. A motion to permit members to remove their hats in the synagogue was tabled. The congregation may have been unwilling to proceed any further along the path of Reform, for in choosing its next two rabbis it consulted Dr. Marcus Jastrow of Philadelphia, a leader of the Conservative movement in American Judaism.[36]

Jacob S. Jacobson was born in Schleswig-Holstein in 1840 and, after graduation from rabbinical academy in 1856, pursued further studies in Hamburg and England, taught English, German, and Hebrew in Flensburg from 1862 to 1864, and received his Ph.D. from the University of Copenhagen. He came to America in 1865 and served congregations in the District of Columbia, Paterson, New Jersey, and Easton, Pennsylvania, before coming to Atlanta. During his seven-year sojourn in the city, no further "reforms" were introduced, and for a brief interval the congregation withdrew from Wise's Union of American Hebrew Congregations. In 1888 Jacobson resigned, probably in the face of uncertain reelection, and assumed a pulpit in Natchez, Mississippi.[37]

Jacobson's successor, Leo Reich, was born in Karacsommezo, Hungary, in 1863 and attended a Budapest rabbinical seminary before emigrating to the United States in 1885. Prior to his election by the Temple in 1888, Reich served congregations in Philadelphia, Brooklyn, and Augusta. During his seven years in Atlanta, the two-day observance of major holidays was restored, the conservative *Minhag Jastrow* replaced Wise's *Minhag America,* and the Temple once again withdrew briefly from the Union of American Hebrew Congregations.[38]

But Reform sentiment continued to grow. At the January 1895 annual meeting, the abandonment of the ritual garb, the reduction of holiday observance to one day, the prohibition of covered heads in the sanctuary, and the adoption of the new Reform *Union Prayer Book* were demanded. Reich refused to accede, and the pulpit was declared vacant. Although the *Constitution* attributed a "restless spirit of dissatisfaction" to Reich's "thoroughly orthodox" sermons, the rabbi's lectures were thoroughly rationalistic in the moderate Reform tradition. Rather, a majority of the voting members opted for a different kind of rabbi and a different brand of Reform.[39]

Ten years after the issuance of the Pittsburgh Platform, the Temple —with its conservative prayer book, bar mitzvah ceremony, two-day observance of holidays, *huppah,* and compulsory wearing of the *yarmulke* (skullcap)—was an oddity among Reform congregations. The delayed move to the left was rooted in the changing composition and religious orientation of the Hebrew Benevolent Congregation and the Jewish community as a whole.

Until 1895, "reform" of the synagogue ritual grew slowly and had been preceded by a steady erosion of personal piety. Strict observance of the Sabbath—abstinence from work from sundown Friday to sundown Saturday—was the most inconvenient of the traditional religious injunctions and the first to be discarded. Sunday closing ordinances prohibited merchants from doing business on the Christian Sabbath, and for a storekeeper to suspend business on both days would have entailed considerable hardship, since workers were paid on Saturday and therefore it was the busiest shopping day. Some Jews did close their stores for the entire weekend, while others either entrusted their businesses to gentile subordinates or opened only after Sabbath morning services. However, most conducted their affairs as usual on Saturday and closed on Sunday. Indeed, when a number of Seventh Day Adventists were imprisoned elsewhere in Georgia for working on Sunday the *Constitution* remarked, "The Jews have never given us any trouble in this matter and the 'Seventh Day [A]dventists' should follow their example for the sake of peace and order."[40]

The need to work on the Sabbath resulted in poor attendance at services. Rabbi Browne observed that the Temple was full on Friday evenings "when business does not interfere" and recognized that those who did come were frequently motivated by other than religious concerns.

> [The Temple] is a beautiful place to meet; the choir is very good; the place has become fashionable, and people like to attend fashionable gatherings. If a young gentleman is not prompted by religious motive to go to the temple, you are sure to find him there—business and other amusements permitting—in order to admire or be admired by somebody. Others may come simply because they have no better way of

> spending the evening. . . . If anything, the "sponger" will make himself more comfortable, criticize the choir, sexton and even the minister. . . . And that gent, curling his moustache, thinks he does the congregation a great deal of honor in visiting the temple. . . .[41]

On another occasion, Browne noted that "New Year's Day and the day [*sic*] of Atonement are the only holidays some so-called Yehudims [*sic*] observe. Those who disregard even these two days need not call upon us. . . ."[42]

In 1886 the *Constitution* remarked that except for the High Holy Days, services were "very slimly attended," a state of affairs which Jacobson attributed to the "strife [*sic*] after material success." Disinterest was especially rife among the young. "Of course we carry all drawing cards," reported a member in 1885,

> a handsome temple, fine organ . . . and the best-trained and best-voiced choir the city affords for the money. The only thing that dampens our ardor is that the choristers, who sing "Sh'ma Yisroel" and "Ayn Kaylohaynu" in our temple on Shabbos, sing "Jesus Lover of My Soul" in the Episcopal and Presbyterian churches, on Sunday. However, the young element in our Jewish circle is, at best, not very religiously inclined, and rather listens to fine music . . . than do the performing itself. . . .[43]

The dietary laws also fell into disuse. Although there were too few Jews in antebellum Atlanta to support a *shohet,* kosher meat could have been imported from Augusta as early as 1851. "While it was impossible to keep a kosher table," recalled Aaron Haas, "there was never a piece of hog in my father's house, nor was milk or butter on the table with meat." Few early pioneers could have claimed more. Rabbis Burgheim and Bonnheim performed the rite of *shehitah* (ritual slaughter) in addition to serving as teacher, reader, and preacher, but in 1874 the board of trustees "found it expedient to separate the kitchen from the pulpit," and the responsibility was transferred to someone else.[44]

Observance of *kashruth* was clearly waning. Gersoni was critical of "kitchen Judaism," and Browne could recommend the practice only for its "great prophylactic virtues."

> We are not one of those who, when the knife used for meat touching a dish containing milk, will stick the blade into the ground overnight. We do not even wait six long hours between a good roast and a cup of cream-capped coffee. Some of our enemies have even gone so far

> as to say that we have occasionally indulged in meat taken from the hindquarter of a beef. But for all that we hold that the sanitary measures aimed at by Moses, are not to be discarded for . . . the principles upon which they are based, challenge not only our admiration as Jews, but the admiration of the gentile world. . . .[45]

Publicity in the local press did contribute to a growing awareness of *kashruth*'s hygenic value, and after a lengthy article appeared in the *Constitution,* one butcher reputedly sold five times as much kosher meat as before, much of it to Gentiles. However, in 1885 the *shohet* slaughtered a weekly average of only six steers, two or three calves, several sheep, and an occasional goat—hardly enough to feed a Jewish community of one thousand persons.[46]

By the mid-nineties, forbidden foods like ham, game, and shellfish were unabashedly consumed in public. Oyster pâté à la Baltimore was served to Rabbi Reich and the leading members of the Temple at the Concordia Hall dedication banquet in 1893, and two years later delegates to the regional B'nai B'rith convention in Atlanta dined on fresh lobster washed down with "Palestine Punch." The local *Jewish Sentiment* carried the advertisements of kosher meat dealer Carl Wolfsheimer, but also those who sold *treif* (unkosher) foods. "Order your . . . Quail, Rabbits, Squirrels, fine Oysters, etc., from us," urged the Dopson Market Company. "Special attention given to the Jewish and retail trade." "Judaism is not unreasonable," explained editor Frank J. Cohen, "and there can flow no possible good from restrictions, ceremonies and laws . . . which so thoroughly separates us from our neighbors. . . ."[47]

The decline in personal piety and the consequent growth of Reform was reflected in the changing character of the Hebrew Benevolent Congregation's membership. The congregation had never been representative of the entire community, and it became progressively less so; only 44 percent of the Jewish males ages 18 and over in 1870 and only 30 percent of those in 1896 belonged. Although 14 percent of the Jewish males ages 18 and over in 1870 were native-born Americans, all of the members that year were foreign-born, and most were sufficiently familiar with the traditional synagogue ritual to result in its adoption with but minor aesthetic changes. Twenty-six years later, as the congregation stood on the brink of radical Reform, a third of the members were native-born, and most of these were ignorant of or alienated from the traditional ritual. The foreign-born members had also changed, for they were older, wealthier, and more americanized than they had been in 1870.[48] Within a quarter of a century, assimilation, the influence of six Reform-minded rabbis, the omnipresent example of Protestant forms, and the gentile Southerner's suspicion of alien ways had transformed many former theological imperatives into embarrassing vestiges of a less enlightened era. (See table 23.)

Since the early seventies, traditionalists like Herman Haas and Jacob Hirschberg had skirmished with Reformers like Abram Rosenfeld and Alex Dittler over changes in the ritual.[49] While the gradual change in the membership finally gave the Reform party the upper hand, its victory was insured by developments outside of the congregation.

In contrast to the port and industrial cities of the East and the Midwest, not until the mid-nineties was Atlanta significantly affected by the deluge of Jewish immigration from Eastern Europe that had begun in 1881. As late as 1890 there were only 126 Russians in Atlanta; but six years later there were 317, and by 1900, almost 500. Together with their native-born children, the Russians constituted nearly 40 percent of the city's Jewish population in 1896 and nearly a majority by 1900.[50] Their arrival in large numbers produced a profound reaction on the part of the established Jewish community. The very foreignness of the newcomers, their Yiddish language, Orthodox religion, Old World ways and physical appearance threatened to give the word "Jew" a connotation that the older settlers had struggled for decades to outgrow. Fearing that their hard-won status was in jeopardy, the "Germans," already committed to acculturation, consciously endeavored to set themselves off from their Orthodox brethren and rushed to embrace American cultural forms. They found an ideal spokesman in David Marx.[51]

A native of New Orleans and a graduate of Hebrew Union College and the University of Cincinnati, David Marx was only twenty-three years old when he became the Temple's youngest and first American-born rabbi. For the next half-century he would lead his congregation along the path of radical Reform.[52]

Soon after his election, the ritual robes and prayer shawls were discarded, holiday observance was again reduced to one day, and the *Union Prayer Book* was adopted. A reporter from the *Constitution* who attended High Holy Day services the following year was astonished to find the worshipers bareheaded, nearly all of the prayers in English, and estimated that only two-thirds of the Jews—"mostly the older element"—were observing the sacred Yom Kippur fast. An attempt in 1897 to do away with the bar mitzvah failed, but early the next year the board of trustees ruled that it was "inexpedient" to confer the rite. When a member demanded that his thirteen-year-old son be bar mitzvah, the rabbi and trustees refused, and after an acrimonious confrontation the dissident member narrowly escaped expulsion.[53] A few members in 1900 spoke of organizing a new congregation that would be "neither orthodox nor ultra-reform," but no action was taken. Four years later, Marx introduced a Sunday service to attract those who neglected to attend the regular Friday evening and Saturday morning services. Unlike some of his Reform colleagues, Marx did not wish to alter the day of Sabbath observance, but the innovation was radical enough to make the Temple one of only nineteen American Reform congregations in 1906 with a Sunday service.[54]

No less than his predecessors, Marx was committed to the survival of Judaism, but the Judaism he espoused, stripped of "foreignism," ritual, and formalism, bore little resemblance to either the ancient Hebrew faith or the religion of Atlanta's Jewish majority. "We stand today for the ideals of Israel spiritually interpreted, a minority of a minority people," the rabbi declared in 1909. "Our services are cast on a high plane of sanity, which while recognizing the importance of sentiment, does not degenerate into hysteria so prejudicial to the intellectual side of man's religious nature." Under his leadership, the congregation conducted its affairs as a religious denomination, in tone and form modeled upon liberal Protestantism. The High Holy Days were referred to as "the great Jewish revival season," and in the "Jewish church," appellations like "minister," "doctor," and "reverend" were increasingly substituted for "rabbi." At the dedication of the new temple in 1902, Massenet's "The Last Sleep of the Virgin" was performed and apparently no eyebrows were raised. Although Marx had only a superficial relationship with the rabbis of Atlanta's three Russian synagogues and never invited their members to participate in Temple functions, he cultivated close ties with several Unitarian, Universalist, Presbyterian, Methodist, and Baptist clergymen. In 1900 they founded the Unity Club and two years later inaugurated the first of several interfaith Thanksgiving services at the Temple.[55]

During his first decade in Atlanta, the young rabbi organized a Temple kindergarten and sisterhood, modernized the religious school, instructed adult Bible classes, conducted services in outlying Jewish communities, and was a driving force behind the establishment of the Young Men's Hebrew Association, the Federation of Jewish Charities, and the local chapter of the Council of Jewish Women. "They did not chain me to the pulpit," he recalled many years later.[56]

Nor did Marx confine his activities to the Jewish community. He wrote for the *Atlanta Journal,* campaigned for free kindergartens, international arbitration, compulsory school attendance laws, manual training, and the prevention of tuberculosis. Frequently he lectured before local church and civic groups. He also welcomed visiting dignitaries on behalf of the city, represented Georgia at several regional conferences, espoused Masonry with great devotion, and delivered the invocation at meetings of the legislature and the city council. In short the rabbi soon became Atlanta's best known and most respected Jew, and as such effectively represented his people before the gentile community.[57]

Marx had a tremendous impact on the Hebrew Benevolent Congregation. During his first decade in the pulpit, the Temple's membership rose from 169 to 289 and for the first time embraced nearly the entire "German" community.[58] Unfortunately, the increase in affiliation was paralleled by a decline in participation, for the rabbi's dynamism seemingly obviated the need for lay leadership. In effect, Marx had become the congregation, and it was sufficient merely to belong. Attendance at services reached a record low in 1908 when, with a membership representing 900 persons of "temple going age," Friday evening services averaged 100 and Saturday morning 137. "A non-worshipping congregation in this generation," cautioned Marx, "begs a non-allegiance to any congregation on the part of the next." But his warning was not heeded. His uplifting exhortations to do good works, live uprightly, and abide by universal ideals and conventional aphorisms failed to strike a responsively Jewish chord. What remained of the once elaborate ritual was now dull and meaningless. Presented with the "distilled essence" of Judaism, members found little that was recognizably Jewish.[59]

Despite the omnipresent signs of spiritual decay, the congregation revered its rabbi and demonstrated its affection by showering him with gifts as well as increasing his salary between 1896 and 1914 from $2,400 to $6,000. He made them proud to be Jews, but their pride was not in the teachings of Judaism, which made increasingly fewer demands upon their lives. It was rather in Marx's acceptance by the gentile community, which they interpreted as acceptance for themselves. As the Russian Jewish population became more numerous and the status of the established Jewish community more precarious, the Temple's members were grateful for even the illusion of acceptance.

# 4

## *The New Immigrants*

The assassination of Czar Alexander II in 1881 marked a turning point not only for Russian Jewry but also for the Jewish community of Atlanta. During the next three decades grinding poverty and governmental anti-Semitism in Russia and Rumania, and severe economic depression in Galicia (Austrian Poland), would send 1,-120,000 Russian, 67,000 Rumanian, and 281,000 Austro-Hungarian Jews fleeing to the United States. Meanwhile, between 1899 and the outbreak of World War I, poverty, a series of natural disasters, and the effects of war and revolution resulted in the immigration of approximately 15,000 Sephardic Jews from the Levant. Although the overwhelming majority of both the East Europeans and the Sephardim settled in the northeastern states, principally in New York City, enough went South to restructure completely Jewish life in the Gate City.

The East European refugees came from a society that had only recently emerged from the Middle Ages. Serfdom had persisted in Russia until 1861 and in Rumania until 1864, while in Austria-Hungary feudal dues and services were not abolished until 1867. Political autocracy, rigid class distinctions, and restraints upon economic activity and physical mobility characterized all three countries. Like the Gentiles among whom they dwelt, most of the Jews maintained an essentially medieval frame of reference. For the vast majority, religion dominated and suffused every aspect of life to a degree perhaps unparalleled in Jewish history. Those affected by the Haskalah (Jewish enlightenment) were not attracted by the Reform Judaism of their western coreligionists but rather sought salvation in the secular messianisms of socialism, Jewish nationalism, and political radicalism. In the multi-ethnic states of the East where Jews constituted a distinct cultural and national group, they could not contemplate becoming simply a religious denomination. Town dwellers in the midst of a predominantly rural population and traders and skilled workers in an overwhelmingly agricultural society, the Jews exercised the same roles of middleman and artisan that had been theirs since the thirteenth century. However, under the delayed impact of the industrial and commercial revolutions and the dramatic increase in anti-Jewish disabilities, the largely middle-class Jewish community underwent a traumatic proletarianization.[1]

Originally united as the Kingdom of Poland, the partitions of the country in the eighteenth century placed the lion's share of the one million Jews under the control of Russia. The ruling classes of the empire viewed with apprehension this new addition to the population. The church, dominated by a religionational outlook, saw them as a threat to the faith of the peasantry. The nationalists considered them aliens incapable of being assimilated with the Russian people, while the autocracy and bureaucracy feared their zeal for education and suspected them of subversive liberalism. To restrict their influence and mark their status as the lowest in the empire, the Jews (with a few exceptions permitted after 1865) were excluded from the Russian interior and confined to the Polish provinces—the Pale of Settlement. During the course of the nineteenth century more than one thousand special laws were enacted to regulate their economic and cultural activities, communal and religious life, military service, and rights of domicile. Without pretensions of consistency, governmental policy alternated between attempts at forcible russification and equally repressive measures which sought to prevent contact between Jews and Gentiles.[2]

Alexander III's ascension to the throne in 1881 marked the beginning of the end for Russian Jewry. The involvement of a Jewish woman in the assassination of his predecessor provided the Czar, long predisposed toward anti-Semitism, with an excuse for a new wave of repression. During the first year of the new reign pogroms erupted in 160 places and left the Jews in a state of stupefaction and horror. Even more devastating pogroms at Kishinev, Gomel, Zhitomir, Odessa, Bialystok, and scores of smaller communities during the first decade of the new century, plus the resurrection of the medieval blood libel, further undermined Jewish security. But the main attack was economic. The "May Laws" of 1882 not only forbade free movement even within the Pale and prohibited Jews from settling anew outside the towns, but were executed in a way that resulted in wholesale expulsions from villages and towns into the already overcrowded cities. In 1891 the twenty thousand Jews of Moscow and the two thousand of St. Petersburg were deported in chains to the Pale. Cut off from their traditional peasant customers, plagued by overcrowding and overcompetition, and at the mercy of arbitrary administrative decrees, the Jews of Russia were driven steadily toward pauperism. Indeed, by the turn of the century an estimated 40 percent were completely dependent upon charity. In the face of economic suffocation and in fear of physical annihilation, one out of every three Jews departed for "The Golden Land" across the sea.[3]

Although they constituted less than 9 percent of the total immigration to the United States between 1881 and 1910, in proportion to their size East European Jews had the highest rate of immigration of any ethnic group. They also had the lowest level of reemigration, the highest proportion of skilled workers, and evidenced the greatest tendency to come in family groups. Arriving at a time when opportunity was greater in the cities than on the rapidly contracting frontier, and accustomed to urban life and a largely Jewish environment, the East Europeans ghettoized themselves in the cities of the Northeast. There, they reestablished familiar religious and cultural institutions and found ready employment in the burgeoning garment industry.[4]

The mass influx of East European Jews posed a critical dilemma for the established American Jewish community, estimated at 250,000 persons in 1880. While deeply sympathetic with the refugees' plight, they feared that the exotic-looking immigrants would imperil their own hard-won status and fuel the fires of emergent anti-Semitism. Furthermore, because most of the newcomers were destitute and nearly 70 percent were women and children, they threatened to create an immense welfare problem with which the established community was economically, organizationally, and psychologically unprepared to deal. Unaware that the dikes had broken, the American Jews of German descent initially endeavored to divert the flow and prevent the *Ostjuden* from clustering in the port cities. It was as a consequence of these early dispersal efforts that the first Russian refugees arrived in Atlanta.[5]

A few East European Jews had resided in Atlanta even before the onset of mass immigration. Bernard Brown, who had moved to the new city in 1851 and remained until 1864, was a native of Prussian Posen. Shortly after the war the Posen-born David Burgheims and the Russian-born William Silverbergs and Morris Wisebergs settled in the community. During the next decade, Max Marcus from Posen, Judah (James) Wolf Hirshfeld from Poland, and Rabbi Henry Gersoni from Lithuania made Atlanta their home. Unlike the mass of East Europeans who were to follow after 1880, these early arrivals had either broken with Orthodoxy in their youth or undergone several years of assimilation elsewhere and acquired a modest competency before coming to Atlanta. As a tiny minority in a small Jewish community composed of people from a variety of national backgrounds, they neither saw themselves nor were perceived by others as being essentially different from their Jewish neighbors. This would soon change.

The arrival of nearly 14,000 Russian refugees at the port of New York in 1881 to 1882 found the local Jewish philanthropies woefully ill equipped to cope with the problem, and in desperation their leaders called upon other Jewish communities to share the burden. By the end of November 1881, the members of the Hebrew Benevolent Congregation raised more than two hundred dollars and forwarded the money to the newly organized Hebrew Emigrant Aid Society (HEAS) with the authorization to send a limited number of able-bodied refugees to Atlanta. Late in December, 4 families consisting of 20 persons arrived, followed by 5 refugees in January, 6 in March, and another 24 during the remainder of the year. After the HEAS disbanded early in 1883, having sent over 2,600 immigrants to 166 cities, its dispersal activities were assumed by the United Hebrew Charities of the City of New York, and presumably some of the 20,000 refugees it relocated during the next decade were dispatched to Atlanta.[6] By 1890 there were 126 Russians plus 55 native-born persons of Russian parentage in Atlanta, nearly all of whom were Jews. A handful of Galician, Rumanian, and Orthodox Hungarian Jews also arrived during the eighties.[7]

The wholesale expulsions from Moscow and St. Petersburg and rumors of new restrictions resulted in a record Jewish immigration in 1891 and 1892 and consequently the establishment of a new dispersal organization, the Jewish Alliance of America. Pioneer Atlantan Aaron Haas, who was president of the Atlanta Hebrew Relief Society and the only southern delegate at the Alliance's inaugural meeting, became a director of the new organization. The Alliance and its Georgia affiliate hoped to colonize Russian Jews on farms near the seaport of Brunswick where they could raise fruits, vegetables, poultry, and dairy products within easy reach of market. The land would be sold on a ten-year mortgage with no interest during the first two years and only 6 percent thereafter. To teach the immigrants American agricultural techniques, the Alliance planned to hire a model farmer and place him in the midst of the settlement. Such talk fitted well into the general nineteenth century idealization of rural life; and Jewish agricultural colonies had earlier been established in such diverse localities as Oregon, Colorado, Louisiana, New Jersey, Kansas, and the Dakotas. Especially in the agrarian South, such measures might enhance the immigrants' acceptability, locate them in areas where they would not threaten the status of the established Jewish community, and enable them to observe traditional religious injunctions without affronting gentile sensibilities or local ordinances. Although the colonization plan generated little enthusiasm among either Russians or native Georgians, the Alliance was responsible for sending 150 Russian families to Georgia in 1891 and perhaps others during the next year.[8]

Atlanta's East European population increased sharply during the nineties. In 1896 there were 317 Russians plus 170 natives of Russian parentage, and by 1900 there were nearly 500 Russians and 400 native Americans of Russian stock. Although Russians and their children had accounted for a mere 2 percent of the Jewish community on the eve of mass immigration, twenty years later they constituted a near majority (45 percent).

The peak years of immigration were still ahead. Sixty-two percent of the total Jewish immigration for the period 1881 to 1910 arrived during the first decade of the new century. Confronted with the increasing congestion and squalor of New York's ghetto district, influential Jewish leaders once again hoped to disperse the newcomers and in 1901 created the Industrial Removal Office. During the next fifteen years the IRO sent 70,000 immigrants to 1,500 communities, including 614 to Atlanta. By 1910 there were 2,300 Jews of East European stock in the city and by 1920, approximately 3,300.[9]

Despite the important contributions of the dispersal agencies, they were directly responsible for only a minority of the East Europeans who came to Atlanta, and the attrition rate among their clients was high. None of the first 5 families sent by the HEAS in the winter of 1881–82 were still in Atlanta at the beginning of 1883, and of 195 males ages 17 and over sent by the IRO between 1901 and 1911, only 30 could be located in the 1912 city directory. Although their low persistence rate was affected by several factors to be discussed later, it is likely that persons who lacked the means to supply their own transportation also encountered difficulty establishing themselves and lacked the commitment to remain.[10]

Most of the East Europeans who settled in Atlanta came without assistance from northern societies. Some were peddlers who had drifted South during the autumn and winter months to sell their wares to the scattered farm population, found business and climatic conditions to their liking, and remained. Others had previously settled elsewhere in the South and, like the Germans before them, decided to try their fortunes in the Gate City. But most appear to have come directly from the North, and in some cases, from Europe, after learning of opportunities in Atlanta from relatives, former neighbors, and *landsleit* (countrymen) who had preceded them.

What kinds of people were they? Census data, naturalization papers, and the records of the Industrial Removal Office provide several clues. While 75 percent of the East European Jews who arrived in the United States between 1881 and 1910 were from Russia, the percentage of Russians in Atlanta was considerably higher. Rumanian-born Karl H. Kieferstein settled in Atlanta in 1883, and Galicians like Wolf Springer arrived later in the decade, but in 1896 there were only 20 Galician, 2 Rumanian, and a handful of Orthodox Hungarian Jews compared to 317 Russians. The proportion of non-Russians increased slightly during the next two decades, and of 270 males ages 17 and over sent by the IRO, 87 percent were Russian, 4 percent Galician, 3 percent Hungarian, and 6 percent Rumanian. Seventy percent of the Russians who came after 1880 were natives of Lithuania, mostly from the provinces of Grodno and Kovno. The Ukraine and southern Russia supplied 17 percent with the remainder coming from Poland and the two Baltic provinces of Courland and Livonia. Although Lithuanians predominated throughout the prewar period, their proportion of the total Russian population declined slightly after 1900. (See table 14.) The unrepresentative character of Jewish immigration to Atlanta was influenced by the multiplier effect of family and regional ties; the early arrivals sent for their relatives and countrymen, thereby perpetuating the proportions of the original groups until the IRO and a new wave of pogroms in southern Russia altered the balance by introducing Ukrainian, Galician, and Rumanian Jews for the first time in large numbers. As will be explained shortly, the changing sources of immigration affected the character of Orthodox Judaism in Atlanta.[11]

Like their fellow refugees, Atlanta's future Russian residents embarked for the New World from Bremen, Hamburg, and to a lesser extent from Antwerp, Rotterdam, and Stettin; a few settled briefly in Germany, England, and Ireland before making the crossing. However, the Russians who eventually came to Atlanta were somewhat less likely to enter the United States at New York than were their fellow Russians. Figures for the total Russian immigration, available only for the years 1886–98 and only for the three ports through which the overwhelming majority entered, indicate that 88 percent came through New York, 8 percent through Philadelphia, and 4 percent through Baltimore. For those who came to Atlanta, the figures were New York, 78 percent; Philadelphia, 6 percent; Baltimore, 10 percent; Boston, 4 percent; Galveston, 1 percent; and miscellaneous northern points, 1 percent. The proportion who landed at New York declined steadily during the period with Baltimore being the major beneficiary.[12]

After a harrowing trans-Atlantic voyage and the strains of adjusting to life in a new country, few immigrants were willing to travel an additional six hundred to one thousand miles overland and settle in Atlanta. For most, New York was America, and the city's Lower East Side nurtured a psychologically supportive atmosphere and a rich variety of religious and cultural institutions. But the same community that sheltered a flourishing Yiddish theater, a vibrant Yiddish press, and hundreds of synagogues was also plagued by the enervating sweatshop and the infamous dumbbell tenement. While Atlanta could not compete with New York's cultural allurements, she did offer the East European newcomer a salubrious climate, superior housing, and significant commercial advantages. David Yampolsky, who experienced both sides of ghetto life before coming to Atlanta in 1905, articulated what for many was a painful dilemma, "In New York I would have found my soul but without my body, and in Atlanta, a body without a soul."[13]

Whatever Atlanta's genuine advantages or disadvantages, the known southern disposition toward disciplining "inferior races" gave the region an unsavory reputation. The murder of Italians in

Louisiana, difficulties encountered by Slovak colonists, wanton lynching of blacks, and unfounded stories of Germans treated as slaves and Jews imprisoned in a mine and forced to "work like mules, under the lash of brutal negroes" were all reported in the Yiddish press. Because of the selective influences of inertia, fear, and the ghetto's sociocultural comforts, most of the few thousand Jews who went South—or at least those who went without outside assistance—were probably more adventurous, independent, and acculturated than the two million who remained in the North.[14]

Like those who stayed in the North, the Russians who came to Atlanta were young. Of 634 who filed naturalization papers in Atlanta between 1883 and 1917, about 33 percent were under the age of 20, nearly 50 percent were in their 20s, 15 percent were in their 30s, and only 4 percent were over 40 at the time they entered the United States. Similarly, 55 percent of the Russians who entered declarations of intention to file for citizenship were between 18 and 29, and about 33 percent were in their 30s. Among the immigrants sent by the IRO, 39 percent were under age 17, and an equal proportion were between 17 and 30 when they arrived in the city. Because of their youth, the Russians were able to adapt more readily to the new conditions they confronted.[15]

The movement of families characterized both the emigration from Russia and the migration to Atlanta. Nearly 80 percent of the 254 Russians who filed naturalization petitions between 1907 and 1917 and 63 percent of the East European males ages 17 and over sent by the IRO were married. However, because of the difficulties and uncertainties entailed in establishing themselves on an economically sound footing, many of the immigrants were forced to leave their families behind, often for periods of several years. Of 172 married males sent to Atlanta by the IRO, only a third were accompanied by their wives, while a fifth of the wives remained in New York and a little less than half stayed in Europe. Most marriages weathered the separation, but in at least one instance, an immigrant who left his family abroad married again in America and, when his bigamy was uncovered in Atlanta, fled from the wrath of the Jewish community.[16]

Although 79 percent of the gainfully employed East European Jews who came to the United States between 1899 and 1910 were artisans and other kinds of manual workers, only about 20 percent of Atlanta's Russians in 1896 were so employed. Most of the Russians who went south (70 percent of those sent by the IRO, but probably less among those who acted independently) apparently had trades, and it was this sort of immigrant that Georgia was anxious to attract. But because wages were low by northern standards and some of their skills did not meet the needs of the local economy, a high proportion of the newcomers returned North or drifted into petty trade.[17]

The refugees who arrived in Atlanta in 1881 and 1882 came almost directly from Europe after only a brief stop in New York. However, by the end of the decade, most had spent at least a few years in another city before settling in Atlanta, thereby enabling the newcomers to acquire some of the skills and perspectives important for success in the South. The IRO records suggest that this pattern was modified after 1900. Of 277 males ages 17 and over sent to Atlanta, 32 percent had been in the United States for less than 6 months, 18 percent for 6 months to 1 year, 28 percent for 13 months to 5 years, and 22 percent for more than 5 years. Because wives and children often arrived after their husbands and fathers had managed to establish themselves in the New World, they tended to be even less acclimated than the men to American conditions.[18]

The desperate plight of East European Jewry received extensive and sympathetic coverage in the Atlanta press. "The persecution of the Jews in Russia is furnishing to the history of fanaticism some of its most shocking details," remarked the *Constitution* in 1882. Noting the success and contributions of the local German Jews, the newspaper urged that Georgia endeavor to attract their Russian coreligionists.

> Jews make excellent American citizens. They have local pride, are enterprising, progressive, and in every way better fitted to enjoy the right of suffrage than some of the hordes of other immigrants. It seems to be the correct thing to offer to Russian Jews, who are daily arriving here, if not "forty acres and a mule," at least the land part thereof. Far-seeing citizens of other states in the south have offered such gifts, but Georgia is yet to be heard from. What does she bid for a class of people estimated to be worth $1000 apiece added to the capital of the State?[19]

Although it was soon evident that the Russians had come with neither capital nor the intention to farm the land, they were fortunate in having arrived at a time when Georgia was still anxious to receive foreign settlers. "I think the Jews a good class of citizens and a desirable element for any country," volunteered Mayor James W. English.

> The gates of Atlanta are open to all such people . . . and I think I speak for the city when I say they are welcome. I never knew a Jew who was a pauper or who could not support himself. Those we have with us—I mean the late immigration—have trades and are willing to work. I am glad to see them come and I hope more will follow.[20]

Not only did they elicit genuine humanitarian concern and appear to be an economic asset, but as victims of gross injustice recounted almost daily by the press, the first Russian arrivals provided Atlanta with an intimate tie to distant, exciting events, and—like the elephant acquired by the city zoo some years before—still another claim to metropolitan status.

However, in response to the onset of the New Immigration,[21] subsequent industrial unrest in other sections of the country, and the activation of sensitive color phobias, enthusiasm for foreign-born settlers soon began to diminish. Vocal opposition to immigration surfaced in several Georgia counties in 1885. The *Atlanta Constitution,* noting its new-found satisfaction with free Negro labor, maintained that only immigrant farmers and capitalists should be encouraged to settle in the state. A month after the Haymarket Affair, the newspaper asserted that the "offscourings of Europe" were threatening the "social and governmental fabric" of some states and proudly boasted that the South was "the only genuinely American section." "The line must be drawn somewhere," declared an editorialist in 1887. "Society must protect itself from these vicious victims of European tyranny. . . . They represent a class which the wonderful assimilating qualities of our native population can neither redeem nor remodel." Italians, whose household effects were said to consist solely of "a stiletto and a brass finger-ring," were accorded special censure.[22]

Traditional American idealism and the feeling that certain kinds of immigrants could contribute to a more prosperous Georgia never disappeared and at times existed uneasily beside blatant nativism. As long as the United States remains "the American Republic," declared the *Constitution* in 1893, "it will continue to fulfill its destiny, a part of which is to afford an asylum to the poor and oppressed of all nations." An immigration convention was convened in

Augusta a year later, and it refuted allegations that immigrant farmers from Europe were unwanted in the South.[23]

But by the mid-nineties, nativism had made notable inroads in Georgia, and even advocates of immigration endorsed the need for restrictive legislation and viewed the New Immigration with disdain. In 1895 the American Protective Association held an "anti-Papist" demonstration outside a Catholic church in Atlanta. The following year an Atlantan was elected national president of the organization, and the local chapter felt confident enough to field a slate of candidates in the municipal election. While it denounced the APA, the *Constitution* in 1897 endorsed the literacy test as a means of curtailing undesirable immigration. As John Higham has observed, "the newcomer's 'in-betweenness' seemed to endanger not only the purity of the white race, but also its solidarity." Southerners feared that the low social and cultural status of the often swarthy-complexioned immigrants and their unfamiliarity with southern traditions and values might imperil the pattern of white supremacy. "Of course the South wants desirable immigrants," noted the *Atlanta Journal,* but not "the Latin elements, which in Cuba, Central and South America have gotten upon such free and easy terms with the negro population as to effect a perfect social equality."

> Georgia emphatically does not want some of the types that have entered the north during the past few decades; she wants people who are capable of taking on American citizenship and entering into the spirit of our institutions in the shortest possible time. . . . The Swedes, Irish, Germans, English, and so forth become Americans very quickly; they are racially akin to us. . . . Besides, Georgia wants agriculturalists, not the type of immigrants given to herding in the cities; given to clannish resistance to the fundamental ideas upon which the Republic is founded.[24]

By the 1900s fear of subversive aliens was endemic in Georgia. Atlanta banker Robert J. Lowry warned against letting "a band of Russian nihilists, Italian mafias, or Spanish anarchists crowd in to contaminate our evolving civilization, and sow the seeds of dissension in the ranks of our people." The Georgia Farmers' Union agreed and termed the state's foreign-born element "unreliable in character, degraded in morals, anarchistic in principle and dangerous to the peace and order of society." Similarly, the Georgia Federation of Labor cautioned against flooding the state "with a population composed of the scum of Europe, a people in no wise in sympathy with the spirit of our institutions . . . and whose presence in our midst will foment race troubles and tend to destroy the cherished ideals of every loyal Southerner. . . ." The intensity of anti-immigration sentiment is especially noteworthy, since only 0.5 percent of Georgia's inhabitants were foreign-born, and in Atlanta, where nearly a quarter of the immigrants were located, less than 3 percent of the residents had been born outside the United States.[25]

Nevertheless, until U.S. Attorney General Charles Bonaparte ruled in March 1907 that state recruitment companies could do no more than advertise, influential Georgians continued to encourage and assist "desirable" immigrants. A bill was introduced into the Georgia General Assembly in 1904 that would have reactivated the office of immigration commissioner, but the proposal died in committee. In 1906 a state immigration conference was held in Savannah, and the following year delegates to the annual convention of the Georgia Immigration Association met in Macon and urged the recruitment of "pure-blooded Celts and Teutons, whose blood flows in the veins of every pure-blooded Georgian." "We favor immigration if we can get the right sort," declared a rural spokesman. "We want the kind that cannot well be spared from home."[26]

Jewish immigrants from Eastern Europe accounted for a tenth of the total immigration to the United States (a proportion surpassed only by the South Italians), and by 1910 constituted a fifth of Georgia's and a third of Atlanta's foreign-born population. Were these Jewish immigrants "the right sort"? Attitudes toward the Russians were clearly ambivalent. The *Constitution* persistently condemned Russian anti-Semitism, defended Jewish immigrants against their detractors, and praised the qualities of the local Russian settlers. The Jews' persecution in Russia "springs from the fact that they are superior to their neighbors," asserted a reporter in 1892, and in "this land of the free there is abundant room for these moral, law-abiding, industrious and brainy people. . . ." "Unlike some immigrants," the editors observed in 1905, "the people of this race come to America determined to become thoroughly identified with the country, and the experience of Atlanta is that they make the best kind of citizens."[27]

Although the *Constitution* praised the Jews and castigated their persecutors, not once after 1882 did the newspaper or other proponents of immigration rank the Russians among those whom Georgia should endeavor to attract. This may be partly attributed to the proponents' objectives, which were to bring into the state persons who could relieve the supposed shortage of servants and agricultural laborers and help develop Georgia's natural resources. Skilled Russian workers might have been welcome—though certainly not by organized labor—and this may explain why Temple president Joseph Hirsch and the local IRO manager Benjamin Wildauer were among the Atlanta delegates to the 1907 Macon convention. But the Russians' suspected unionist proclivities and a tendency to drift into petty trade made them unattractive to prospective employers.[28]

Although the immigration of Russians was not encouraged, they were neither singled out as undesirables (as were the South Italians, Greeks, Slavs, Hungarians, and Chinese) nor exempted from general condemnations of the New Immigration. Georgians' preferences were influenced as much by culture and "race" as by economic considerations. They subscribed to the popular notion that "Celts and Teutons," the Old Immigration, were superior to the "lesser breeds," the New Immigration, and Jews were implicitly grouped among the latter. And when Georgians spoke with alarm of the "changing complexion of America's largest cities," they understandably thought of the "Hebrew Conquest of New York." Atlanta editors, to be sure, had greater contact with Jews and more respect for their commercial expertise than did spokesmen in rural parts of the state, and the substantial influence of Jewish advertisers, no less than the admirable qualities of the city's Russian residents, affected editorial policy.[29]

The Russians themselves were largely unaware of the debate, and few had been in America long enough to acquire a sense of public relations. The conditions they fled had imperiled both their lives and livelihoods, and whatever prejudices they encountered in Atlanta were benign by comparison. The thoughts of most were preoccupied with establishing themselves economically and transplanting some of the supportive communal institutions they had known in Europe.

Religion lay at the core of Jewish life in Eastern Europe, minutely regulating daily activities and providing the principal source of authority, consolation, and even recreation. Even the humblest *shtetl* (Jewish townlet) maintained a house of worship, while in more populous communities small prayer halls existed in addition to the central synagogue. Power within the Jewish community was vested in a board of lay leaders who appointed the rabbi, regulated religious observances, and coordinated charitable and other associational activities. The early East European immigrants understandably desired to transplant their familiar institutions in the New World but, like their German cousins one or two generations earlier, were thwarted by the vicissitudes of readjustment, the absence of generally recognized sources of authority, and the secularism, voluntarism, and congregational autonomy that characterized life in America.[30]

It was largely because the organization of the Hebrew Benevolent Congregation and its affiliated charities had antedated their arrival and could provide kosher food, funds, and other assistance to cover the exigencies of resettlement, as well as a place to worship that the first Russian refugees were able to establish themselves in Atlanta. However, the condescending Germans made the Russians uneasy, and while the immigrants initially worshiped at the Temple, its moderate Reform service struck them as shockingly impious. As soon as there were enough Russians for a *minyan* they met together for prayer. By 1886 they were numerous enough to rent Concordia Hall for Rosh Hashanah and Yom Kippur services and for the first time were treated by the local press as a distinct religious entity.

> There are in Atlanta a community of Israelites, principally from Poland and Russia, who do not subscribe to the reformed or American ritual, the one followed by the temple . . . and who will have services of their own, conducted after the old orthodox ritual, as followed by them in Europe. . . . There are many of these people who are thorough [*sic*] in Hebrew lore, and they will see to it that all the ceremonies are closely observed. . . . They eschew instrumental music in their services.[31]

One year later, Congregation Ahavath Achim (Brotherly Love) was incorporated. Like the Temple, the new congregation led an itinerant existence during its early years, shuffling between second-story halls along Decatur and Gilmer streets and renting larger quarters such as Concordia Hall and the Lyceum Theater for the High Holy Days. After fourteen years of wandering, an onion-domed brick synagogue was erected at a cost of $20,000 on the southeast corner of Piedmont Avenue and Gilmer Street in the heart of the "ghetto district" bounded by Edgewood Avenue and College Street on the north, Pratt Street on the east, Decatur Street on the south, and Ivy Street on the west.[32]

Unlike the Hebrew Benevolent Congregation, which had hired a rabbi a mere two years after its reestablishment, for nearly a decade

Ahavath Achim did without the services of a paid minister. The relatively inferior economic status of the Russians—most of whom were grocers, petty dry goods dealers, and peddlers—the disinclination of qualified candidates to seek pulpits in the *treif* South, and the presence of several members competent enough to lead the congregation in prayer were largely responsible for this condition. Furthermore, in Eastern Europe the rabbi functioned as an interpreter of the Law for the community rather than as a preacher or reader, and it took time for the newcomers to adopt the American notion that every respectable synagogue required a rabbi.

At first, the Sabbath service was chanted by laymen and on holidays the *shohet* sometimes officiated as *hazan.* In 1896 following a marked increase in membership, Jacob Simonoff was elected rabbi. Born in Kovno in 1860, he arrived in the United States in 1892 and came to Atlanta the following year. Although a student of the Talmud, Simonoff, like the Hebrew Benevolent Congregation's first rabbi, David Burgheim, had never been ordained. In 1902 Simonoff was succeeded by Berachya Mayerowitz, a thirty-seven-year-old native of Kovno who had received *semikhah* from the Kovno Theological College and then continued his education in Riga. Mayerowitz had published a book on the ethics of the Talmud and served congregations in Kansas City and Toledo before commencing his five-year tenure in Atlanta. Fluent in English, the rabbi actively participated in communal affairs and was praised by the *Atlanta Constitution* as being "fully imbued with the spirit of American liberty." In 1907 the congregation elected Julius M. Levin, who had previously filled pulpits in Fall River, Massachusetts, and Bayonne and Jersey City, New Jersey, and Wilkes-Barre, Pennsylvania. Levin was followed in 1913 or 1914 by H. Yood. Among the cantors who served Ahavath Achim between 1900 and 1915 were I. M. Lubel, N. Abramson, and Salo H. Goldstone, the latter also advertising himself as "positively the only antiseptic surgeon Mohel in the South."[33]

Because children constituted a large proportion of the Russian community, and Jewish males reached their religious majority at age thirteen, a religious school was necessary if Orthodoxy was to be perpetuated. A Talmud Torah (Jewish elementary school) was established under private auspices prior to 1892. However, when an attempt was made in 1893 to bring the school under congregational control, half the voting members disapproved because such action would have entailed an increase in dues. A congregational Sunday

School was organized in 1898, weekday instruction added three years later, and further improvements undertaken in 1912. Although it was claimed that "many of the brightest young men in the city give this school credit for a large share of their equipment for a successful career," most of Atlanta's Russian children received little or no formal Jewish training. Enrolled in the city's public schools and eager to embrace American patterns of living, only a minority had either the time or the inclination to pursue separate Jewish study. Furthermore, until free Jewish education was inaugurated under communal auspices in 1914, most parents could not afford to send their children to synagogue schools.[34]

Not only a place to worship and a religious school but also a *shohet, mikvah* (ritual purification bath), and cemetery were required if the Russians were to be true to the commandments. The rite of *shehitah* had been performed in Atlanta since 1869, but the Russians may have had reservations concerning the *shohet*'s qualifications until one of their number assumed the office in the early eighties. Ahavath Achim attempted with little success to regulate the *shohet*'s operations, and when a member who was a butcher tried to induce the *shohet* to work solely for him, the congregation disapproved and appropriated fifty dollars to open a butcher shop under its own control.[35]

The construction of a *mikvah* was discussed in 1891, but when a ritual bath was finally opened in 1896, it was under private rather than synagogue auspices. Despite the financial assistance of wealthy Temple members who felt that periodic baths would do the Russians much good, the venture was apparently short lived, and not until the following decade was a *mikvah* established on a secure foundation. The need for a cemetery was more pressing, since the infant mortality rate was high and the risk of burial in unsanctified ground was a frightening prospect. When a Russian child died in June 1891, the Temple provided a grave site in its section of Oakland Cemetery but cautioned that because of limited space, further burials would not be permitted after ninety days. The following year Ahavath Achim purchased from the Temple one-fourth of a newly acquired $2,000 tract in Oakland, and subsequent acquisitions were made as the Russian population increased.[36]

Because many of the Russians were poor, the congregation was necessarily involved in assisting the needy. A *hevra kaddisha hesed shel emeth* (Merciful and Holy [Burial] Society of Truth) was organized in 1887, and free cemetery plots were provided for impoverished nonmembers. When informed of the "distressful condition [of] one of our brothers," the congregation voted to lend the member twenty-five dollars. The death of a member or someone in his family invariably resulted in an assessment of the membership to cover funeral and related expenses. Early in 1891 the congregation called a "mass meeting" of the East European community to discuss the creation of a relief fund. The association that emerged from the meeting was unable to supply assistance to more than a fraction of those in need. In 1893 a committee appointed by Ahavath Achim met with the officers of the larger Temple-affiliated Hebrew Relief Society to request (with no apparent success) that charity be withheld from Russian Jews whose petitions did not first receive the approval of the Orthodox congregation. This action was motivated by the congregation's desire to regulate the conduct of Russians who were not otherwise subject to its discipline. A further deviation from the traditional Jewish conception of charity characterized by "obligation, complementary function, formal subordination and functional interdependence," is found in the stated purposes of the Montefiore Relief Association, incorporated by Ahavath Achim members in 1896:

> dispensing and distributing charity, aid, relief, and assistance to such persons, who by reason of sickness, abject poverty or other causes, may be deemed worthy of relief or assistance as the Association . . . may deem advisable to bestow upon them.[37]

In the secular, materialistic, and voluntaristic atmosphere of Atlanta, such attempts at social control were considered necessary by those concerned with maintaining communal solidarity; yet this goal was beyond their grasp. For economic and other reasons, only a minority of the city's East European households were affiliated with the synagogue. The initiation fee of three dollars and dues of fifty cents per month prevented many of the poor from joining. Until 1895 all applicants for membership were subjected to scrutiny by a committee and balloted on by the congregation; some were rejected. Successful applicants were expected "to take the obligation," an oath which bound them to abide by the decisions of the congregation and to attend all meetings under penalty of a two-dollar fine. Expulsions and suspensions were not uncommon.[38]

The biweekly meetings provided the Russians with a major social outlet. In the absence of generally recognized authority and under the influence of petty differences and still novel democratic forms, the name Ahavath Achim was sometimes more indicative of the body's aspirations than its substance. Louis Grudzinsky was repeatedly accused at meetings of having gone "around this town cursing and denouncing the officers and members of the congregation," a claim which the arraigned member denied with a thunderous, "You're a G . . . d[amned] liar!" On another occasion, Jacob Berenstein, who did not belong to Ahavath Achim, was charged with having insulted several members of the congregation "in their capacity as officers of the latter, said insults having been prompted by sheer malice." After a "thorough, fair and impartial vindication [*sic*]," Berenstein was found guilty and it was decreed that should he ever apply for membership he would have to pay a fine of ten dollars. Antagonism between two leading members, Odessa-born Leon Eplan and Warsaw-born Abe Posner, enlivened several meetings. In the course of a debate Eplan was recognized:

> But no sooner had he opened his mouth to speak upon the question in issue than Pres[iden]t Posner ordered him to take his seat upon pain of carrying him out with the assistance of a policeman. Brother Eplan silently took his seat and said no more.

This may not have been an idle threat, since the congregation's Decatur Street hall was situated only a few doors away from police headquarters. However, the following week Eplan was revenged after Posner discharged

> a flood of abuses directed towards several members of the congregation whose names the president thought wise to avoid. . . . When at last the document of abuses was read through the prest decended [*sic*] the chair.

Posner's resignation was followed by an "ugly debate full of bitter feelings and disorderliness."[39]

In view of these conflicts it is not surprising that other congregations soon appeared. Congregation B'nai Abraham (Children of Abraham) was chartered in September 1890 by natives of Kovno, quite likely from the same town. In January 1893 B'nai Abraham purchased a half-interest in Ahavath Achim's recently acquired cemetery plot, and seven months later "a permanent and unconditional consolidation" was negotiated between the two congregations to eliminate "all strife, ill feelings and unpleasantness due to the existence of a separation. . . ." However, the union was unstable and in 1897 B'nai Abraham reappeared only to be reabsorbed shortly thereafter by Ahavath Achim. Another group of Ahavath Achim members who had been born in Kovno seceded in 1896 and organized Congregation Chevra Kaddisha (Holy Brotherhood), which survived until 1898.[40]

Although all three congregations adhered to the Orthodox ritual, under economic pressure and the influence of American ways, the manifold injunctions of Orthodoxy began to fall into disuse. As Joshua Trachtenberg has written of the East European settlers of Easton, Pennsylvania:

> They too drifted in time from the letter of the law—beards grew shorter and eventually vanished; the *kosher* diet, away from home, made room for delicacies that were *treif;* the Sabbath and workday became indistinguishable—but they could never presume to flaunt such defections in the face of tradition. Deep at heart they remained "orthodox" however unorthodox their action. The open perversion of the "Deitschen" [Germans] was unforgivable.[41]

The dietary laws were generally, if not punctiliously, obeyed, and even the peddlers who were away from the city for days at a time avoided unclean food, often by carrying a supply of cooked vegetables and hardboiled eggs. But observance of the Sabbath entailed considerable hardship for all but the peddlers whose work week was flexible. Workers received their wages on Saturday, making it the busiest shopping day, and because local ordinances prohibited business from being conducted on Sunday, Jewish storekeepers were obliged to violate the sanctity of the Sabbath or court economic ruin. Consequently, the nominally Orthodox Jew pursued his economic self-interest without divesting himself of the notion that Saturday was a sacred day. Yiddish poet I. J. Schwartz, who settled in the South in 1918, observed:

> The joke was:
> That one worked on the Sabbath
> Even harder than on the week-day,
> Because on Saturday people got their wages;
> They fitted shoes and pants on Negroes,
> And talked their hearts out—
> But as soon as the stars appeared,
> The merchant immediately stopped his business,

Withdrew quickly behind the partition
And said the *Havdoleh* [prayer at the end of the Sabbath] out loud.

If a man "stands by his convictions and observes the Sabath [*sic*]," declared Benjamin Wildauer in 1907, "there is nothing for him to do in Atlanta." Such persons generally drifted back North. Rabbi Tobias Geffen, who settled in Atlanta in 1910, recalled that at the time of his arrival only eight of the several hundred Jewish-owned businesses remained closed for the Sabbath.[42]

Lapses from the traditional norm were most common among the senior members of the Russian community, those who had resided in Atlanta the longest, had the greatest exposure to American ways, and having acquired wealth and influence were the leading members of Congregation Ahavath Achim. They were beardless and worked on the Sabbath, and although the congregation had ruled otherwise in 1894, such men could hardly be denied the honor of reading from the Torah at services. This was taken as an affront by the poorer, more pious members who were further enraged when the congregation, burdened by the debt of its newly constructed synagogue, denied admission to High Holy Day services to nonmembers who could not afford to purchase tickets. Shortly thereafter, several of the more pious members resigned and, together with a number of previously unaffiliated Jews, founded a new congregation in 1902, which was incorporated two years later as Shearith Israel (Remnant of Israel).[43]

During its first four years, the new congregation worshipped in a small rented building on Butler Street near Coca-Cola Place, and met in the Fulton County Court House, the Armory Building, the Edgewood Avenue Theater, and the Red Men's Hall on the High Holy Days. In 1905 the congregation purchased a wooden antebellum building on East Hunter and Bell streets that had formerly been occupied by St. Paul's Methodist Church. After they expended $3,-200 for the property and $8,000 on improvements, the new synagogue was dedicated in 1907. The same year, Shearith Israel hired its first rabbi, a young graduate of the Isaac Elchanan Yeshiva named Zvi Elchanan Gutterman. Gutterman was succeeded in 1909 by Philip Kaufman, who in turn was followed the next year by Tobias Geffen. Geffen had been born in Kovno in 1874, attended *yeshivoth* (Jewish religious academies of higher learning) in Kovno and Slobodka, and received *semikhah* in 1903, just prior to embarking for America. During the next seven years the rabbi served congregations in New York City and Canton, Ohio. Already an active participant in Zionist affairs and a contributor to several Hebrew periodicals, Geffen attempted to regulate the conduct of the Atlanta *shohetim,* improved the community's education facilities, and supervised the construction of a *mikvah.* As one of the few ordained Orthodox rabbis in the Southeast, he was frequently called upon to adjudicate disputes in other communities and during his more than four decades of active service to the congregation, authored several volumes of responsa, sermons, and talmudic discourses.[44]

The Ahavath Achim from which the founders of Shearith Israel seceded in 1902 was in nearly every respect an Orthodox congregation. While many of the recent arrivals from Russia objected to the former congregation's minor deviations from the traditional norm, many of the more settled and prosperous members found fault with its old-fashioned ways. They desired to belong to a congregation that would reflect their americanized outlook and newly won economic status while retaining the loyalty of their native-born children to Judaism. In 1905 after some had joined, or attempted to join, the Temple and were cooly received, they organized Congregation Beth Israel (House of Israel). Of the fifteen charter members, at least four were former presidents of Ahavath Achim.[45]

Beth Israel's founders called their congregation "Conservative," by which they meant a vague compromise between Orthodoxy and Reform rather than a commitment to any precise theological position. At first they worshiped in a hall on Decatur Street, but in July 1907 laid the cornerstone of an impressive $35,000 neoclassical synagogue on the corner of Washington and Clarke streets. Nearly all of the Jews who lived in the area belonged to the Temple, and the choice of the location mirrored the social aspirations of the new congregation's members. Governor Hoke Smith and Mayor W. R. Joyner spoke at the dedication, but the collapse of the roof during the ceremony augured ill for the future.[46]

In 1907 Julius T. Loeb was elected rabbi. An ardent Zionist, Loeb founded and edited a local Jewish weekly called the *Southern Guide* and involved himself deeply with communal affairs before accepting a position in Birmingham in 1909. His successor, Alexander S. Kleinfeld, had been born in Austria-Hungary in 1876 and had attended both public school and *yeshiva* before moving to Vienna to study music. He came to the United States in 1893 and after a brief course of study at Columbia University was appointed cantor and then rabbi of several congregations in New York and Paterson, New

Jersey. After Kleinfeld left Atlanta in 1912, the congregation experienced difficulty filling the pulpit. Loeb returned to conduct Rosh Hashanah services in 1913 and the following year, Louis J. Goetz, formerly a rabbi in Jersey City, New Jersey, was hired. Two years later Beth Israel elected Hyman Solomon, a twenty-six-year-old native of New York, who had graduated from City College, Columbia University, and Conservatism's Jewish Theological Seminary, and was active in Zionist and settlement work. Solomon served only one year. By 1916 Beth Israel was disbanding. Several of its most affluent members had joined the temple. The remaining members, under fire from the Orthodox congregations for "getting away from Judaism," showed little enthusiasm to carry on and formally disbanded around 1920.[47]

The founders of Ahavath Achim, B'nai Abraham, Chevra Kaddisha, Shearith Israel, and Beth Israel—like three quarters of Atlanta's East European Jews—were from Lithuania and as such were mostly Mitnagdim, adherents of the rationalistic and legalistic party within Orthodoxy. With the increase in Galician and Ukrainian Jewish settlers after 1900, Hasidism made its appearance in Atlanta. Hasidism, a pietistic movement of religious revival founded in the eighteenth century, emphasized mysticism and personal spontaneity rather than fixed practice and talmudic discourse. The Hasidim tended to be less learned and sophisticated than the Mitnagdim, and the two Orthodox groups differed further in their liturgies, folkways, and views of traditional Judaism.[48]

Although a few traces of Old World suspicion remained, the early Hasidim attended services at Ahavath Achim and Shearith Israel. By 1911 they were numerous enough to hold their own services and two years later incorporated themselves as Beth Hamedrash Hagodol Anshe Sfard (Great House of Study of the Men of Spain). Ahavath Achim lent the congregation one of its Torahs, and Rabbi Levin provided further assistance. At first the congregation met in the Red Men's Hall on Central Avenue, but by the end of 1913 a wooden building at the corner of Woodward Avenue and King Street was secured. A few years later the congregation moved several blocks west to the corner of Woodward and Capital avenues. Too poor to engage a rabbi and more disposed to follow the prophetically inspired than the rabbinically ordained, the congregation of Anshe Sfard was initially served by several cantors, two of whom were Rev. Stein and Jacob Taratoot.[49]

However great the distinction between Orthodox and Reform,

Russian and German, Hasid and Mitnaged, and Litvak (Lithuanian Jew) and Galitzianer (Galician Jew), they all had much in common. The Germans, however much they chose to ignore the fact, were but a few generations removed from the Yiddish language, Orthodox faith, and ghetto roots of their East European cousins. Among the immigrants, small numbers and a common culture, language, and shared experiences in Europe and America made differences of nativity, liturgy, and pronunciation lose much of their significance. Yet just as the various East European factions were becoming aware of their common identity and the first bridges were being built between the immigrant and native communities, a third Jewish group entered Atlanta, one with a far greater claim than the Hasidim to the label *anshe sfard* (literally "men of Spain," referring not to the Hasidim's ancestry but rather to elements of their liturgy).

Sephardim, natives and descendants of the Jews who had lived on the Iberian Peninsula prior to the expulsions of the fifteenth and sixteenth centuries, were among the first settlers of the New World. Coming either directly from Spain or Portugal, or via Holland and England, they possessed a vibrant cultural heritage and, in many cases, arrived with capital, valuable commercial connections, or professional experience. Although they initially composed a majority of North America's few hundred Jews, by the mid-eighteenth century their immigration had virtually ceased, and they were soon overwhelmed by Ashkenazic Jews from Central and Eastern Europe.

A new wave of Sephardic immigration began at the end of the nineteenth century. Turkey's wars with Russia, Italy, and the Balkan states had left that country in a precarious state, physically and economically. Military conscription was introduced after the Young Turk's revolt of 1908, and finally a series of natural disasters occurred. All this only exacerbated the difficulties of supporting a family and resulted in ever increasing immigration to the United States. However, these immigrants not the prosperous assimilated descendants of the refugees who had settled in Western Europe but rather those whose forebearers had found sanctuary in the Ottoman Empire. After an initial cultural renaissance, Jewish life in the East had sunk into social and intellectual stagnation. Although they were obligated to pay a special tax as an acknowledgement of their inferiority, unlike their brethren in Russia and Rumania, the Jews of the Levant were not subject to religious persecution and shared a cultural affinity with their Muslim neighbors. Superstitious and highly devout, most were petty traders, artisans, and laborers. Their Orthodox services differed in liturgy, ritual, and Hebrew pronunciation from those in the West, and their complexion, culinary preferences, and outlook were, by European standards, distinctively Oriental. But their most distinctive trait was linguistic. Whereas the Central Europeans spoke German and the Russians Yiddish (literally, "Jewish"), the Sephardim spoke Ladino, a tongue that bore the same relationship to Spanish as Yiddish did to German.[50]

Most of the newcomers preferred familiar saltwater climes. However, two Levantine Jews arrived in Atlanta in 1906, and by 1912 the city contained approximately one hundred Sephardim (a figure equalled only by San Francisco, and surpassed by New York and Seattle).[51] Two years later, at the outbreak of World War I, the number had increased to perhaps as many as one hundred and fifty. Slightly more than half were natives of Rhodes, about a third came from Bodrum and Izmir, a tenth from Constantinople, and the remainder from Magnesia, Crete, and the Dardanelles. Most were desperately poor, in their twenties and thirties, and nearly two-thirds were unmarried. Several had spent time in Palestine and Egypt. They embarked for the United States from Patras, Marseilles, and Naples, and nearly all arrived at New York. Why the initial settlers decided to go South remains unclear. Perhaps like the founders of the Seattle Sephardic community, they were directed to the city by Greek acquaintances who had preceded them. As soon as a few families had arrived, the multiplier effect and the work of the IRO led to further growth.[52]

At first the Sephardim worshiped at Ahavath Achim and Shearith Israel, but the Ashenazim were suspicious of the swarthy-complexioned newcomers from the Levant. The Sephardim reciprocated with aloofness, partly in an attempt to maintain their self-respect but also out of an impoverished hidalgo's sense of inner superiority. Even had relations been better, the Sephardim's strong religious and linguistic traditions necessitated the creation of their own synagogue. Congregation Ahavat Shalom (Love of Peace) was founded in 1910 with a membership of forty, mostly natives of Rhodes. But because of slight differences in *minhag* (rite) and their keen sense of provincialism, a group of members—mostly from the Turkish mainland—withdrew in 1912 and established Congregation Or Hahayim (Light of the Living). Two years later the rival groups recognized the trivial nature of their division and combined to form the Oriental Hebrew Association Or Ve Shalom, shortened soon thereafter to Congregation Or Ve Shalom (Light and Peace). In 1916 property was purchased at the corner of Central and Woodward avenues, and in 1920 the new synagogue was dedicated. Within the next five years a rabbi was engaged, and welfare, burial, and Sunday school societies were organized.[53]

In merely thirty years, profound changes had occurred. At the start of the 1880s, the Jews of Atlanta were a relatively prosperous, assimilation-minded people of Central European descent who worshiped at the same synagogue. By 1915 the Germans and their children had been reduced to a minority, and there were now six congregations, mirroring the community's deep national, economic, social, and religious divisions.

# 5

## *The Divided Community*

The East European and Sephardic immigrants entered Atlanta during a period of tremendous development for both the city and its Jewish community. Between 1880 and 1910 Atlanta's population and area quadrupled to 155,000 persons and 26 square miles. The increase of paved streets from 3 to 166 miles, a corresponding expansion of the streetcar network, and the construction of a dozen viaducts and bridges provided a previously unknown internal unity. The western boom town appearance and social fluidity of the seventies succumbed during the following three decades to tall office buildings, functional differentiation, and the emergence of an institutionalized social elite. The value of manufactured output increased almost ninefold and local property more than sevenfold. A series of locally sponsored international expositions in 1881, 1887, and 1895, and the entrance of nine more railroads enhanced further Atlanta's preeminence as a trade and distribution center. By 1910 trade amounted to nearly $312 million per year, and more than half the merchants in the Southeast were customers of the city's manufacturers, wholesalers, and agents.[1]

Jewish immigration from Central Europe declined sharply after 1880. Between that year and 1910 Atlanta's "German" Jewish population increased at half the rate of the total population, from 600 to about 1,400. Meanwhile, the number of Jews of East European descent increased from less than a dozen to approximately 2,400. Although the demographic, occupational, and residential structure of the Jewish community continued to differ in most respects from that of the city as a whole, considerable differences also existed between the established and immigrant Jewish communities.

In 1896 there were approximately 1,500 Jews in Atlanta. Nearly 60 percent of these—mostly children and young adults—had been born in the United States, 21 percent in Russia, 13 percent in Germany, and 4 percent in Austria-Hungary. Although the percentage of native-born was roughly the same as in 1880, the proportion of Central Europeans declined by nearly 50 percent, while the proportion of Russians increased forty-three fold. (See tables 15 and 5.) Despite the high proportion of native-born, only 5 percent of the city's Jews were of native parentage, while 40 percent were of Russian, 25 percent of German, 7 percent of Austro-Hungarian, and the remaining 23 percent of mixed German, Austro-Hungarian and native stock. (See table 16.) In contrast, during the years 1890 to 1910, 97 percent of Atlantans were native-born and 92 percent were of native stock.[2]

As in 1880, the Jews in 1896 were young; nearly 50 percent were under the age of 20, compared with 40 percent of the total and 42 percent of the native white population of the city. The age profile of the various Jewish groups differed considerably. The youngest Jews were native-born, 66 percent being under age 20 and only 6 percent over age 39. The Russian immigrants were also young, 29 percent under age 20, 57 percent between 20 and 39, and only 14 percent ages 40 and older. Because few young Jewish natives of Central Europe settled in Atlanta after 1880, the age level of this group naturally rose. Twenty-one percent of the Austro-Hungarians (including the young recent immigrants from Galicia) were under age 20 and 35 percent over age 39, while only 15 percent of the Germans were under age 20 and 64 percent ages 40 and over.[3] (See tables 17 and 7.)

Because of opportunities in manufacturing and domestic service, women outnumbered men in Atlanta at the turn of the century. The sex ratio in 1900 was 91 for the entire population, 95 for native-born whites, 71 for blacks, and 139 for the foreign-born. In contrast, the Jewish community's 1896 sex ratio was 111, even higher than in 1880. This figure obscured considerable variety within the Jewish community whose native-born constituents had a sex ratio of 96, compared with 121, 168, and 235 respectively, for those born in Russia, Germany, and Austria-Hungary. (See table 17.) The disparity was closely related to the circumstances of immigration. As noted previously, young unmarried males outnumbered females among the early Jewish immigrants from Central Europe, for young men were more vulnerable to the disruptive influences of economic revolution and resurgent anti-Semitism. As these settlers grew older, husbands tended to predecease their younger spouses, thereby widening further the sex ratio. In contrast, the enormity of czarist persecution uprooted entire families and even villages. Consequently, the Russian Jewish population of both Atlanta and the nation as a whole was characterized by a larger proportion of females than any other immigrant people except the Irish.[4]

Marital patterns were affected by nativity, age, and sex. As in earlier years, economic insecurity discouraged marriage among those ages 18 to 29, while mortality made widowhood more likely for those ages 50 and over. The growth of both groups between 1880 and 1896 resulted in the proportion of married adult Jewish males declining from 64 to 59 percent and the number of widowers rising from 3 to 6 percent—precisely the same figures for the city as a whole in 1900. Bachelorhood was most common among native-born Jewish adults, only one-third of whom were married, primarily because two-thirds of this group were under age 30. In contrast, 81 percent of the Austro-Hungarian-born and 90 percent of the German-born adult males were ages 30 and over, and their respective marriage rates of 63 and 76 percent, and widowhood rates of 9 and 8 percent, were correspondingly high. Although nearly 40 percent of the adult Russian males were under age 30, 79 percent were married. This reflected not only a favorable sex ratio, but also the family character of Russian immigration and a socially sanctioned predisposition toward early marriage. (See tables 17 and 18.) For these reasons and also the considerable differences which separated them from Gentiles and other Jews, the Russians were the most endogamous immigrant group in the city, nearly 95 percent being married to other Russians. The little exogamy that did occur involved Russian men and took place during the eighties and early nineties when there was a relative shortage of eligible Russian women and before class lines hardened.[5] (See table 19.)

Several changes in the Jewish community's occupational and industrial profile occurred between 1880 and 1896. Although nearly identical proportions of Jews were to be found in trade, transportation, public service, manufacturing, domestic and personal service, and in clerical positions, the percentage of Jewish professionals, manual workers, and peddlers increased from 3, 6, and 0 percent to 6, 9, and 4 percent respectively, and the proportion of proprietors declined from 60 to 49 percent. Meanwhile, the proportion of

Atlantans in trade and in domestic and personal service declined markedly and the proportion in transportation rose. The occupational and industrial profile of the Jewish community continued to differ sharply from that of the total male population of the city. Jews were four times more likely than Gentiles to be engaged in trade (71 percent), half as likely to be in manufacturing and mechanical pursuits (15 percent), and one-tenth as likely to provide domestic or personal service (2 percent). Approximately equal proportions performed clerical (6 and 10 percent), professional (5 and 6 percent), and public services (0.5 and 0.7 percent), but only 0.5 percent of the Jews were in transportation and none in agriculture compared with 16 percent and 1 percent of all Atlantans. Furthermore, while the overwhelming majority of Atlantans in trade, manufacturing, and the crafts were employees, 56 percent of the Jews in these categories were the proprietors of shops and stores or officers of corporations. (See tables 20 and 21.)

Industrial distribution and occupational status were closely related to nativity. The proportions of Jewish males engaged in trade and manufacturing were substantially higher for the Russians (79 and 18 percent) and Germans (77 and 16 percent) than for the native-born (62 and 12 percent), while the percentage in clerical and professional pursuits was highest for the Americans (11 and 12 percent) and lowest for the Russians (0 and 1 percent) and Germans (3 and 2 percent). Similarly, the native-born had the smallest proportion of proprietors (40 percent) and the largest of white-collar workers (44 percent); the Germans had the highest proportion of proprietors (59 percent); and the Russians had the highest proportion (19 percent) of manual workers—skilled, semiskilled, and unskilled workers—the lowest of white-collar workers (17 percent), and 16 of the 18 peddlers.[6] (See tables 20 and 21.)

The high economic status of the Germans was in large measure due to their entrepreneurial background, age, and early arrival in the United States. Lacking the predisposition, training, or capital necessary to enter the professions or engage in agriculture, most began their careers in America as peddlers, petty merchants, and clerks. Many had settled in Atlanta shortly after the war, and as the city prospered they reaped the rewards of the pioneer.

By 1896 nearly one-quarter of the German Jews were officers or proprietors of factories and wholesale houses. Jacob Elsas's Fulton Bag and Cotton Mill and Sigmond Landauer's Southern Agricultural Works (formerly the Haiman Plow Works) were two of Atlanta's leading factories. Other firms owned or administered by German Jews manufactured straw hats, whiskey, cottonseed oil, paper bags, and furniture, and the wholesale clothing house of M. and J. Hirsch and the millinery business of J. Regenstein and Co. were still among the city's largest. German retailers sold dry goods, fruit, groceries, shoes, paper, and drugs, and among the leading clothiers were Hirsch Brothers, Eiseman and Weil, and Eiseman Brothers. The service sector included such prominent German Jews as Aaron Haas, president both of the Atlanta and Florida Railroad and the Atlanta City Street Railway; and his cousin Jacob Haas, who was president of two banks, cashier of a third, and an officer of both the Atlanta Railway Company and the Atlanta Baggage and Cab Company.[7]

One-third of the Germans were white-collar workers, mostly store clerks and commerical travelers. Most, like twenty-five-year-old Nathan Kahn, who clerked for Eiseman and Weil, were upwardly mobile young men. Others, like thirty-seven-year-old dry goods clerk Louis Bebro, had resided in Atlanta for decades but failed to rise economically. Although technically ranked below proprietors, some of the German white-collar workers filled positions which demanded considerable responsibility and which offered more prestige and financial security than some of the retail proprietorships. Only 5 percent of the Germans were manual workers. (See table 21.)

The early settlers were often able to pass along entrepreneurial aspirations and opportunities to their native-born children. However, most of the native-born in 1896—because of their youth, superior education, or lack of capital—were professionals or held white-collar positions that promised future upward mobility. Only 4 percent were manual workers. Seventeen of the twenty Jewish professionals were American-born, and their number included three rising stars of the local bar: Henry A. Alexander, a future member of the Georgia House; and Benjamin Z. Phillips and Arthur Heyman, whose respective partners John M. Slaton and Hugh M. Dorsey would eventually become governors of Georgia. Nearly half of the Jewish white-collar workers had been born in the United States, and most of these were clerks, bookkeepers, and commercial travelers for Jewish-owned firms. Only 40 percent of the native-born were proprietors but among these were several leading manufacturers: Victor H. Kriegshaber, president of the Atlanta Terra-Cotta Works; Isaac H. Haas, president of the American Upholstery Company; Louis Newelt, president of the Southern Furniture Company; and Simon Montag of Montag Brothers (stationery). Some younger Jews like the Hirsch cousins entered their fathers' businesses, but others set out on their own and established such firms as Schoen Brothers (wholesale hides), Gershon Brothers and Rosenfeld (wholesale woodenware), and Byck Brothers (retail shoes).

Among the most innovative local businessmen was Joseph Jacobs, a native of Jefferson, Georgia, who had moved to Atlanta in 1884 and established Jacobs's Pharmacy on the corner of Peachtree and Marietta streets. Prior to 1885 the nickel was the smallest coin in general circulation in the city, and odd-cents transactions were usually rounded-off to the nearest five-cent piece; but shortly after opening his store, Jacobs ordered $1,000 in new pennies (which resembled five-dollar pieces) and began giving exact change. As a result, many goods were reduced in price, and his competitors pressured wholesalers and manufacturers not to sell to him. Jacobs successfully filed several suits under the Sherman Antitrust Act and by 1910 had established ten branches of his pharmacy. Despite usually good judgement, early in his career Jacobs made an almost unforgivable mistake when he exchanged a one-third interest in a new syrup preparation for some stock in a glass factory and a few bedpans, syringes, and pill boxes. Asa G. Candler proceeded to make millions with Coca-Cola.[8]

The Russian immigrants shared the Germans' predisposition toward commerce and industry: 79 percent were engaged in trade and 16 percent in the crafts. However, lacking capital, language skills, and the kinds of opportunity available a generation earlier, they began their careers in the city on a very modest scale. Those with trades, mostly tailors and shoemakers, found employment in establishments owned by the German Jews, and in time many accumulated sufficient capital to open their own shops. For the majority, who either had no trades or did not wish to pursue them, the peddler's pack was the passport to opportunity. "This sack will teach you to talk," a novice was informed, "will give you food to eat, will give you an opportunity to emerge from your greenness, will teach you to integrate yourself into American life." One of the relief agencies or supply stores usually advanced initial credit to the newcomer, and the high mark-up on goods, low capital investment, and flexible work schedule made peddling attractive to those willing to carry a pack. Thirteen percent of Atlanta's Russians in 1896 were peddlers, and by foot, wagon, and railroad they distributed spreads,

FIGURE 6.

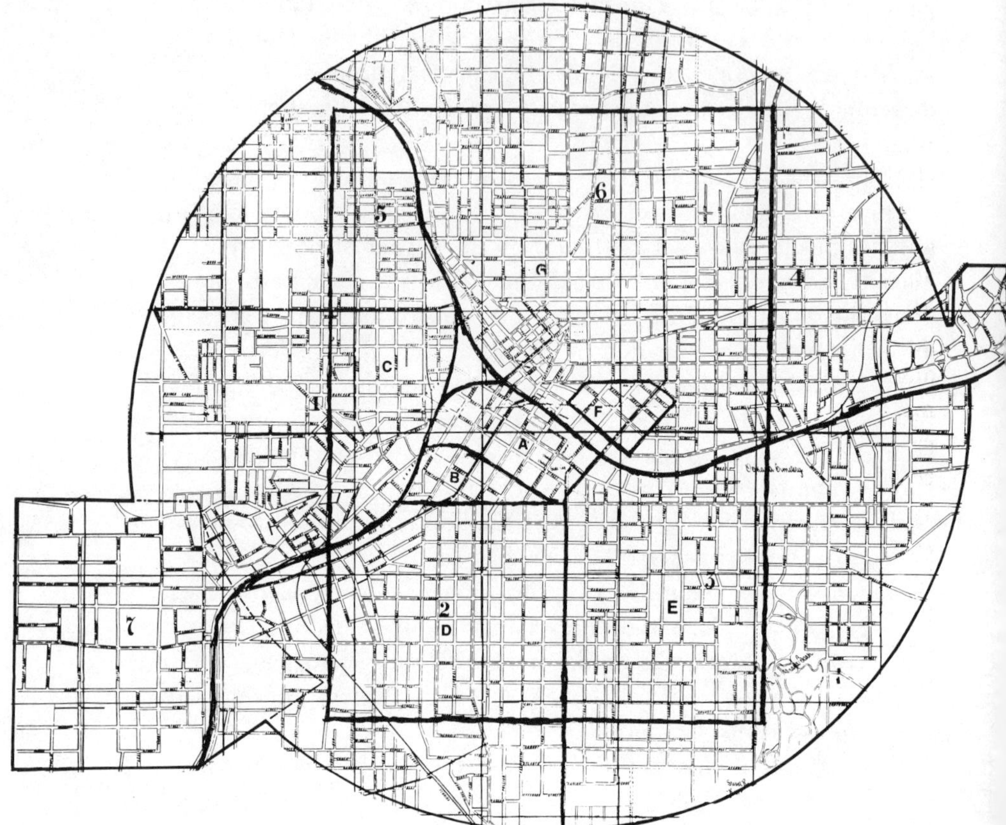


FIGURES 6 and 7. *Atlanta in 1896 and 1911.*

*Legend:*

The large rectangular areas outlined in black correspond to the sections of the city depicted in figures 8 and 9, pages 106–7 and 108–9 (numbers signify wards). The smaller areas represent the following sections of the city:

A bounded by the Central Railroad of Georgia, the Georgia Railroad, Trinity Avenue, Fair, and South Butler streets

B bounded by the Central Railroad of Georgia, Trinity Avenue, and Fair Street

C north and west of the Central of Georgia and the Western and Atlantic railroads tracks

D south of Fair Street and the Central of Georgia tracks and west of Capitol Avenue

E south of the Georgia Railroad tracks and east of South Butler Street and Capital Avenue

F bounded by Edgewood Avenue, Ivy, Decatur, Pratt, and College Streets

G east of the Western and Atlantic and north of the Georgia Railroads tracks

For an 1882 map indicating these same areas see figure 3, page 45.

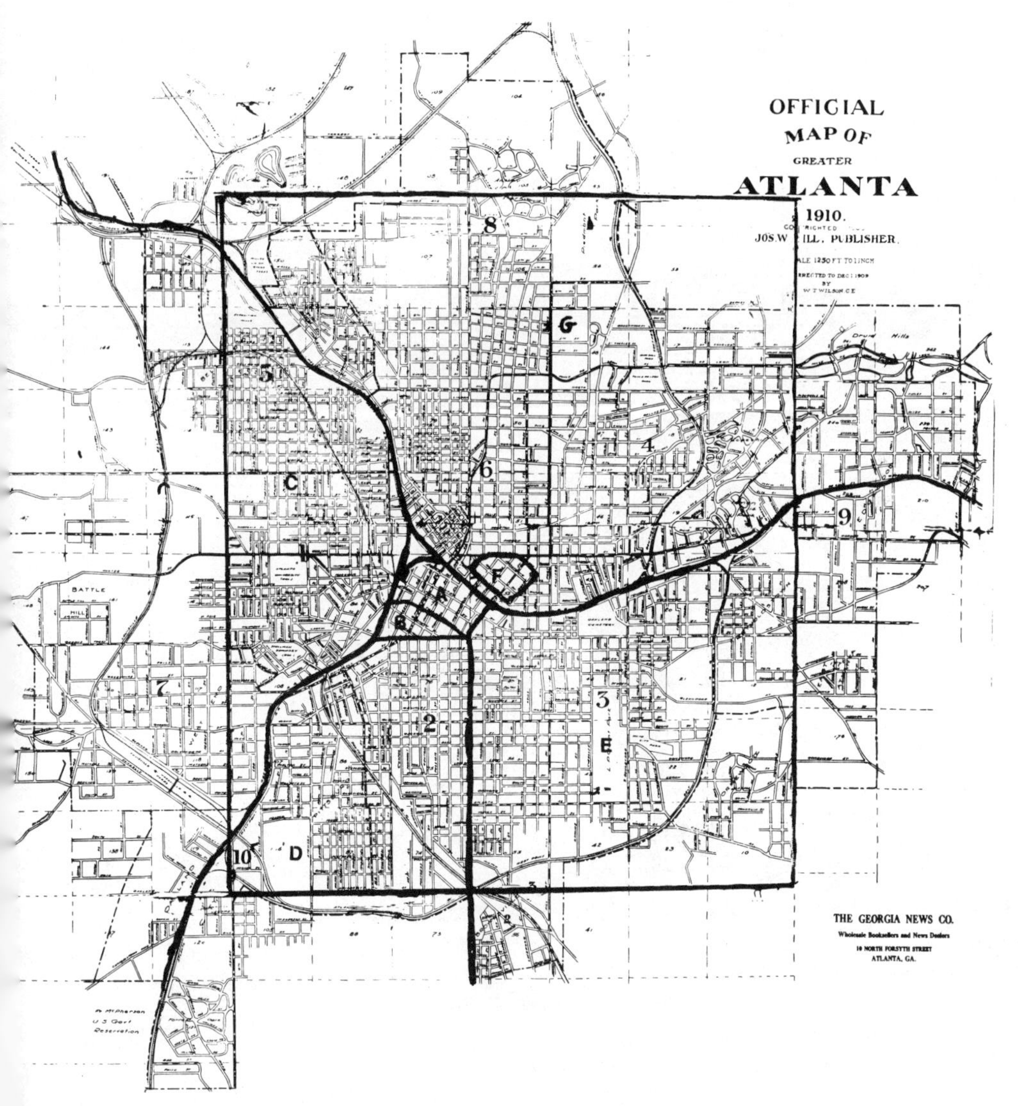


FIGURE 7. *Atlanta in 1911.*

FIGURE 8. *Jewish Institutions and Residential Patterns of Identifiable Jewish Males (Ages 18 and Over) by Country of Birth, 1896.*

*Legend:*

A Hebrew Benevolent Congregation
B Concordia Hall
C Hebrew Orphans' Home
D Hebrew Association
E Congregation Ahavath Achim

■ Austria-Hungary
● Germany
✪ Russia
0 Europe Other

★ United States
✱ Unknown

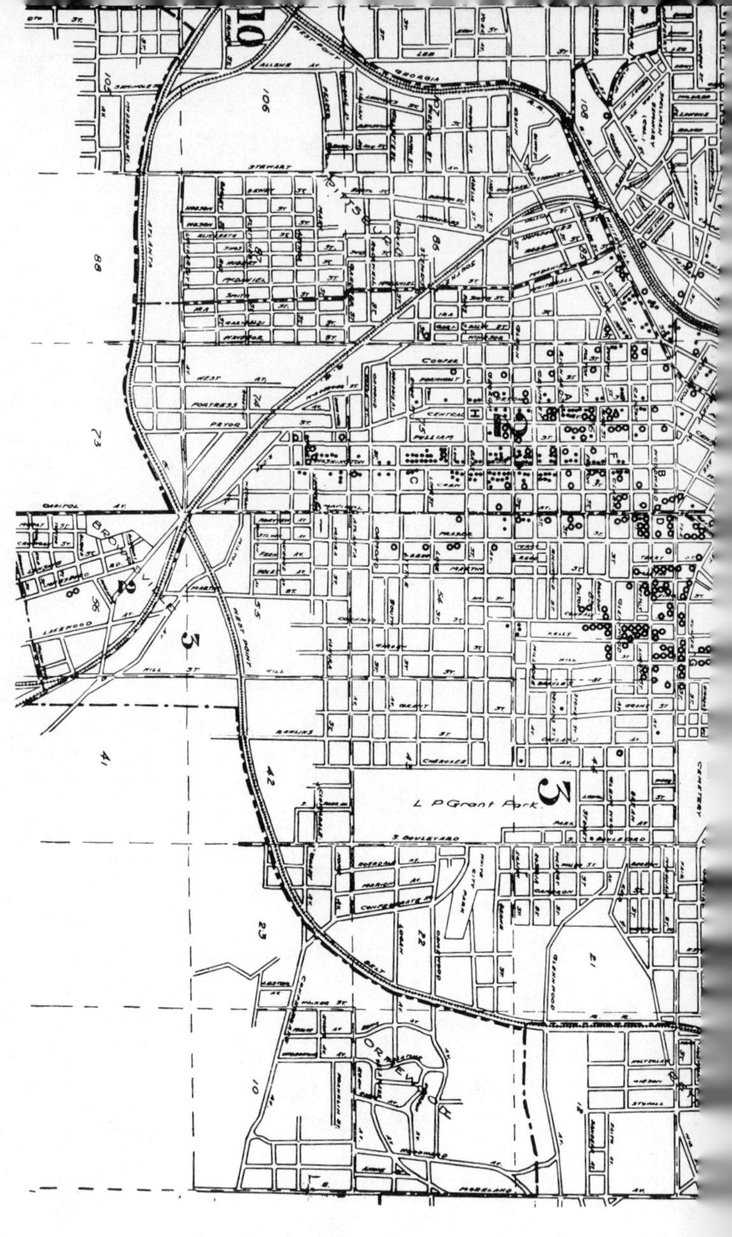


FIGURE 9. *Jewish Institutions and Residential Patterns of Selected Jewish Males (Ages 18 and Over) by Parentage, 1911.*

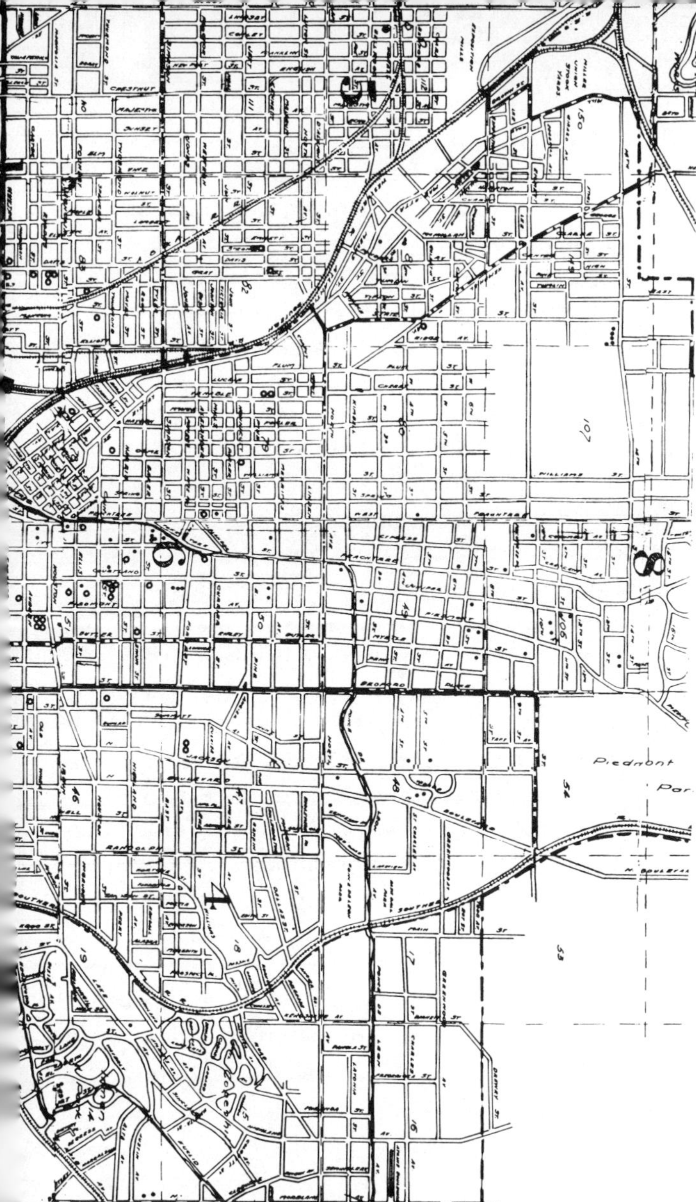


*Legend:*

A Hebrew Benevolent Congregation
B Standard Club
C Hebrew Orphans' Home
D Jewish Educational Alliance
E Congregation Ahavath Achim
F Congregation Beth Israel
G Congregation Shearith Israel
H Progress Club

- ● "German" (includes persons of German, Austro-Hungarian, native-born and mixed parentage)
- ✪ Russian

*Note:* Data for 1911 include all males ages 18 and over in 1896 who were still present 15 years later, and all Russians not present in 1896 and present in 1911 who filed naturalization papers in Atlanta between 1897 and 1917. (Numbers signify wards.)

blankets, towels, and curtains in both the Negro districts on the edge of town and the surrounding farm communities.[9]

A successful peddler might soon exchange the peripatetic existence for a more stationary one. Half of the Russians in 1896 were proprietors, but except for pioneer bonnet maker Morris Wiseberg, jeweler Abe Holzman, and leather dealer H. Wilensky, none were wholesalers or manufacturers. Nearly all the others were Decatur Street vendors of dry goods, used clothing, and shoes to local blacks and farm folk of both races, and grocers who worked within or on the fringes of black neighborhoods. While retailers such as Hyman Mendel, Philip Elson, Joseph Saul, and Jacob Chomsky would soon accumulate sufficient credit to enter wholesaling, only 37 of the 142 Russians had property assessed at over $50, and of the 6 who were worth over $1,000, 5 were members of the temple.[10]

The economic status of Atlanta's Russian Jews was different from, and probably superior to, that of their compatriots in America's fifteen largest cities. The local Russians were only one-third as likely to be employed in manufacturing and the crafts and three times more likely to be engaged in trade. (See table 22.) Furthermore, 26 percent (New York) to 55 percent (Milwaukee) of the Russian-Jewish male heads of household engaged in business for profit compared to 72 percent of Atlanta's adult Russian males.[11]

With their strong craft tradition, the Levantine Jews who began arriving after 1906 had an occupational profile which differed markedly from that of their Ashkenazic brethren. In 1914 two-thirds of the local Sephardim were shoemakers, nearly all with their own shops or stands on Decatur Street or elsewhere in the downtown area. One-fifth ran delicatessens, lunch rooms, beer saloons, and fruitstands patronized largely by blacks, and most of the remaining were white-collar workers.[12]

After 1880 Jews continued to exhibit a high degree of residential clustering, but because of the considerable cultural, economic, and temperamental differences separating the "Germans" and "Russians," the two Jewish groups tended to live in different sections of the city.

As the business district expanded during the eighties and nineties, the German Jews who lived on its southern fringe pushed deeper into the southwest quarter of the city. The area bounded by Trinity Avenue, Fair Street, and the Central of Georgia tracks (area

B), which had encompassed 50 percent of Atlanta's Jews in 1880 included only 25 percent of the German and 14 percent of the total Jews in 1896. Fifty-four percent of the Germans now resided south of Fair Street between Capitol Avenue and the Central of Georgia tracks (area D). Forsyth Street between Garnett and Fair streets was still almost solidly Jewish, but most Jews now lived along lower Whitehall, South Pryor, Pulliam, and Washington streets, and to a lesser extent on Woodward Avenue, Fair, Rawson, Orange, Richardson, and Crumley streets. As in earlier years, the southside Jews and their vastly more numerous gentile neighbors occupied detached one- and two-story single family frame dwellings which were located on spacious lots. Aaron and Jacob Haas were among the major developers of southside real estate, and as the streetcar lines they controlled extended farther south, the neighborhood became one of Atlanta's most prosperous and attractive.[13] (See figs. 6 and 8; tables 23 and 24.)

One-fifth of the Germans resided north of the railroad tracks (areas F and G). The Alexander and Weil families continued to live on Forrest and Merritts avenues respectively as they had for a quarter century. Employees of the Fulton Bag and Cotton Mill, such as Isaac Elsas and Benedict Stahl, resided near the factory; and entrepreneurs like plow manufacturer Sigmond Landauer, terra-cotta works owner Victor Kriegshaber, candy maker Harry L. Schlesinger, and Atlanta Telephone Company president Simon Baer had homes on Baltimore Place, West Peachtree, and Peachtree streets.

Only a handful of Russian Jews lived on the southside prior to 1900; all but one family lived north of Fair Street. Although the refugees felt somewhat more akin to their prosperous Reform coreligionists than to the Gentiles, the cost of southside rentals was prohibitively high. Moreover, their ghetto background, need for proximity both to their synagogues and places of business, a common language, culture, and outlook, and a shared sense of insecurity and alienation resulted in voluntary segregation. As Louis Wirth has observed, "The tolerance that strange ways of living need" often results in the creation of "separate cultural areas where one obtains freedom from hostile criticism and the backing of a group of kindred spirits."[14]

When the first Russian refugees arrived in the early eighties, the Germans, hoping to avoid the reghettoization so evident in the Northeast, purposely found lodgings for the newcomers in scattered sections of town. But as their numbers increased, the immigrants began to cluster in a small area just east of the Union Depot in the vicinity of Decatur Street (area F), and by 1896, 76 percent of the Russians resided there. (See figs. 6 and 7; tables 24.)

The Decatur Street, or ghetto district, was one of the city's oldest neighborhoods, and by the nineties was undergoing physical deterioration and racial transition. One of Atlanta's four major commercial thoroughfares, Decatur Street ran east from the center of town to Decatur, the seat of De Kalb County. It was via this route that much of the farm trade entered the city, and the surrounding area was dotted with wagon yards, saloons, boarding houses, and small stores. Several planing mills, two medical schools, Grady Hospital, Boys High School, and the Lyceum Theater were also located there. The street was lined with two-story, attached, brick buildings, stores alternating with saloons and poolhalls, which, together with the segregated vice district on nearby Collins Street, gave the neighborhood an unsavory reputation. More than one local writer expressed disdain at the "long rows of dingy shops below and dingier dwellings above—markets where everything from eggs, overripe, to women's caresses have their recognized price and alleged value."[15] (See fig. 10.)

Many of the same factors that led to the exodus of the original native-born white inhabitants attracted the newly arrived Russian Jews. Long accustomed to acting as middlemen for a depressed peasantry, the low rents and bustling country trade enticed the nascent immigrant storekeeper. Furthermore, since most property in the area was owned by absentee landlords, there was little if any resistance to the influx of Russians. Obliged to remain behind their counters from dawn to dusk in order to make as many sales as possible, the struggling merchants could live either above their Decatur Street stores or rent rooms on nearby Gilmer, Jenkins, and Pratt streets, or on Piedmont and Courtland avenues. Living conditions in the small frame houses were crowded, and the average Russian household contained 5.5 persons compared to 4.2 for the city as a whole. But even though an Austrian-born Jewish physician asserted that the neighborhood was characterized by "dirt, filth, putrefaction and noxious emanations," and lamented that in the dusty, poorly ventilated rooms "millions of deadly microbes held unmolested their murderous sway," the dwellings occupied by the newcomers were superior to those which they had known on the Lower East Side or in the *shtetl.*[16]

Although the Russian Jews in the Decatur Street district were clustered far more tightly than the Germans on the southside, they constituted only a large minority of the neighborhood's inhabitants. Blacks had established themselves in the area long before the arrival of the East Europeans, and there were two dozen "negro tenements" in the alleys of the heavily Jewish block bordered by Piedmont Avenue and Gilmer, Butler, and Decatur streets. (See fig. 10.) Moreover, the blocks north of Edgewood Avenue between Piedmont Avenue and Hilliard Street, and also those east of Pratt and north of Decatur streets, were overwhelmingly black. Greeks, Syrians, Chinese, Italians, and Hungarians also lived in the district, but Jews were the largest white group.[17]

One-quarter of the Russians in 1896 lived outside the ghetto. Some, like baker Morris Scrochi and grocer Sam Gottlieb, lived on its fringe, on Decatur and Gilmer streets east of Pratt. Others, such as Sol Aronson, lived more than half a mile north, near his Peachtree Street ladies tailor shop. One-tenth of the Russians lived west of the Central of Georgia tracks in the vicinity of Peters Street (area C). Like Decatur Street, Peters was a major gateway for farmers and was lined with stables, small stores like Jacob Finkelstein's, and establishments of more questionable character. Similarly, the area was undergoing racial transition and offered low-priced housing and easy access to the business district. Only 8 percent of the Russians resided on the southside (areas A, B, D, and E). Some of these were early arrivals who had acquired the economic and psychological means to leave the ghetto: Asher L. Feurstenberg, who resided on Pulliam near Fulton Street and owned property assessed at $2,500; and Judah W. Hirshfeld, who lived next to the Temple, had arrived in Atlanta twenty years earlier and was worth $13,700. Others, such as Madison Avenue tailor Max Sirkin and Cooper Street junk dealer Frank Revson, were proprietors of southside businesses and sought proximity to their establishments. (See figs. 6 and 8; table 24.)

Jewish residential patterns changed substantially between 1896 and 1911. The southward expansion of the business district was accompanied by a steady deterioration of the contiguous neighborhoods north of Fair Street (areas A and B). As stately old homes were converted into boarding houses, all but the least affluent German Jews, such as shoemaker Morris Lang and gas-fitter Fred Saloshin, evacuated the area. The use of the automobile and farther extension of the streetcar lines brought the outlying areas of the city within easy reach of the center, and in 1902 the Temple followed

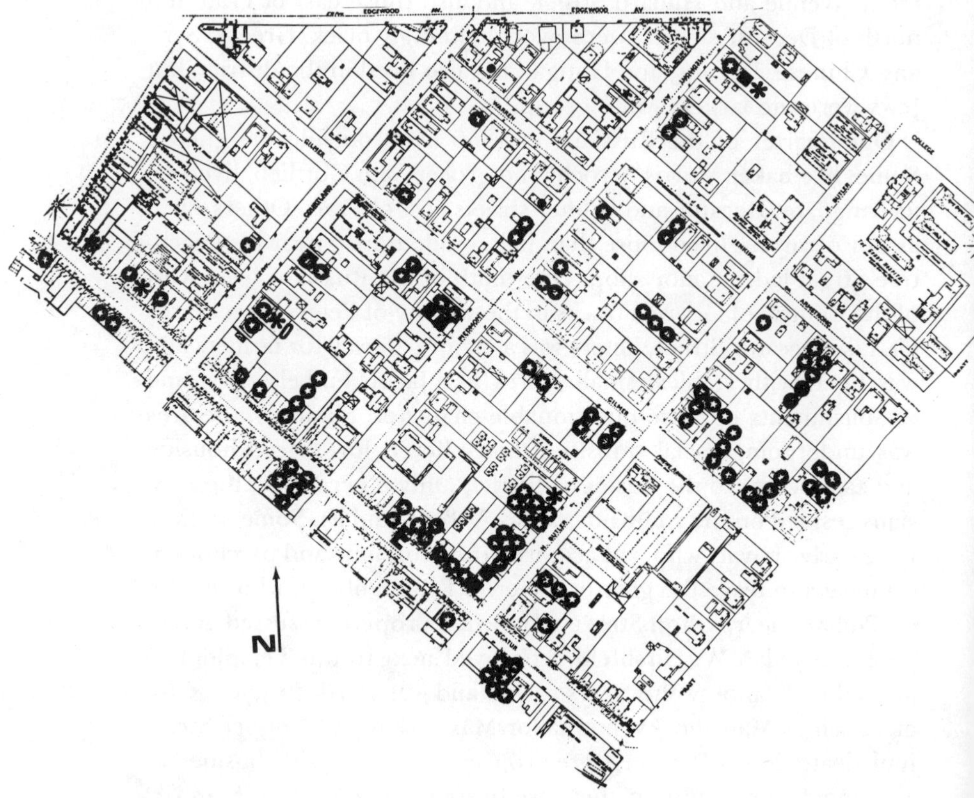


FIGURE 10. *Identifiable Jewish Males (Ages 18 and Over) in "Ghetto District" (Area F) by Birthplace, 1896.*

Legend:

■ Austria-Hungary
● Germany
✪ Russia
0 Europe Other and n.s.
⋆ United States
✱ Unknown
E Congregation Ahavath Achim

*Note:* Base map is a greatly reduced composite of seven plates from *Insurance Maps of Atlanta Georgia 1899* (New York: Sanborn-Perris Map Co., 1899). n.s.—non-specified.

its members southward to Pryor and Richardson streets. By 1911 more than two-thirds of the Germans lived south of Fair Street and west of Capitol Avenue (area D). Substantial numbers continued to live on Whitehall and Pryor streets, but more than half lived on fashionable Washington Street which, for the half-mile stretch between Clarke and Little streets, was mostly Jewish. Here resided some of the most prominent members of the Jewish community: Herbert J. Haas, Isaac Schoen, Isaac Liebman, Jr., Louis Newelt, Isaac H. Hirsch, and David Marx. Although predominantly southsiders, nearly a quarter of the Germans—a greater proportion than in any previous year—lived on the northside (area G). The elegant Inman Park section included the families of Victor Kriegshaber, Aaron Haas, and Harold Hirsch; Oscar Pappenheimer had a huge residence on Ponce de Leon Avenue, and Joseph Jacobs and Harry L. Schlesinger lived on Peachtree Street. Other prosperous Germans, such as Joseph Hirsch, Armand May, B. F. Joel, and Eugene Oberdorfer, lived on the northern edge of the city, more than three miles from the Temple. They constituted the vanguard of what would soon become a major migration from the southside, impelled in large measure by the southward expansion of the ghetto district. (See figs. 7 and 9; table 24.)

The fivefold increase in the Russian-Jewish population between 1896 and 1911, the advance of the business district on the ghetto's western flank, the encroachment of Negroes on the northern and eastern perimeters, and the Russians' growing prosperity resulted in the disintegration of the ghetto. Only 13 percent of the Russians in 1911 resided in the Decatur Street district (area F), while another 19 percent lived on its fringes (area G), many in areas populated largely by blacks. These tended to be the poorer and more recent arrivals such as peddler Morris Weiner and shoemaker Philip Yellen. However, 57 percent now lived on the southside where only 8 percent had resided fifteen years earlier. Half of the southside Russians lived east of Capitol Avenue along the parts of Woodward Avenue, Hunter, Fair, South Butler, Rawson, Connally, Fraser, and Hill streets that lay just across the Georgia Railroad tracks from the former ghetto (area E). Most of the Jews in this area were either recent arrivals, like tailor Sam Isecoff, or less affluent old-timers, like bookkeeper Morris Ney. It was here that Congregation Shearith Israel was located. Capitol Avenue itself was the home of several prominent Russians, including wholesale grocer Charles Goldstein and wholesale dry-goods merchant Hyman Mendel. To the west (areas B and D) lived most of the prosperous Russians, many on streets populated largely by Germans: physician Louis Rouglin, leather dealer H. Wilensky, and frame manufacturer Herman Binder on Washington Street; tailor Joseph Gross, wholesale clothier Joseph Saul, and pawnbroker Isaac Sinkowitz on South Pryor Street; and shoe store owner Jacob Heiman and dry goods merchant Joseph Buchman on Whitehall Street. Other successful Russians like pawnbroker Leon Eplan, wholesale notions dealer Philip Elson, and harness manufacturer Morris Frankel lived on Central Avenue and Pulliam Street, which were between the streets favored by the Germans. Conservative Congregation Beth Israel was also located in this area. As in 1896 a tenth of the Russians lived west of the Central of Georgia tracks (area C). This section of the city was now heavily black, and most of the Jews who lived there were grocers. (See figs. 7 and 9; table 24.)

There were no Levantine Jews in Atlanta in 1896 and only a handful in 1911. But of the 46 adult males (out of 69) in 1914 for whom addresses are known, 17 lived on Gilmer Street between Courtland and Piedmont avenues, 13 on Central Avenue between Fair and Fulton streets, and the remaining 16 were scattered throughout the center of town. Their clustering patterns bore less resemblance to those of other Jews than to the Greeks with whom they shared a cultural affinity and occupational similarity.[18]

The demographic, economic, and residential differences between the Germans and Russians reflected and were partially responsible for an almost total absence of social interaction. Separated by a wide cultural and temperamental gulf, the two groups were generations apart. By the mid-nineties, nearly all the members of the established Jewish community were either native-born or had lived in the United States for several decades; some ranked among Atlanta's pioneer settlers. Heirs to the age of science and reason, they identified strongly with American ways and with the interests of their city. While some still clung to a vague sense of Jewish peoplehood, their Jewish identity was primarily denominational and their "progressive" Judaism was shedding the last of its "foreignisms."

The East Europeans were of a different breed. Refugees from a land in which they had constituted as genuine a national group as the Poles, Lithuanians, and Ukrainians among whom they dwelt, few of the Russian Jews had been affected by the Enlightenment. Those who had, tended to be nationalists or radicals of various persuasions; but for the vast majority Orthodoxy enveloped their lives and governed a large part of their behavior. Their distinctive language, "un-American" appearance, and "backward" ways did not endear them to their Reform coreligionists. The uncouth foreignness of the Russians provided the prosperous Germans with a disquieting reminder of their own humble origins and, by conforming closely to the popular Jewish stereotype, threatened the status of the established community. Although the ratio of Russian to German Jews never became as great in the South as it did in the northern port cities, the visibility of the newcomers was magnified by the overwhelmingly Protestant and old-stock character of the region's population and its sensitivity to deviations from the norm. Like their counterparts in the North, Atlanta's German Jews sympathized with the Russians' plight, provided them with material assistance, and endeavored to americanize them. But at the same time they regarded the newcomers as social inferiors and sought to place as much distance as possible between themselves and the immigrants.

The institutional structure of the German-Jewish community became increasingly complex and restrictive during the period of Russian immigration. In 1880 the Hebrew Benevolent Congregation, which was open to all who wished to join, was the unquestioned center of Jewish communal life; three decades later Rabbi Marx had to remind his flock that "the Congregation, not the Club nor the Lodge nor any other organization is the representative body in Israel."[19]

More discriminating, less demanding, and offering more tangible benefits, the social club gradually eclipsed the Temple in the competition for Jewish time and money. The Concordia was the most prestigious of the city's Jewish associations during the nineteenth century. Its supremacy was unsuccessfully challenged in 1893 when a group of former Concordians established the Harmony Club for "literary and social purposes." The new club acquired rooms on Whitehall Street between Hunter Street and Trinity Avenue (Peters Street) but disbanded prior to 1900. The Concordia passed into receivership in 1901 and was succeeded four years later by the Standard Club. Established as "a high class social club. . . . devoted to entertainments of high order," its organizers constituted the social and economic elite of Atlanta Jewry. The *Journal* observed:

> The auspices under which the Standard starts, make it certain that the new club will at once take high rank among the social organizations of the city. The members are great lovers of music, art and social pleasures, and it is certain that the Standard will be the scene of many notable receptions and musicales.

The club purchased a spacious colonnaded mansion on Washington Street near Woodward Avenue and provided facilities for poker, bridge, dancing, and bowling. Dues were high and membership was limited to 150. Younger and less affluent Jews who could not afford to join the Standard organized their own exclusive clubs. The Progress Club was founded in 1909, purchased a house the following year on Pryor Street between Georgia and Bass avenues, and survived about four years. In 1913 the Phoenix Club was organized, but it too was short lived. The Standard Club is still the leading social institution of the Atlanta Jewish community.[20]

Several ephemeral cultural and athletic organizations were also founded during the last quarter of the nineteenth century. A debating society called the Young Israels' Association appeared in 1877; two years later the Atlanta Hebrew Literary Association and the Young Men's Hebrew Literary Association made their debut. The Crémieux Literary Club, named after the great Franco-Jewish statesman, was organized in 1881 by young men and women in their late teens and early twenties who met in each other's homes for musical and literary entertainments. On a grander scale was the Hebrew Association, which was chartered in 1896 by leading members of the community to promote "moral, intellectual and physical improvement." "As a general thing the Jews do not indulge sufficiently in exercises," observed one of the sponsors, "and physical development is as essential as the intellectual. . . ." On the corner of Pryor and Garnett streets the association erected a two-story building containing a gymnasium, billiard room, bowling alley, hot water baths, library, and reading rooms. It also issued the *Jewish Tribune,* a weekly newspaper edited by George W. Markens. Although it had 175 members in 1898, the Hebrew Association disbanded in January, 1900.[21]

Women participated either as members or guests in most organized communal activities, but rarely did they hold office. Although a Hebrew Ladies Aid Society had been established in 1871, its worthy but limited objectives afforded affluent and leisured women little opportunity to fulfill their capacity for leadership or need for independent social recognition. In 1887 the Tuesday Afternoon Club was organized by a dozen prominent women, including the wives of cotton mill owner Jacob Elsas, brewery president Albert Steiner, former state legislator Adolph Brandt, and the three Hirsch brothers. New members were accepted only upon the death or resignation of one of the founders, and during its two-decade existence the club held weekly kaffeeklatsches and engaged in a variety of benevolent activities. A similar society of somewhat briefer existence was the Grandmothers' Club, founded in 1894 by several grande dames including Eliza (Mrs. David) Mayer, Caroline (Mrs. Jacob) Haas, and Georgia (Mrs. Jacob) Steinheimer. Meetings were devoted to recitations, euchre, and whist; ailing members were comforted and dues were applied to charitable purposes. "The organization," remarked the *Constitution* in 1898, "is one of the most exclusive in the city." A chapter of the Council of Jewish Women was founded in 1895 and is still active today. Under the leadership of Rebecca (Mrs. Julius M.) Alexander and Clara (Mrs. Julius E.) Sommerfield, the Council acted as the sisterhood and social action arm of the Temple, organized Bible study classes for members, gave charity balls, conducted musical and literary programs, rendered considerable service to immigrant families, and campaigned for free kindergartens, the eight-hour day, and for the abolition of child labor.[22]

Teen-age children also formed their own societies, often emulating the pleasures and pretensions of their elders. The Lucky Thirteen Club was begun in 1898 "to give functions of which only a few select couples can indulge," and the following year the Nameless Club was organized. The Girls' Amusement Society included the younger Haases, Riches, Cohens, and Rosenfelds. The Players' Club, a dramatic society, had a similarly elite membership. Purim, Hanukkah, and New Year masquerade balls at the Concordia and Standard Clubs, Sunday school picnics at Ponce de Leon Springs, dances at the lodge halls, and confirmation and debut parties at the Kimball House provided further diversion for the younger set for whom calling cards and dance programs were *de rigueur.*[23]

The increasing prosperity of the German Jews and the consequent development of elite social clubs detracted from the appeal of the Jewish fraternal orders. Because the well-to-do did not need sickness and death benefits, the relative affluence of lodge members declined. By 1900, except for a few older members who remained active in the politics of the district grand lodges, the lodges had become social centers for the managers, white-collar workers, smaller proprietors, and younger professionals. Although the local chapter of the Free Sons of Israel persisted into the twentieth century, the Kesher Shel Barzel Lodge did not. Largely because of its strong national and regional organization, the B'nai B'rith Gate City Lodge continued to flourish even though a group of younger members seceded in 1903 and for three years held a charter as the Atlanta Lodge. Despite the social focus of its activities, the major achievement of Atlanta's B'nai B'rith was its role in the creation of the leading Jewish benevolent institution in the South Atlantic states: the Hebrew Orphans' Home.[24]

The suggestion to establish a Jewish orphan asylum was first made at the 1870 convention of B'nai B'rith District Grand Lodge No. 5, but little was accomplished until 1877. In 1886 it was decided to begin construction as soon as $50,000 was raised and to locate the institution either in Atlanta, Richmond, or the District of Columbia, whichever contributed the greatest amount of money. Within two years Atlantans donated more than half the $62,000 eventually required to build the home. Joseph Hirsch, Morris Adler, Isaac May, and Jacob Elsas each contributed $1,000, and more than $5,000 came from Gentiles like Samuel N. Inman, who felt that the acquisition of the home would be still another sign of Atlanta's greatness. The Hebrew Orphans' Home was dedicated in March 1889 amid laudatory addresses delivered by Mayor John T. Glenn and Governor John B. Gordon before an audience estimated at three thousand persons. Located on Washington Street between Love and Little streets near what was then the southern border of town, the home was of Venetian style, built of brick trimmed with granite and terra cotta; the central building, clinic, dairy, servants' cottage, and playground occupied an entire square block. Under the superintendency of R. A. Sonn, nearly four hundred children passed through the home between 1889 and 1915, approximately two-thirds of these coming from outside Atlanta and most of East European parentage. The children attended the Fraser Street Public School, received religious instruction at the Temple or Ahavath Achim, and were trained to be typists, stenographers, plumbers, and printers. Uniforms and military discipline were abolished shortly after 1900, and by the standards of the day the orphans fared very well. Although financial support was technically the responsibility of the district grand lodge, Atlanta shouldered much of the burden. With funds raised through fairs, dances, and card parties, the Tuesday Afternoon Club, Ladies Sewing Society, and Orphans' Aid Society provided the children with clothing, toys, and personal attention. In response to increasing costs, around 1910 the directors began providing subsidies to foster parents and widows, and by 1930 the home was vacant, its role eventually supplanted by the Jewish Children's Service.[25]

Except for the fraternal lodges and benevolent societies, German-Jewish institutional life in Atlanta during the late nineteenth and early twentieth centuries was characterized on every level by the growth of social exclusivity. The Jewish conception of "club life" was influenced deeply by the emergence in the eighties of elite social associations such as the Capital City Club and Gentlemen's Driving Club. Manifestations of the "general struggle for place and privilege" which followed the Civil War, these organizations attempted to safeguard the status of their members by refusing to admit Jews. Status-conscious Jews responded to this discrimination and to the widening economic and social divisions within the community by endeavoring to create their own version of "high society" and provide themselves with opportunities to express their affluence and refinement. Yet while the gentile clubs strove to erect nonpecuniary standards for social acceptance—largely in an effort to exclude wealthy Jews and other social climbers—wealth was initially the primary criterion for admission to the Jewish clubs. However, as Atlanta's Russians acquired wealth and their native-born children entered the universities and the professions, the same status considerations which had resulted in the exclusion of German Jews from the Capital City Club led the Germans to bar Russians from the Standard. Only when the Great Depression severely eroded the Standard's fiscal stability were the first Jews of East European descent admitted.[26]

The Hebrew Benevolent Congregation did have East European members: 7 out of 184 in 1896 but only 5 out of 295 in 1911. The decline was probably attributable to Ahavath Achim's acquisition of a permanent synagogue in 1901 and to the establishment of Beth Israel in 1905. The 7 who belonged in 1896 had much in common with the Germans. Six had settled in the United States prior to 1880; 4 were married to native-born women, and a fifth to a German; they included the first, second, fifth, and sixth wealthiest Russians in the city; and only 1 resided in the "ghetto district." Although some were alienated from Orthodoxy and found Reform more attractive, most had joined because the Temple provided more substantial material benefits and conferred higher social status than did the other congregations. On the whole, Reform Judaism held little appeal for the Russians, and while the Temple was willing to accept them as members, it did not encourage them to affiliate. "As an exponent of progressive Judaism, accretions to our ranks have been few from the large number of our immigrant brethren," declared Rabbi Marx in 1909. "We have sacrificed no principles to secure numerical strength."[27]

Because the Jewish national fraternal orders had explicit Jewish objectives but were unconnected with any faction within Judaism, they were more hospitable than the Temple or the social clubs to Russian membership. Moreover, the lodges' sickness and death benefits offered newcomers protection against some of the vicissitudes of resettlement. Between 1882 and 1896, of the 127 men who joined the Gate City Lodge, 11 had been born in Eastern Europe, and several Russians later joined the Atlanta Lodge. However, whether because of discrimination or an inability to pay their dues, few Russians remained in the predominantly German lodges for more than three or four years. Even in the absence of discrimination, the economic and cultural differences between the two groups impeded the growth of fraternal bonds. In 1896 the first of several immigrant lodges, Kadisha Lodge No. 216 of Independent Order B'rith Abraham, was organized, and by 1907 it had 300 members and paid sick benefits of $7.50 per week and death benefits of $500. Two other B'rith Abraham chapters, Georgia Lodge No. 493 and Capital City Lodge No. 554, were founded during the next few years. In 1905 Theodor Herzl Lodge No. 596 of the Independent Order of B'nai B'rith was organized, but its charter was revoked four years later, after which Russians became increasingly numerous in the Gate City Lodge. Order B'rith Shalom established a local lodge in 1913 and within eight months attracted 250 members, nearly all between the ages of eighteen and twenty-five. Members of Conservative Congregation Beth Israel attempted to start a new national fraternity to be called Order B'nai Israel, but it had little appeal.[28]

The two most dynamic immigrant lodges were Arbeiter Ring (Workmen's Circle) Branch No. 207 and Farband (National Workmen's Alliance) Branch No. 71, organized in 1908 and 1913 respectively. Like the other fraternal societies, the Ring and the Farband provided sickness and death benefits, but in addition promoted Yiddish culture and Socialist doctrine and held strongly differing views on the issue of Zionism. The Ring members were predominantly free thinkers who had been associated with the Bund in Russia and, imbued with proletarian ideals, despised Zionism as "bourgeois utopianism." Under the leadership of Samuel Yampolsky and M. J. Merlin, the Ring started a Yiddish library at 86 Central Avenue and later established a lyceum and *folks-shule* (people's school). In contrast, the Farband members were Labor Zionists and fairly religious. Although there was some initial antagonism between the two groups, they cooperated in bringing to the city such prominent Yiddish speakers as Baruch C. Vladeck, "the young LaSalle"; Peretz Hirschbein, the dramatist and novelist; Chaim Zhitlowsky, the socialist philosopher; and Joel Entin, editor of the *Warheit.* Despite their proletarian outlook, Atlanta's Jewish socialists were almost all small businessmen: peddlers, grocers, and clothiers. Unlike the industrial cities of the North where the Jewish workers' movement had its greatest strength, there was little incentive for Jewish proletarians to settle in Atlanta unless they eventually hoped to become proprietors; wages were low and working conditions unattractive.[29]

Orthodox Hungarian Jews—there were several dozen families in the city—founded their own society in 1910, the Hungarian Benevolent Association, to which Russians and Galicians were also admitted. The association paid sick benefits of three dollars per week for a maximum of thirteen weeks and one dollar per week thereafter.[30]

In 1904, four years after the dissolution of the Hebrew Association, several influential Russians including Leon Eplan, Morris Lichtenstein, and D. Zaban secured a charter for a Young Men's Hebrew Association. Established "to promote the cause of the Jewish religion, social intercourse and the intellectual development of its members," the "Y" emphasized athletic activities and "Americanization." During the first two years it rented quarters on Edgewood between Courtland and Piedmont avenues, later moving to a small building on Piedmont just below Auburn Avenue. An affiliated society, the Young Men's Hebrew Literary Association, which met Sunday afternoons at the nearby Lyceum Theater, had been in existence over twenty years. The immigrants also organized several amateur theatrical groups such as the Jewish Progressive Dramatic Club, which performed the works of Sholom Asch and other Yiddish playwrights.[31]

To meet the needs of the growing immigrant community, two Yiddish weeklies made their debut later in the decade. The *Southern Guide* was inaugurated in March 1908 by the International Printing

Company, which engaged Rabbi Julius Loeb of Congregation Beth Israel as editor. Billed as "The First and Only Yiddish Publication in the South," it failed to survive Loeb's departure for Birmingham the following year. Not easily discouraged, the publishers established the *Jewish Star* and hired Dr. Charles Wortsman, who had earlier edited Yiddish periodicals in New York, Boston, and Cleveland, to direct the enterprise. An ardent Zionist, Wortsman nonetheless recognized that until the distant day when Palestine would pass into Jewish hands, America would have to serve as a temporary shelter for persecuted European Jewry. With this in mind and also in the hope of boosting his paper's circulation, he tried to convince IRO general manager David Bressler that the South was the only region with sufficient room to absorb the immigrant masses and that a migration southward could best be encouraged by IRO subsidization of the *Jewish Star.* Bressler was not convinced, and within a year the itinerant journalist left for greener pastures. Wortsman was succeeded by Dr. Henry Fueher, who guided the paper until its demise in 1911.[32]

The local Jewish community proved to be no more receptive to Yiddish journalism than it had been to earlier efforts of Browne, Markens, and Cohen. While a demand did exist for news of exclusively Jewish interest, the community was not large enough to support a local newspaper profitably, especially since Jewish newspapers could be imported from the North. Moreover, the small size of the Russian colony accelerated its acculturation and, in turn, lessened its dependence on the ethnic press.[33]

Excluded from the German clubs and alienated from the "old fashioned" fraternal lodges of their fathers, the sons and daughters of the early Russian immigrants founded more than a dozen short-lived social clubs during the years 1910 to 1913. These included the Don't Worry Club, Eagle Social Club, Henry Grady Debating Society, Harmony Social Club, Little Women, South Side Club, High School Graduates Club, Wide Awake Club, Progressive American Club, Jolly Fifteen, and the Osceola Club. The most successful of the Russian societies was the Jewish Progressive Club, similar in name but not in intent to the previously mentioned Jewish Progressive Dramatic Club, which was founded in 1913 and is still in existence today. Most of the early members were successful men in their twenties and thirties who were affiliated with Congregation Beth Israel. Under the leadership of Joseph "Billy Sunday" Lazear, Benjamin J. Massell, and Ike Eplan, the club quickly raised $25,000 and in 1916 dedicated a newly constructed clubhouse on Pryor between Rawson and Eugenia streets. Under the direction of Massell, who would later make his mark as Atlanta's preeminent real estate developer, the building was equipped with spacious reception, dining, and billiard rooms, as well as a library, theater, gymnasium, and swimming pool.[34]

Although there was little social contact with the Russians from the beginning, prominent members of the established German Jewish community were outspoken on their behalf. When a local reporter suggested to Rabbi Jacobson in 1882 that the refugees were "rather a peculiar lot," the rabbi replied that they were "thrifty, hardworking people. . . . sober and industrious [who] will work when you would play." Ten years later Levi Cohen, Joseph Steiner, and others petitioned the Georgia House to repeal an 1891 statute which subjected all peddlers to a fifty dollar license fee per county, claiming that the Russians carried only fifty dollars worth of goods and could not afford to purchase licenses in four to ten counties. The previous winter, it was alleged, "these poor strangers were *molested* or to say *robbed,* by some so-called bailiffs" who were enforcing the law. Editor Frank J. Cohen of the *Jewish Sentiment* recognized the low esteem in which the newcomers were held, but insisted that "any asylum for the oppressed Jews should be welcomed by every other Jew" and that "our Russian co-religionists number good, bad and indifferent just as any other people."[35]

As czarist persecution intensified, Temple members became increasingly aware that they shared a common destiny with their Orthodox brethren. As early as 1880, the Atlanta Young Men's Hebrew Literary Association cosigned a memorial to the United States government on behalf of Russian Jewry. Ten years later, a committee consisting of Aaron Haas, Joseph Hirsch, Jacob Elsas, Samuel Weil, and Rabbi Leo Reich was appointed to organize a public meeting to protest Russian anti-Semitism, but apparently the meeting was never held. The Kishinev massacre in 1903 generated a more effective reaction. At the initiative of Rabbi Mayerowitz of Ahavath Achim, a fund was created to aid survivers of the pogrom. Leaders of the two congregations worked side by side to insure an effective solicitation, and the Bijou Theater agreed to donate the receipts from two matinee performances. At one of the benefits, Henry A. Alexander, scion of one of the oldest Jewish families in the

South, delivered an eloquent plea on behalf of his downtrodden coreligionists:

> I grant you that their garb may be outlandish, their speech unintelligible and their ways and manners wholly foreign to this country; but do not forget that through the veins of the humblest Jew who lands at the port of New York, there flows the unsullied blood of priests and prophets, and, though his bearing be ungainly and his presence uncouth, his fundamental conceptions are identical with your own.

Nine hundred dollars was raised within three weeks, and the IRO was notified to send Kishinev refugees to Atlanta as soon as they arrived at New York. Similarly, the Odessa pogrom two years later was followed by a mass meeting at Ahavath Achim which netted eight hundred dollars, and leading members of the German and Russian communities served together on the collection committee. "It is one of the most beautiful and enviable traits of this particular people," observed the *Atlanta Constitution,* "that they are never lacking in generosity and initiative, both of purse and effort when misfortune strikes members of their faith. . . ." Several years later, when unrestricted Jewish immigration was threatened by the proposed enactment of the literacy test bill and a pending decision to place the Bureau of Immigration under the control of an independent Department of Labor, both Germans and Russians vociferously voiced their objections.[36]

Despite common opposition to infringement of Jewish rights, members of the community sometimes differed regarding the nature of an effective response. For example, at the outbreak of the Russo-Japanese war, some Jews—mostly Russians—wanted to raise money to purchase a battleship for Japan and thereby "strike [the] enemy whenever and however the opportunity is presented." Another faction, led by Rabbi Marx but also with some immigrant backing, opposed this plan on the grounds that it would not only engender further pogroms but also improperly enmesh the United States in the war. Nor did opposition to anti-Semitism dissolve the social barrier separating the established and immigrant communities. When services were held at the Temple "in memory of our massacred brothers in Russia," the "minister" and president—but not the members—of Ahavath Achim were invited to attend.[37]

The Germans recognized an obligation to assist the Russian refugees who were arriving in ever growing numbers. If they had little patience with the immigrants' Orthodoxy and backward ways, they had genuine compassion for them as human beings and fellow Jews. Money raised by the Temple paid for the transportation and resettlement of the first refugees in 1881 and 1882, and the Germans subsequently participated in the dispersal programs of the Jewish Alliance of America and the Industrial Removal Office. The Hebrew Relief Society, a Temple-affiliated group which received most of its income from an annual Purim ball and Yom Kippur appeal, was reorganized in 1883 and again in 1889 to handle the growing welfare problem. The Hebrew Ladies Benevolent Society, which had over one thousand dollars in its treasury by 1889, supplied coal to needy families, provided small sums to men who wished to enter peddling, and taught Russian women how to prepare the unfamiliar foods available in the South. Upon application from a "russian [*sic*] committee" in 1891, the Temple permitted the newcomers to use its basement for a night school which lasted for about five years.[38]

The initial objective of the Germans was to make the newcomers self-sustaining by securing them employment and providing loans for those who wished to strike out on their own. Not only was this goal consonant with the ideals of *tzedakah* (righteousness), but the Germans also recognized that from the standpoint of public relations it was imperative that poor Jews not become a burden to the general community. "We see beggars of every other nationality and religion by scores in the street," observed the *Atlanta Constitution,* "but we see Jews never. If Jews do beg, they beg of Jews . . . and there is every apparent reason to believe . . . that Jews take care of their own. . . ." "Did you ever see a poor Jew?" a Christian merchant asked several friends in 1890. None had. "It is because they are thrifty. And then because their charity to the poor of their race is, as true charity should be, kept hidden from the world. No religion has such well-organized, such beautiful charities." However, the generosity of the Germans was limited by the widely accepted notion that a too liberal dispensation of charity would undermine initiative and foster dependence. "He has never been sensational or promiscuous in his benefactions," noted a gentile observer, "for above all, the Jew is a good business man [*sic*]. He has seen that his largess will not be wasted and has striven scrupulously not to encourage mendicancy or pauperism."[39]

It was not sufficient that the immigrants be self-supporting; they also had to be americanized as quickly as possible. Like all acculturated members of a minority group, the Germans feared that they would be judged by their lowest representatives. Moreover, they were acutely conscious of the Southerners' sensitivity to cultural differences and the consequent necessity for conformity. At the same time, the Germans sincerely believed in the superiority of American ways and failed to appreciate the depth and richness of the East European tradition. Our "duty does not rest with saving them [the Russian Jews] from starvation," insisted a prominent Temple member, "we must raise them from intellectual and physical destitution and decay, teach them and enlighten them . . . and make them a desirable element, worthy to inhabit this great country. . . . Have mercy upon him and teach him to become like you."[40]

Like the blacks of a later period, the Russians responded to the well-intentioned paternalism of their benefactors with both gratitude and resentment. None denied that the Temple-affiliated charities had been of assistance, but the continued insensitivity and condescension of the Germans evoked considerable bitterness, especially among the more established members of the immigrant community. Tensions that had been simmering for a decade came to a head in 1896 when the local *Jewish Tribune* reviewed the charitable activities of the Council of Jewish Women and the Hebrew Ladies Benevolent Society. Editor George W. Markens explained that in response to complaints from public school teachers about the appearance of the Russian children, and also from the feeling that the young Russians knew little about "true Judaism," the HLBS had opened a cheap bathhouse and the CJW started a Sabbath school on Decatur Street.

> A strenuous effort to instill patriotism into these young minds is made, and "America" is most heartily sung by all. Generally speaking, the ignorance of these people is sadly striking. They know nothing at all of the ten commandments and the fall of Adam and Eve is a news story to them.[41]

Leon Eplan and Morris Lichtenstein responded to this public washing of the community's dirty linen by closing the Sabbath school and accusing the Germans of seeking unnecessary publicity. "We do not need force [*sic*] baths, nor do we need a guardianship as to our lavatory exercises. . . . Charity is a great virtue," declared the two Russian spokesmen, "but the charity which seeks notoriety in newspapers ceases to be a virtue, and becomes a simple advertizing medium, repulsive even to those who, by force of circumstances, are compelled to accept it." They staunchly denied the charge of religious ignorance, noted their appreciation of the Germans' past help, but insisted that "we need not cling to the apron strings of Mrs. Eichberg [president of the HLBS] forever. . . . Let us work our way to prosperity and American citizenship in our own humble way. Be charitable to our needy, if you wish, but do not publish us as barbarians, constantly inviting the contempt of our fellow citizens."[42]

In reply Markens accused Eplan of robbing the children of enlightenment and "grossly insulting the philanthropic women." However, he believed Lichtenstein to be a gentleman "under the magic spell of Svengali's baton," and therefore not deserving of censure. "Probably Mr. Eplan is afraid of reforms and prefers orthodoxy, with all its sacred yet out of date platitudes." The question was not one of nativity or rite, the editor claimed, but "between an educated, refined man and an ignorant, coarse one. . . . We want to make good American citizens out of our Russian brothers. . . . However, if they prefer merely to exist, instead of living and expanding in the broad light of day, so be it." At this point a third Russian, junk dealer Frank Revson, entered the fray. Revson, who had resided in Atlanta since 1883, stoutly denied the editor's imputations and alleged that Markens sat up nights searching through magazines looking for "something to strike the Russian Jew with." The Russian Jews of 1896, he declared, were no longer the poverty-striken refugees of 1882.

> They claim to be able and willing to care for the poor that are among them and thereby repay the charity that has been extended to them. No longer will they have the name Russian Jew to be the emblem of helplessness and imposition. They assert to have grown into manhood and it is but meet and proper that they should be given the right to exercise the same. The motherly care of Mrs. Eichberg is thankfully appreciated, but she must admit that it is utterly impossible to keep grown up boys (and sometimes even under age) under perpetual vigilance. . . . Let the noble ladies look for other quarters to bestow charity and lavish their tender affection where it is wanted and needed, but in passing we would suggest not to itemize their deeds before the public.[43]

At about the same time that the bathhouse and Sunday School controversy erupted, Markens disclosed that "Svengali" Eplan had organized nearly all the Russian voters into an Independent Citizens' Club and was allegedly bartering their votes for cash. After "escaping from the iron heel of the merciless czar," declared the editor, the Russian Jews "find themselves in the clutch of a scheming, cunning politician who trifles with their suffrage under the guise of religious fellowship." Eplan acknowledged that he played a leading role in naturalizing immigrants but denied Markens's charges. "I believe that it is the right way to make them a respected part of our population," said the Odessa-born pawnbroker, "and that it is the best way to make them take a pride in their new home." The real basis for Markens's concern was that the ICC met to endorse candidates in Ahavath Achim's hall and in so doing was imprudently mixing religion and politics.

> It is just such uncalled-for demonstrations which create prejudices against the Jewish race, and with justice. Nor is this all, for this political meeting, which, at times became extremely passionate . . . was in a Jewish temple of religion on Decatur Street. A more undignified proceeding has never been recorded in the annals of progressive Judaism, and . . . we bow our heads with shame. . . .[44]

In the same manner that the Germans felt threatened by Russian involvement in local politics, immigrant support for political Zionism aroused the concern and opposition of the established community. Jews had yearned for a return to Palestine since the beginning of the Diaspora. Despite a separation of two millenia and thousands of miles, pious Jews prayed thrice daily for the Restoration, measured their lives by the chronology of ancient Palestine, and considered themselves to be a nation in exile. This conception of Jewish peoplehood came under attack during the nineteenth century. To achieve political equality and demonstrate their loyalty to the countries in which they lived, the Jews of the West rejected the concepts of Exile and Return, and proclaimed Judaism to be a religion with a universal ethical message. According to this reasoning, the "mission of the Jews" was to propagate the teachings of the Hebrew prophets, and the dispersion was a necessary means of achieving this end. In both Central Europe and the United States, Reform rabbis successfully urged the elimination of the many liturgical references to an ingathering of the exiles, the restoration of Jewish sovereignty, and the rebuilding of the Temple in Jerusalem. During the 1880s the pendulum began to move in the opposite direction, as the optimism which had characterized earlier decades was eroded by the growth of ideological anti-Semitism in the West and the outbreak of pogroms in the East. As Jewish life in Europe became less secure, Jews took a cue from the German and Slavic nationalists about them and yearned increasingly for a land of their own where they could evolve according to their own destiny. This messianic yearning was accelerated and transformed in 1896 by Theodor Herzl, whose *Jewish State* propelled Zionism into the arena of international politics.[45]

While Atlanta's secular and prosperous German Jews had scant interest in a messianic restoration, they maintained a sentimental attachment to Palestine. When Rabbi Nathan N. Notkin, a *meshullah* (emissary) from the Ashkenazic community of Jerusalem, passed through the Gate City in August 1867, he received a contribution of fifteen dollars from the Hebrew Benevolent Congregation. Three months later, his colleague Rabbi Arya Loeb Cohen called upon synagogue president Isaac Steinheimer and was given eighteen dollars plus a recommendation "To the kind consideration of all our coreligionists through out [*sic*] the Southern States." Another *meshullah,* perhaps a fraud, appeared in 1871, allegedly soliciting contributions "for the rebuilding of Jerusalem." Five years later, "a genuine article" called upon Rabbi Gersoni—"who is generally a little prejudiced against such applicants"—and a "handsome collection" was taken up. While Gersoni was not adverse to assisting the pious Jews of the Holy Land, he believed that without the Diaspora, the Jews could never fulfill their mission of diffusing the knowledge of God among men. Gersoni's successor, Edward Benjamin Morris Browne, was of a similar bent and several years later wrote:

> America is our "promised land," we are *permanent* and happy citizens of the United States, and as such we must pray for the prosperity of *our* country, and not for Palestine of old; especially after we know full well, that a "restoration" and return to Jerusalem would not be accepted if offered us, with all the promises strictly fulfilled.[46]

Given the opposition of the Reform leadership, it is not surprising that Zionism was brought to Atlanta by the Russian immigrants. Six months after the first Zionist Congress convened in Basle in August 1897, a Zionist society was organized in the Gate City with fifty charter members and Louis Charnason, a twenty-six-year-old clerk who had emigrated from Kovno in 1890, as president. Despite this auspicious beginning, the society was dormant by 1901. After a lull of two or three years, the Ahavath Zion Society and the Daughters of Zion were founded and joined the Federation of American Zionists. Within a decade, an Atlanta Zionist Society, a Dorshei Zion Society, and a branch of the Labor Zionist Farband were established, and in 1914 they participated in the first Southeast Zionist Convention. Few, if any, of the early Atlanta Zionists ever settled in *Eretz Israel* (the Land of Israel). Rather, they hoped to provide a sanctuary for their oppressed brethren in Europe and resurrect Palestine as the major center of Jewish life. They studied Hebrew and Jewish history, collected money for the Jewish National Fund, and publicized their cause by staging plays like "The Promised Land" and hosting lectures by well-known Zionists like Henrietta Szold.[47]

Prior to the First World War, nearly all of Atlanta's Zionists were young men and women of East European parentage. Although they made up only a minority of the immigrant community and were bitterly opposed by the Arbeiter Ring, their influence was magnified by the leadership of such prominent personalities as Joel Dorfan, Morris Lichtenstein, and Louis J. Levitas. Rabbi Geffen of Shearith Israel, Rabbi Levin of Ahavath Achim, and Rabbis Loeb and Solomon of Beth Israel were also ardent Zionists, though critical of the movement's secular tone. The Yiddish-language *Southern Guide* and *Jewish Star* provided valuable editorial support, and Frank J. Cohen of the *Jewish Sentiment* observed:

> When the Jews learn that in unity only lies their safety will they be able to cope with opposition. To advocate and aid Zionism does not necessarily prove lack of patriotism . . . or the desire to remove to Palestine.[48]

Few Temple members shared Cohen's assessment, for Zionism ran counter to the principles adopted by the American Reform conferences of 1885, 1890, and 1898. Not only did Reform Jews view the dispersion as a necessary means of propagating Judaism's universal message, but they also accepted the widely held belief that immigrants must adopt American customs and ideals; they minimized the significance of anti-Semitism; and they feared that Zionism would imperil their position as loyal Americans. At a Chautauqua meeting in 1900, Rabbi David Marx "discussed zionism [*sic*] from the stand point [*sic*] of the American Jews," and in 1907 defined "The Mission of Israel" from the anti-nationalist perspective of classical Reform:

> Israel is the leaven of civilization. Its position is unique: a nation in name only, a people whose home is everywhere—in America, Americans; in Germany, Germans; in Russia, despite oppression, Russians. A people not shaped by destiny for a separated isolated existence, nor formed to be a political power amidst the nations of the world. A religious congregation whose survival is a mystery; a martyr-people that four thousand years after its inception but begins to have the recognition due its genius and to receive the homage that is its own by virtue of the benefits it has conferred upon men.[49]

During his remaining four decades in the pulpit, Marx became increasingly intractable on the subject of Zionism, and the Temple remained opposed to one of the most vital movements within Jewish life long after the national bodies of Reform had reversed their earlier stand. Walter W. Visanska, a prominent attorney who belonged to the Temple, spoke for his fellow members when he observed in 1914 that "if it were possible to run a Pullman train from Atlanta to Jerusalem today, with free tickets and free lunch, it would not be necessary to reserve a lower berth in advance."[50]

The attitude of the established community reflected its assimilation, desire for acceptance, and belief that Zionism would compromise its hard-won status. Three decades before the Basle congress, Rabbi Max Lillienthal's exclamation that "America is our Palestine; here is our Jerusalem," was hailed by the *Atlanta Constitution.* "Israelites," noted the newspaper, "are constantly subjected to the charge that they do not consider themselves permanent citizens of the country where they reside but that they are awaiting the coming of a temporal messiah, who will establish the nation in Palestine." The testament of the distinguished Cincinnati rabbi was expected to quash such accusations. Only when Jewish immigration from Russia reached a new peak in 1891 could the *Constitution* envision the establishment of a Jewish state, primarily because "It would neither be prudent nor politic to bring so many [Russian Jews] to the United States." Later in the decade, the paper endorsed the anti-nationalist statements of the Reform leadership and remarked that few prominent American Jews were "anxious to forfeit the sure birthright of liberty vouchsafed to them under the American flag." Max Nordau's claim that "Jewish liberty hangs by a thread in most civilized countries" was labeled a gross exaggeration, and the editors resented even the slightest implication that Jews suffered any discrimination in America. "The Constitution [*sic*] has never been a keen sympathizer with the Zionist propaganda," observed an editorialist in

1913. "We believe there is plenty of room in America for the right sort of Jews, as for the right sort of Greeks, French, English and Germans." After waxing eloquent about Jewish generosity, morality, hospitality, business acumen, and respect for the law, the writer concluded:

> And yet it is this splendid class of citizenry that some of their own number would remove from this country and set to blaze in what is to them now a strange land. Were the advice followed universally it requires no imagination to see that the machinery of civilization would be, temporarily at least, paralyzed.[51]

Conflicts over philanthropy, politics, and Zionism widened the gulf between the native and immigrant communities and were responsible for the establishment of Russian-controlled associations which, by virtue of their greater familiarity and empathy with conditions in the ghetto, were able to deal more effectively with the newcomer's problems. Nevertheless, the Temple-affiliated organizations continued to provide much of the needed relief services. At the urging of Victor Kriegshaber and David Marx, the Hebrew Relief Society, Free Kindergarten and Social Settlement, Council of Jewish Women, and the Central Immigration Committee (the local IRO affiliate) organized the Federation of Jewish Charities in 1906 to coordinate their overlapping responsibilities better.[52]

In response to a dramatic increase in immigration, the Federation was reorganized in 1912 to include the Montefiore Relief Association, the Free Loan Association, and the newly created Jewish Educational Alliance. During its first three years, Temple vice-president Isaac Schoen served as president of the Federation and Leon Eplan as vice-president. The objectives of the expanded Federation were to systematize the distribution of relief, discourage pauperism, grant loans to meritorious persons, encourage thrift, aid the poor in obtaining employment, and provide social, ethical, and educational opportunities for the deserving. Through a network of interlocking directorates and representation on the board of trustees by each of the constituent agencies, the FJC balanced the interests of the native and immigrant communities, and effectively coordinated welfare activities.[53]

The Federation prided itself on its "scientific" approach to philanthropy. "You are a stockholder in this corporation which shapes and rehabilitates human lives," declared the compilers of the 1914 annual report.

> The dividends are men and women and children made happier, self-sustaining and self-respecting. Is the work worth while? Does it not pay. What is the work? Adequate relief for those who need it. Elimination of the professional schnorror [beggar], the dead-beat and the worthless. Application of the money, which they do not get, to those who are entitled to receive it. Protection of the community against promiscuous and generally inefficient and pauperizing giving. Conservation instead of reclamation. Independence instead of dependence. Social responsibility and obligation instead of shifting responsibility and a dole to relieve the conscience. Justice instead of charity. Knowledge of the causes that produce poverty and a sane effort to remove the cause rather than sentimental giving which makes donor and recipient the poorer.

"Oft-times we fear to extend aid," explained Federation investigator and Alliance superintendent H. Joseph Hyman, "lest we break down the individual's power of resistance." As a disciple of Jewish social work pioneer Boris D. Brogen, Hyman insisted that "The destinies of the poor are too precious to be placed in the hands of persons whose only qualifications are their willingness to act as social workers." The charity worker must be a trained professional, "sympathetic, but not too sentimental; gentle; but firm."[54]

The Federation budget for 1914 was $15,000, raised almost entirely through subscriptions. Of this amount, $4,200 was allocated to the Montefiore Relief Association, which aided 747 cases representing 2,119 souls. In addition to supplying rent money, groceries, transportation costs, and coal, it also handled 13 cases of desertion, 14 pension cases; supplied Passover provisions to the Jewish inmates of the nearby federal prison, and provided school books for 78 children. The Free Loan Association used its $100 allocation to make $2,200 worth of interest free, short-term loans. The Schoen Free Kindergarten received $700. On its budget of $1,300 the staff of the Morris Hirsch Free Clinic handled 3,455 office calls, made 536 house calls, and performed 124 operations. The Jewish Educational Alliance, whose activities will be discussed shortly, received $5,200. Most of the remaining $3,500 paid for administrative expenses, was applied to special local cases, or was contributed to national Jewish charities.[55]

The extent of Jewish philanthropy can best be understood by comparing the income and membership of the Federation of Jewish

Charities with the nonsectarian Associated Charities of Atlanta. The ACA's 1912 budget amounted to $14,800, and while 10 percent of its contributors were Jewish, Jews constituted only 7 of the 570 cases handled in the six months following December 1, 1908 (the only period for which data are available). In contrast, virtually all of the FJC's $13,300 was raised by 426 Jewish subscribers, more than half of whom were Russians. Hence, although Jews constituted only 3 percent of the city's population, they contributed more than half of the charity funds. "Jewish charity never has to beg for existence," observed the *Atlanta Constitution.* "The Jew gives and he gives *continuously, religiously.*"[56]

The Jewish Educational Alliance, which represented the first major cooperative achievement of the immigrant and established communities, had its origin in the separate but parallel action of the two groups. Early in 1906 a "mass meeting" at Ahavath Achim raised $1,700 for a Hebrew Institute that would house a gymnasium, kindergarten, night school, Hebrew school, classes in "domestic arts" and meeting rooms for Jewish organizations. Several months later, thirty-one German Jews raised $1,500 for the erection of a building to shelter the Free Kindergarten and Social Settlement. After two years of independent and inefficient fundraising, the Germans and Russians agreed to combine their efforts and objectives. In May 1909 they chartered the Jewish Educational Alliance and two years later dedicated its two-story colonial style headquarters on Capital Avenue between Fair Street and Woodward Avenue. Because the Germans raised most of the $35,000 required, they were initially accorded two-thirds of the seats on the board of trustees. Morris Lichtenstein, Joel Dorfan, Hyman Mendel, J. J. Saul, and Samuel Yampolsky also sat on the board, and in 1915 Lichtenstein, who had long since attained the respect of the Germans, was nominated by the outgoing president to lead the organization. Several women, notably Melanie Feibelman, Bertha Montag, and Clara Sommerfield, played a leading role in both the founding and leadership of the Alliance.[57]

The Alliance quickly became the focus for Russian communal activity. The fraternal lodges, two-dozen clubs, and a dozen societies made it their home. "It is a school, recreation center, club and shule for our people," boasted a spokesman in 1915. "You can not explain it on paper. You must see it and catch the spirit of the hive." In the preceding year the JEA hosted 95 general recreation affairs, 5 concerts, 11 plays, 13 mass meetings, 13 dances ("The public dance hall is no longer a problem with us."), 2 outings, 34 debates, and 17 lectures (e.g., Leon Zolotkoff on "The Future of the Jew in America" and Dr. R. R. Daly on "The Care of the Eyes, Ears, Nose and Throat"). The religious school had an enrollment of 200; 120 girls received instruction in home economics; 54 children attended the kindergarten; and 35 pupils were taught stenography. Seventy-nine men and women attended the Alliance Night School, which had just been incorporated into the public school system as the Capital Avenue Night School. "To learn the language of the country of their adoption," observed superintendent Hyman, "means bread and butter, opportunity and a better life."[58]

Unlike the insensitive attempts at rapid americanization that had characterized the German philanthropy of the nineties, the Alliance was committed to pluralism. "Among Jewish settlements," noted Hyman, "the tendency is . . . the Judaization of its constituency rather than Americanization, although the latter is not neglected." The newcomers received instruction in English and civics, but great stress was also placed upon folk dancing, Yiddish theater, and the observance of religious festivals. To narrow the widening gap between the americanized children and their traditionalist parents, the Alliance emphasized respect for Orthodox customs while encouraging the parents to adopt more modern ways.[59]

Although the Germans demonstrated a willingness to work on a basis of equality with the leaders of the immigrant community, like many Russians, they remained adamantly opposed to the radicalism represented by the Arbeiter Ring. When the *Constitution* commented upon the sizable number of northern Jews who voted the Socialist ticket, a member of the Council of Jewish Women hastened to reassure the public that Jews were "too civilized and just a people to sympathize with socialist notions." Although the Ring was permitted to meet in the Alliance, two Russian trustees were delegated to audit its lectures. When the Ring petitioned to store its books in the building, the board of trustees, objecting to what it suspected to be subversive literature, replied that the "jargon [Yiddish] books" would first have to be approved by the library committee.[60]

Despite claims that in the Alliance "the foreigner meets his American brother on equal terms [and] the rich mingle with the poor," the JEA represented only the first step on the long road to communal unity. The Alliance was more a settlement house than a center for the entire community. The Germans had little need for its facilities and participated only in a supervisory capacity. At the end of 1914 editor Albert J. Herskowitz of the *American Jewish Review* lamented the continued existence of a Jewish "caste system" and asked rhetorically whether "the 'isky' at the end of your friend's name ever made you ashamed to introduce him into polite society."

> We pick flaws and find endless criticism. One is German, another is Russian; and because the fates decreed that a mere imaginary boundary line should come between them, each thinks the other eternally chosen to see to it that neither crosses the line of demarkation.[61]

It would take another generation and the shared agony of the Holocaust before a divided community became whole.

# 6

## *Making It: Parameters of Geographic Persistence and Economic Mobility*

Atlanta's dramatic increase in population from 22,000 in 1870 to 155,000 in 1910 was largely the result of immigration from the economically depressed rural sections of Georgia and neighboring states. Although the pace of urbanization was slower in the overwhelmingly agrarian South than elsewhere in the nation, the new southern urbanites, like their northern and midwestern cousins, were drawn to nearby cities by the lure of opportunity.

Jews too sought success in coming to Atlanta, and it would appear that they found it. Two-thirds of the Gate City's adult Jewish males in 1870 and 1880 and more than 50 percent in 1896 were professionals, proprietors, managers, and officials, and approximately 30 percent in each year were white-collar workers. Even in 1896, with recently arrived Russians constituting 30 percent of the work force, only 14 percent of the city's Jews were manual workers or peddlers. However, these figures reflect the community's occupational structure at only three widely separated points in time and may be less indicative of success achieved or maintained in Atlanta than of status acquired prior to arrival. Likewise, changes over the course of a quarter-century might be more attributable to the in-migration of newcomers than to economic mobility.

The quest for success lies at the heart of the immigrant experience, and the notion that the United States has long been "the land of opportunity for the common man" is one of the most enduring of popular American maxims. One way of ascertaining the availability of opportunity is to measure the extent of geographic stability and economic mobility. Considering their special religious and cultural needs, Jewish immigrants and their offspring had little noneconomic incentive to leave the supportive environments of the northeastern urban centers and settle in *treif* places such as Atlanta. The degree to which they chose to remain in such communities tells much about the quality of their experience, an indication of satisfaction with present place and future prospects. Even more revealing is a study of whether those people who remained managed to improve their economic status by acquiring additional wealth or by moving up in the occupational hierarchy. Every Jewish community can boast of its own Horatio Alger heroes or David Levinskys, and these have seldom escaped the notice of local historians. But while recounting the struggles and achievements of poor immigrants who became merchant princes tells much about the ambition, ability, and luck of certain individuals, it indicates little about the fortunes of the great mass.[1]

To determine the extent to which Jews realized the ambitions which had drawn them to the Gate City, all adult Jewish males present in 1870 were traced through city directories, manuscript census schedules, and tax digests to 1880, 1890, 1900, and 1911; those present in 1880 to 1890, 1900, and 1911; and those present in 1896 to 1911.

Given the tendency among writers of local Jewish history to emphasize the continuity between generations and within families, an examination of geographic mobility in Atlanta yields surprising, perhaps even disquieting, findings. After adjustments are made for death, it appears that 42 percent of the adult Jewish males who resided in Atlanta in 1870 and 38 percent of those in 1880 moved away within ten years. After three decades, only one-third of the 1870 and one-fourth of the 1880 cohort remained in the city. Similarly, 46 percent of the Jews in 1896 were no longer present in 1911. However, this figure is not corrected for death, and approximately 20 percent of the cohort members were initially ages 50 or over. Thus the adjusted rate of out-migration was probably lower than for the 1870 and 1880 groups. (See table 25.)

Geographic stability was directly related to occupational status. Proprietors in all three groups had a lower attrition rate than white-collar workers during the initial intervals. The difference was greatest during the economically depressed seventies, when 30 percent of the proprietors and 74 percent of the white-collar workers left the city, and smallest during the period 1896 to 1911 when 40 percent of the proprietors and 44 percent of the white-collar workers (who tended to be younger than the proprietors) were no longer present. Professionals in 1896 had the lowest attrition rate (30 percent) and manual workers the highest (50 percent). (See table 26.)

Just as persons of high occupational status generally remained in the community and those of lower status did not, the wealthy were more likely to stay than the poor. Fifty-two percent of the men in 1870 and 45 percent of those in 1880 who had taxable assets valued at under $600 left the city within a decade. In contrast, only 20 percent of those worth $600 or more were no longer present after at least ten years. The ownership of real estate had an even greater effect on geographic stability. Only 8 percent in 1870 and 17 percent in 1880 of those who owned realty departed during the initial ten-year periods, compared with 55 and 58 percent respectively of those who did not.[2]

Occupational status and wealth were closely related to age and marital status; that is, married and older Jews tended to occupy a higher economic position than those who were single and younger. Consequently, it is not surprising to find a strong association between geographic mobility and these ostensibly noneconomic variables. Forty-four percent of the 18- to 29-year-old males in 1870 and 57 percent in 1880 left the city within ten years, compared with 23 and 24 percent respectively of those ages 30 and over. Similarly, 44 percent of the single males in 1870 and 61 percent in 1880 migrated during the first interval decade, compared with 35 and 22 percent respectively of the married males. Because the figures for 1896 are not corrected for death, which naturally affected the persistence of older more than younger men, they are less clear-cut than those for 1870 and 1880. Nevertheless, they confirm the previously observed trend: 51 percent of the 18- to 29-year olds and 49 percent of the single males in 1896 were no longer present in 1911, compared with 40 percent of those over age 29 and 36 percent of those who were married.[3] The tendency for young unmarried men to leave the city in disproportionate numbers was probably indicative not only of their economic circumstances but also of a shortage of eligible Jewish women (who were outnumbered 5 to 1 in 1870 and 2 to 1 in 1880) and the greater ease with which unattached men could pull up stakes and move on.

Young, unmarried white-collar workers without property, men such as Herman Rothman and Isador Bandman, were not the only

Jews to leave the city after less than a decade. Petty proprietors like dry goods merchant Isaac Hirsch and dairyman Jacob A. Franklin also found it difficult to survive in Atlanta's intensely competitive atmosphere. Nor were the economically unsuccessful the only ones to move. Several of the most enterprising Jewish businessmen—such as Moses Frank, B. F. Friedman, and William Rich—left Atlanta after one or more decades. As Stephan Thernstrom explains, in the case of men on the lower end of the economic scale, those who left "had made the least successful economic adjustment to the community" and had little incentive to remain, while the out-migration of middle-class people was "often in response to greater opportunities elsewhere."[4]

Geographic stability was directly related to the amount of time spent in the community, since the consequent changes in age, marital status, and economic circumstances often resulted in deeper roots. While the corrected first decade out-migration rates for 1870 and 1880 were 42 and 38 percent, only 19 percent of those present in both 1870 and 1880 and 13 percent of those present in both 1880 and 1890 died or moved away by 1890 and 1900 respectively.

Although the 1870 and 1880 cohorts suggest an apparent relationship between stability and nativity—the foreign-born remaining at a higher rate than native-born Americans—this is really a function of the former's older age. The 1896 enumeration, with its sizable contingent of Russians, provides better evidence of nativity's possible effect. Whether the entire adult male community is considered or only those ages 18 to 39, Russian-born Atlantans stayed in the city at approximately the same rate as the "Germans." Russian proprietors and white-collar workers did leave at a slightly higher rate than their "German" counterparts, but Russians on the lower end of the occupational spectrum remained to a greater degree.[5] All this is surprising, since the Russians' relatively inferior economic status, youth, and recent arrival in the city should have resulted in a substantially greater degree of out-migration than was the case for their more affluent, older, and more americanized coreligionists. The Russians' greater tendency to be married (55 percent) may have contributed to their stability, but even more important was the rapidity with which they attained economic security.

What do these figures demonstrate about the Jewish encounter with Atlanta? If urbanization is considered to be primarily a process of ingathering, then the fact that large numbers of Jews—especially those on the lower rungs of the economic ladder—did not remain in Atlanta for even a single decade would lead to the conclusion that Jews failed to realize the hopes which had drawn them to the Gate City. But an examination of data from other communities reveals the opposite may have been true. Recent studies have shown that nineteenth-century cities were like "busy railroad stations, into which many travelers poured but in which few stopped for long."[6] Out-migration occurred on a fantastic scale. For example, approximately 800,000 people moved into Boston between 1880 and 1890 to yield a population increase of only 65,179 for the decade. Nor was this turnover exceptional. Among Poughkeepsie males ages 16 and over in 1870, 64 percent of the native-born, 60 percent of the Irish, and 56 percent of the Germans were no longer present in 1880. In Omaha, 60 percent of the 20- to 45-year-old males present in 1880 moved away from the city by 1891. In New York City, a staggering 67 percent of the Russian Jewish families sampled in 1880 could not be located a decade later.[7]

Atlantans, however, demonstrated a greater tendency to stay than did residents of these other cities, and the Gate City's Jews were even more stable than their gentile neighbors. Forty-five percent of the city's native-born white and 40 percent of her immigrant males ages 16 and over in 1870 were still present in 1880, and 24 and 16 percent remained in 1896. In contrast, 56 percent of the Jewish males ages 18 and over living in Atlanta in 1870 were there ten years later, and 36 percent were still there in 1896.

In terms of both age and occupational status, Jews exhibited superior stability. Although the young of all three groups (Jews, native-born whites, immigrants) were most likely to leave the community, young Jews remained in greater numbers than the others. In the 20- to 29-year-old age group, 56 percent of the Jews in 1870 and 43 percent in 1880 remained for at least one decade, while 30 and 23 percent were still present in 1911. In comparison, 47 percent of the native-born whites and 51 percent of the foreign-born in 1870 stayed until 1880, and 16 and 15 percent stayed until 1910. Among native-born whites and immigrants in 1880, 43 and 32 percent remained to 1890, while 22 and 13 percent still resided in the city in 1910.[8] (See table 27.)

Just as more young Jews stayed than young Gentiles, more Jewish proprietors remained than their gentile counterparts, though Jewish white-collar workers were somewhat less prone to remain than Gentiles. (See table 28.) Interestingly, for neither Jews nor Gentiles was there a significant correlation between the decision to remain or depart and particular periods of boom or depression. Native-born whites who began their careers during the unsettled seventies remained at virtually the same rate as those who started work in the prosperous eighties, while the rate at which the 20- to 29-year-old members of the 1870 immigrant and Jewish cohorts stayed was higher than for their counterparts in 1880.[9]

Their relatively high stability rates suggest that Jews were largely satisfied with what they found in Atlanta. Although there is a clear correlation between geographic stability and economic mobility, it would be unwarranted to conclude that all Jews who remained in Atlanta succeeded economically. The degree of economic success or failure they encountered can be seen in the changes in occupational status and wealth of employed adult males living in the city in a base year (1870, 1880, or 1896) and remaining one decade.

Mobility, however, is a two-way street, and the direction in which an individual moves is obviously influenced by where he begins. Most historical studies of occupational mobility have focused on predominantly blue-collar populations. Theoretically at least, in such cases there was considerable room for upward movement. In contrast, most Jewish Atlantans were proprietors, professionals, managers, and officials (proprietor-professional class) for whom there was considerable potential for skidding but few higher occupational statuses to which they could aspire. Consequently, there is the possibility of a smaller amount of upward and a greater amount of downward mobility among Jewish Atlantans than for most other groups. Indeed, retention of proprietary or professional status—that is, the absence of occupational mobility—would itself be an indication of economic success in an intensely competitive milieu.

The importance of these cautionary words is apparent from an examination of the different degrees of occupational mobility experienced by the three Jewish populations. During each of the four decades through which the 1870 cohort was traced, there was more downward than upward movement, the difference being 2 percent in 1880, 5 percent in 1890, 19 percent in 1900, and 5 percent in 1911. Although a sizable 83 percent of the persisting proprietor-professional class managed to keep their high status in 1880, the proportion dropped to 77 percent in 1890 and 64 percent in 1900 before rising to 88 percent in 1911. (See table 29.) Members of the 1880 group fared somewhat better. During the first interval decade,

17 percent achieved higher status while 9 percent "skidded," but in 1900 "skidders" outnumbered the climbers 27 to 11 percent and 11 to 6 percent in 1911—almost identical to the respective figures for the 1870 cohort. Meanwhile, the proportion of those who remained in the proprietor-professional class was 87 percent in 1890, 64 percent in 1900, and 88 percent in 1911—only slightly better than for 1870. (See table 30.) In contrast, members of the 1896 group did quite well, climbers outnumbering skidders 25 to 7 percent, while a staggering 92 percent of the proprietor-professional group retained their high status over the 15 year interval. (See table 31.)

What do these figures indicate? At first glance, the fact that skidders outnumbered climbers during most of the decade intervals over which the 1870 and 1880 cohorts were traced suggests that the economic position of Atlanta's Jews underwent deterioration during the late nineteenth century. Yet no such thing occurred. Between one-half and three-quarters of those Jews who were theoretically capable of rising in status did so, in most cases moving into the proprietor-professional class. However, this pool was relatively small, and its upwardly mobile constituents were outnumbered by a small, but relatively larger, number of skidders. For example, of the 9 men who were *not* in the proprietor-professional group in 1870 but stayed in Atlanta until 1880, 7 achieved this status by the latter year and none declined though their remarkable performance was outweighed by 8 of the 48 who remained in the city, but who slipped in occupational status. Considering the high rate of upward mobility in the non-proprietor-professional class in the 1870 and 1880 groups, the general tendency of proprietors and professionals to retain their high status, and the considerable upward and slight downward mobility that characterized members of the 1896 cohort (with its relatively large proportion of theoretically upwardly mobile men), the Atlanta Jewish experience was clearly an economic success. A closer examination of this process is revealing.

The most upwardly mobile Jews were white-collar workers, men such as brothers-in-law David Kaufman and Leon Lieberman, who clerked for Jewish dry goods dealers in 1870 before becoming successful trunk manufacturers later in the decade. For some, like Max J. Baer, success came slowly. Baer opened a meat market in the nineties, but only after having worked as a clothing store clerk in 1870, a traveling salesman in 1880, and a clerk once again in 1890. For others, like Louis Newelt, success was meteoric. A lowly dry goods clerk in 1880, ten years later the young Hungarian was president of the thriving Southern Furniture Company. Similarly, Emanuel Guthman, a bookkeeper in 1880, became a partner in a spring bed factory and later in a steam laundry. But success was not always lasting. Daniel Klein, a commercial traveler for a safe manufacturing firm in 1880, opened a grocery during the following decade, did poorly, and was a salesman in 1900.

Those in the proprietor-professional group were the most likely to retain their initial status. However, considerable movement also took place within this category and is not reflected statistically, mostly as a result of retailers expanding their businesses, some becoming wholesalers, and a few entering manufacturing. For example, Morris Rich established a small dry goods business in 1867 which, as mentioned earlier, became one of the largest retail emporiums in the Southeast. Meyer Wellhouse, a retail produce merchant in 1870, shortly thereafter became a wholesale paper dealer and in the eighties began to manufacture boxes. During the same period, Jacob Elsas and Julius Dreyfus rose from owners of a warehouse to paper bag manufacturers and eventually proprietors of one of the South's largest cotton mills. Of course, not all those who remained proprietors managed to improve their lot. Levi Cohen, one of the Jewish community's leading members and a successful wholesale liquor dealer in 1870 and 1880, fell upon hard times during the next decade, lost his fortune, and barely remained in business. Professionals were more adept than proprietors at maintaining their high position; none ever fell to white-collar or manual status. While most white-collar workers eventually moved into the proprietor-professional group and only two ever skidded to manual positions, some failed to demonstrate any significant mobility. Typical of this small group were Joseph Auerbach, Louis Bebro, and David Rosenberger, who shifted between various white-collar jobs during their more than three decades in the city.

Interestingly, all of the skidders in the 1870 and 1880 cohorts and two-thirds of those in the 1896 group were proprietors. Most of the proprietary skidders were petty retailers who had been lured to the expanding city with high hopes of success but were unable to withstand the fierce competition. "We have only one answer to the numerous requests of Israelites who solicit our advice concerning removal to Atlanta," wrote Rabbi Browne in 1879. "If you can start a wholesale house or factory, hurry up and come, for this is the place, but do not venture yourself into the retail trade which is already overcrowded."[10] Most merchant skidders became white-collar workers.[11] For example, rag dealer Morris Barwald, grocer Edward B. Cohen, and saloonkeeper Aaron Gershon declined during the depressed 1890s to the positions of commercial traveler, salesman, and bookkeeper respectively. Only a handful of proprietors ever fell to manual status. Among these was clothier Gustave Saloshin, who became a bartender; saloonkeeper George Kleinart, who became a beer bottler; and California Wine House owner Jacob Morris, whose political influence earned him the post of courthouse janitor.

Because of the extraordinary proportion of Jews in the proprietor-professional group and the fact that nearly all skidders came from this category, it might be useful to exclude momentarily initial holders of this status from the calculations and to focus on those theoretically capable of upward movement. During the four decades over which members of the 1870 cohort were traced, considerable upward but only negligible downward movement can be seen. An average of 70 percent achieved higher occupational status while 30 percent remained stable; the 1880 cohort was evenly divided between climbing and stable men; and among those in the 1896 group, the status of 58 percent improved, 36 percent remained the same, and 6 percent declined.[12]

Though an individual's initial occupational status was apt to affect greatly his future occupational mobility, such movement was also seemingly affected by such noneconomic variables as age and marital status. During each of the eight interval periods over which the three groups were traced, members of the initial 18- to 29-year-old cohort manifested more upward and less downward movement than did men ages 30 to 39 or 40 and over.[13] Furthermore, during six of the eight periods, the youngest cohort in the proprietor-professional group demonstrated the greatest degree of stability. There was also a tendency for single men to be more upwardly mobile than married ones. Both relationships were rooted in the generally lower initial occupational status held by the young and unmarried and perhaps also in their greater amount of resilience, which enabled them to cope more effectively with economic vicissitudes. Initial wealth affected occupational mobility in the same way inasmuch as the ownership of small amounts of property generally reflected a lower occupational status from which their holders could climb. However, among the proprietor-professional group, initial possession of real estate or substantial amounts of personal property were often crucial to the retention of high status.

It might be assumed that there was some connection between economic mobility and place of birth: that native-born Jews would do better than those born abroad. The experiences of the 1870 and 1880 cohorts appear to indicate this, but the relationship—like those between occupational mobility and initial age, marital status, and wealth—is misleading. Native-born Jews in the 1870 and 1880 groups were more upwardly mobile than foreign-born ones, primarily because the former were almost always younger and therefore more likely to be initially in a lower occupational status from which they could climb. Indeed, many were white-collar workers, essentially merchants-in-training, employed by older, foreign-born relatives.

Rather than look for differences between the mobility patterns of German-born fathers and American-born sons, it would be more productive, as in the case of geographic stability, to compare the experiences of the Russians and "Germans" in the 1896 enumeration. Despite the "Germans" initially higher age and occupational status, which should have limited their upward and facilitated their downward mobility, members of the established community had a more favorable mobility profile than their immigrant cousins. Although 25 percent of both groups were upwardly mobile during the period 1896 to 1911, 15 percent of the Russians but only 4 percent of the "Germans" skidded, while 95 percent of the "Germans" compared to 84 percent of the Russians in this proprietor-professional class managed to retain their high status. (See table 32.) Very similar results were obtained for 18- to 29-year-olds in the two groups. While one-third of both young Russians and young "Germans" were upwardly mobile, 11 percent of the Russians but none of the "Germans" moved downward. The data do not explain why the "Germans" fared better than the Russians, but it is reasonable to assume that their greater acculturation, familiarity with local and American business and social practices, access to credit, and family connections gave them an advantage over their more recently arrived brethren.

The fact that the "Germans" had a more favorable mobility profile than the Russians does not mean that the Russians did poorly. On the contrary, the Russians fared quite well in comparison to members of the 1870 and 1880 cohorts; and whereas 34 of the 35 upwardly mobile "Germans" in 1896 rose only one step from white-collar worker to proprietor-professional status, 11 of the 15 upwardly mobile Russians climbed 2, 3, 4, or even 5 steps. Some marginal Russian proprietors such as Harris Rouglin and Morris Mendel skidded to white-collar status and an occasional clerk like Abraham Rogowski might be only a traveling salesman fifteen years later, but many of the new immigrants made substantial improvements in their status. For example, policeman Benjamin Wildauer became a dentist, umbrella repairer David Berger became a grocer, peddler Joel Dorfan opened a successful ladies and gents furnishings store, and Simon Abelman rose from clerk to wholesale grocer. There were also notable advances within the proprietor-professional category: retail merchants Hyman Mendel, Joseph Saul, Philip Elson, and Jacob Chomsky each entered the wholesale trade, and secondhand furniture dealer Tobias Borochoff established the Southern Wire and Iron Works.

Studying changes in occupational status represents the conventional means of ascertaining economic mobility. But as stated earlier, such an approach has the disadvantage of employing a scale closed at its upper end, thereby artificially restricting the mobility of the initially large proportions of Jews in the proprietor-professional category. Measuring economic mobility in terms of significant changes in wealth avoids this problem, since the potential for upward movement is theoretically limitless. During the first decade over which the 1870 cohort was traced, twice as many men substantially increased their property holdings than suffered serious reverses, and for the second and third decades gainers outnumbered losers four to one. (See table 33.) During both of the decades over which the 1880 cohort was followed, there were twice as many climbers as skidders. An average of approximately one-third of the members of the two cohorts neither substantially increased nor decreased their holdings. (See table 34.) Among the Russians in the 1896 cohort, a staggering 60 percent achieved a substantial increase in wealth, 34 percent experienced little change, and a mere 6 percent suffered a serious loss. (See table 35.)

The greatest increase in wealth was achieved by those who initially possessed the least property. Sixty-two percent of the persisters who owned $500 or less in 1870, 54 percent of those in 1880, and 55 percent of the Russians in 1896 were worth $600 or more after the first interval period. Some of these gains were modest. For example, David Rosenberger, who had no property in 1880, was assessed at $650 in 1890. However, most increases in wealth were more dramatic. During the same period, August Abraham's assessed worth increased from $390 to $6,175, David Kaufman's from $475 to $7,512, Isaac Liebman's from $420 to $4,475, and Henry Wellhouse's from $50 to $25,225. Some of the most impressive gains were made by Russians in the 1896 cohort. While only 10 percent of the Russians who remained in Atlanta initially had assets in excess of $500, in 1911 63 percent were worth over $500, and 30 percent over $3,000. Among the most successful were Jacob Chomsky, whose holdings increased from $50 to $18,300; Jacob Heiman, from $50 to $21,700; Harris Clein, who climbed from $350 to $13,100; and Hyman Mendel, from $350 to $14,000. Most of the initially affluent Germans continued to increase their fortunes. For example, stove manufacturer Herman Franklin's holdings increased in value from $8,100 to $13,200 between 1880 and 1890.

Although men initially worth under $600 achieved the greatest upward mobility, many others in this category failed to improve their condition appreciably. Of those who were initially assessed at $500 or less, 38 percent in the 1870 cohort and 46 percent in the 1880 cohort failed to reach the $600 level after ten years. For example, bookkeeper Louis Bebro did not declare any taxable assets in either 1880, 1890, or 1900, while bookkeeper Monte Hustler was assessed at $200 in both 1880 and 1890.

Downward mobility was most characteristic of those initially worth $10,000 or more. In the case of Levi Cohen, who was assessed at $18,000 in 1870, $12,100 in 1880, and zero in 1900, the decline was precipitous. However, for the vast majority of skidders the loss was less dramatic, as exemplified by hardware merchant Adolph J. Brady, whose holdings dropped from $15,300 in 1880 to $7,000 in 1890.

Not only were Atlanta Jews generally adept at increasing their wealth; they also invested much of it in local real estate, a wise decision considering the rapid inflation in land values. Whereas only 27 percent of those remaining in the 1870 cohort initially owned realty, 57 percent did so by 1880 and 88 percent by 1890. Real estate acquisitions by members of the 1880 cohort and the 1896 Russian cohort were more modest, but nearly 50 percent the men who initially lacked such holdings soon gained their "piece of the rock."[14]

The economic experience of Atlanta's Jews was clearly uneven. While the overwhelming majority of those who stayed either improved their condition or retained already high status, the position of a small minority deteriorated. Unfortunately, there are little data with which these findings may be compared, and much of what does exist must be viewed with at least a modicum of caution.[15]

Recent studies of occupational mobility in Poughkeepsie and Boston take into consideration the influence of religioethnic factors on economic success, though the small size and probable unrepresentativeness of the Jewish samples cast doubt upon the authors' conclusions. Methodological objections aside, Jews in both cities seem to have achieved greater upward mobility than their gentile neighbors. According to the Poughkeepsie study, 55 percent of the young German Jews in 1850, 1860, and 1870 began, and 90 percent ended their careers in white-collar (that is, nonmanual) positions. In contrast, 17 percent of the young German Protestants and 15 percent of the German Catholics began, and 37 and 35 percent respectively ended in white-collar jobs. The Boston study yields similar results. Among Bostonians born between 1860 and 1879, 73 percent of the Jews, 41 percent of the Catholics, and 65 percent of the Protestants began their careers in white-collar positions, while 84 percent of the Jews, 43 percent of the Catholics, and 64 percent of the Protestants ended their careers in this classification. For those born during the next decade, 43 percent of the Jews, 32 percent of the Catholics, and 41 percent of the Protestants began, and 60, 44, and 50 percent respectively ended in the white-collar category. Despite the impressive gains Jews registered in both cities, the Atlanta experience was more conducive to economic success. All 18- to 29-year-old Jewish Atlantans in 1870, 93 percent in 1880, and 88 percent in 1896 held white-collar positions, and by 1911 all of those in the first two cohorts and 90 percent of those in the third wore white collars. Furthermore, most of the Jews in this classification, in both base and subsequent years, were in the proprietor-professional group.[16] (See table 36.)

Whereas the examination of Jewish mobility in the Poughkeepsie and Boston studies was incidental to some broader purpose, a recently completed work focuses squarely on the mobility of East European Jews in New York City. Tracing for one decade representative samples of Jewish household heads drawn from the 1880 federal and the 1892 and 1905 state censuses, the author finds that 27 percent improved their occupational status, 7 percent skidded, and 66 percent remained stable—almost matching the performance of the 1896 Atlanta Russian-Jewish cohort. Moreover, he observes an impressive amount of movement across the collar line: 46 percent of Jews beginning and 64 percent ending their careers in white-collar positions. But despite representative samples and generally trenchant analysis, the author's choice and definition of occupational status categories distorts his findings and militates against comparing the New York and Atlanta experiences. By placing peddlers (a low status group requiring little skill or capital) in the "lower white-collar" category along with more settled small proprietors, semiprofessionals, and clerks, the author may have mistakenly interpreted movement from skilled artisan to peddler status as upward mobility, and movement from petty proprietor to peddler and vice versa as occupational stability.[17] (See table 37.)

In their economic performance, the Jews of Atlanta surpassed not only their northern cousins but also their gentile neighbors. Among 20- to 29-year-old Atlantans in 1870, all the Jews began and ended their careers in white-collar positions, while only 55 percent of the native-born whites and 63 percent of the immigrants started in white-collar jobs and 61 and 69 percent ended that way. The figures are similar for 20- to 29-year-olds in 1880.[18] The favorable Jewish mobility profile is even more evident when the movement between individual occupational categories is examined. In three of the four decades over which the 1870 population was traced, Jews manifested less skidding and Jews in the proprietor-professional group demonstrated greater stability than both native whites and immigrants. Jews in the 1880 cohort did even better: none declined in status as opposed to a skidding rate of 13 percent for native-born whites and 11 percent for immigrants.[19] (See tables 38 and 39.)

The widely observed tendency for Jews to succeed economically may be attributed to several sociohistorical factors. Heirs to a centuries-old tradition of commerce, industry, and scholarship, long predisposed to minority status, and in many cases having experienced urban life prior to immigration, Jews were unusually well prepared to deal with the economic opportunities and vicissitudes encountered in the American metropolis. Desirous of independent status which would both shield them from discrimination by employers and permit the fulfillment of religious obligations, they sought early entry into callings for which they were uniquely qualified. Skills that had been marginal in one setting became highly useful in another. As Miriam Slater has written, "Jews who were commercial *faute de mieux* in manorial Europe were as peripheral as the first mammals among the dinosaurs, but fortuitously advantaged later."[20] Furthermore, a plethora of philanthropic and mutual benefit societies eased the hardships of transition from Old World to New and in some cases provided assistance to prospective businessmen. Those who could not achieve economic independence generally found employment in Jewish-owned firms, and a policy of ethnic recruitment and family sponsorship furthered the Jews' upward mobility. Even the impoverished Russians who began to arrive in large numbers during the eighties carried with them the values of literacy, thrift, foresight, moderation, and a positive orientation toward worldly success, the complex of habits generally associated with middle-class life. Like the Germans who had preceded them, the newcomers were characterized by a high degree of achievement motivation, and if the first generation failed to succeed, the expectations were intensified and projected onto the second.[21] As Nathan Glazer has observed, the proletarianized Russians did not share the limited horizons of most other immigrants.

> The Jewish workers were the sons—or the grandsons—of merchants and scholars. . . . This background meant that the Jewish workers could almost immediately turn their minds to ways and means of improving themselves that were quite beyond the imagination of their fellow workers. Business and education were, for Jews, not a remote or foreign possibility, but a near and familiar one.[22]

But granting the assumption that there are elements in the Jewish sociohistorical experience that are conducive to upward mobility does not account for the fact that Atlanta's Jews outdistanced not only their gentile neighbors but also their northern coreligionists. Indeed, their astonishing success might not have been anticipated, for unlike the Jews in the major northern cities, those in Atlanta were relatively isolated from the mainstream of Jewish life and competed not against other first and second generation Americans but rather against old stock whites presumably better prepared to confront the Gate City's challenges.

The economic success of Atlanta's Jews was rooted not only in their cultural baggage but also in a fortuitous confluence of economic, demographic, and migratory factors. The Jews who settled in Atlanta were not typical immigrants, for Jewish migration southward was highly selective. In contrast to the uprooted farmers and freedmen who comprised the bulk of the Gate City's population, prospective Jewish settlers had to travel far greater distances, face an unfamiliar region's unsavory reputation, and accept greatly limited opportunities for Jewish fellowship and expression. Few were tempted to take the risk. Moreover, remoteness from the dominant East-West transportation routes, the distributive orientation of the local economy, and the presence of a large pool of black "surrogate immigrants" discouraged the in-migration of "greenhorns" who lacked capital and marketable skills. Indeed, those Jews who came were often uniquely equipped to make the most of local opportunities, were already somewhat conversant with American ways, and were less dependent than their northern coreligionists upon traditional norms and institutions. The fact that the overwhelming majority of Atlantans were native Southerners also furthered Jewish mobility. Unlike the Yankees of Boston, or even the Germans of Poughkeepsie and New York, the bulk of Atlanta's black and white in-migrants were so ill-educated and otherwise unprepared to cope with the realities of an urban commercial society that they provided the Jews with less than formidable competition.

The small size of the Jewish population also contributed to its success. On one level, small numbers fostered assimilation and facilitated acceptance by Southerners who might otherwise have been less tolerant of Jewish assertiveness and cultural nonconformity. On another level, it enabled a greater percentage of Jews to penetrate into the upper reaches of the occupational pyramid. Jews as a group may aspire to high status, but where they constitute a considerable proportion of the population, as in the major cities of the Northeast, there is insufficient room at the top to absorb all those who wish to become professionals and proprietors. Because Atlanta's Jews never comprised more than 3 percent of the population, however, half or even two-thirds could occupy positions of high status without dominating either the commercial or professional sectors of the economy.

For the Jews of Atlanta, America was indeed the land of opportunity. It was primarily the promise of economic success that drew them to the Gate City, and it was the fulfillment of this promise that convinced them to remain. But to weigh the promise of America by purely materialistic standards is to overlook some of the less tangible, but nonetheless powerful, aspirations which a persecuted people brought to America and also to forget that economic success does not necessarily guarantee acceptance, social status, political recognition, or physical security.

*Atlanta, German-Jewish Settlement , 1871 (center of photo)*

*Atlanta, Decatur St. 1892 (lower center of photo)*

*The Hebrew Benevolent Congregation, 1877*

*The Concordia Club, 1893*

*Ahavath Achim Synagogue, Constructed in 1902*

*The Hebrew Benevolent Congregation, circa 1905*

*Atlanta in 1866*

*Jewish-owned Businesses in Atlanta on E. Alabama Street, 1876*

*Jewish-owned Businesses in Atlanta on S. Whitehall Street, 1875*

*Decatur Street Dry-goods Store, circa 1900*

*Jewish Residences in Atlanta, 1900*

*on Capitol Avenue*

*on S. Pryor Street*

*on Washington Street*

*The Hebrew Orphans' Home, circa 1890*

*Atlanta Jewish Educational Alliance, 1910*

*The Standard Club, circa 1915*

The Don't Worry Club Dinner, 1916

Farband Branch No. 71, circa 1913

# 7

## *Citizen and Symbol*

It is a matter of local history, remarked the *Atlanta Constitution,* "that no element in our varied population has been more conservative, enterprising, patriotic and profitable to the city than [our] Jewish citizens. They have always stood for pure homes, for clean government, for civic progress, for education and for the moral advancement of Atlanta. They have been honored with the foremost positions in our commercial, financial, social and political life. And no single betrayal of public trust and honor has ever been chargeable to one of them."[1] Without forsaking their religious identity, the Jews of Atlanta participated extensively in the affairs of the general community and achieved a level of integration that their northern cousins could well envy.

This involvement was facilitated by several factors discussed earlier: The Jewish community's small size and limited institutional variety were unable to satisfy completely the status and associational needs of its members. Their small numbers accelerated their acceptance. Furthermore, Jews lived in close proximity to Gentiles of similar means, and their role as merchants brought them into still greater contact and helped erode mutually unfavorable stereotypes. The desire for acceptance and assimilation received support from Reform Judaism's de-emphasis of ethnic particularism. Moreover, the fact that Jews were white in a society which attached great importance to color elevated their position.

But there were also other forces at work. The Jews' remarkable economic success was often translated into equally notable civic-mindedness—a recognition of their stake in the welfare of the city and the realization that their interests could be furthered by actively participating in its affairs. For their part, gentile advocates of economic development recognized that Jewish entrepreneurs could contribute to Atlanta's prosperity, and this perspective was reinforced by the Jews' conservatism, respect for the law, quiet demeanor, and the symbolic role they played in fundamentalist eyes. Yet, there were limits to this acceptance. Attitudes toward Jews were always ambivalent, and as Atlanta matured, the status of her Jewish citizens and the amount of esteem accorded them declined.

Although the proportion of Jewish Atlantans never exceeded 3 percent of the total population, Jews played a major role in local politics. Significantly, it was suspicion of Jewish intentions which was responsible for the first known reference to their political involvement. The presidential election of 1868 pitted Ulysses S. Grant against Horatio Seymour, and local Democratic leaders were worried about how the city's largely northern and foreign-born Jewish population was going to vote. For months preceding the contest, the Democratic press repeatedly reminded Jewish voters that six years earlier, General Grant had ordered the expulsion of Jews, "as a class," from the Department of the Tennessee. "The man of that race, who, after reading the following order, will vote for Grant," asserted the *Constitution,* "becomes the instrument of his own degradation, and is unworthy longer to be called an Israelite." Jews were quick to demonstrate their opposition to the Republican candidate. Five Jews served on the arrangements and reception committees for the Democratic mass meeting and parade at the end of July, and on Whitehall Street a transparency proclaimed: "The Jews will defeat Grant as they defeated Haman. The Jews will elevate Grant to office as they elevated Haman." In response to an election eve inquiry from the Atlanta Democratic Executive Committee, president L. L. Levy of the Hebrew Benevolent Congregation gave his assurance that only one or two local Jews were not Democrats and that even they planned to vote for Seymour. "They [the Jews] have an account to settle with General Grant, personally," prophesied an observer. "At the elections in November their influence will be felt."[2]

Whether Atlanta's Jews were indeed unanimous in their opposition to Grant is a matter of conjecture. But their need to proclaim vocally solidarity with the interests of their ex-Confederate neighbors bespeaks both a sense of insecurity and a desire for acceptance.

Three years later, when German editor Otto Palmer criticized conditions in the South, Samuel Weil spoke for many of his fellow Jews in maintaining that "a man has no right to abuse the country he lives in." While Jews joined with other foreign-born Atlantans in protesting the disinclination of local politicians to nominate naturalized citizens for public office, unlike many of their fellow Germans, Jews remained loyal to the Democracy.[3]

Jewish steadfastness was rewarded in 1873 when Aaron Haas was elected first ward alderman and then reelected the following year as alderman-at-large. During the eighties, Elias Haiman, Max Kutz, Joseph Hirsch, and Jacob Haas each served one or more terms on the city council, and Samuel Weil represented Fulton County in the Georgia House.[4] In addition, Jacob Haas presided over the park commission and was a member of the water board; Aaron Haas served as vice-president of the water board and a member of the board of health; and Aaron Elsas and Simon Einstein served respectively on the water board and park commission.[5]

After 1890 Jewish aspirants for office were less successful. When first ward voters met in 1893 to select delegates to the city-wide nominating convention, one of those present allegedly declared that no Jew should be allowed on the delegation or permitted to hold public office. Although Joseph Hirsch, Isaac Liebman, and Aaron Haas were among the twenty-seven men vying to be among the fifteen delegates, for the first time in twenty years no Jews were chosen. Hirsch, who was perhaps Atlanta's preeminent philanthropist, did manage to get reelected to the city council in 1892, 1894, 1896, 1904, and 1907, but Aaron Haas was defeated in his bid for Democratic endorsement in 1897, as was his cousin Jacob in 1899. "There is not a Jew holding office in Atlanta," observed Frank J. Cohen in 1900, and added that two "of the best men in Atlanta were [recently] defeated for office because of their religious affiliations." Cohen urged his readers

> to combat prejudice at the polls by voting for men of broad and liberal minds; men who have advanced beyond the stage of fanaticism and ignorance. . . . Numerically, we are painfully week [*sic*], but if a solid line is taken in politics, the number of our votes and the influence wielded by Jews will tell in our favor.

Whether or not his advice was followed, Jewish candidates continued to suffer defeat. During the next eight years, Isaac Liebman,

Henry Wolfe, Harry L. Silverman, and Joseph Loewus were all unsuccessful in their bids for seats on the council, and Loewus was reputedly called "a d . . . Jew" by his opponent. Perhaps more invidiously, in 1900 an attempt was made to reschedule the Democratic primary for Yom Kippur, and in 1915 the primary was set for Rosh Hashanah, effectively disfranchising hundreds of Orthodox voters.[6]

Even the durable Joseph Hirsch went down to defeat in 1908 when he sought the Democratic mayoral nomination. Hirsch's promise of a "clean, honest and economical business administration" had little appeal for most Atlantans, who preferred James G. Woodward, the recognized candidate of the workingman. However, when Woodward, for the second time in his public career, was found drunk and disorderly in the city's red-light district, a group of prominent citizens, which included Jacob Haas and Victor H. Kriegshaber, nominated Robert F. Maddox, who went on to defeat the Democratic nominee.[7]

With the exception of Hirsch, the only Atlanta Jew elected to public office in the quarter-century after 1890 was Henry A. Alexander. In 1908 he and two others were nominated, and subsequently elected, out of a field of ten candidates to represent Fulton County in the Georgia House. Despite his active participation in Jewish affairs, as a fifth generation Southerner whose grandfather had settled in Atlanta in 1848, the young attorney's religious affiliation was not widely known at the time of his election. However, when Alexander and his two colleagues ran for reelection in 1910, he alone was defeated.[8]

None of the eleven Jews who ran for the city council or the legislature were politicians in the sense that public affairs was their primary interest or source of income. Except for Alexander and Weil, all were prominent businessmen. One had been born in the South, two in the North, and the remainder abroad; but each had resided in the South for at least two decades prior to entering public life. All were active in the affairs of the Jewish community, and Hirsch, Weil, Liebman, and Jacob Haas each served as president of the Hebrew Benevolent Congregation. All were Democrats and had they been asked to summarize their political views in two words, most would probably have chosen "conservative" and "progressive." Each spoke for the interests of the business community, and their gentile fellow entrepreneurs were generally more concerned with the effectiveness rather than the religion of their representatives. Of course, slate-makers recognized that Jewish candidates would receive support from their coreligionists, but the size of the Jewish constituency was small, and its favor had to be weighed against the number of voters who would refuse to cast their ballots for a Jew.[9]

The political consciousness of the average Atlanta Jew never approached that of the community leadership. This was especially true of the Russian immigrants whose experience with the democratic process was limited and who were too busy trying to scratch a living out of their small stores to concern themselves with civic affairs. During the nineties, Leon Eplan and Morris Lichtenstein did endeavor to encourage naturalization, and in 1896 their Independent Citizens' Club reputedly controlled 250 Russian votes. Nevertheless, while it was possible to petition for citizenship after five years of residence in the United States, 54 percent of the Russians who filed for naturalization between 1883 and 1917 had been in the country for nine or more years.[10]

Vulnerability to anti-Semitism, as exemplified by the Leo Frank case, was attributed by some members of the community to the relative disinclination of Jews to register to vote, seek office, or serve on juries. Attorney Walter W. Visanska claimed in 1914 that less than half of those Jews who were qualified to vote were registered "and not one-half of those who register vote on occasions where the public welfare is at stake." To combat this apathy, Visanska and four other Jewish lawyers organized the Civic Educational League. At a mass meeting convened at the Jewish Educational Alliance, the founders carefully avoided potentially dangerous appeals for Jews to vote as a bloc. Instead they stressed civic obligation and urged those assembled to exercise all of their duties as citizens. Yet, behind the vague call for civic usefulness and purity was an unmistakable trace of insecurity. When one speaker remarked that the privileges and liberties guaranteed by the Constitution applied to Jew as well as Gentile, few mistook the reference to Leo Frank, who was awaiting execution in the Fulton County Tower. "We [must] combat prejudice with unselfish service as citizens," insisted Leonard J. Grossman.

> The cur dog only bites and yelps at the man who is afraid. . . . . We Jews now have the only thing that the nonchalant politician wants—the vote. This power is ours to use, [and the] bigot and anti-Semite will find us a bitter foe.

During the next two years, the League sponsored debates and lectures on political issues and endeavored to increase the number of Jewish naturalized citizens and registered voters. While it never became a major force in local politics, in the first three months of its existence, fifty-four Jews signed declarations of intention—double the number in any previous twelve month period—and twenty-four filed naturalization petitions, exceeding the total of the previous four years.[11]

While the Frank case provided the Jewish community with the most serious threat to its existence and resulted in the only instance of Jews acting in political concert as Jews, the political issues of prohibition and free silver also elicited uniform responses from Atlanta Jewry.

The liquor question was a perennially divisive factor in Georgia politics during the fifty years after the Civil War. The temperance movement had its greatest strength in the rural sections of the state and had the wholehearted support of the influential Baptist and Methodist clergy. By the mid-1880s, the position of these denominations had shifted from that of persuading individual Christians to abstain from intoxicants to declaring that it was the moral duty of society to enact prohibition legislation. The objective of the prohibitionists was not simply to curb individual sin and preserve the integrity of the family but also to control the actions of the more volatile elements in the community, especially the blacks.[12]

Following the enactment of a state-wide local option law in 1885, prohibition became the central issue in the Atlanta elections of 1885–88. Among the leaders of the wet party were attorney Adolph Brandt (formerly a member of the legislature from Richmond County), manufacturers Elias Haiman and Julius Dreyfus, and merchants Jacob Menko and Isaac H. Haas. Despite their efforts, Fulton County went dry by a margin of two hundred votes in 1885. But prohibition proved less salutary in reality than in theory, and after two years the experiment ended. Jacob Haas was elected alderman-at-large on the antiprohibition ticket in 1887, and the wets consolidated their gains the following year when Joseph Hirsch was elected to the council.[13]

The local correspondent of the *Jewish Messenger* characterized the drys as "country yokels" and "religious fanatics without reference to color or previous condition [of] morality and virtue." Jewish opposition was based on both economic and cultural concerns. Jewish businessmen—and many of their gentile counterparts—

feared that prohibition would have an injurious effect on the town's economy. Also, between 5 and 6 percent of the employed Jewish males in 1870 and 1880, slightly more than 2 percent in 1896, and probably close to 5 percent a decade later, were directly involved in the production, distribution, and sale of intoxicating beverages. However, a Jewish observer noted that these few people kept "their nests nicely clean and well feathered" and did not play a leading role in the controversy. On a different level, Jews objected to what they perceived as interference with their ritual observances and social customs. Even so, the *Messenger* exaggerated the extent of the imposition when it reported:

> our responsible and law-abiding citizens, if they feel like making *Kiddish* and *Habdolah,* must do so on the sly; henceforth they are forbidden to invest a spare nickel, that threatens to burn a hole in their pants-pocket, in a glass of beer, but they are compelled to lay in their wiskey [*sic*] (a quantity of beer might sour on their hands) by the additional expense of expressage from Macon or Chattanooga, hide the demijohn under the bed, and go through their sacramental ablutions on the sly.

"You seldom see a Jew prohibitionist," remarked George W. Markens ten years later. "He believes in home rule and usually rules his own house." Frank J. Cohen echoed this sentiment and advised prohibitionists to organize "a mothers' temperance society on the Jewish plan."[14]

The antiliquor crusade of the eighties engendered few if any outbursts against Jews, but anti-Semitism clearly played a role in the successful 1907 campaign to reimpose prohibition. This time, it was not the German brewers and distillers, but rather the Russian saloonkeepers who evoked the public ire. Atlanta's rapid increase in population after 1900 was accompanied by a soaring crime rate. Much of the blame was wrongly placed on saloons which catered to blacks, and a sizable minority of these enterprises were owned by the new immigrants. "Loafers hanging around barrooms develop into criminals—expecially when these loafers are negroes," warned the *Constitution* on the morning before the 1906 race riot. Idleness "breeds viciousness, and . . . loafing vagrants are the class that are assaulting white women." "As to white foreigners [Russian Jews and Greeks] who cater to the negro trade and negro vice in this locality," observed another journalist, "it is left to the judgement of the reader which is of the higher grade in the social scale, the proprietors or their customers." The call to "CLEAN OUT THE DIVES" was directly responsible for the lopsided defeat of Col. Harry L. Silverman when he sought the Democratic nomination for second ward alderman in 1907. One year later, a pulpitless Methodist minister known as "the Carpenter Evangelist" denounced the "flat headed, flat nosed, course [*sic*] haired, cross eyed slew footed Russian Jew whiskey venders." "The seed of Abraham, Are, The Protected of God," declared the minister, "but Commercialism controlled by these pagan devils called Jews . . . disgraces the good name of Abraham."[15]

As was the case with prohibition, Atlanta's Jews took a strong stand during the free silver controversy of the nineties, and their image did not emerge unscathed. Initially one of several planks in the Populist program, bimetalism was endorsed by the national and Georgia Democratic parties in 1896 in an effort to undercut the Populist opposition and weld a new electoral majority. A major theme of the Populist rhetoric—and also of some silver Democrats—was the notion that Jewish finance capitalism was in large measure responsible for America's economic woes. Accordingly, cachets such as "Rothschild," "Belmont," and "Shylock" were frequently used as ethnic symbols of hated plutocracy.[16]

Despite considerable strength in the countryside, Populism had little appeal for urban Atlantans. However, the Gate City was the home of the South's leading Populist journal, Tom Watson's *People's Party Paper.* Not once during the period 1891 to 1896 did the paper publish anything that might be considered anti-Semitic. Indeed, Jews as a group, as opposed to Jewish bankers, received sympathetic treatment. When several Protestant divines claimed that the Jews were dispersed because they had rejected Jesus, Watson praised Rabbi Leo Reich's able "intellectual refutation of this unfounded charge." Watson's friendly attitude—in sharp contrast to the virulent anti-Semitism he would display twenty years later—may have resulted from the large number of Jewish merchants who advertised in his paper as an ideal means of soliciting the country trade. Watson shamelessly endorsed the products and services of his patrons. However, while a Jewish clothier could impishly advocate "16 ounces of wool to 1 pound of cloth," the inflationary program of the People's Party, no less than its antiurban and Christ-tinged rhetoric, made Populism anathema for most Jewish businessmen.[17]

The Gate City's prosperous Jews were staunch fiscal conservatives. "Atlanta's rapid growth and reputation for solidity and prosperity would suffer vastly by the advocacy of . . . free silver coinage," declared M. L. Adler of the Atlanta Paper Company. "An honest dollar is the noblest work of trade," echoed Harry Silverman, "I am unutterably [*sic*] opposed to the silver movement." "If Atlanta goes for free silver it will have a bad effect financially," predicted Joseph Hirsch, while Joseph Jacobs observed that "it will be worth a considerable amount to the commercial interest of Atlanta if the sound money men win. . . ." Jacob Haas and Oscar Pappenheimer actively campaigned for the gold standard, and furniture manufacturer Otto Schwalb was among the ten sound money men who sought to represent Fulton County at the 1896 Georgia Democratic Convention. But despite strong opposition from the business community, the silver forces carried the county.[18]

The *People's Party Paper* carefully avoided offensive Jewish characterizations, but the prosilver and Democratic *Constitution* was less scrupulous. A cartoon published in 1895 pictured President Grover Cleveland pawning the United States to John Bull while a grotesquely stereotyped character labeled "Ickelheimer" swept out the shop. Ickelheimer, a New York Jewish banker, was also the subject of a float designed to popularize the silver cause. Jacob Haas angrily accused the *Constitution* of using the Jew as a scapegoat and rebuked Senators Tillman of South Carolina and Morgan of Alabama for their claims that the Jews were responsible for demonetization. When the *Constitution* declared the currency question to be a matter of "money against patriotism; the flag against the three balls," the *Jewish Tribune*—aware that nearly all the city's pawnbrokers were Jews—protested against what it saw as an impugnation of Jewish devotion to the commonweal.[19]

If Jewish participation in politics was motivated, at least in part, by the desire to safeguard certain basic interests, their commitment to public education had similar roots. The traditional Jewish respect for learning, together with a desire for acceptance and zeal for assimilation, made Atlanta's Jews ardent advocates and grateful beneficiaries of the public school system. "All the [Jewish] children visit the public schools where they get their English education," noted an observer from Cincinnati in 1874. "This is right; we want no sectarian schools for this purpose. Our children must grow up as Americans, and as such they shall mix with American children." Jewish students tended to excel academically, and in some years more than a fifth of the Boys and Girls High graduates were Jews.

Jewish women, mostly unmarried graduates of Girls High, were first hired as teachers in the eighties and by 1896 taught in seven of the city's seventeen public schools. One of them, Annie Teitlebaum Wise, became the first principal of Commercial-English High School in 1910.[20]

Despite their assimilative outlook, Jewish parents desired that their children be excused from classes on religious holidays and insisted that the Bible not be read in school. Initially, Jewish wishes were respected, largely because of David Mayer's influence. A resident of Atlanta since 1847, Mayer was one of the architects of the public school system and served as a member or officer of the board of education from its creation in 1869 until his death in 1890. During this period, Jewish absences for religious reasons were always excused, and Mayer led the battle against a division of school funds for sectarian purposes. When the city council voted in 1873 to require mandatory Bible exercises, Mayer persuaded his fellow board members to resist the intrusion. "Now, the Jews and Catholics are tax payers just as Baptists and Methodists are," reasoned board president and ex-governor Joseph E. Brown,

> and the schools are supported in part by their money; and if they cannot conscientiously send their children to a school where they are taught our version of the Bible, is it right that we should tax them to support the schools where we teach our children these doctrines?[21]

Upon Mayer's death in 1890, the city council recognized the Jewish stake in nonsectarian education and nominated three Jews to fill his seat: Aaron Haas, Jacob Elsas, and Joseph Hirsch. Hirsch was elected and served until 1897, when he was succeeded by Oscar Pappenheimer who remained on the board until 1904.[22] Unfortunately, Pappenheimer lacked the influence of his predecessors and was unable to block the board's 1899 decision not to excuse religious absences. Rabbi Marx, a Catholic priest, and the Episcopal bishop protested the action, but the board adamantly maintained that since the overwhelming majority of the city's population did not observe any holy day other than Sunday, it would be wrong to permit religious absences. Upon the expiration of Pappenheimer's term, the "Jewish seat" went unfilled until 1913, when Walter H. Rich was elected for three years. Meanwhile, local ministers pressured the board to include the Bible in the curriculum, and a member of the state legislature introduced a bill to require compulsory Bible instruction in the public schools.[23]

The civic-mindedness of Atlanta's Jews was not limited to activities in which they had vested economic or cultural interests. "The Jews of Atlanta do not confine their philanthropic energies to institutions within their own creed," observed the *Constitution* in 1914. "They are liberal, even lavish, supporters of every deserving and constructive charity. . . . [The Jew] has been keen upon his private business, but no less keen upon the public welfare. He has entered into every movement making for the general good."[24]

In the years immediately following the Civil War, David Steinheimer, Isaac Steinheimer, Sigmond Rosenfeld, Joseph Hirsch, and Marcus Hartman were volunteer firemen, and Max J. Baer was president of Robert E. Lee Fire Co. No. 4. During the seventies, Jews contributed to the erection and repair of several churches; when a yellow fever epidemic struck the lower Mississippi Valley, Jews raised $500 to help the victims. Rabbi Browne returned to the lecture circuit and the Concordia staged a benefit to augment the collection. David Mayer served as treasurer of the Atlanta Benevolent Home during the eighties, and after the Jewish charity ball in 1884, contributions were made to various denominational charities.[25]

Involvement in philanthropy became especially notable after 1890. In 1892 Jewish merchants participated in the program to give food, fuel, and clothing to the poor for Christmas, and the following year Harry L. Schlesinger led the campaign to aid the yellow fever sufferers in Brunswick. Several Jews also contributed generously to the construction of a juvenile reformatory in 1894. During the Spanish-American War, the Council of Jewish Women raised money to aid the wounded soldiers hospitalized near the city, and Mrs. Joseph Hirsch chaired the state executive board of the Woman's National War and Relief Association.[26] In the first decade of the next century, a meeting at the Temple raised $200 for the victims of the Galveston hurricane; East Europeans joined Temple members in aiding residents of a nearby town that had been devastated by a tornado; Jews generously supported the campaign to build a Presbyterian University in Atlanta; physicians Lee Ben Clarke and Samuel Visanska led the fight for pure milk; David Marx campaigned for free kindergartens and playgrounds; the Associated Charities of Atlanta engaged the energies of Jewish leaders; and the Council of Jewish Women supported the Home for the Incurables, the Home for Old Women, and child labor laws.[27] Between 1911 and 1915, Jews supported the YMCA, the Boys Club, and the Buy a Bale of Cotton Movement; Albert Steiner and Jacob Elsas were major donors to the Georgia Tech Fund; the wives of Victor H. Kriegshaber and Julius E. Summerfield participated in the work of the Atlanta School Improvement Association; Henry Schaul was among the leaders of the Oglethorpe College fundraising drive; and Julian Boehm headed the Red Cross Christmas Seal Campaign. In addition, Wesley House (Methodist), Atlanta's only social settlement, received the free services of Jewish physicians and a monthly subsidy from the Fulton Bag and Cotton Mill on whose property it was located.[28]

Perhaps the greatest monument to Jewish philanthropy was the Henry Grady Memorial Hospital. The idea for the hospital was first suggested in 1888 by Jacob Elsas, who inaugurated the building fund with a contribution of $1,000. Joseph Hirsch persuaded his fellow city council members to vote a large appropriation, after which he supervised the hospital's development, first as chairman of the building committee and until his death in 1914 as chairman of the board of trustees. While Atlanta "is filled with Christian churches," editorialized the *Constitution* in 1891, "she owes the existence of her only great charity to Hebrews, to such men as Hirsch, Elsas and Mayer." In their generosity was a lesson for every businessman: "It follows without argument that to the community in which a man has prospered he owes a return."[29]

Atlanta's Jews heartily endorsed this credo. Heirs to a heritage of persecution, they were profoundly grateful for the physical security and economic opportunities they found in the Gate City. In addition, participation in city-wide charity drives provided a means of furthering their integration by emphasizing what they had in common with their gentile neighbors.[30]

However, Jewish generosity was not always solicited or even welcome. Rabbi Reich voiced the resentment of many Jews when he criticized the repeated appeals in the local press for "Christian ladies" to meet and raise money for the Industrial School and the Home for Fallen Women. Jews, the rabbi insisted, had never restricted their beneficence to Hebrews and did not wish to be excluded from any worthy cause. Two decades later, when the Associated Charities of Atlanta was formed to coordinate local benevolent activities, several Protestant clergymen insisted that the designation "Christian" be included in the organization's name. Since this would have precluded Jewish participation, it was rejected by a majority of the organizers. Yet, one-quarter of the members of the Evangelical Ministers' Association continued to demand that charity be dispensed in the name of Christ, and Rev. E. C. Crock of the Evangelical Lutheran Church declared:

> If he [the Jew] is willing to lay aside as much as we are asked to lay aside, namely, his religious belief, and come in on a platform where Christ is honored as lord and Savior, I suppose no one will oppose his coming. . . . We are not dictating to people of other religions how they shall dispense their charities. If they do not want to do it in the name of Christ we are only sorry for it, but it is asking too much that Christians should haul down the Christian banner and march under a Christless flag in order that others who deny him should be admitted.[31]

A similar incident occurred in 1911. For nearly three decades Jews had generously contributed to the Young Men's Christian Association but were barred from serving on its board of directors. An attempt was made to admit them, but a majority of the directors, led by Rev. Len G. Broughton, refused to accede. The Baptist minister insisted that the purpose of the organization was "to save young men . . . not by giving them a room with a bath, but by bringing them to accept Jesus Christ as Savior." To give Jews or Catholics a voice in setting policy would result in "a medly which is paganism." Even Rev. John E. White, the staunchest advocate of Jewish participation, spoke in terms that were not likely to please his Jewish friends. White urged that no action be taken "which tends to drive the Jew further from Christ." Jewish participation, he suggested, would lessen anti-Christian feeling among Jews and facilitate their conversion.[32]

The participation of Jews in politics and philanthropy was of two sorts. On the one hand, a small number—no more than two dozen—were civic leaders, while Jews were more commonly involved only in the impersonal roles of voter and donor. In their public capacities, only members of the elite had much contact with Gentiles, and even these relationships tended to be formal and goal directed. The only noneconomic activities which brought large numbers of Jews and Christians together revolved around the lodge hall.

The nineteenth century was the golden age of fraternal associations, and Jews were attracted to the mystic brotherhoods for many of the same reasons as their neighbors. In addition to providing sickness and death benefits, the lodge offered a refuge from the loneliness and anonymity wrought by rapid urbanization. The ritual expressed the corporate sense of the group, reaffirmed fundamental patterns of belief, supplied emotional and aesthetic satisfaction, and also provided a sense of anchorage through identification with some larger entity. Members of the fraternal tribe were expected to practice an ethical code among themselves, and in the privacy of the lodge hall could indulge in grandiloquent titles, ceremonials, and eccentric behavior which would not be tolerated elsewhere. Moreover, affiliation might further one's political or economic ambitions. For Jews in particular, the lodge afforded opportunity for personal relationships with members of the ethnically predominate group, and it was perhaps a manifestation of their insecurity, no less than their sociability, that impelled some Jews to join a multiplicity of brotherhoods. Atlanta Jews belonged to the Elks, the Shrine, the Royal Arcanum, and Civitan International; but their presence was most notable in the Odd Fellows, the Knights of Pythias, and above all, the Free and Accepted Masons.[33]

Schiller Lodge No. 71 of the Independent Order of Odd Fellows was founded in 1872 by Jews and Gentiles of German extraction, with offices generally divided between the two groups. German remained the official language of the lodge for two decades, but by 1903 at least two East Europeans, Leon Eplan and N. A. Kaplan, had served as noble grands. During the seventies, Jewish women were among the leaders of Miriam Lodge of the Rebekahs, the order's ladies auxiliary. Adolph Brandt was elected grand master of the Georgia Odd Fellows in 1878 and remained active after he moved to Atlanta in 1885. Alex Dittler and Dr. Lee Ben Clarke, both members of the Schiller Lodge, were elected to the top state office in 1899 and 1911 respectively.[34]

At the time of his death in 1889, Brandt was also captain of the Capital City Division of the Knights of Pythias. Subsequently, Alex Dittler, Joseph Hirsch, and Samuel Weil all served as chancellors of the lodge that was named in his honor. On the state level, Herman Cronheim was elected grand master of the exchequer in 1888 and later held other offices in the grand lodge.[35]

More than any other fraternal order, Freemasonry provided a hospitable and attractive haven for Atlanta's Jews. Many clearly accepted Isaac Mayer Wise's assertion in 1855 that Masonry was a Jewish institution "whose history, degrees, charges, passwords, and explanations are Jewish from the beginning to the end with the exception of only one by-degree and a few words in the obligation." Two years later, David Mayer and Simon Frankfort became charter members of Fulton Lodge No. 216, Atlanta's second oldest Masonic body. As the lodge grew from 54 members in 1860 to 100 in 1867, 121 in 1878, and 250 in 1913, the proportion of Jews respectively rose from 6 percent to 13, 26, and 36 percent. Although Jews were always in the minority, David Mayer occupied the highest lodge office from 1859 to 1863; Levi Cohen held it from 1870 to 1873 and from 1891 to 1892; Joseph Fleishel in 1874; Aaron Haas in 1878; David Marx in 1899; and Samuel Boorstin in 1913. Jewish participation was less notable in Georgia Lodge No. 96, which grew from 64 members in 1870 to over 400 in 1913, but whose Jewish contingent remained at 3 percent. Similarly, as the membership of Atlanta Lodge No. 59 increased from 205 in 1870 to 507 in 1913, its proportion of Jews climbed from 3 to 5 percent. Despite their small number of Jews, Georgia Lodge elected Alfred Eichberg as its worshipful master in 1885, and the Atlanta Lodge bestowed the same honor on Isaac Steinheimer in 1900. On the state level, both David Mayer and Levi Cohen chaired the finance committee of the grand lodge and Max Meyerhardt, an attorney from the north Georgia town of Rome, served as grand master from 1900 to 1907.[36]

It is significant that Jewish membership in the nonsectarian brotherhoods was not to the exclusion of participation in specifically Jewish fraternities like the B'nai B'rith. Moreover, while the fraternal lodges remained the only sphere of local associational life in which large numbers of Jews and Gentiles could mix comfortably, the trend was for Jewish activity to be ever more centered in the Schiller, Brandt, and Fulton lodges.

In contrast to their prominence in fraternal affairs, relatively few Jews participated in the cultural life of upper middle-class Atlanta, and those who did tended to be American-born. Aaron Haas was vice-president of the Young Men's Library Association in 1877, and in 1901 Aaron A. Meyer became a trustee of its successor, the Carnegie Library. Isaac Schoen and Leon Lieberman belonged to the Kentucky Society, and Victor Kriegshaber served as its vice-president in 1907. A man of diverse interests, Kriegshaber mixed membership on the executive committee of the Music Festival Association with the presidency of the Chamber of Commerce. He and I. H. Oppenheim also belonged to the Atlanta Gun Club and the Atlanta Lecture Association. Mrs. Oppenheim and Mrs. Jacob Elsas were members respectively of the Daughters of the American Revolution and the Atlanta Woman's Club. While Jews were starkly under-represented in most cultural associations, a disproportionate number found a comfortable niche in the Burns Club, which was founded in 1896 to perpetuate the legacy of the "wee bard of auld Scotia." Joseph Jacobs and Aaron Meyer were among the charter members; Harry Silverman, Eugene Oberdorfer, and Otto Schwalb joined soon afterward.[37]

During the first two decades following the Civil War, Atlanta's raw and bustling commercial atmosphere cast a blanket of relative social equality over the city's white businessmen. Unlike their counterparts in the older southern cities, "they have no long line of ancestry to keep up," declared the *Constitution* in 1879. "They keep no stylish turnouts, with expensive accompanyments. They live to drive their businesses." There is "no city in this or any other country more free from the domination of caste," a local booster proudly asserted in 1881, "admission to society being based on character alone." Outsiders also remarked about the city's distinctiveness. A correspondent for the Louisville *Courier-Journal* observed in 1875 that "the very rapid growth of the place has caused its society to be very much mixed" and that several years would have to pass for it to become "properly stratified." "There is little distinctively Southern in Atlanta," lamented an Englishman who characterized the city as "the antithesis of Savannah . . . eminently modern and unromantic," while a fellow-countryman complained that conversation was confined to talk of religion, money, and politics. Atlanta's materialistic ethos and youth—the fact her old families were pioneers rather than patricians and that some of these were Jews—delayed the introduction of the kind of social discrimination already rampant in the North. The highly publicized exclusion in 1877 of Jewish banker Joseph Seligman from Saratoga's Grand Union Hotel could still elicit from an outraged Jewish clothier the exclamation that "such a thing would be literally impossible in this city or state. The sentiment here is purely cosmopolitan. There is no distinction of race [that is, nationality] or religion. Jews who are respectable go everywhere." "So long as the scrawl of a Jew on the back of a piece of paper is worth more than the royal word of three kings," added the *Atlanta Daily Herald*, "it will be vain to try to limit them to two dollar hotels."[38]

But the immunity of Atlanta's Jews was not permanent. As elsewhere, the major manifestation of growing exclusivity was in the membership policy of the new elite clubs. John Higham has noted that these clubs were products of "a general struggle for place and privilege" that followed the Civil War. In a society in which wealth itself could confer and perpetuate elite social status, social climbing became a genuine problem. In order to protect their gains from newcomers, successful social climbers strove to erect nonpecuniary standards for social acceptance: elite clubs, formalized etiquette, social registers, and an emphasis on pedigree. "The Jews," Higham continues,

> symbolized the pecuniary vices and entered more prominently than any other ethnic group into the struggle for status. Practically, anti-Semitic discriminations offered another means of stabilizing the social ladder, while, psychologically, a society vexed by its own assertiveness gave a general problem an ethnic focus.[39]

Many Atlanta Jews acquired wealth more rapidly than culture, and their interest, affluence, and talent continued to enable them to participate deeply in the civic and fraternal life of the general community. Nevertheless, it did not matter that influential and cultured men like Joseph Hirsch, Jacob Haas, Joseph Jacobs, and Victor Kreigshaber might socialize with equally prominent Gentiles as guests in their homes and clubs; club membership was a symbolic triumph that remained beyond their grasp. Since its creation in 1883, no Jew has belonged to the Capital City Club, although Sam Massell was asked to join after he was elected mayor in 1969. Aaron Haas was a founding member in 1887 of the Gentlemen's Driving Club (after 1895, the Piedmont Driving Club), but no other Jew has since been admitted. Each club had approximately six hundred members in 1915. The Commercial Club, started in 1892, did have ten Jews among its two hundred charter members, but since it was an adjunct of the Chamber of Commerce, the parent body's most prominent members could hardly be excluded.[40]

Although the Gate City's Jews were victims of social discrimination, they fared better than their northern and midwestern brethren. No evidence could be found to indicate discrimination in housing, employment, education, or public accommodation, and their participation in political, philanthropic, and fraternal affairs remained relatively high. The old-line Jewish elite maintained contact with its gentile counterpart and acted as an informal intermediary between the Jewish and general communities. Several other factors accounted for the continued high status of Atlanta's Jews. First of all, they were more fully integrated into the local culture and achieved prominence long before the status rivalries began to crystalize in the eighties. The pervasiveness of the business culture, though affected by growing refinement, remained receptive to entrepreneurial talent irrespective of religion. The advent of East European immigration, which paralleled and to an extent accelerated the pace of discrimination, did not come with disruptive force. Moreover, the proportion of Jews in the total population remained small, and there was no danger of being overwhelmed by upwardly mobile (or politically assertive) Jews. Perhaps most important of all, the overriding preoccupation with maintaining white supremacy tended to blur distinctions between different kinds of white men.[41]

Despite their continued high status, by the beginning of the twentieth century, Atlanta's Jews had clearly experienced a dimunition in political, civic, fraternal, and social prominence. In part, this decline mirrored new perceptions of immigration in general and Jewish newcomers in particular. On another level, it reflected changing attitudes toward Judaism and the Jewish businessman.

The attitude of Christianity toward Judaism has always been ambivalent: Jews were both God's chosen people and rebels against His purpose; Judaism was both the mother religion of Christianity and a repudiation of its legitimacy; Jesus was a Jew and Jews were his murderers. Nowhere was this ambivalence greater than in the fundamentalist South.[42] Jewish religious observances attracted more than passing curiosity, but while the local press always maintained a respectful tone, the public image of Judaism underwent a steady erosion as the nineteenth century passed into the twentieth.

A common journalistic refrain during the seventies was that the survival of the Jewish people was a confirmation of biblical verities. "Though modern religionists complain that they [Jews] do not go far enough in recognition of divine revelation," observed the *Constitution,* "the Israelites are living witnesses to the truths of Holy Writ as handed down to them through successive generations of the faithful." The *Daily New Era* evidenced a similar view in noting that

> the annual recurrence of the Jewish festivals . . . is well calculated to impress all thinking men with the truth [and] Divine inspiration of the Holy Scriptures, especially when an opportunity is afforded to witness their celebration by a considerable body of intelligent descendants of Abraham, of whom there are a very respectable number in Atlanta.

Jewish religiosity was often favorably compared to the prevailing mode of Christian observance. "We can but admire the devotion of the Jews to their church and the fidelity with which they observe all its festivals," declared an editorialist in 1878.

> In these respects they set a noble example which Christians might follow with profit to themselves and to the liveliness of their faith. Christian feasts are never observed with the strictness, or apparently, with the joy which always characterize the . . . Jewish festivals.

In a city noted for its rowdiness, prosperous and conservative Gentiles recognized the value of religion as a mechanism for social control and welcomed all agencies—including the synagogue—which might foster order. The *Constitution* remarked that Jews seemed to enjoy Rosh Hashanah as much as the Gentiles did Christmas, but added that "none of them [Jews] have been seen reeling with intoxication upon our streets, [and] none have been carried to the lock-up by our police for violation of law and order during the whole time." Jewish holy days were not occasions for "reveling and hilarious enjoyments," but rather for "rational feasting" and solemn introspection. Yet, praise for Judaism to the contrary, the local press and public officials customarily used the designation "Christian" to describe American civilization, government, morals, and education.[43]

Like other Americans, Atlantans esteemed organized religious life and accepted the legitimacy of denominationalism. The erection of a synagogue was both an act of piety and patriotism, testimony to the freedom of America. During the seventies, Jews contributed to the construction and repair of local churches, and Christians responded in kind. A reporter who attended Easter services at the Church of the Immaculate Conception in 1877 remarked that "casting your eyes to one side you would have thought yourself in the synagogue, so many Jews were there. . . ." Many Christians attended High Holy Day and Passover services, and when the annual Baptist Convention met in Atlanta in 1879, several preachers lodged with David Mayer.[44]

Ecumenicalism began to fade when East European Orthodoxy preempted Reform as the prevailing mode of local Jewish observance. The press continued to mark the occurrence of Jewish holidays, but it was the quality of the Temple's musical program rather than the virtues of Judaism that it deemed worthy of notice. Pronouncements by local preachers claiming that the Jews were forever cursed and had been scattered because they rejected Christ were so common in the nineties that Rabbi Reich was impelled to issue a public rebuttal. A decade later, the *Constitution* reprinted a defamatory article from a northern magazine; this time it was Rabbi Loeb who took to print in defense of Judaism. Belief that the Jews were doomed to suffer did not preclude sympathy with their plight. Rev. Broughton loudly condemned the perpetrators of the Kishinev massacre and even urged President Theodore Roosevelt to send a note of protest to the Russian government. However, he added that the slaughter confirmed the prophecy that "the Jewish nation should be trampled under foot because of a rejected Christ. And to more or less a degree it will be so until He comes again and is crowned by his chosen people."[45]

Until recently, the ultimate conversion of the Jews was an end prayerfully desired by nearly all Christians, and the Baptist and Methodist denominations, which held the allegiance of most Atlantans, attached particular eschatological importance to bringing the elect of God to Christ. This attitude was by no means anti-Semitic; all men were deemed in need of salvation. However, the steps undertaken to accomplish this goal do provide an index of Judaism's legitimacy in the eyes of non-Jews.[46]

No serious attempt was made to evangelize Atlanta's Jews during the nineteenth century. A man claiming to be a Jewish-born Methodist preacher visited the city in 1860 and solicited funds "to facilitate the Christianization of his countrymen," but was denounced as a fraud by a local clergyman and hastily left town. Seven years later, the Southern Baptist Convention unanimously resolved to "labor and pray more earnestly for the conversion of the Jews," but it appropriated no funds for the purpose. Abraham Jaeger, who had served as rabbi in Selma and Mobile before embracing the Baptist faith in 1872, addressed packed church meetings in Atlanta in 1873 and 1874, but while "members of the Ancient House of Israel [were] especially invited" to attend, none apparently did. Nor was the Board of Domestic Missions willing to engage Jaeger as a missionary to his former coreligionists. The Board of Foreign Missions was instructed in 1882 to "seek missionaries to Israelites in this and other countries," but this had no effect in Atlanta. Another apostate, Rev. Sigmond Rogowsky, preached before the First Baptist Church in 1897 on the theme, "Our Obligations to the Jews and How to Pay Them." Rogowsky, who had spent the previous eight months in Georgia seeking converts, urged that Jews be treated kindly and responsibly, but nonetheless brought within the Protestant fold.[47]

The sharp increase in the local Russian Jewish population after 1895 stimulated more energetic conversion efforts. In 1904 Rev. Dr. Julius Magath was employed by the South Georgia Methodist Conference as a missionary to the Jews of the Southeast, and he urged Conference delegates to invite Jews to their services, prepare sermons suitable to their needs, deal kindly with them, and pray for their speedy conversion. An Orthodox Jew by birth and a persistent critic of anti-Semitism, Magath maintained that a Jew need not forfeit his Jewishness by accepting Jesus Christ. A similar stand was taken a few months later by Rev. Mark Levy, a converted English Jew who spoke before local Episcopal and Methodist congregations. Other converts, including Philip Sidersky, "the Yiddish evangelist," preached in Atlanta during the next few years, but the most influential was Rev. A. Litchenstein. Litchenstein, who was superintendent of a Jewish-Christian mission in St. Louis, persuaded local Baptists to establish the Atlanta Hebrew Christian Association in 1905. By 1912 the Association had a Hebrew Christian Gospel Hall of Forsyth Street, and the following year a Jewish Christian Mission was opened on upper Whitehall Street, apparently under separate auspices. Partly because they were located in a neighborhood long since vacated by its Jewish residents, neither mission achieved much success and both were defunct by 1917.[48]

Despite their apparent failure, the missionaries nonetheless disconcerted the Jewish community. Rabbi Marx, who had converted six women and one man to Judaism between 1898 and 1914, warned his congregation in the latter year that "the missionary plys his trade and sooner or later will reap, if we do not bestir ourselves." Similarly, reports that "a great many" Jewish children were attending Bible classes and a vacation school at the Wesley Memorial Church persuaded the trustees of the Jewish Educational Alliance to organize a Jewish summer school the following year. But perhaps even more disturbing than the threat missionaries actually posed to Jewish youth was the realization that, in the eyes of the general community, Judaism had lost some of its legitimacy.[49]

The economic stereotype of the Jew, no less than the religious one, embodied friendly and hostile elements. If Jews could be both God's chosen people as well as Christ-killers, they could also be both enterprising and avaricious, agents of commercial progress and also cunning parasites. These conflicting attitudes often existed side by side, not only within the same community but also within the same mind, and for practical or opportunistic reasons were not always acted upon. Adherents of the New South Creed recognized the contribution Jewish entrepreneurs could make to city building and were accordingly hospitable to Jewish settlement and investment. But even their admiration might turn to envy in light of the "mysterious" Jewish ability to succeed. The gentile capitalist, subconsciously uneasy over his own success, could find in his Jewish counterpart an ideal object upon whom he could project his own guilt. Members of the newly urbanized working class were even less likely to respect Jewish achievement. Victims of an agrarian depression which they attributed to the machinations of financiers and greedy middlemen, the heirs of the Populists continued to distinguish between the producing and nonproducing classes. Jews, who had no organic tie to the land, seemed to thrive off the labor of others. They were ethnic and religious aliens and represented the vanguard of a new culture that was destroying time-honored ways.[50]

During the three postwar decades, Jews were frequently commended for their industry, integrity, prosperity, thrift, and enterprise. "Jews never fail to build up a town they settle in," remarked the *Atlanta Daily Herald* in 1875. "Look around you in every business and in every walk of life," suggested a Christian merchant fifteen years later, "and you will see that the leaders are Hebrews. Everyone must admire the wonderful business capacity with which the race seems imbued." Jews were often cited as Atlanta's most enthusiastic boosters and prophets of her future greatness. To "no other element of its population is Atlanta more indebted than to those of the Jewish faith," commented the *Constitution* in 1897. "They have contributed their energy, their business acuteness and their money to the building up of Atlanta, and have been constant factors in its progress."[51]

Yet even in the seventies and eighties, uncomplimentary references to Jewish economic activity were not unknown. The success of Jewish merchants sometimes engendered envy among their competitors, and a business dodger distributed by an unidentified firm in 1876 concluded with the admonition: "Remember that we are no Jews." This, in turn, impelled the *Constitution* to remind its readers that

> the Jews with which the people of today are made brethren are an honest, laborious, productive and noble class of people. They have never proven a burden to the public purse, a curse to society, enemies to law and order, or drones in the hive of industry. . . . Against such a people no unjust and sneering epithet should be hurled.

But there were occasions when even the *Constitution* spoke of "a Jew of tobacco" or used the word "Jew" as a verb. Perhaps more significantly, an article about commercial traveler Solomon Dewald mentioned that he was known to everyone as "the honest Jew," implying that Jews were commonly considered to be less than ethical in their business dealings.[52]

Meanwhile, the growing prominence of Russian immigrants as owners of pawnshops and saloons patronized by blacks provided grist for the mills of those who believed that Jews thrived on the misfortune of others and in a manner antithetical to community interests.[53] In 1897, advertising solicitors for the *Jewish Sentiment* were "told pointedly" by a shoe dealer, fish seller, and milliner that they did "not cater to or want the Jewish trade." Two years later, a liquor store owner placed a sign in his window which read: "No Jew Trade Wanted." The ever ambivalent attitude toward Jewish economic achievement perhaps reached its fullest expression in Lucian Lamar Knight's 1907 essay, "The Twentieth Century and the Jews." Though at times almost embarrassingly philo-Semitic, the Georgia historian nonetheless emphasized the Jew's peculiar ability to gain advantage. Jews, he observed, "are money makers to such an extent that the roll-call of the entire Hebrew population can be made from the tax-book." Eventually, the Jew "owns the grocery-store, the meat-market, the grog-shop, the planing-mill, the newspaper, the hotel and the bank." At about the same time, one of the local dailies found cause to refute "the ancient mockery that the Jew is 'tricky.' "

> Well then, does he monopolize this quality? Were you ever fleeced by a Methodist class leader in a trade? Did you ever come out of the little horn at the hands of a Baptist horse trader? Did a Presbyterian speculator ever get the best of your pocket book, or did an Episcopalian broker ever unload upon you a worthless mining stock? . . . When you answer

> these questions, you will realize that this criticism of the Jew is half nonsense and half falsehood mixed with prejudice.[54]

The status of Atlanta's Jews was greatly enhanced by their orderliness. Although the Gate City had one of the highest crime rates in the country, it was rare for a Jew to run afoul of the law. A careful examination of the local press between 1865 and 1900 reveals that except for a case of assault and battery, Jews were accused of only minor offenses: peddling without a license, obstructing the sidewalk, failure to pay a hotel bill, swindling, disorderly conduct, violating the Sunday closing law, and "lynching" a cat.[55] As the immigrant population increased during the next decade and a half, juvenile delinquency emerged as a minor problem, and a few Jews were charged with more serious crimes: receiving stolen property, theft, violating the prohibition law, and running a disorderly house.[56] This still represented such a low level of criminality that Governor J. M. Terrell could report in 1907 that only one Jew was among the 3,500 inmates in Georgia prisons, and six years later the *Constitution* could declare:

> Turn where you will, the Jew makes a desirable citizen of the finest type. You do not find many Jews in the penitentiary or many Jews lined up with the vicious or predatory class. The Jew is essentially law-abiding. This is part of his religion. Where he breaks over the line it is probably in smaller proportion than would be found in the offenses of the people of any other creed.[57]

Despite this record, when Leo Frank was charged with murder in May 1913, a well-known Atlanta woman observed that while this was the first time a local Jew had ever been in serious trouble, everyone was prepared to believe the worst of him.[58]

If attitudes toward the Jew were always more or less ambivalent, not until the turn of the century did Jewish leaders express their concern. In 1898 Frank Cohen exclaimed that "the feeling against the Jew exists to as great an extent in America as anywhere else on earth. It is dormant, not dead and will never die." Two years later, Rabbi Marx, whom Cohen claimed seldom "rubs up against the world or express[es] a conclusion on subjects of this nature," told his congregation that while little prejudice was entertained for the individual Jew, there existed "widespread and deep-seated prejudice against Jews as an entire people."[59]

The motivating factors behind these declarations are not all known. Certainly, defeats of Jewish aspirants for office, constricting social opportunities, revived missionary activity, the board of education's decision to discontinue its policy of excused religious absences, and the increasing disparagement of Jewish character were all partly responsible. Further cause for reflection was provided in 1914, when the warden of the federal prison withdrew his permission allowing Jewish inmates to abstain from work and attend services on the High Holy Days.[60]

Even more disturbing to some was the increasing popularity of plays, movies, and newspaper features which appeared to burlesque the Jew and Judaism. During the nineteenth century, Jewish stage roles, drawn largely from the Old Testament, tended to be philo-Semitic, and as late as 1904 local audiences flocked to "The Peddler," which concerned a "hard-working man of the East Side . . . who has a heart for the poor and unfortunate." A locally made film, "A Thousand Dollar Bet," which appeared in 1913, was of a different sort. Its central figure was Izzy Cohen, who, excited beyond measure by money, agreed to marry an unseen woman whose complexion turned out to be "just a few shades darker than midnight." At about the same time, the movie "Shylock" and the stage musical "Buzzy Izzy" amused local audiences. Jews were no more pleased to read about Ikey Schwartz, a shady New York real estate man whose apartment buildings came with "hot and cold windows, running gas and noiseless janitors." The vaudeville routines of Weber and Fields, and Montague Glass's play "Potash and Perlmutter," also utilized stereotypes that many Jews considered objectionable.[61]

At a time of rapid change, the employment of stage stereotypes reduced the anxieties of the white gentile majority to more managable proportions. Although Irishmen, Yankees, and other groups were also stereotyped, except for the Negroes, Jews were most vulnerable to the effects of ridicule. While it was the East European immigrant who was most frequently lampooned, Atlanta's Russians were still too isolated from their gentile neighbors to be anxious about what seemed, at worst, to be a relatively benign version of a familiar malady. On the other hand, the Temple members—native-born, assimilated, and prosperous—perceived a threat to their hard-won status and carefully cultivated public image. At the regional B'nai B'rith convention in 1910, an Atlanta delegate introduced a resolution protesting the "so-called humorous articles appearing in magazines and vaudeville acts" which grossly exaggerated and misrepresented Jewish behavior and tended "to cast discredit on Jews as a whole. . . ." In 1914, Rabbi Marx went a step further and urged the members of his congregation to boycott and protest against the "vulgar stage misrepresentations of the Jew and Judaism, the reprehensible moving picture 'hebrew' singer, [and] the unwarranted press inference." A year earlier, the president of the B'nai B'rith Gate City Lodge had appointed a committee "to investigate the complaints against Jewish caricatures that are becoming so frequent on the local stage." The president's name was Leo M. Frank, and within two months he would be arrested on the charge of murder.[63]

When, in the aftermath of Appomattox, substantial numbers of Jews first began to settle in Atlanta, their presence was hailed as an auspicious sign of commercial growth and future greatness. "In our cosmopolitan city," remarked the *Constitution* in 1870, "but little of that general prejudice against Jews is ever demonstrated." Slightly more than four decades later, the Gate City became the focal point for a manifestation of anti-Semitism that has been ranked with the Dreyfus Affair and the Beiliss case.[64]

# 8

## *Jews and Blacks*

The economic mobility, assimilation, and social status of Atlanta's Jews were strongly affected by the city's large black population. Jews, in turn, provided Negroes with useful services and what appeared to be a viable model for group advancement. Relations between the two communities were highly ambivalent and influenced by circumstances beyond their control. While cordiality was the norm, resentments, frustrations, and attitudinal changes weakened what was, on the whole, a mutually advantageous arrangement. This interaction was probably quite typical in the South during the fifty years after Appomattox, yet little of the voluminous literature on Jewish-black relations deals with the phenomonon.[1]

The first sustained contacts between Jews and blacks in Atlanta were between masters and slaves. Slavery probably had a deterrent effect on antebellum Jewish immigration to the South. Between 1830 and 1860, Europeans and Northerners came increasingly to regard Negro slavery as an anachronistic and reprehensible institution, and Jewish immigrants were undoubtedly influenced by this attitude. Moreover, the growth of abolitionist and free soil thought intensified sectional strife and transformed southern fear of abolitionists into distrust of all outsiders. Slavery was the pillar of southern civilization, and the region was more likely to attract immigrants who had no strong objections to the "peculiar institution" and were willing to adapt themselves to the prevailing orthodoxy. This was more a matter of unconscious accommodation than mere protective coloration. As members of a success-oriented but economically vulnerable and isolated minority, Jews were likely to adopt the attitudes and practices of their gentile neighbors and customers. Blacks also acted as a lightning rod in deflecting prejudices which might otherwise have been manifested against Jews, and by parenthetically ordaining the equality of all whites, slavery conferred indirect benefits even on poor Jewish newcomers.

While opposition to slavery was reputedly one of the reasons why David Steinheimer resisted conscription into the Confederate Army in 1862, on the whole there was no discernible difference between local Jewish and gentile attitudes. Those Jews who had the desire and means to purchase Negro servants generally did so. Four of the six Jewish households in 1850 contained slaves, and this figure corresponded favorably to the 75 percent of Jewish households in Charleston, Richmond, and Savannah which had slaves three decades earlier. Local Jews also participated in the slave trade: the auction and commission house of Mayer and Jacobi dealt in slaves as in other commodities; Levi Cohen purchased slaves in several Georgia counties during the war; and Solomon Cohen offered "75 LIKELY NEGROES" for sale in 1862.[2]

Jews continued to employ Negro servants after the abolition of slavery. Indeed, the low cost and abundance of free black labor placed the employment of servants within reach of the lower middle-class. Fifty percent of Atlanta's Jews in 1870 and 42 percent in 1880 resided in households which also included black domestics. Presumably, many other Jewish households employed nonresident blacks, since the trend during the postwar period was for domestics to live outside their places of employment. Most of the blacks in Jewish homes were girls or young women, sometimes with children, who worked as maids, cooks, and nurses. A few, like Mollie Alexander and her children, bore the surname of their Jewish employer. Only rarely did adult black males live on the premises. The average Jewish household contained only one live-in servant, but some had as many as four, and there was a clear association between Jewish economic status and the employment of domestic labor: 52 percent of the Jewish heads of household in 1880 with assets of at least $1,100 employed live-in help, compared with only 29 percent of those worth under that amount.

Commerce provided additional interracial contacts. Jewish peddlers and petty traders who filtered south after the war eagerly courted the patronage of blacks, willingly bargained over prices, "showed infinite patience in dealing with simple people in small business affairs," and treated their customers with a civility that the latter rarely received from white Southerners. This commercial intercourse was rooted in the marginality of both vendor and purchaser. The Jew had little capital, spoke broken English, was unfamiliar with regional mores, and in some cases was perceived as an intruder by native whites. Similarly, the freedman was disdained and feared by ex-Confederates. Perhaps more importantly, prior to going South, few of the newcomers had encountered blacks, and this made them "more willing to respond out of actual experience with the Negro than out of a twisted history of slavery, guilt and pathological hate." "When the Negro smiled at the Jew," notes Eli Evans, "the Jew smiled back."[3]

Many of the Central European Jews who settled in Atlanta during the sixties and seventies previously had extensive experience selling to blacks in the countryside. Some, like Gustave Saloshin, who had a secondhand clothing business on Decatur Street, and Alex Dittler, whose grocery and home were located in the Negro neighborhood of Summer Hill, continued to service a predominantly black clientele. Other German Jewish merchants were patronized by both races to the extent that the price of their goods and location of their stores allowed. As late as 1913, the city's three leading Jewish-owned emporiums and numerous lesser enterprises advertised regularly in the local black press. Jewish businessmen also employed a substantial number of black porters and draymen, and at least one owned houses which he rented to Negroes.[4]

As the Germans acquired the capital and skills required to tap the more lucrative white market, their former dependence on the Negro trade was inherited by newly arrived immigrants from Eastern Europe. Peddling, either in the country or the outlying sections of the city, was commonly the initial occupation of the Russians, 13 percent of whom in 1896 earned their livelihood in this way. *Landsmen* (countrymen), the Jewish relief societies, and wholesalers willingly advanced the goods and funds which they hoped would transform the destitute refugee into a nascent merchant.

Country peddlers, who carried their assortment of dry goods and notions in a sack or valise, generally spent a week at a stretch in the rural townships of Georgia and Alabama. For many immigrants like Charles Greenberg, this experience provided their initial contact with blacks and an introduction to southern racial mores. "I got off at the first station and walked a few miles until I saw black men working in the fields, carrying the same kind of bags white people in Russia would carry," Greenberg recalled.

> I walked over and greeted them as I had been instructed. So, they all stopped working and looked at me, not because I was carrying a pack, but, as I found out later, [because] I, a white person, had greeted them. It was my good luck that no white person had seen me, because no white person [in the South] greets a black one.

As dusk began to fall, the young peddler looked for a place to spend the night. "Having been advised that I should not lodge with blacks, for a white person must not lodge in a black home, I kept walking after nightfall till I reached the home of a white." Before retiring for the evening, he mused that he was no longer a "greenhorn." Not only had he made his first sale, but also learned a fundamental lesson about deportment in the South.[5]

Aside from being a seasonal activity confined largely to the autumn months when farmers had money to spend, country peddling entailed problems of finding shelter, avoiding unfriendly dogs, and keeping kosher. More convenient but less profitable was the routine of the urban basket peddler. The basket peddler learned the English names of his wares, memorized the words "Look in the basket," took one of the streetcar lines to the last stop, got off, and knocked on doors. Once again, blacks were his main customers, and after a while he might accumulate savings sufficient to advance them credit, would inscribe their names in a small book, and return after a specified time to collect. "On the Monday of the following week I went out like a businessman, now without a pack, only to collect," recalled a former practitioner of the trade. Like his colleagues, he discovered that it was easier to make sales than make collections, not only because the blacks were poor, but also since "till one gets to know them, they all seemed to have the same face."[6]

Since the peddler had little overhead and the mark-up on his goods was between fifty and one hundred percent, his peripatetic livelihood often provided the capital required to open a retail grocery or enter the dry goods or clothing business. Blacks remained his primary customers. The ownership of saloons and pawnshops—two other enterprises heavily patronized by blacks and frequently owned by Jews—required greater capital than most recent immigrants could muster, and their proprietors constituted a large share of the Russian community's economic elite.[7]

Several factors accounted for the Jews' extensive economic involvement with blacks. The destitute Russian newcomers possessed all the prerequisites essential to entrepreneurial success save capital and familiarity with American ways. Having arrived in Atlanta substantially poorer than had their now prosperous German coreligionists, they were able to enter the overcrowded retail market only at the lowest and most stigmatized level. By necessity, the Russians were compelled to court the patronage of those whose business was scorned by more established merchants. Long accustomed to providing goods and services for a brutalized peasantry, they had few if any temperamental objections to dealing with blacks and, unlike their white gentile counterparts, had no deep-seated compulsion to manifest anti-Negro prejudice. Indeed, Jews aggressively sought the blacks' trade and treated their customers with unaccustomed courtesy.

Central to the popularity of the Jewish merchant was his willingness to extend credit—even at a personal sacrifice—to often impecunious blacks; and his ability to do so reflected, in turn, the availability of credit from benevolent societies, friendly wholesalers, and banks. In contrast, the prospective black businessmen found credit and capital more difficult to obtain and generally lacked commercial experience. The black's consequent reluctance to advance credit limited his customers to those who could pay in cash. In addition, while many blacks preferred to patronize merchants of their own race, many others suspected that merchandise sold by a Negro was bound to be inferior. The willingness of blacks to "walk three blocks or more to trade with a white man, when there is a Negro store at their door" engendered the resentment and envy of Atlanta's nascent black business class. "We have aided the Jew from the time he came into our neighborhood with his store on his back," complained one of their spokesmen in 1899,

> until now he has a large brick building, a number of clerks, and he and his family ride in a fine carriage . . . driven by a Negro. Why can we not help our brother who is struggling with all the odds against him . . . ? I am sure that what we might buy from the Negro could be no more inferior than some of the things we have bought from the Jew, and I suspect his recommendation of the article would be as truthful as that of the Jew.[8]

Finally, the commercial bond between Jew and Negro was reinforced by a vague sense of empathy between the two persecuted peoples. The New York Yiddish press, to which many of Atlanta's Jews subscribed, was very sympathetic toward the plight of blacks and frequently compared their suffering with that of the Jews in

Europe—an analogy made even more often by Negro journalists. Yiddish poet I. J. Schwartz caught the flavor of this feeling.

> And it was noteworthy: how soon
> The people without a tongue understood—
> Or more clearly stated—smelled, felt,
> The naked nature of the strange Negro—
> . . . . . . . . . . . . . . . . . . . . . . . . . . . . . . . .
> And it was natural, that the Negro
> On his part, also immediately sensed that these
> Were somehow people closer to him,
> Belonging, indeed, to the white race,
> But a white race of another kind.[9]

Native-born white Gentiles looked with disdain upon Jewish dealings with blacks which, they suspected entailed breaches of southern etiquette. Alan Rogers, a local feature writer, drew upon a mixed bag of stereotypes in describing Decatur Street's Jewish businessmen in 1906.

> Hugging the very curbstones for a football, this same indomitable race of nationless wayfarers withstand the crush and crowding of the black denizens quite long and strong enough to ply their natural gifts for trade, and prey upon African weaknesses and prejudices for profits in percentages sufficiently large enough to [reprieve?] the very city of Jerusalem itself.

Pawnbrokers were suspected of receiving stolen property and, much worse, selling weapons to blacks. The hero of one of Rogers's stories is a pawnbroker named Levi Eichenstein, who is initially seen anxiously awaiting the birth of his first child. Suddenly, the bell rings in his shop below, and "the natural inclination and heritage of a thousand generations . . . asserted themselves." His customer is a Negro who wishes to purchase a revolver. Eichenstein instinctively begins to praise his stock of firearms, but then hears his baby's birthcry, realizes the possibly tragic consequences of the sale, and sends the Negro from the store.[10]

The arrest in 1896 of a Decatur Street furniture dealer and a Negro employee on the charge of burglary engendered speculation that criminally inclined Jews and blacks were in collusion; both men were subsequently acquitted. Jewish-owned saloons, some of which advertised in the Negro press, were deemed even graver threats to public order. After the 1906 race riot, several saloon licenses held by Jews were revoked, and a journalist suggested that those "who catered to negro trade and negro vice" were on an even lower social level than their customers.[11]

Unlike Harlem's Jewish merchants of a later period, Jewish Atlantans who catered to a predominantly black clientele lived in close proximity to their customers. In 1896 blacks were concentrated in four sections of the city: Mechanicsville, west of the Western and Atlantic tracks in the low area near the railroad shops; the neighborhoods farther west and south near Atlanta University and Spelman Seminary; Summer Hill, southeast of the business district between Martin and Hill streets; and Shermantown, which encompassed the bottom lands in the vicinity of Houston, Wheat, and Butler streets in the northeast quadrant of the city. Smaller pockets of blacks were to be found in the alleys of otherwise white neighborhoods and bore such descriptive appellations as Hell's Half Acre and Niggertown. (See fig. 11.)

Atlanta's Jews in 1896 resided in two distinct areas: the Germans, along the streets just south of the business district, and the Russians, in the vicinity of Decatur Street where most of them worked. Except for a few blocks of Orange and Crumley streets and Woodward Avenue, few Negroes lived among the prosperous southside Germans. Conditions were quite different in the Decatur Street area, where small numbers of blacks had settled prior to the arrival of the Russians. College Street and Edgewood Avenue formed the boundary between the ghetto and Shermantown, and blacks lived along Gilmer, Courtland, Butler, and Pratt streets. Negro and Jewish proprietors shared occupancy of several two-story buildings on Decatur Street, and twenty "negro tenements" (one room shacks) clustered in the alleys behind the Jewish homes on the block bordered by Decatur, Piedmont, Gilmer, and Butler streets. (See figs. 11 and 12.)

Between 1896 and 1911, Atlanta's Negro neighborhoods all expanded under the influence of immigration from the rural sections of the state, and the advance of the business district pushed the Germans even further south. The Decatur Street ghetto's Jewish and black populations also increased. The consequent congestion, closer proximity to blacks, expansion of the business district, and growth of prostitution were responsible for the migration of Russian Atlantans to the streets just across the Georgia Railroad tracks. There, on the fringe of Summer Hill, they remained until further intrusions of blacks sent them into the German neighborhood to the west. Russian Jewish grocers were an exception to this tendency to cluster near but not within Negro neighborhoods. They generally lived above their small stores located inside black districts, in some cases miles from the nearest concentration of Jews.

While relations between Jews and blacks were usually amicable, this was not always the case. One major cause of friction was the high prices often charged for inferior goods, the blame for which may be attributed to the high cost of credit and the cupidity of dishonest proprietors.[12] The ensuing resentment was sometimes exacerbated by high pressure salesmanship. Such was the case with Sam Clark, who was fined $5.75 in 1900 for cursing a Decatur Street used-clothing dealer. The young Negro maintained that his language was justified by the merchant's overly aggressive attempt to induce his patronage:

> Meester Aldyman, yer hain't 'quainted lak Judge Briles widde way folks does on Decatey Street, fer ef yer wus yer nebber would be axin' me erbout cussin' de dago what tried ter drag me inter his ole shop. Des dagos habs er way ob takin' hol' ob de niggers and jest er draggin' em inter de shop and makin' em buy dey ole close. . . . I mout er sed perflamed language, but de sitterwashun was de proper time for mos' enny gemmen ter cus er leetle.[13]

Residential proximity and commercial intercourse also produced situations in which Jews were victimized by black criminals. Joe Poolinski was stabbed in his Decatur Street used-clothing store in 1898, and four years later, Peters Street clothier Morris Greenblatt fatally shot a black man whom he allegedly caught stealing for a second time.[14] Saloonkeeper A. Smullyan and several of his customers were threatened by a knife-wielding Negro in 1903, and in 1907 two Jewish women were stabbed outside Grady Hospital. The following year, Jacob Hirsowitz, one of the leading members of the Russian community, was murdered by several Negroes who attempted to steal a revolver from his pawnshop.[15] Perhaps the most tragic incident was the 1912 murder of Aaron Morris, a recently arrived barber, who had come to the aid of his landlady who was being assaulted in her Gilmer Street home.[16] Crimes of a less serious variety were even more common.[17]

Although such incidents were exceptional, they doubtlessly affected the manner in which Jews viewed their black neighbors and

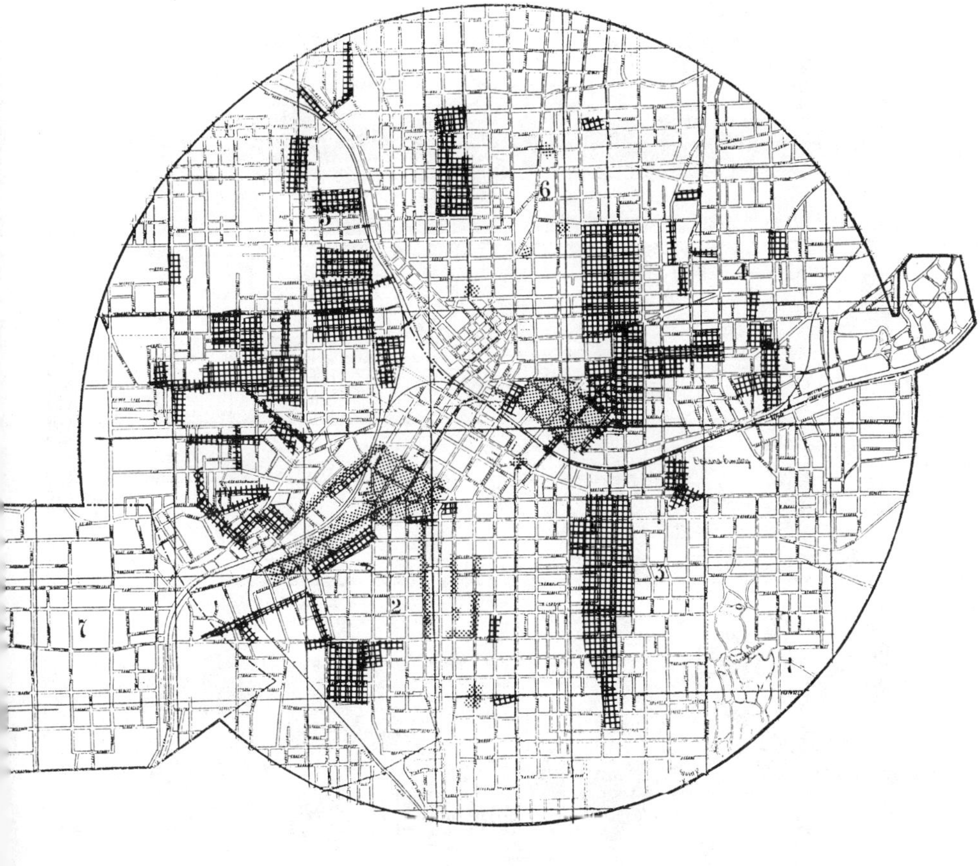

FIGURE 11. *Jewish and Black Residential Patterns, 1896.*

*Note:* Numbers signify wards.

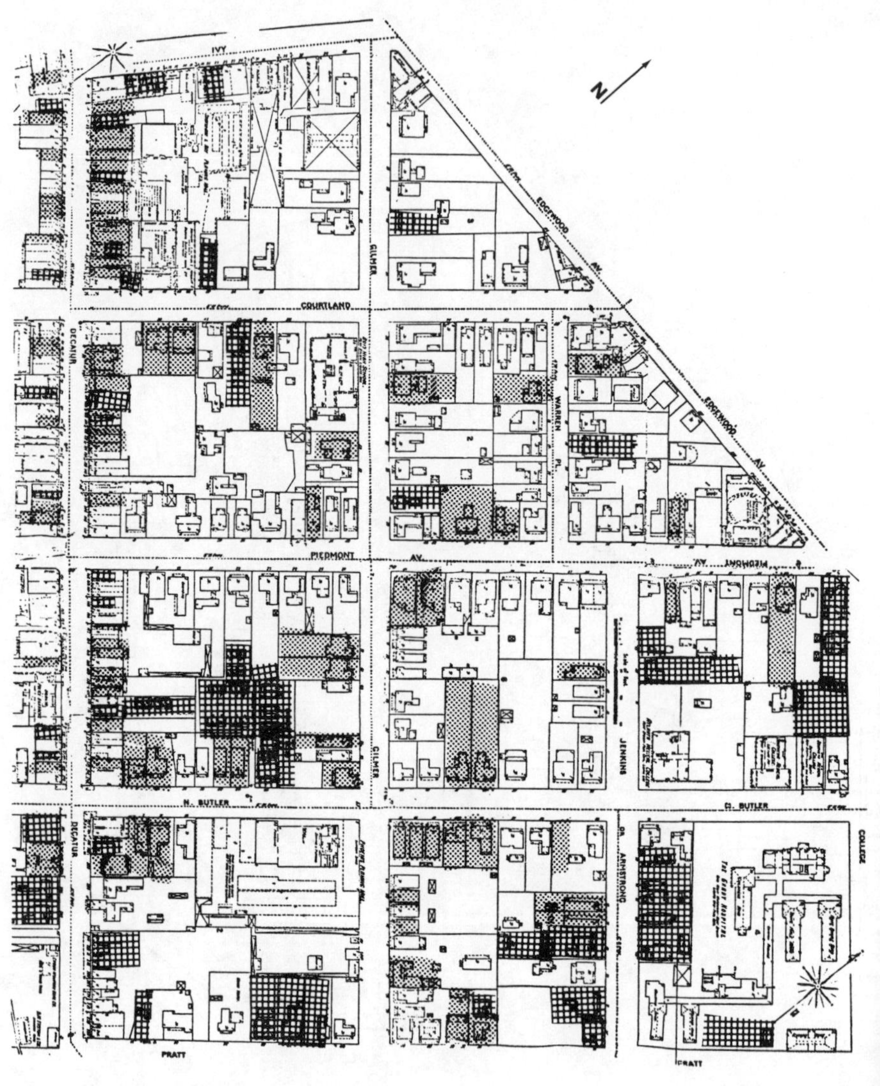


FIGURE 12. *Jewish and Black Occupancy in Decatur Street Area, 1896.*

Jewish Black

vice versa. Moreover, given the superficial level upon which they interacted and the Jews' ignorance of Negro history and culture, there seemed to be little that was ennobling about the black man's attributes. To Jews who respected piety, moderation, intellectual accomplishment, and material achievement, the Negro's seemingly loose sexual behavior, physicality, lawlessness, and improvidence made him the consummate Other. But if the Russian Jew was not predisposed to respect the Negro, his own recent experience with persecution enabled him to sympathize with the black man's plight. Young David Yampolsky, shocked by the Negroes' "terrible, slavish, oppressed condition"—worse than that of his brethren in Russia—described the 1906 race riot as a "pogrom on the blacks." Inclined toward socialism, Yampolsky regretted that his poor English prevented him from expressing solidarity with his black fellow proletarians.[18]

In general, the degree of sympathy which Jews had for blacks was inversely related to the amount of time the former had spent in the South. The process of americanization entailed adopting the normative traits of the white gentile majority, and these included negative attitudes toward blacks. Negrophobia made slower headway among the Russians, whose own recent experience with oppression militated against manifesting the more vicious forms of racism. Moreover, many were dependent upon black patronage and were relatively unconcerned with appearing "right" on the race question. However, Russian children who attended the city's segregated public schools were less immune to the corrosive influence of racial prejudice. When twelve-year-old Horace Mann Bond passed by a Jewish grocery in his neighborhood in 1916, the grocer's son chanted through the picket fence: "Nigger, Nigger, Nigger, Nigger." Rock-throwing fights between Negro and Jewish children also broke out occasionally, and a native of Poland recollects that he "heard the term 'nigger' used by Jewish sons of immigrant parents with the same venom and contempt as the term 'Zhid' was used in the old country."[19]

Members of the established Jewish community responded even less sympathetically to the condition of their black fellow citizens. By the turn of the century, nearly all of the former had either been born in the South or lived there for many years; even those who had been born abroad had neither experienced the kind of persecution nor been exposed to the radical ideologies which affected the refugees from Russia. The Germans tended to share the racial views of their gentile socioeconomic counterparts, and while this was primarily a consequence of assimilation, it was also related to the Germans' insecure status and desire for acceptance by their gentile peers.

At one extreme among the Germans was editor Frank Cohen of the *Jewish Sentiment.* A distinctly personal journalist not adverse to defying popular opinion, Cohen's pronouncements on the race question differed little from those of the *Atlanta Constitution* and did not necessarily reflect the views of his readers. When racial violence flared in North Carolina at the end of 1898, Cohen observed that "the laws of nature cannot be reversed by 'an act of Congress' and the white man is not only superior to the black man, but will assert his supremicy [*sic*] at the proper time and in the proper manner. . . ." Two weeks later he wrote:

> North Carolina has recently done herself proud while several other states have had dignified hanging bees—provoked by the usual cause. . . . Those negroes who conduct themselves properly, are respected and protected, but the lawless brute who violates the sanctity of the white man's home deserves death and usually receives it with electrical swiftness.

And again:

> The primary needs of the negro race is [*sic*] obedience to the law and recognition of the rights of others. . . . If law abiding and worthy, every opportunity will be accorded him short of social equality and this no self-respecting white man can endure. If the unmentionable crime against women is persisted in [,] mobs in the future will deal with him as they have in the past.

On two occasions the *Jewish Sentiment* condemned anti-Negro violence, but the exceptions confirm the rule. When "a negro desperado" allegedly murdered several New Orleans policemen and reprisals were made against innocent blacks, Cohen remarked that the murders "did not in the most remote manner licence whites to reck [*sic*] revenge upon the entire race." Similarly, the lynching of nine Negroes in a Georgia town was labeled a crime "without parallel or palliation" by the editor, who insisted that "there is but one provocation for lynch law." However, when such provocation presented itself in Columbus, Cohen congratulated the citizens of Columbus and Georgia "upon being forever rid of two such scoundrels as those negroes who were hung," and suggested that the governor had been too prompt in offering a reward for the capture of the mob's leaders.[20]

At the other end of the spectrum, probably more representative of popular Jewish opinion, were moderates whose support for white supremacy was tempered by a sense of paternalism and desire for racial harmony. Mrs. Victor Kriegshaber urged Atlantans to "take up the white man's burden" and establish boys clubs and summer camps for Negro youths, while Oscar Pappenheimer, wishing to distinguish between industrious and vagrant Negroes, suggested that all blacks be compelled to carry documents which would indicate their appearance, employment, abode, and prior conduct. In the wake of the 1906 race riot, David Marx was appointed a member of the Civic League, which endeavored to prevent a recurrence of the catastrophe. Two decades later, he became a leader in the Georgia Commission on Interracial Cooperation.[21]

On at least two occasions, other leaders of the Jewish community endorsed racial discrimination. Just prior to the construction of their new temple, the trustees of the Hebrew Benevolent Congregation decided in 1901 that their outmoded house of worship on Garnett and Forsyth streets should not be sold or rented to a black congregation. And the following year, the Jewish member of the Carnegie Library Board of Trustees voted to reject the petition of W. E. B. Du Bois and others that the library admit Negroes.[22]

While the Jew looked upon the Negro primarily as a customer and had almost no contact with blacks prior to settling in the South, blacks perceived Jews to be far more than mere purveyors of goods and services and were indirectly acquainted with them long before actual contact was made. Even the most unlettered knew of Moses, Joshua, David, Daniel, and Job, whose exploits provided the inspiration for innumerable spirituals and folk songs. The Negro identified strongly with the longing, suffering, and striving of the Old Testament Hebrews. Their bondage in Egypt, trek through the wilderness, conquest of the Promised Land, and punishment when they whored after false gods were highly relevant symbolic images for a people newly freed from slavery and struggling for equality. But however durable the analogy, it had its limits; when a local Negro informed members of his church that the Lord had appeared to him in a vision and revealed that Negroes were really Jews and therefore God's chosen people, he was run out of town.[22]

If the Old Testament predisposed the Negro to look upon the Jew with reverence, the New reminded him—as it did white Christians—that Jews were rebels against God's purpose. Recalling his childhood in Mississippi and Arkansas, novelist Richard Wright remarked that all of his neighbors hated Jews, not because Jewish merchants exploited them but because they had been taught at home and in Sunday School that Jews were Christ-killers. "To hold an attitude of antagonism or distrust toward Jews was bred in us from childhood" and manifested in folk ditties such as

Bloody Christ killers
Never trust a Jew
Bloody Christ killers
What won't a Jew do?

Similarly, an Atlanta reporter in 1875 heard an old woman sing,

I hear a rumblin' in de skies,
Jews, screws, de fi dum?
I hear a rumblin' in de skies,
Jews, screws, de fi dum.

When asked the meaning of the reference to Jews the woman replied: "Jews crucified him." Four decades later, young Horace Mann Bond, stung by the epithet of "Nigger," instantaneously retorted: "You Christ-killer!" As late as 1965, Bond suspected that the phrase had "hung imminent in the Atlanta air," a legacy of the Leo Frank case that had entered his subconscious and remained, waiting only for an opportune moment for release. "But of course the thought that Christ had been killed, and by the Jews, and that this little boy was such a one, may have had a more ancient basis in my-twelve-year-old mind than I can now bring myself to admit." Just as the Jews' acquisition of race prejudice was a by-product of the assimilative process, anti-Jewish prejudice was normative in a Christian society and provided blacks with a means of manifesting something they had in common with other Gentiles.[23]

Blacks could identify not only with the biblical Hebrews, but also with the Jews of the Diaspora. In an era of lynching and disfranchisement, local and national black spokesmen came to the defense of Alfred Dreyfus and expressed sympathy for the victims of Russian pogroms. These declarations of concern were motivated not only by genuine humanitarianism but also as a means of winning the support of Jews and other whites for their own cause by demonstrating the similarity between conditions in Russia and America. The failure of most whites to perceive any similarity led to black accusations of gross hypocrisy.[24] When, in the aftermath of the Bialystok pogrom, the U.S. Senate passed a resolution expressing the horror and sympathy of the American people, the editors of the local *Voice of the Negro* remarked: "With the Jews all lovers of justice are bound to sympathize. . . . But what right has the United States Senate to be horrified? . . . We are having here in America Kishinevs and Bialystoks every day." Similarly, when representatives of the Episcopal and Methodist churches declared their solidarity with oppressed Russian Jewry, Benjamin Jefferson Davis, editor of the *Atlanta Independent,* wrote: "We have but little patience in the statesmanship or religion that is so solicitous about saving the Jews of Russia, while the Negroes in their back yards . . . are dying and perishing for [want of] Christian help."[25]

The superior claim that the foreign-born seemed to exert on the American conscience reinforced an existing nativist strain in Negro thought. In his widely hailed 1895 Atlanta Exposition speech, Booker T. Washington urged the white South to "cast down your bucket where you are. . . . among the eight millions of Negroes whose habits you know," rather than look to whites of alien ways and dubious loyalties to bring prosperity to the region. Black nativism resulted principally from the apprehension that foreign laborers would take jobs away from native blacks. To combat this threat, Negro spokesmen endeavored to tap the wellspring of white xenophobia and readily distorted the characteristics of the New Immigrants. In "The Crocodile Tears of Inconsistency," a cartoonist for the *Voice of the Negro* depicted a teary-eyed Uncle Sam kneeling on top of a prostrate Negro (labeled "American born citizen") and reaching out to embrace highly stereotyped figures labeled "Nihilist," "Socialist," "Anarchist," and "Jew" who are being expelled from Germany, Italy, and Russia. "Why not offer the Negro at your door some of the plausible opportunities you are now painting for the foreigner," queried the *Atlanta Independent,* which went on to prophesy that immigration would have a harmful effect on racial and industrial tranquility.

> These foreigners will put the devil in the Negroes' heads and another menace will be added to our labor and race problem. . . . The white man will [then] be perfectly willing to exchange his overpaid anarchist laborer for his old, under-paid and half-fed Negro service [*sic*].

Even more outspoken was the *Voice of the Negro,* which ridiculed the notion of replacing the "sunniest-dispositioned, most patient, most law-abiding, the meekest and the best working people in the world" with "the scum of Europe."

> The men who are plotting this immigration scheme do not stop to think how, in filling the South with cheap labor from Europe, they would thrust wages down lower and lower; how the immigrants would come here with their anarchist ideas; how the Negroes and low laborers of Europe would clash at every point, and how the very integrity of the pure white South would be threatened by intermingling with this semi-white class of people. These immigrants would be a serious factor in any national crisis. Aliens always are.[26]

While the foregoing characterization of a "semi-white class of people" was a reference to Italians, the local Negro press frequently distinguished between the Jew and the white man. This resulted from a number of factors. The new Jewish immigrant had little conception of himself as a white man; his primary self-identification was as a Jew, and he probably found cause to make this clear to his Negro customers. Second, the Jew dealt with blacks in a more civil fashion than did native-born white Gentiles and was, in turn, perceived as an outsider by the dominant group. Finally, the Negro's habit of distinguishing between the Jew and the white man paralleled the Jew's tendency of differentiating between the *shvartze* (black) and the *goy* (Gentile).[27]

However real the cultural differences separating the immigrants from their native-born white neighbors, Jews were undeniably graced with the color of privilege, and in a society preoccupied with maintaining the subordinate status of blacks, differences between kinds of whites could usually be submerged. But not always. Italian tenant farmers were often ranked with nonwhite laboring groups, and one southern writer insisted that Jews were of Negro descent. There is no indication that the Caucasian standing of southern Jews was ever seriously challenged. However, when Booker T. Washington published an article characterizing Jews as nonwhite, it was perhaps with such an eventuality in mind that Isaac Mayer Wise sternly suggested "the Rev. Prof." needed "a lesson in primary ethnology."[28]

Despite the Jew's sometimes unethical business dealings, implication in deicide, status as an alien, and ambivalent racial standing, many articulate blacks saw in him a model for their own upward mobility. This sense of identification was not only rooted in the relevance of scriptural allegories and a shared experience of exile and rejection, but also in the initial low status of both groups in America. The fact that Jews seemed to overcome the disabilities of poverty and prejudice while blacks had not, suggested that prosperity and equality could be achieved by adopting certain "Jewish qualities." However, there remained considerable disagreement over the specific characteristics and strategies responsible for Jewish success.

Booker T. Washington, who between 1895 and his death in 1915 was the most influential Negro spokesman in America, aimed to improve the economic and moral condition of the Negro through a program of racial solidarity, industrial education, and economic nationalism. Though he looked forward to a day when blacks would eventually attain their constitutional rights, he couched his program in conciliatory terms, depreciated politics, denied interest in social equality, and stressed racial harmony. Washington believed that the black man would never achieve any great success in America until he learned to follow the Jew's example of unity, pride, and economic assertiveness. "The Jew that was once in about the same position as the Negro," observed the Alabama educator, "now has complete recognition because he has intertwined himself about America in a business and industrial sense." T. Thomas Fortune, a prominent northern proponent of Washington's philosophy of "uplift," stressed a similar need for the black man to emulate the Jew in "beating down opposition gradually by high character, great abilities in all directions, the accumulation of wealth and by sticking together."[29]

Washington's most articulate Atlanta supporter was Davis of the *Atlanta Independent,* a keen admirer of Jewish self-esteem, respect for law, and skill in business—qualities in which he believed blacks were woefully deficient. "The Jew is proud that he is a Jew," Davis observed, "and he teaches his children to love the Jews and have more pride in a Jew's achievement, and points to Jewish history as the highest possibility of the human family." Other nationalities do this too, though to a lesser degree, while "the Negro is the only race that has an element in it that is ashamed of itself." As a spokesman for Atlanta's nascent Negro middle-class, Davis was embarrassed and dismayed by the depredations of less orderly blacks, and pointed to the conduct of Jews as worthy of emulation.

> The Jew is known the world over as a good and law abiding citizen. . . . The Independent holds them up to all other citizens as a model. . . . It is so rare for a Jew to commit a crime and be brought into the courts for heinous ones, that when he does commit one, every reasonable doubt is in his favor. The Independent regrets that this is not true of the Negro folks. We are all too prone to commit crimes. . . .

Moreover, unlike the indolent Negro, Jews strove "to lift themselves above the conditions that invite the white man's prejudice" by founding and patronizing their own businesses. But while Davis was a staunch advocate of "race enterprises" and urged his readers to support Negro-owned establishments, his dependence upon Jewish advertising revenue restrained him from calling for a boycott against Jewish merchants.[30]

While most articulate blacks prior to 1915 endorsed Washington's essentially accommodationist program, others—notably W. E. B. Du Bois and Kelly Miller—vigorously dissented. They too recognized the value of racial pride and group solidarity in economic matters, but also came to the defense of liberal education and believed that without political rights blacks could not secure or maintain economic prosperity. Like Washington, they saw relevant parallels in the Jewish experience. Du Bois, who taught sociology at Atlanta University between 1897 and 1910, was an ardent admirer of Jewish philanthropy, political influence, and organizational vitality. Through their vast organizational network, the Jews have made themselves a "tremendous force for good and for uplift," remarked Du Bois. "Let black men look at them with admiration and emulate them."[31]

Midway between Washington's Tuskegee Machine and Du Bois's Niagara Movement was Atlanta's monthly *Voice of the Negro,* edited by J. W. E. Bowen and J. Max Barber. Unlike the Bookerite *Atlanta Independent,* the *Voice of the Negro* was open to divergent viewpoints and even published an article by Daniel Murray who insisted, in true

Bookerite fashion, that "prejudice cannot stand against self-interest. . . ."

> We have a lesson in the experience of our Jewish neighbors. I venture to say that the Negro is not more the object of dislike and prejudice than the Jew, and yet by shrewdly seeking to control all handicrafts and manufacturing processes, the Jew has forced prejudice to be silent in this country. . . .

But Bowen and Barber rejected the assumption that economic power alone would render blacks immune from bigotry. "It is [the Jews'] wealth and beautiful women that made them the object of cruel race prejudice," the editors declared. "In other words, wealth is valuable in its place, but it is not going to solve the race problem." Like Washington, they too admired Jewish industry, orderliness, thrift, passion for liberty, and ("barring financial transactions") morality, but what they esteemed most was the Jews' ability to become socially acceptable to white people without forfeiting their "racial integrity." This, they contended, disproved the Anglo-Saxon's belief that "every other race is fairly crazy to marry into his race."[32]

Black analogies with the Jewish experience were understandable, but also simplistic. Both Washington and his critics underestimated the depth of anti-Jewish prejudice and the reasons why Jews enjoyed greater success than blacks in America. Washington was furthest off the mark. Self-help and ethnic solidarity *had* improved the Jews' economic position and widened their influence, but at the expense of increased hostility from Gentiles. Du Bois and his followers recognized the insufficiency of economic power as a solution to the race problem. However, their adulation of Jewish zeal for education, institutional strength, and political influence contrasted with gentile white fears of these same Jewish predispositions. Though more muted than Negrophobia, anti-Semitism reached a peak in the United States during the first decade and a half of the twentieth century; to an increasing pattern of social discrimination were added restrictive policies in employment, housing, and college admission, and a belief that there existed a subversive international Jewish conspiracy. The Jews' adaptable cultural tradition was certainly responsible for much of the success that they achieved, but blacks would require more than mere will in order to undo the destructive effects of slavery on their history and culture. Moreover, in the South more than elsewhere, the fact that the Jews shared the color of privilege affected their performance. Even the most versatile leopard could not change its spots.

Analogies aside, black leaders still felt betrayed by the unwillingness of Jews to speak out against racism. When Isador Rayner, the Jewish U.S. Senator from Maryland, died in 1912, Benjamin Davis commented, "Though of a race itself beaten by stripes, he invoked upon his colored neighbor the terrors of Kishinev." Nor is there evidence to suggest that any of Atlanta's Jews desired a greater amelioration in the condition of blacks than would have been acceptable to the more enlightened upholders of white supremacy. This is not surprising, for aside from a small conservative elite whose interests generally coincided with those of the business community, Atlanta's Jews kept a low political profile. Only in the case of the prohibition, free silver, and Leo Frank controversies did Jews take the unpopular side of an emotionally charged question. In each instance, their interests were directly affected, and they found themselves singled out for criticism. Even as honorary white men, sharing the color of privilege, Jews were not free to speak their minds. More than anything else, support for white supremacy was the test of a true Southerner. It was perilous enough for a southern-born white Christian to challenge the prevailing system of race relations. For a Jew to have done so would have jeopardized the position of the entire Jewish community, especially at a time when the group's status was being undermined on other fronts.[33]

There was one occasion, however, when a Jew did ally himself with the interests of Atlanta's blacks only to meet with opposition from Benjamin Davis. In 1912 a northern Jew named Rhodes visited the Gate City to popularize a new secret order called the Knights of Moses and ostensibly dedicated to the political, industrial, and social advancement of the Negro race. Davis was not only suspicious of Rhodes's sincerity but also hostile to the very idea of a secret political order, something which might weaken the Georgia Republican Party and the Negro Odd Fellows—in both of which the editor played a leading role. "They may be honest," cautioned Davis, "but it is a little out of place for a Jew to spend his money and time, without some hope of financial return."[34]

On the whole, Atlanta's blacks enjoyed better relations with Jews than with native white Gentiles. Whatever hostilities were engendered by the cupidity of Jewish merchants, the depredations of black criminals, unfavorable stereotypes, and the effect of residential proximity were mitigated by mutual economic dependence, the Jews' sensitivity to the Negroes' condition, and the symbolic role which the Jew played in black eyes. But in 1913 a respected Jewish businessman was convicted of murder, largely on the testimony of a Negro, severely straining the relationship and forcing the Jews to question the immunitive properties of their white skin.

# 9

## *The Leo Frank Case*

The 1913 murder of fourteen-year-old Mary Phagan resulted in one of the great *cause célèbres* of the twentieth century and perhaps the most lurid manifestation of anti-Semitism in American history. Like the Sacco-Vanzetti, Scottsboro, and Rosenberg cases of later decades, what became known as the Leo Frank case was far more than a judicial proceeding. Mary's death channeled the fears and disillusionments of a society undergoing industrial transformation and rapid social change and projected these collective resentments onto a northern Jewish industrialist who had settled in Atlanta only six years earlier.[1]

Except for the fact that Leo Frank was the superintendent of the factory in which Mary Phagan worked, the two inhabited almost different worlds. The son of moderately well-to-do German Jewish parents, Frank received a middle-class upbringing in Brooklyn and attended Pratt Institute and Cornell University before accepting the invitation of his uncle, Moses Frank, to settle in Atlanta and superintend the operations of the newly established National Pencil Company. In 1910 he married into the wealthy and established Selig family and two years later was elected president of the B'nai B'rith Gate City Lodge. Like most other Jews of his class, he resided on the fashionable southside, belonged to the Temple and the Standard Club, was an enthusiastic bridge player, and had few material cares.[2]

The daughter of a dispossessed tenant farmer, Mary Phagan had none of Frank's advantages. Together with her parents and five brothers and sisters, she lived in a three-room cabin in Bellwood, a mill village on the outskirts of Atlanta. Her father worked fourteen hours a day as a "linthead," and rather than accept the niggardly five cents an hour which the cotton mill paid child labor, Mary found more remunerative and salubrious employment at the National Pencil Company.[3]

The world of Mary Phagan was one with which neither Atlanta's prosperous German Jews nor the Gentiles with whom they associated had much experience. For them, Atlanta's continued growth had meant increased prosperity and sophistication; but for the great majority, it decreed frustration and bewilderment. Among leading southern metropolises, only Birmingham outpaced Atlanta's 93 percent increase in population between 1900 and 1913. Most of the newcomers exchanged rural squalor for urban blight. Educational, recreational, police, and other public services failed to expand quickly enough to meet the needs of the burgeoning population, half of whom lived on streets without water mains and more than a third without sewers. Affluent Atlantans were embarrassed, but not overly perturbed, by the fact that the city's crime and death rates were among the highest in the nation and that the cost of living was the second highest.[4]

Lured to Atlanta by the prospect of employment in the growing regional center, the uprooted tenant farmers were ill-prepared for the vicissitudes of urban existence. Their Baptist and Methodist ministers continued to preach the godliness of the agrarian way of life and inveigh against the wickedness of the city. Inherently hostile to innovation, they were deeply suspicious of the New South leaders who endeavored to industrialize the region. Factory work for women was regarded with especial horror, for it not only altered the woman's traditional role but also brought wives and children into intimate association with strange men and compromised the virility of the male breadwinner. Always acutely conscious of their Anglo-Saxon heritage, the new urbanites grew more xenophobic after 1890 and viewed outsiders as threats to the purity of southern blood and values. Meanwhile, the ever ambivalent religious and economic image of the Jew became increasingly negative. Not only were Jews the largest foreign-born group in both Georgia and its capital city, but more than any other people, they personified the subversive values of the emerging urban, commercial, and industrial age.[5]

The brutal murder of a factory girl in a factory made good copy, and in their competition for new readers, Atlanta's three daily newspapers exploited the slaying for all it was worth. Local journalists resorted to sensationalism, slander, and misrepresentation in portraying an archetypical crime: "the young virgin violated in the wood by the dark assailant, the primordial fear of the American South." The press, public, and mayor challenged the inefficient and corrupt police force to apprehend quickly the killer, and under intense pressure, seven men were arrested, including Leo Frank. Despite the lack of incriminating evidence, the fact that Frank was a Yankee Jew and also the last person to admit having seen Mary Phagan alive made him a prime suspect. Because the police committed themselves prematurely to proving Frank's guilt, it became both psychologically difficult and politically inexpedient for them to alter their assessment later when contrary evidence was uncovered.[6]

During the two months between his indictment on May 24 and the commencement of the trial, rumors circulated throughout the city that Frank was a sexual pervert, that he had sired numerous children out of wedlock, that he had killed another wife in Brooklyn, and that Judaism condoned the violation of gentile women. The *Constitution* assumed Frank's guilt from the moment of his arrest, and while the *Journal* and the *Georgian* took a more judicious view, their sensationalist coverage had undesirable consequences. Meanwhile, Solicitor-General Hugh M. Dorsey took charge of the state's case. A politically ambitious lawyer who had recently lost several important cases, Dorsey viewed the pending trial as a vehicle for his own advancement. With this end in mind, the solicitor manufactured evidence to support the contentions of the prosecution and suppressed other material which might have exonerated the accused. Frank's attorneys were confident of an acquittal and naively assumed that they were handling a routine murder case. They completely misjudged both Dorsey's unscrupulousness and the amount of prejudice against their client.[7]

The prosecution attempted to prove that Mary had been murdered in the workroom across from Frank's office, that Frank had the opportunity to kill her, that he had previously acted in a familiar manner with other female employees, and that he had a reputation for lascivious behavior. Except for the testimony of Jim Conley, the pencil factory's Negro sweeper, the evidence against Frank was entirely circumstantial. But Conley, who had served several jail terms for petty thievery and been fined numerous times for disorderly conduct, not only introduced the damning charge of sexual perversity but also claimed to have assisted Frank in carrying Mary's body to the coal cellar where it was later found. In rebuttal the defense called over two hundred witnesses who vouched for Frank's good character and testified that he had conducted himself in his usual manner on the day of the murder and was not alone long enough to commit the crime. However, the defense attorneys failed to crack Conley and overlooked the significance of crucial evidence which might have vindicated their client.[8]

The jury needed less than four hours to find Frank guilty. Outside the courthouse, a mob of over three thousand greeted the verdict with shouts of joy, and an excited public tripled the number of telephone calls made on any previous day in the city's history. The general antipathy against Frank may well have influenced the jurors. For a month they had passed through angry crowds and heard epithets such as "The Jew is the synagogue of Satan," "Crack that Jew's neck," and were themselves threatened with lynching if they failed to "hang that 'damned sheeny.' " The judge and the defense attorneys were also warned that they would not leave the courtroom alive if Frank was turned loose.[9]

The impassioned trial "opened a seemingly impassable chasm between the people of the Jewish race and the Gentiles," reported the *Macon Daily Telegraph* the day after Frank was sentenced to hang.

> It has broken friendships of years, has divided the races, and brought about bitterness deeply regretted by all factions. The friends who rallied to the defense of Leo Frank feel that racial prejudice has much to do with the verdict. They are convinced that Frank was not prosecuted but persecuted. They refuse to believe he has had a fair trial.

The *Constitution* and the *Journal* attempted to counteract the anti-Semitism that they had inadvertently kindled by printing laudatory editorials concerning Jewish generosity and accomplishments, but to little avail. As the *Southern Ruralist* observed, under normal circumstances Atlanta's Jews and Gentiles lived together "in perfect harmony," but when their relationship was subjected to sudden strain, "dormant prejudice flares up with explosive force."

> Let anyone who doubts the significance of this fact—or that prejudice has played an important part in this case—board an Atlanta street car filled with home-going working people. . . . Not a week ago we personally heard this remark under such circumstances: "If the Court don't hang that *damned Jew,* we will."[10]

Almost immediately after the verdict was announced, the defense initiated a round of appeals which lasted nearly two years. The state constitution stipulated that appeals in a capital case could only be based on errors in law and that newly uncovered evidence could not be considered. Therefore, in their hearing before trial judge Leonard Roan, Frank's attorneys stressed procedural irregularities, the alleged prejudice of two of the jurors, and possible intimidation of the jury by the mob. They argued that Conley's testimony regarding Frank's supposed sexual perversion should never have been permitted and that the verdict was not supported by the evidence. In October, Roan denied the appeal but expressed personal reservations concerning Frank's guilt. The following month the defense presented similar arguments before the Georgia Supreme Court, which upheld the verdict by a vote of 4 to 2. Still undaunted, Frank's attorneys filed an extraordinary motion for a new trial based upon the discovery of new evidence and the recantation of testimony by several key prosecution witnesses. When their appeal was rejected, the defense appealed unsuccessfully to the United States Supreme Court, first for a writ of error and then for a writ of habeas corpus. With all court action exhausted, Frank's attorneys petitioned the prison commission and then the governor for clemency.[11]

Although the Phagan murder and Frank trial had received extensive coverage in the Georgia press, not until the spring of 1914 did the case attract national attention. In September 1913 Rabbi David Marx and several other local Jews appealed for assistance to Louis Marshall, the respected constitutional lawyer who was president of the American Jewish Committee. Marshall and the AJC leadership agreed with their Atlanta correspondents that sensationalist publicity and anti-Semitism had been responsible for the verdict, but also recognized southern sensitivity to outside interference and did not wish to exacerbate Frank's difficulties by imprudent meddling. Therefore, Marshall and his associates resolved to take no official action, but rather to endeavor as individuals to persuade potentially sympathetic journalists and public figures of Frank's innocence. By the middle of 1914, newspapers throughout the country, including several in the South, were urging that Frank be given a new trial, while a number of wealthy and influential men were contributing substantial amounts of money to the defense fund. Louis Marshall himself coordinated the legal strategy, and Albert D. Lasker, the

Chicago advertising genius, used his considerable talents to create a climate of opinion conducive to granting a new trial.[12]

A fact that occurred to many at the time was that Leo Frank may have been the only white man in Georgia ever convicted of a capital offense largely upon the testimony of a Negro. Leonard Dinnerstein has argued that "resentment against a symbol of alien industrialism took precedence over the usual Negro prejudice," and Harry Golden has suggested that Atlantans saw Conley as someone who *"belonged"* to them testifying against an outsider. While neither of these explanations is entirely satisfactory, the willingness of Southerners to take the word of a Negro with a criminal record over that of a Jew with an unblemished reputation indicates the depth of their prejudice against Frank. Thirty years after Mary Phagan's death, her former pastor recalled:

> My feelings, upon the arrest of the old negro nightwatchman, were to the effect that this one old negro would be poor atonement for the life of this innocent girl. But, when on the next day the police arrested a Jew, and a Yankee Jew, at that, all the inborn prejudice against Jews rose up in a feeling of satisfaction, that here would be a victim worthy to pay for the crime.[13]

If Frank was innocent, Conley had to be guilty, and even as the superintendent's supporters criticized those who spoke of the "damned Jew," they characterized the sweeper as a "black monster." "No white man killed Mary Phagan," Frank declared one week after his indictment, "It's a negro's crime through and through." Defense attorney Luther Rosser referred to Conley as a "dirty, filthy, black, drunken, lying nigger," and even Louis Marshall—who later joined the NAACP's board of directors—spoke privately of the "degenerate negro, of criminal antecedents." Similarly, in their effort to help Frank and incriminate his chief accuser, the major metropolitan dailies often employed the crudest anti-Negro stereotypes. To black editors, it appeared that whites were again looking for a Negro scapegoat, and while Conley was not made into a hero by the black press, his story was accepted.[14]

Interestingly, the only Negro editor who rejected the sweeper's tale and endorsed Frank's appeal for a new trial was Benjamin Davis of the *Atlanta Independent.* Davis, who in some ways was more of a class man than a race man, maintained that Frank had been the victim of anti-Jewish prejudice and insisted that Conley was unworthy of belief.

> Under ordinary circumstances the public conscience is such that it is impossible to convict a white man upon the testimony of a Negro unsupported, and it is easily within the purview of reason that a native white man would not have been convicted upon the evidence of a discreditable Negro like Jim Conley. . . . His evidence is not sufficient to take the life of an individual.

However, many of Davis's readers were critical of this breech of race unity, and lower-class blacks regarded the sweeper as a hero. "Well, boss, dem niggers down on Decatur Street, day ain't talken of nothing but Jim Conley," a bootblack confided to a reporter. "He got de best of de smartest of 'um. Nobody can fool er nigger like Jim!"[15]

While Negroes resented the attempt of Frank's supporters to incriminate Conley, whites interpreted other elements of the press campaign as an attack on Georgia justice. Many Georgians wondered whether the clamor for a new trial would have been as great had the defendant been a Gentile, and some suspected that Jews had purchased the pro-Frank editorials and bribed prosecution witnesses to repudiate their original testimony.

Those outraged by the specter of outside influence and alien money found their spokesman in Tom Watson. The embittered ex-Populist had an immense following among rural Georgians, and though he had recklessly denounced Catholics for more than a decade, not until 1914 did he find cause to vilify the Jews. Watson entered the controversy obliquely. In March 1914 the *Atlanta Journal,* which was generally recognized as U.S. Senator Hoke Smith's organ, demanded that Frank be given a new trial and asserted that the execution of the condemned prisoner would be judicial murder. Watson was opposed to Smith's reelection and, misinterpreting the *Journal*'s editorial as an attempt to drag the Frank case into politics, lashed back at his political adversary. However, readers of Watson's *Jeffersonian* responded more positively to the attack on Frank, and by April Watson was vituperatively assailing the Jew without any reference to Smith or the *Journal.* Playing upon the fears, hatreds, and prejudices of his readers, he asked two questions which had occurred to other Georgians: "Does a Jew expect extraordinary favors and immunities *because* of his race?" and "Who is paying for all this?" "Here we have the typical young libertine Jew," he wrote, "who . . . [has] an utter contempt for the law, and a ravenous appetite for the forbidden fruit—*a lustful eagerness enhanced by the racial novelty of the girls of the uncircumcised.*" Former governor Joseph E. Brown, Jr., soon added his considerable support to those calling for Frank's blood. "Are we to understand that anybody except a Jew can be punished for crime?" he queried. "If so, Georgia will soon become the exploiting ground for every Jew who is criminally inclined."[16]

The debate escalated toward the end of 1914 as Frank's appeals were rejected by the Georgia courts and the prospects in the federal courts looked uncertain. As a last resort, Frank petitioned the Georgia Prison Commission and Governor John M. Slaton for clemency, and his supporters endeavored to rally public opinion. The *Atlanta Journal,* the *Atlanta Georgian,* and the *North Georgia Citizen* were among the scores of newspapers which urged the commutation of Frank's sentence to life imprisonment. In addition to the press campaign, efforts were made to induce distinguished Gentiles to come to the condemned man's aid. Jane Addams, the president of the University of Chicago, nine governors, seven senators (including Georgia's Thomas Hardwick), scores of congressmen, and six state legislatures urged commutation, while more than one million persons (ten thousand of them Georgians) signed petitions on Frank's behalf. The opponents of clemency were also busy. As Watson's crusade against the "jewpervert" entered high gear, the *Jeffersonian*'s circulation tripled to 87,000, and the angry editor warned that commutation would result in *"the bloodiest riot ever known in the history of the South."* In response to his call, anticommutation rallies were held throughout the state, and in Atlanta mass meetings occurred almost every day during the first three weeks of June.[17]

When the prison commission, meeting within hearing distance of the demonstrations, rejected Frank's petition by a vote of 2 to 1, the ultimate decision fell to outgoing Governor Slaton. Slaton had been one of the most popular governors in Georgia history, and though narrowly defeated in his bid for the Democratic senatorial nomination, it was widely acknowledged that he would succeed on his next try if he let Frank hang. Rather than bow to expediency, Slaton immersed himself in the record and recognized the significance of important evidence which had been overlooked by the defense. Convinced that Frank was innocent, the governor commuted his sentence to life imprisonment and confided to friends that a full pardon would undoubtedly be forthcoming as soon as the public could view the facts objectively. A ten-thousand-word review of the evidence accompanied the release of the order.[18]

Although most newspapers approved Slaton's action, commutation engendered violent protest in Georgia. Throughout the state, mobs burned the governor in effigy, and in Mary Phagan's hometown of Marietta, he was denounced as "King of the Jews and Georgia's Traitor Forever." A mob of several thousand men armed with guns and dynamite marched on Slaton's home just north of Atlanta but were repulsed by the state militia. Threatened with lynching, Slaton left Georgia at the end of June and did not return until after World War I. Jews, too, received their share of abuse. In La Grange a mass meeting resolved that the Jews of Georgia should either deny the charge that they had been subjected to "race hatred" or be encouraged to seek "more congenial climes." The Jews of Canton were threatened with "summary vengeance" if they failed to quit town within twenty-four hours, and the Marietta Vigilance Committee warned the community's Jewish merchants to close their businesses and depart by the end of the week. Jewish merchants in Clark County were boycotted and a correspondent proudly informed Tom Watson that his neighbors would make sure

> that the vast slush fund given by the Jews all over Georgia to defeat the ends of justice, and make a joke and laughing matter of Georgia people and Georgia laws, will loose [*sic*] many times more than they gave for the cause of saving the neck of Leo Frank. . . . All other Jews in any kind of business in Athens are feeling the coldness and antagonism they have wrought. . . .[19]

For Frank, the consequences of commutation were fatal. Eight weeks after he was transferred to the state prison farm at Milledgeville, he was abducted by twenty-five men who styled themselves the Knights of Mary Phagan and early the next morning was hanged from a massive oak not far from Mary's birthplace in Marietta. Although their identities were known, none of the members of the lynching party was ever brought to justice.[20]

The turmoil engendered by the Leo Frank case affected the Jews of Atlanta more than those of any other community. Harry Golden has written that initially, with the exceptions of Rabbi Marx, attorneys Leonard and Herbert Haas, and the accused man's family, Jewish

Atlantans "felt no sympathy" for Frank, who in being implicated in a heinous crime, compromised the community's security. According to Golden, not until Tom Watson commenced his crusade and thousands of Gentiles rallied to Frank's side did local Jews join the fight.[21] But, on the contrary, while they recognized the delicacy of the situation, Atlanta's Jews early demonstrated their solidarity with Frank. The day after his arrest, several—including Solicitor Dorsey's law partner, Arthur Heyman—publicly protested his detention and characterized him as "a clean-cut manly man, with a real zeal for doing good for others. . . . The very idea that he could be implicated in this horrible affair is simply preposterous." Although Frank had lived in Atlanta for only six years, his leadership of the B'nai B'rith lodge provided him with a wide range of acquaintances and his cell was usually crowded with friends and well-wishers. Dozens of Jewish businessmen, including several Russians, testified on his behalf, thereby exposing themselves to possible economic retaliation. Even two Levantine immigrants signed affidavits supporting the contentions of the defense. Moreover, not long after the jury returned a verdict of guilty, the imprisoned Frank was unanimously reelected president of the Gate City Lodge—an expression of confidence in his innocence which former governor Brown termed an open defiance of the state and its laws.[22]

While the intermittent outbursts of anti-Semitism never imperiled their physical security, Jewish Atlantans were sufficiently apprehensive that editor Albert Hershkowitz of the *American Jewish Review* could rhetorically inquire whether they were embarrassed to read a Jewish newspaper on the streetcar. The Russians, who accepted anti-Semitism as a fact of life and had less contact with Gentiles, were less affected by the manifestations of prejudice than were the acculturated Germans who became acutely self-conscious and endeavored to maintain a low profile. Anxious not to lend credence to the charge that "Jews held a Jew above the law," none of the communal agencies (the Federation, the Alliance, and the congregations) commented on the merits of the case, though their leaders labored in an unofficial capacity on Frank's behalf. Aware of southern sensitivity to outside criticism, local Jews attempted unsuccessfully to restrain well-intentioned but ill-advised northern observations concerning Georgia justice and anti-Semitism.[23] For similar reasons, the *American Jewish Review* never explicitly affirmed Frank's innocence, but instead repeatedly expressed doubt that he was guilty and reprinted the more strongly worded editorials of other journals.[24]

In March 1914 shortly after Tom Watson began his crusade, four local Jewish attorneys organized the Civic Educational League. The founders hoped to bolster the community's security and avoid any future judicial travesty by raising the Jews' civic consciousness and encouraging them to fulfill previously neglected obligations to petition for citizenship, vote, serve on juries, and seek public office. Although the League obliquely worked for Frank's vindication, its leaders carefully avoided making declarations which might antagonize their gentile neighbors. "It is not for us as citizens of Georgia to impugn any judge who has passed on this case, nor should we attribute any ignoble motive to a single juror or a somewhat zealous prosecution," asserted Leo Grossman before a meeting of six hundred members. "Whatever prejudice exists is mostly in our imagination, and to call attention to it is to encourage it. . . . [As] Georgians we must protect our institutions, our courts and judges from unfair criticism and abuse."[25]

Despite the League's failure to increase substantially Jewish political influence or assist Leo Frank, it became the only nonphilanthropic organization to include all members of the community,

> from the ultra-orthodox to the extreme radical, from the strictly pious worshipers of the old Synagogue to the most liberal wing of the reformed Temple, the street vendor and the prosperous looking gentleman of the upper spheres—all were there, side by side, engaged in friendly discussion of the subject before them.[26]

Declarations of unity to the contrary, the solidarity created by Watson's tirades was short-lived. In the depths of their hearts, the Germans suspected that the Russians had been indirectly responsible for the growth of anti-Jewish prejudice. When, in the emotionally charged aftermath of the Frank lynching, David Marx alluded to these suspicions in an address to the League, Leon Eplan denounced the rabbi in an "incendiary speech," which in turn led to Eplan's resignation as vice-president of the Federation of Jewish Charities.[27]

The years 1913 to 1915 were not a time of unremitting trauma for Atlanta's Jews. The shock and apprehension engendered by Frank's arrest and conviction subsided over the next few months until revived by the *Jeffersonian's* attacks the following spring. The summer hiatus brought a relaxation of tension, but the judicial proceedings during the autumn and winter of 1914–15 led to a resumption of the anti-Semitic campaign, which intensified as the decision over commutation drew near. Immediately after Slaton issued his controversial order, a hostile mob gathered at the state capitol, and Jews were uncertain whether the mob was going to march on the governor's mansion or invade the southside Jewish district. The sheriff warned Jewish leaders of an incipient riot and authorized some of them to carry firearms. Harry Golden has written that all the Jewish businessmen closed shop, locked their homes, and checked into hotels, most remaining for several days. However, while some Jews undoubtedly preferred the safety of hotel rooms and a few sent their families out of the state, there was no dramatic exodus or panic. The Jews were frightened, but most went about their business as usual and no serious incidents occurred.[28]

The problem of determining precisely how the Jewish community was affected is complicated by attempts of the local press to discredit reports of anti-Semitism and the tendency of northern journals, few of whom had correspondents on the scene, to exaggerate what occurred. One Anglo-Jewish newspaper even alleged that a pogromlike atmosphere had prevailed: grocers refusing to deliver goods to Jews, Jewish children being beaten on the streets, and nine-tenths of the Jewish businessmen on the verge of leaving the city. In contrast, the *American Jewish Review* acknowledged that there had been acts of anti-Semitism, but asserted that their magnitude had been grossly exaggerated. The one indisputable manifestation of hostility was the attempted boycott of Jewish merchants. Thousands of Atlantans received cards which read:

> Carry me in your purse. Stop and think. Before you spend your money, shall it go to a fund to protect murderers, to buy Governors? Stop and think. Now is the time to show your true colors; to show your true American blood. Is it streaked. Can't you buy clothing from an American? Can't you buy the necessities of life from an American? American gentiles, it is up to you. This little card is only a little ant hill to start with. Help it grow into a mountain.

Fortunately, the boycott was less effective in Atlanta than in the countryside. No demonstrations against the Jewish community accompanied the lynching of Frank seven weeks later.[29]

An unofficial referendum on the Frank case was held at the end of 1915, when the sudden death of the second ward councilman-elect resulted in the nomination of two candidates to fill his seat: Jewish manufacturer Joseph Loewus and railway conductor Oscar H. Williamson. Alluding to recent events, Loewus campaigned on the slogan of "peace and harmony" and claimed that a vote for him would be a repudiation of the "fanaticism . . . which has libelled the good name of our city." Williamson, capitalizing on the resentment of "Jew money," made an issue of Loewus's wealth, and though the conductor solicited support from "men of all nationalities," he would not do so "at the sacrifice of principle." Given the public temper, the results of the balloting surprised few Atlantans: Williamson, whose job required frequent absences from the city, received twice as many votes as his Jewish opponent and carried all but one ward. Not until the thirties would an Atlanta Jew again run for office.[30]

At almost the same moment that Loewus was defeated, Victor Kriegshaber, the Jewish community's foremost lay leader, was elected president of the Atlanta Chamber of Commerce. The *New York Times,* which had earlier been a strong critic of Georgia justice, cited Kriegshaber's election as conclusive proof that Atlantans felt no antagonism toward Jews. What the *Times* failed to appreciate was that while the Chamber's members may have been horrified by the murder of the pencil company superintendent, their sentiments were not shared by most local residents. Nor were Atlanta's leading businessmen willing to deprive themselves of the services of a city builder like Kriegshaber simply because he was a Jew. Electing him to membership in their social clubs remained a different matter.[31]

During the quarter-century preceeding the Frank case, the once highly secure position of Atlanta's Jews underwent steady erosion. Jewish political candidates received dwindling support at the polls; the emotion-laden free silver and prohibition controversies left a legacy of bitterness and suspicion; the public schools were subjected to sectarian influence; growing social discrimination isolated the Jews from their neighbors; Judaism lost much of its legitimacy in the eyes of evangelical Protestants; uncomplimentary references to Jewish economic activity became more frequent; and the Jews were increasingly burlesqued in local theaters. Meanwhile, the once relatively homogeneous Jewish community was beset by internal religious and ethnic divisions.

Though the Frank case would have been impossible three decades earlier, it would be erroneous to project a sense of inevitability on the events of 1913 to 1915. Had Frank been a merchant and scion of one of Atlanta's established Jewish families, rather than an industrialist, an employer of underpaid child labor, and a recent arrival from the North, it is unlikely that he would have been subjected to the calumny which eventually took his life. But the fact that Frank's Jewishness was held against him and that the antipathy toward him was readily transferred to the Jewish collectivity demonstrated the vulnerability of Atlanta's Jews.

For several decades the Frank case hung like a threatening cloud over the Jewish community, confirmation that economic success was no protection against bigotry. Ten years after the Phagan murder a Canadian journalist working for the *Constitution* uncovered new evidence documenting Frank's innocence, but prominent Atlanta Jews, fearing repercussions, persuaded the editors to suppress the material. And when Warner Brothers in 1937 released a film dealing with the Frank case, Jewish leaders successfully petitioned the distributors not to show it in Atlanta. Five years later, Rabbi Marx refused a Jewish graduate student permission to examine Marx's records of the case, claiming that further public discussion would only stir up trouble. Even in the 1960s, Harry Golden encountered some Jewish opposition to his research.[32]

Nor were the aftereffects confined to the local Jewish community. The anti-Semitism generated by the trial gave final impetus to the establishment of the Anti-Defamation League, and the Knights of Mary Phagan provided the nucleus for a new organization of a different sort: the revived Ku Klux Klan. Both Hugh Dorsey and Tom Watson reaped political rewards for their roles in the case. In 1916 the popular solicitor-general was overwhelmingly elected to the first of two terms as governor, and in 1920 the vituperative ex-Populist won election to the U.S. Senate. Both died in their beds.[33]

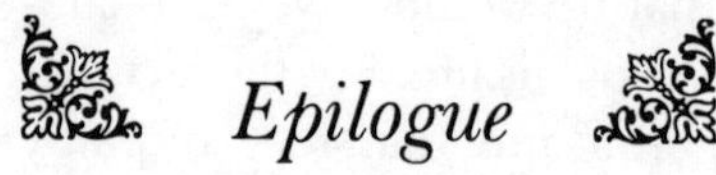

# Epilogue

## From Fragmentation to Integration

Atlanta changed markedly during the six decades following the Leo Frank case, fulfilling the dreams of her most sanguine boosters. Except for the depressed 1930s, the population grew unabated, from 155,000 in 1910, to 331,000 in 1950, and nearly one-half million in 1970. Unlike many older cities which could accommodate new residents within their tightly sealed borders only by expanding skywards, Atlanta spread out over the north Georgia hills, increasing from 26 to 131 square miles, and providing the core of a five-county metropolitan area with a population of 1,400,000.

Population growth contributed to a booming construction industry, which in turn stimulated other sectors of the economy. Local merchants accounted for one-eighth of the South's total wholesale sales, and more than a thousand manufacturing plants produced steel, paper, chemicals, furniture, fertilizers, candy, textiles, and processed foods. Of the nation's five hundred leading industrial corporations, over 80 percent had operations in Atlanta, and the city had one of the lowest unemployment rates in the country. The railroad network which had made the Gate City the transportation hub of the Southeast continued to function but was increasingly complemented by an elaborate system of interstate highways and the nation's second-busiest airport. Blessed with major league baseball, football, basketball, and hockey teams, Atlanta in the 1970s exerted a lure that could be matched by few other cities.

On a more subtle level, Atlanta changed from a crude and materialistic overgrown town into a sophisticated and cosmopolitan metropolis with a respected art museum, an accomplished symphony orchestra, a futuristic skyline, and even a black mayor. The difficult transition from being one of the most segregated communities in the nation into what longtime Mayor William B. Hartsfield called "the city too busy to hate" was accomplished under the progressive, if paternalistic, guidance of a powerful coalition of political, media, and business leaders. It is significant that during the interim between the electoral defeat of the "white power structure" in 1969 and the ascendency of Atlanta's black majority in 1973, City Hall was presided over by a Jewish mayor, Sam Massell, Jr.

The Jews of Atlanta, no less than their neighbors, share in the city's material and cultural development. Like Gentiles, Jews continue to be drawn to the Gate City, but they now arrive carrying attaché cases rather than peddler's packs, and are mostly native-born professionals, managers, and technicians, instead of marginal immigrant traders. From 4,000 in 1910, the Jewish population rose to 10,000 in 1948, 16,500 in 1968, and 21,000 in 1976. In addition to the forces which affected the lives of all Atlantans, the internal dynamics of the Jewish community were transformed by the federal restriction of immigration during the 1920s, the Holocaust of the Second World War, and the creation of the State of Israel in 1948.

At the time of Leo Frank's death, the Jewish community was deeply divided along ethnic lines. Although a handful of Russians belonged to the Temple, and the German and Russian leaders had for several years worked together on the boards of the Federation of Jewish Charities and the Jewish Educational Alliance, there was little social contact. Even the more affluent and assimilated Russians were barred from the precincts of the Standard Club, "intermarriage" was rare, and the newly arrived Sephardim were almost completely isolated from the rest of the Jewish community.

Six decades later such barriers are all but forgotten. A majority of the members of both the Standard Club and the Temple are of Russian descent, and hardly anyone is concerned whether a prospective son-in-law had Yiddish-speaking grandparents or German-speaking great-grandparents. During the past fifteen years, even Congregation Or Ve Shalom has lost its solidly Levantine character as a result of marriages with Ashkenazim, and Sephardim have joined the ranks of the communal leadership.

The changes occurred slowly. During the 1920s and 1930s, the legacy of the Leo Frank case, the resurrection of the Ku Klux Klan, and especially the federal restriction of immigration combined to limit the southward flow of recently arrived East European and

Levantine Jews. As Atlanta's Russians and, to a much lesser extent, Sephardim steadily accommodated themselves to local conditions, the economic and cultural gap between immigrant and native communities narrowed. After the Great Depression damaged the fortunes, if not the pedigrees, of many of the more established families, the social barriers also began to fall. The real watershed came, however, with the rise of Hitler and the onslaught of World War II. Now it was German-Jewish refugees who were arriving in Atlanta destitute, bewildered, and in need of social services. Soon the entire community—German, Russian, and Levantine—would share the collective agony of the Holocaust.

The trauma of the Holocaust unified the Jewish community, but the postwar creation of the State of Israel threatened to disrupt the fragile rapprochement. Zionism had the support of only a small minority of Atlanta Jews in 1915, almost all of them of East European descent, while the Reform community was steadfastly opposed to Jewish nationalism. During the next three decades, as a result of the Balfour Declaration, Jewish achievements in Palestine, and especially the post-Holocaust refugee problem, most Atlanta Jews slowly came to recognize the feasibility and desirability of Jewish statehood. But Rabbi David Marx and most members of the Temple demurred. At a time when other Reform leaders and congregations were beginning to show enthusiastic support for Israel, Marx grew increasingly intractable and became a prominent figure in the anti-Zionist American Council for Judaism. It took more than a decade of skillful maneuvering by Rabbi Jacob M. Rothschild, who succeeded Marx in 1946, to bring the Temple into the Jewish mainstream.

The emergence of a Jewish state beset by enormous problems actuated an unprecedented philanthropic vision and marshaling of economic support on both the national and local levels. Atlanta's Jews had always been known for their liberality. The $13,300 they donated in 1913 to the Federation of Jewish Charities represented approximately one-half of the charity funds raised in the city. But this was a pittance compared to the five million dollars raised by the Atlanta Jewish Welfare Federation in 1975, nearly two-thirds of which was forwarded to Israel. As elsewhere in the United States, the annual Federation campaign constitutes the central activity of the organized Jewish community, a unifying ritual embracing diverse economic, social, and religious groups, and Atlanta is known as one of the most generous communities of its size.

In its operational scope as well as fundraising effectiveness, the Federation has come a long way since the beginning of the century, when the attempt was made to systematize the distribution of relief and provide opportunities for "the deserving" in accordance with the new principles of "scientific philanthropy." The Atlanta Jewish Welfare Federation resulted from a merger in 1967 of the Jewish Social Service Federation, the Jewish Welfare Fund, and the Jewish Community Council. The new AJWF did more than raise and allocate funds for dozens of national and overseas community relations, service, and cultural agencies. It also performed the delicate task of local intergroup relations, handled the community's social planning, and supported and coordinated eleven local service agencies ranging from Jewish day schools to a home for the aged, from an employment service to a family and children's bureau. As Atlanta Jewry's "central address," the Federation touches more lives and has more members than all the city's temples and synagogues combined.

Congregational life has also changed. At the time of Leo Frank's death, the Reform Temple was the preeminent Jewish congregation in the city, with not only the largest membership but also a monopoly of the socially and economically prominent. Of the four Orthodox synagogues, Or Ve Shalom and Anshe Sfard worshiped in rented halls, Ahavath Achim and Shearith Israel having ended their wanderings during the previous decade. Beth Israel, the Conservative congregation which included the more assimilated and economically successful Russians, occupied an imposing southside edifice but was destined to survive for only another five years. With this exception, all of Atlanta's pioneer Jewish congregations continue to exist—but not as they were.

The Temple, with a membership of 1,450 families, continues to adhere to Reform, but not the classical Reform of David Marx. The service now includes Hebrew prayers, the ancient language is taught in the religious school, and in 1970 the bar mitzvah ceremony was reinstated. Though the Temple is perhaps still Atlanta's most prestigious Jewish congregation, the claim does not go undisputed. A second Reform congregation, Temple Sinai, was founded in 1968 and has a membership of over four hundred mostly younger families. Or Ve Shalom and Anshe Sfard are still Orthodox, but the original character of the former has been leavened by Ashkenazim and assimilation and has a membership of approximately 400 families, while the latter has a membership of less than 75, mostly elderly and foreign-born. Beth Jacob, a third Orthodox congregation, was founded in 1943 and has a membership of nearly 500. Ahavath Achim, with a membership of 1,800 families, is Atlanta's largest Jewish congregation, but it drifted from Orthodoxy to Conservatism during the 1930s. Shearith Israel with 635 members, while still traditionally oriented, is no longer affiliated nationally with the Orthodox movement. Two new congregations, Etz Chaim and Beth Shalom, consider themselves Conservative.

Congregational movement has been geographic as well as spiritual, for Atlanta's Jewish congregations have long since followed their members from the inner city to the periphery. At the time of the Frank case, approximately three-quarters of the German Jews resided on the southside, especially along Washington, Whitehall, and Pryor streets, while a quarter were dispersed across the northside. More than half of the Russians also resided on the southside, mostly on streets east of the German neighborhood, with the remainder in the Decatur and Peters street areas and scattered thoughout the city's black neighborhoods.

During the next two decades, the Germans evacuated the southside for the more fashionable northeast, while the Russians, under the pressure of an expanding black population on their eastern flank, pushed westward into the area being vacated by the Germans. But soon they too joined the migration northward, and by 1945 two-thirds of Atlanta's Jews were living in the northeast, one-quarter on the southside, and most of the remainder in the northern suburbs. During the following decade, the southside settlement disappeared, and Jews increasingly concentrated in the Morningside and Johnson Estates neighborhoods of northeast Atlanta and the Briarcliff-La Vista section of adjoining De Kalb County. The sixties witnessed a phenomenal expansion of Atlanta's boundaries, and Jews poured first into the newly annexed northwest section of town, and later into the northern suburbs of Sandy Springs, Chamblee, Dunwoody, and Doraville—more than fifteen miles from what had been the center of Jewish settlement at the time of the Frank case.

The suburbanization of Atlanta Jewry has been a function of both growing affluence and a desire (shared with other middle-class whites) to escape the perceived ills of urban life, particularly the problems associated with the city's increasing black population. During the half-century prior to the Frank case, the presence of a substantial Negro population tended to further the economic mobility, assimilation, and social status of Atlanta's Jews. Blacks not only comprised a large share of the clientele of many Jewish businesses but also deflected prejudices which might otherwise have been vented against Jews, while the system of white supremacy represented a pattern of life to which Jews had to adjust. For the Negro, the Jew was not simply a vendor of necessary goods and services, but also a model for group advancement and a white man with whom he shared a bond of empathy. The relationship was not one of equals and was marred by misconceptions and resentments, but it was fairly cordial and mutually beneficial.

The Frank case placed a heavy if temporary strain on this relationship, and during the next few decades Jewish economic presence in the black community gradually decreased as Jews found new opportunities elsewhere. Meanwhile, the web of racial segregation grew ever tighter, and though Rabbi David Marx and other progressive leaders of the Jewish community cautiously championed the cause of interracial cooperation, there was little challenge to the prevailing orthodoxy. Marx's successor, Rabbi Rothschild, was less circumspect. Beginning in 1948, and especially after the 1954 Supreme Court desegregation decision, Rothschild spoke out forcefully and frequently in support of civil rights, earning the respect of black leaders and the enmity of diehard segregationists. Rothschild's pleas for racial justice initially caused a good deal of consternation among Jews who had been conditioned to keep a low profile, but most eventually closed ranks behind him. The Jewish community's liberal political stance, reflected in the overwhelming black support for Sam Massell in 1969, alleviated but failed to eliminate tensions between the two groups. The rise of strident black militancy during the 1960s and the accompanying accusations of exploitation leveled against white merchants in the ghetto engendered a Federation-sponsored attempt to buy out the few remaining Jewish grocers and transfer ownership of their stores to blacks. While this program had only limited success, and black anti-Semitism remains a minor problem, Gary Marx has shown in *Protest and Prejudice* that Atlanta blacks are better disposed toward Jews (including Jewish merchants) than are blacks in the North.

During the emotion-charged 1950s, Jewish support for civil rights was a risky business, and on the morning of October 12, 1958, a dynamite explosion ripped into the Temple, inflicting approximately $100,000 in damages. Jews were again reminded that bigotry and violence were not reserved only for Negroes. But 1958 was not

1915, and the Jewish community no longer had to face adversity in isolation. The bombing acted as a catalyst. Eager to prove that their city was not simply another hate-ridden southern metropolis, gentile Atlantans responded with an outpouring of sympathy, grief, anger, and financial assistance. Instead of intimidating the Jewish community, the bombing marked a watershed in the struggle for integration and heralded the active reentry of Jews into local politics.

During the two decades since the bombing, Atlantans have elected not only a Jewish mayor, four state legislators, and a number of judges, but also Georgia's first Jewish congressman, Elliot Levitas. When Jimmy Carter launched his drive for the presidency, the leaders of the Atlanta Jewish community did missionary work on his behalf among their Yankee brethren, and President Carter subsequently appointed several of them to high-ranking White House positions. The Capital City Club and the Piedmont Driving Club are still closed to Jews, but such vestiges of an earlier era may be more embarrassing to club members (even those not appointed to top cabinet posts) than they are irritating to the Jewish community.

The Jews of Atlanta have not forgotten the Leo Frank case, but they no longer live in its shadow. The oak tree in Marietta from which Frank was hanged no longer stands. The site is now an empty lot occupied by weeds and discarded beer cans, flanked by a Lum's restaurant and the Interstate-75 overpass. A few blocks from the lot there is a large SoLo grocery on whose shelves in recent years (and during the appropriate season) can be found a large assortment of Passover foods—by no means a symbol of triumph, but certainly one of renascence.

# APPENDIXES, SELECTED BIBLIOGRAPHY, NOTES, AND INDEX

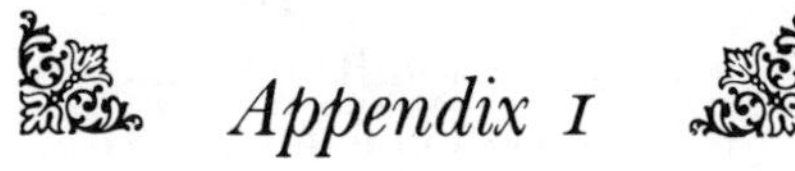

# Appendix 1

## The Sources and Techniques Used to Identify Jews and Their Characteristics

Central to understanding what the people of a community were like is knowing who they were. Therefore, one of the first steps in the preparation of this study was the identification of nearly every Jew who resided in Atlanta in 1870, 1880, and 1896.

The basic sources for the 1870 and 1880 enumerations were the ledgers, minute books, and occasional membership lists of the Hebrew Benevolent Congregation. Besides indicating who the members were, these records often identified renters of seats for the High Holy Days and also unsuccessful petitioners for membership. Other fruitful sources of information were 236 membership applications filed with the B'nai B'rith Gate City Lodge and a typed summary of the contents of applications filed with the local Free Sons of Israel lodge. Not only did the lodge applications provide additional Jewish names, but they also contained a considerable amount of demographic material.[1]

The federal manuscript census schedules for 1870 and 1880 and the respective city directories were then consulted to determine which of the individuals who could be identified as Jews had resided in Atlanta during these two years.[2] Where there was no reason to suspect intermarriage, the spouses, other family members, and seemingly unrelated persons in their households who bore Jewish names were assumed to be Jews, and their demographic characteristics were recorded. The census manuscripts and directories were then examined a second time and data were collected on persons whose names, nativity, or other factors indicated the possibility of being Jewish, but for whom corroborative evidence was lacking.

After careful consideration, it was determined that some of these people were indeed Jews, generally younger relatives of persons already identified as Jews, but whose age, economic circumstances, brief residence in the city, or personal inclination had resulted in their failure to affiliate formally with the Jewish community. However, there were few such exceptions. The small size of the Jewish community and the strong southern tradition of denominational identification apparently engendered a higher degree of affiliation than may have been the case in more secular locales with large Jewish or German-Gentile colonies.

The census and directory canvasses were separated by a space of several months, and some members of a given enumeration were not present at both times. Nevertheless, it was necessary to utilize both sources because many Jews known to have been present at the time of the census could not be found in the schedules either due to illegibility or accidental omission. This problem was especially acute in the case of the 1870 schedules. Because the canvasses were conducted at different times and for dissimilar purposes, there were also several cases of contradictory or otherwise varying data, usually regarding occupation or place of residence. In all such instances, the directory information was accepted as valid.

The same sources and techniques used to compile the 1870 and 1880 enumerations were also used for 1896, and the 1896 local census and directory were checked to determine which of the members of the earlier enumerations were still present in the city. A fragmentary set of minutes and the 1900 membership list of Congregation Ahavath Achim were useful in identifying East European Jews. Even without them, however, it was evident from the 1896 census schedules, naturalization records, and the tables on nativity and mother tongue in the 1900 and 1910 census reports that prior to 1896 nearly all Russian Atlantans were Jews.[3]

The major problem in identifying the characteristics of Jewish Atlantans in 1896 involved the shortcomings of the 1896 census. Unlike the federal returns, which grouped people into households and provided considerable demographic data, the individuals enumerated by the municipal census takers were listed alphabetically by ward and lacked indications of their marital status, parentage, and occupation. Furthermore, the spelling of names was often ingeniously garbled, and the birthplaces of many of the foreign-born were incorrectly noted. The elimination of a relatively large number of duplicate entries, careful cross-checking against other sources, and a partial reconstruction of households was required before this census could be mined systematically.

The 1870 Jewish enumeration included 284 persons, the 1880 cohort had 570, and the 1896 had 1,501—or a total of 1,934 individuals who were present in at least one of the three years. While a few Jews no doubt escaped identification and some unwary Gentiles were probably included, reliable local estimates of 336 Jews in 1872, 525 in 1878, and between 1,500 and 2,000 in 1900 suggest a very slight margin of error.[4]

To ascertain the extent of geographic and economic mobility, all Jewish males ages 18 and over in 1870 were traced through the city directories to 1880, 1890, and 1911; those in 1880 to 1890, 1900, and 1911; and those in 1896 to 1911.[5] Because of spelling changes and the in-migration of men who shared names with persons already in one of the three groups, it was frequently necessary to check the directories during the intervening years in order to insure firm linkages. The county death certificates and the Oakland Cemetery interment records were examined to determine whether disappearance from the city was a consequence of death or voluntary removal.[6]

After establishing who was present in a given year and in what occupational capacity, data were collected on the wealth of the cohort members. The sources for this information were the 1870 census schedules and the county tax digests for 1880, 1890, 1900, and 1911.[7] Property assessment data are a helpful indication of wealth but must be used with caution. While local real estate was assessed at full value and could not be hidden from tax collectors, the assessment of personalty was based entirely upon the estimates of its owners. Not only was there a consequent tendency to undervalue property, but it is apparent that some people of means managed to avoid assessment entirely. Even had estimates of local holdings been correct, business assets were often listed separately from the other property of proprietors, and investments outside the county and corporate stock were not subject to assessment.[8]

To cope with these deficiencies, several crude but unavoidable rules of thumb were laid down. In the case of independent proprietors, personal and business assessments were combined to yield an adjusted assessment. Where businesses or parcels of realty were owned jointly by two or more persons, the shared property was divided equally in order to derive adjusted valuations. This was also done in the case of corporations whose officers also appeared to have been the owners. In addition, property owned by married women was included under the holdings of their husbands'. At best, the result was an approximation of actual wealth, and at worst, a lesser distortion of reality than would have been the case had not the rules been applied.

Between twelve and fifty pieces of information were recorded for each of the 1,934 identifiable Jews in the three enumerations. To facilitate analysis, this material was translated into machine readable numbers and then transferred to computer tape.[9] Most of the operations performed on the data were cross-tabulations using "canned" SPSS programs.[10]

The major problem was coding and classifying nearly 200 occupations by status, skill, and industrial group. After considering a number of systems, I adopted a modified version of the one employed by Richard Hopkins in his examination of mobility in Atlanta.[11] This involved assigning a separate four-digit code derived from a 1915 Census Bureau publication for each occupation, and then grouping these occupations into skill/status categories similar to those used in the 1900, 1910, and 1920 censuses.

Unranked and Indeterminate Designations
(student, minor, unemployed, or retired)
Professionals
Proprietors, Managers, and Officials
White-Collar Workers
Self-Employed Artisans
Skilled Workers
Peddlers
Semiskilled Workers
Unskilled, Personal, and Domestic Service Workers
Not in Enumeration

These two systems of classification provided an accurate description of the Jewish occupational structure and facilitated comparison with data found in Hopkins's work and in the published census reports.[12]

# *Appendix 2*

## *Tables*

## · TABLE 1 ·

TOTAL, NATIVE-BORN WHITE, FOREIGN-BORN WHITE, AND NEGRO POPULATION OF GEORGIA, 1860–1910

| *Year* | *Total Population* | *Native-born White* | | *Foreign-born White* | | *Negro* | |
|---|---|---|---|---|---|---|---|
| | | *No.* | *%* | *No.* | *%* | *No.* | *%* |
| 1860 | 1,057,286 | 580,881 | 54.9 | 11,671 | 1.1 | 465,698 | 44.0 |
| 1870 | 1,184,109 | 627,799 | 53.0 | 11,127 | 0.9 | 545,142 | 46.0 |
| 1880 | 1,542,180 | 806,573 | 52.3 | 10,333 | 0.7 | 727,113 | 47.0 |
| 1890 | 1,837,353 | 966,465 | 52.6 | 11,892 | 0.6 | 858,815 | 46.7 |
| 1900 | 2,216,331 | 1,169,273 | 52.8 | 12,021 | 0.5 | 1,034,813 | 46.7 |
| 1910 | 2,609,121 | 1,416,730 | 54.3 | 15,072 | 0.6 | 1,176,987 | 45.1 |

*Note:* Percentages are rounded off to nearest 0.1 of 1%.

## · TABLE 2 ·

TOTAL AND ESTIMATED JEWISH POPULATION OF SOUTHERN STATES AND SELECTED CITIES, 1878

| *State* | *Total Population** | *Jewish Population* | | *City* | *Total Population** | *Jewish Population* | |
|---|---|---|---|---|---|---|---|
| | | *No.* | *%* | | | *No.* | *%* |
| Alabama | 1,262,505 | 2,045 | .16 | New Orleans | 216,090 | 5,000 | 2.3 |
| Arkansas | 802,525 | 1,466 | .18 | Louisville | 123,758 | 2,500 | 2.0 |
| Florida | 269,493 | 772 | .29 | Nashville | 43,350 | 2,100 | 4.8 |
| Georgia | 1,542,181 | 2,704 | .17 | Richmond | 63,600 | 1,200 | 1.9 |
| Kentucky | 1,648,690 | 3,602 | .21 | Knoxville | 9,693 | 1,085 | 11.2 |
| Louisiana | 939,946 | 7,538 | .80 | Galveston | 22,248 | 1,000 | 4.5 |
| Mississippi | 1,131,597 | 2,262 | .20 | Shreveport | 8,009 | 900 | 12.4 |
| North Carolina | 1,399,750 | 820 | .06 | Charleston | 49,984 | 700 | 1.4 |
| South Carolina | 995,577 | 1,415 | .14 | Little Rock | 13,138 | 655 | 5.0 |
| Tennessee | 1,542,359 | 3,715 | .24 | Savannah | 30,709 | 603 | 2.0 |
| Texas | 1,591,749 | 3,300 | .20 | Montgomery | 16,713 | 600 | 3.6 |
| Virginia | 1,513,565 | 2,506 | .16 | Atlanta | 37,409 | 525 | 1.4 |
| TOTAL | 14,639,937 | 32,145 | .22 | TOTAL | 634,701 | 16,868 | 2.7 |

*Figures are for 1880.

*Note:* Percentages are rounded off to nearest 0.1 of 1%. Maryland (10,400), Missouri (7,380), West Virginia (511), and Delaware (585) are generally not considered part of the postwar South.

## · TABLE 3 ·

TOTAL, NATIVE-BORN WHITE, FOREIGN-BORN WHITE, NEGRO, AND ESTIMATED JEWISH POPULATION OF ATLANTA, 1860–1910

| Year | Total Pop. | Native-born White No. | % | Foreign-born White No. | % | Negro No. | % | Estimated Jewish No. | % |
|---|---|---|---|---|---|---|---|---|---|
| 1860 | 9,554 | 7,015[a] | 73.4 | 600[a] | 6.3 | 1,939 | 20.3 | 50 | 0.5 |
| 1870 | 21,789 | 10,770 | 49.4 | 1,090 | 5.0 | 9,929 | 45.6 | 300–400 | 1.4–1.8 |
| 1880 | 37,409 | 19,663 | 52.6 | 1,416 | 3.8 | 16,330 | 43.7 | 600 | 1.6 |
| 1890 | 65,533 | 35,569 | 54.3 | 1,847 | 2.8 | 28,098 | 42.9 | 1,200–1,500 | 1.8–2.3 |
| 1900 | 89,872 | 51,632 | 57.5 | 2,458 | 2.7 | 35,727 | 39.8 | 2,000 | 2.2 |
| 1910 | 154,839 | 98,451 | 63.6 | 4,410 | 2.8 | 51,902 | 33.5 | 4,000 | 2.6 |

[a]Estimate

*Note:* Percentages are rounded off to nearest 0.1 of 1%.

## · TABLE 4 ·

FOREIGN-BORN WHITE POPULATION OF ATLANTA, 1870–1910

| Country | *1870*[a] No. | % | *1880* No. | % | *1890* No. | % | *1900* No. | % | *1910* No. | % |
|---|---|---|---|---|---|---|---|---|---|---|
| Austria-Hungary | n.s. | . . . | 52 | 3.7 | 60 | 3.2 | 100 | 4.0 | 105 | 2.3 |
| Canada | 40 | 3.4 | 72 | 5.1 | 112 | 6.0 | 202 | 8.0 | 257 | 5.7 |
| Germany | 346 | 29.3 | 471 | 33.3 | 616 | 33.0 | 672 | 26.6 | 729 | 16.2 |
| Great Britain | 208 | 17.7 | 190 | 13.4 | 316 | 16.9 | 358 | 14.1 | 595 | 13.2 |
| Greece | n.s. | . . . | . . . | . . . | 7 | .4 | 44 | 1.7 | 388 | 8.6 |
| Ireland | 470 | 39.9 | 465 | 32.8 | 413 | 22.0 | 286 | 11.3 | 302 | 6.7 |
| Italy | n.s. | . . . | 23 | 1.6 | 43 | 2.3 | 42 | 1.7 | 95 | 2.1 |
| Russia | n.s. | . . . | 3 | . . . | 126 | 6.7 | 531 | 21.0 | 1,342 | 29.8 |
| Other | 105 | 8.9 | 140 | 9.9 | 178 | 9.1 | 296 | 11.7 | 688 | 15.3 |
| TOTAL | 1,179 | 100.0 | 1,416 | 100.0 | 1,871 | 100.0 | 2,531 | 100.0 | 4,501 | 100.0 |

n.s.—nonspecified

[a]1870 figures are for Fulton County which included Atlanta's 1090 foreign-born.

*Note:* Percentages are rounded off to nearest 0.1 of 1%.

## · TABLE 5 ·

BIRTHPLACES OF IDENTIFIABLE ATLANTA JEWS
1870 AND 1880

| Birthplace | *1870* No. | *1870* % | *1880* No. | *1880* % |
|---|---|---|---|---|
| Austria-Hungary | 26 | 10.5 | 37 | 6.7 |
| Bohemia | 3 | 1.2 | 5 | .9 |
| Hungary | 23 | 9.3 | 32 | 5.7 |
| Germany | 86 | 34.7 | 143 | 25.3 |
| Baden | 4 | 1.6 | 3 | .5 |
| Bavaria | 7 | 2.8 | 26 | 4.6 |
| Hamburg | 2 | .8 | 3 | .5 |
| Hanover | 2 | .8 | 3 | .5 |
| Hesse | 20 | 8.1 | 28 | 5.0 |
| Prussia | 9 | 3.6 | 28 | 5.0 |
| Wurttemburg | 21 | 8.5 | 16 | 2.8 |
| Germany n.s. | 21 | 8.5 | 36 | 6.4 |
| Great Britain and Ireland | 2 | .8 | 7 | 1.2 |
| Russia | 5 | 2.0 | 3 | .5 |
| United States | 128 | 51.8 | 369 | 65.7 |
| Europe n.s. and misc. | ... | ... | 1 | .6 |
| TOTAL | 247 | 100.0 | 562 | 100.0 |
| Unknown | 37 | 9.6 | 8 | 1.4 |

n.s.—nonspecified

*Note:* Percentages are rounded off to nearest 0.1 of 1%.

## · TABLE 6 ·

PARENTAGE OF IDENTIFIABLE ATLANTA JEWS
1870 AND 1880

| Parentage | *1870* No. | *1870* % | *1880* No. | *1880* % |
|---|---|---|---|---|
| Austro-Hungarian | 35 | 14.8 | 54 | 10.0 |
| German | 162 | 68.3 | 308 | 57.2 |
| Russian | 12 | 5.1 | 11 | 2.0 |
| United States | 9 | 3.8 | 30 | 5.6 |
| Mixed foreign | 3 | 1.3 | 29 | 5.4 |
| Mixed native and foreign | 16 | 6.8 | 106 | 19.7 |
| TOTAL | 237 | 100.0 | 538 | 100.0 |
| Unknown | 47 | 16.5 | 32 | 5.6 |

*Note:* Percentages are rounded off to nearest 0.1 of 1%.

**· TABLE 7 ·**

AGE AND SEX OF IDENTIFIABLE ATLANTA JEWS, 1870 AND 1880

| | *1870* | | | | | | *1880* | | | | | |
|---|---|---|---|---|---|---|---|---|---|---|---|---|
| | *Males* | | *Females* | | *Total* | | *Males* | | *Females* | | *Total* | |
| *Age* | *No.* | *%* | *No.* | *%* | *No.* | *%* | *No.* | *%* | *No.* | *%* | *No.* | *%* |
| 0–9 | 37 | 24.7 | 41 | 40.2 | 78 | 30.9 | 93 | 31.8 | 92 | 34.1 | 185 | 32.9 |
| 10–19 | 17 | 11.3 | 17 | 16.7 | 34 | 13.5 | 44 | 15.1 | 62 | 23.0 | 106 | 18.9 |
| 20–29 | 45 | 30.0 | 21 | 20.6 | 66 | 26.2 | 43 | 14.7 | 51 | 18.9 | 94 | 16.7 |
| 30–39 | 29 | 19.3 | 14 | 13.7 | 43 | 17.1 | 56 | 19.2 | 30 | 11.1 | 86 | 15.3 |
| 40–49 | 17 | 11.3 | 4 | 3.9 | 21 | 8.3 | 34 | 11.6 | 19 | 7.0 | 53 | 9.4 |
| 50–59 | 3 | 2.0 | 4 | 3.9 | 7 | 2.8 | 16 | 5.5 | 8 | 3.0 | 24 | 4.3 |
| 60–69 | 2 | 1.3 | 1 | 1.0 | 3 | 1.2 | 5 | 1.7 | 8 | 3.0 | 13 | 2.3 |
| 70–80 | ... | ... | ... | ... | ... | ... | 1 | .3 | ... | ... | 1 | .2 |
| TOTAL | 150 | 59.5 | 102 | 40.5 | 252 | 100.0 | 292 | 52.0 | 270 | 48.0 | 562 | 100.0 |
| | Unknown | | | | 32 (11.3%) | | | | | | 8 (1.4%) | |
| | Average age | | | | 21.4 | | | | | | 21.6 | |
| | Sex ratio | | | | 147 | | | | | | 108 | |

*Note:* Percentages are rounded off to nearest 0.1 of 1%.

**· TABLE 8 ·**

MARITAL STATUS OF IDENTIFIABLE MALE ATLANTA JEWS (AGES 18 AND OVER), 1870 AND 1880

| | *1870* | | | | | *1880* | | | | |
|---|---|---|---|---|---|---|---|---|---|---|
| | *Married* | *Single* | *Widowed* | *Total* | | *Married* | *Single* | *Widowed* | *Total* | |
| *Age* | *%* | *%* | *%* | *No.* | *%* | *%* | *%* | *%* | *No.* | *%* |
| 18–19 | ... | 12.0 | ... | 6 | 5.9 | ... | 16.1 | ... | 8 | 5.3 |
| 20–29 | 20.4 | 70.0 | ... | 46 | 44.6 | 6.3 | 62.0 | ... | 37 | 24.5 |
| 30–39 | 38.8 | 18.0 | ... | 28 | 27.7 | 43.8 | 18.0 | ... | 51 | 33.8 |
| 40–49 | 30.6 | ... | 100.0 | 17 | 16.8 | 28.1 | 4.0 | 60.0 | 32 | 21.2 |
| 50–59 | 6.1 | ... | ... | 3 | 3.0 | 15.6 | ... | 40.0 | 17 | 11.3 |
| 60–69 | 4.1 | ... | ... | 2 | 2.0 | 5.2 | ... | ... | 5 | 3.3 |
| 70–79 | ... | ... | ... | ... | ... | 1.0 | ... | ... | 1 | .7 |
| TOTAL % | 49.0 | 49.0 | 2.0 | | 100.0 | 63.6 | 31.1 | 3.3 | | 100.0 |
| No. | 50 | 50 | 2 | | 102 | 96 | 50 | 5 | | 151 |
| Unknown | | | 11 | (9.8%) | | | | 9 | (5.6%) | |

*Note:* Percentages are rounded off to nearest 0.1 of 1%.

### · TABLE 9 ·

EMPLOYED MALE JEWS (AGES 18 AND OVER) IN 1870 AND 1880, AND EMPLOYED MALE ATLANTANS (AGES 16–59) IN 1880, BY INDUSTRIAL GROUP

| *Industry* | *Jews 1870* | | *Jews 1880* | | *Atlantans 1880*[a] | |
|---|---|---|---|---|---|---|
| | *No.* | *%* | *No.* | *%* | *No.* | *%* |
| Agriculture | ... | ... | ... | ... | ... | 2.2 |
| Clerical | 3 | 2.8 | 10 | 6.6 | | |
| Domestic and personal service | 2 | 1.9 | 5 | 3.3 | ... | 27.2 |
| Manufacturing and the mechanical arts | 3 | 2.8 | 22 | 14.7 | ... | 29.3 |
| Professional service | 3 | 2.8 | 5 | 3.3 | ... | 5.0 |
| Public service | 1 | .9 | 1 | .7 | | |
| Trade | 95 | 88.8 | 107 | 71.3 | ... | 24.9 |
| Transportation | ... | ... | ... | ... | ... | 11.4 |
| TOTAL | 107 | 100.0 | 150 | 100.0 | 10,224 | 100.0 |
| Unknown | 5 | 4.5 | 10 | 6.3 | | |

[a]Figures for Trade, Transportation, and the service categories were derived through interpolation.

*Note:* Percentages are rounded off to nearest 0.1 of 1%.

**· TABLE 10 ·**

OCCUPATIONAL DISTRIBUTION OF EMPLOYED AND IDENTIFIABLE ATLANTA JEWISH MALES (AGES 18 AND OVER), 1870 AND 1880

| Occupation | *1870* No. | *1870* % | *1880* No. | *1880* % |
|---|---|---|---|---|
| *Professional* | 3 | 2.8 | 5 | 3.4 |
| Architect | ... | ... | 1 | .7 |
| Lawyer | 1 | .9 | 2 | 1.3 |
| Physician | ... | ... | 1 | .7 |
| Principal, private school | 1 | .9 | ... | ... |
| Rabbi | 1 | .9 | 1 | .7 |
| *Proprietor-manager-official* | 71 | 66.4 | 90 | 60.4 |
| Manufacturing | | | | |
| Agricultural implements | ... | ... | 1 | .7 |
| Hats and bonnets | ... | ... | 4 | 2.7 |
| Hoop skirts | 1 | .9 | ... | ... |
| Leather trunks | ... | ... | 2 | 1.3 |
| Paper bags | ... | ... | 5 | 3.4 |
| Stoves | 1 | .9 | 1 | .7 |
| Wholesale | | | | |
| Cigars and tobacco | ... | ... | 3 | 2.0 |
| Clothing and dry goods | 4 | 3.7 | 4 | 2.7 |
| Liquor, beer, wine | 2 | 1.9 | 5 | 3.4 |
| Millinery | 1 | .9 | 3 | 2.0 |
| Notions | ... | ... | 1 | .7 |
| Paper | ... | ... | 2 | 1.3 |
| Tea and spices | ... | ... | 1 | .7 |
| Warehouse owner | 2 | 1.9 | 1 | .7 |
| Real estate agency | ... | ... | 1 | .7 |
| Produce and commission broker | 1 | .9 | 4 | 2.7 |
| Cotton broker | 1 | .9 | 1 | .7 |
| Cotton shipper | ... | ... | 1 | .7 |
| Retail | | | | |
| Cigars and tobacco | 1 | .9 | 5 | 3.4 |
| Clothing and dry goods | 41 | 38.3 | 24 | 16.1 |
| Dairy | ... | ... | 1 | .7 |
| Eyeglasses | 1 | .9 | ... | ... |
| Fruits and confectionery | ... | ... | 1 | .7 |
| Grocery | 4 | 3.7 | 2 | 1.3 |
| Hardware | 2 | 1.9 | 3 | 2.0 |
| Jewelry | 1 | .9 | 1 | .7 |
| Junk | ... | ... | 1 | .7 |
| Liquor, beer, wine | 1 | .9 | 1 | .7 |
| Lumber | 1 | .9 | ... | ... |
| Rags | ... | ... | 2 | 1.3 |
| n.s. and misc. | ... | ... | 3 | 2.0 |
| Agent, Liquor or wine | 2 | 1.9 | ... | ... |
| Auctioneer | ... | ... | 1 | .7 |
| Manager, store or factory | ... | ... | 1 | .7 |
| Pawnbroker | ... | ... | 1 | .7 |
| Pharmacy | 1 | .9 | ... | ... |
| Saloon | 2 | 1.9 | 2 | 1.3 |
| Gauger, internal revenue | 1 | .9 | 1 | .7 |

· **TABLE 10**—*(Continued)* ·

OCCUPATIONAL DISTRIBUTION OF EMPLOYED AND IDENTIFIABLE ATLANTA JEWISH MALES (AGES 18 AND OVER), 1870 AND 1880

| ***Occupation*** | ***1870*** | | ***1880*** | |
|---|---|---|---|---|
| | ***No.*** | ***%*** | ***No.*** | ***%*** |
| *White-collar worker* | 32 | 29.4 | 45 | 30.2 |
| Bookkeeper or accountant | 1 | .9 | 9 | 6.0 |
| Clerk, store | 30 | 28.0 | 19 | 12.8 |
| Clerk, postal | . . . | . . . | 1 | .7 |
| Commercial traveler | . . . | . . . | 13 | 8.7 |
| Insurance agent | 1 | .9 | 2 | 1.3 |
| Salesman | . . . | . . . | 1 | .7 |
| *Self-employed artisan* | 1 | .9 | 1 | .7 |
| Plumber or gas-fitter | 1 | .9 | . . . | . . . |
| Tailor | . . . | . . . | 1 | .7 |
| *Skilled worker* | . . . | . . . | 3 | 2.0 |
| Printer | . . . | . . . | 1 | .7 |
| Tailor | . . . | . . . | 2 | 1.3 |
| *Semiskilled worker* | . . . | . . . | 3 | 2.0 |
| Bottler | . . . | . . . | 1 | .7 |
| Brewer | . . . | . . . | 1 | .7 |
| Cigar maker | . . . | . . . | 1 | .7 |
| *Unskilled worker* | . . . | . . . | 2 | 1.3 |
| Janitor or sexton | . . . | . . . | 2 | 1.3 |
| TOTAL | 107 | 100.0 | 149 | 100.0 |
| Unknown | 15 | 4.5 | 11 | 6.9 |

***Note:*** Percentages are rounded off to nearest 0.1 of 1%.

· TABLE 11 ·

ASSESSED WEALTH OF IDENTIFIABLE JEWISH MALES (AGES 18 AND OVER), 1870 AND 1880

| Wealth (in dollars) | *1870* No. | *1870* % | *1880* No. | *1880* % |
|---|---|---|---|---|
| 0– 50 | 46 | 63.0 | 72 | 46.2 |
| 100– 500 | 1 | 1.4 | 18 | 11.5 |
| 600– 1,000 | 3 | 4.1 | 5 | 3.2 |
| 1,100– 3,000 | 6 | 8.2 | 13 | 8.3 |
| 3,100– 5,000 | 4 | 5.5 | 9 | 5.8 |
| 5,100–10,000 | 8 | 11.0 | 25 | 16.0 |
| 10,100–15,000 | 4 | 5.5 | 6 | 3.9 |
| 15,100–20,000 | 1 | 1.4 | 6 | 3.9 |
| 20,100–30,000 | . . . | . . . | 2 | 1.3 |
| TOTAL | 73 | 100.0 | 156 | 100.0 |
| Unknown | 39 | 34.8 | 4 | 2.6 |

*Note:* Percentages are rounded off to nearest 0.1 of 1%. Wealth is rounded off to nearest $100. The property holdings of married women are included with the holdings of their husbands.

· TABLE 12 ·

RESIDENTIAL PATTERNS OF IDENTIFIABLE ATLANTA JEWS, 1870 AND 1880

| Area | *1870* No. | *1870* % | *1880* No. | *1880* % |
|---|---|---|---|---|
| A | 71 | 25.4 | 37 | 6.5 |
| B | 96 | 34.4 | 280 | 49.4 |
| C | 5 | 1.8 | 25 | 4.4 |
| D | 45 | 16.1 | 135 | 23.8 |
| E | . . . | . . . | . . . | . . . |
| F | . . . | . . . | . . . | . . . |
| G | 62 | 22.2 | 90 | 15.9 |
| TOTAL | 279 | 100.0 | 567 | 100.0 |
| Unknown | 5 | 1.8 | 3 | 0.5 |

*Note:* Percentages are rounded off to nearest 0.1 of 1%.

### · TABLE 13 ·

IDENTIFIABLE JEWISH MALES (AGES 18 AND OVER) AND MALE MEMBERS OF THE HEBREW BENEVOLENT CONGREGATION 1870 AND 1896

| *Birthplace* | *1870* | | | | *1896* | | | |
|---|---|---|---|---|---|---|---|---|
| | *HBC* | | *All* | | *HBC* | | *All* | |
| | *No.* | *%* | *No.* | *%* | *No.* | *%* | *No.* | *%* |
| Austria-Hungary | 7 | 16.3 | 16 | 16.5 | 15 | 11.2 | 33 | 7.1 |
| Germany | 34 | 79.1 | 63 | 64.9 | 64 | 47.8 | 104 | 22.5 |
| Europe, n.s. and misc. | ... | ... | ... | ... | 2 | 1.5 | 10 | 2.2 |
| Great Britain and Ireland | 1 | 2.3 | 1 | 1.0 | 3 | 2.2 | 5 | 1.1 |
| Russia | 1 | 2.3 | 3 | 3.1 | 6 | 4.5 | 144 | 31.1 |
| United States | ... | ... | 14 | 14.4 | 44 | 32.8 | 167 | 36.1 |
| TOTAL | 43 | 100.0 | 97 | 100.0 | 134 | 100.0 | 463 | 100.0 |
| Unknown | 6 | 12.2 | 15 | 13.4 | 10 | 6.9 | 24 | 4.9 |

n.s.—nonspecified

*Note:* Percentages are rounded off to nearest 0.1 of 1%.

· TABLE 14 ·

BIRTHPLACES OF RUSSIAN JEWISH IMMIGRANTS BY YEAR "DECLARATION OF INTENTION TO PETITION FOR CITIZENSHIP" FILED IN ATLANTA

| *Birthplace* | *Total* No. | % | *1881–1890* No. | % | *1891–1900* No. | % | *1901–1906* No. | % | *1907–1917*[a] No. | % |
|---|---|---|---|---|---|---|---|---|---|---|
| Lithuania | 173 | 70.3 | 7 | 53.8 | 64 | 77.1 | 34 | 69.4 | 68 | 67.3 |
| Grodno | 53 | 21.5 | ... | ... | 12 | 15.5 | 17 | 34.7 | 24 | 23.8 |
| Kovno | 79 | 32.1 | 5 | 38.5 | 41 | 49.4 | 10 | 20.4 | 23 | 22.8 |
| Minsk | 16 | 6.5 | 2 | 15.4 | 1 | 1.2 | 4 | 8.1 | 9 | 8.9 |
| Mohilev | 2 | .8 | ... | ... | 1 | 1.2 | ... | ... | 1 | 1.0 |
| Vilna | 19 | 7.7 | ... | ... | 9 | 10.8 | 1 | 2.0 | 9 | 8.9 |
| Vitebsk | 4 | 1.6 | ... | ... | ... | ... | 2 | 4.0 | 2 | 2.0 |
| Poland | 16 | 6.5 | 2 | 15.4 | 4 | 4.8 | 6 | 12.2 | 4 | 4.0 |
| Poland n.s. | 5 | 2.0 | 2 | 15.4 | ... | ... | 2 | 4.0 | 1 | 1.0 |
| Lomza | 6 | 2.4 | ... | ... | 4 | 4.8 | 2 | 4.0 | ... | ... |
| Lublin | 1 | .4 | ... | ... | ... | ... | 1 | 2.0 | ... | ... |
| Warsaw | 4 | 1.6 | ... | ... | ... | ... | 1 | 2.0 | 3 | 3.0 |
| Ukraine and South Russia | 41 | 16.7 | 3 | 23.0 | 10 | 10.1 | 7 | 14.3 | 21 | 20.8 |
| Bessarabia | 4 | 1.6 | ... | ... | ... | ... | ... | ... | 4 | 4.0 |
| Kherson | 21 | 8.5 | 2 | 15.4 | 3 | 3.6 | 4 | 8.1 | 12 | 11.9 |
| Kiev | 8 | 3.2 | 1 | 7.7 | 3 | 3.6 | 2 | 4.0 | 2 | 2.0 |
| Podolia | 5 | 2.0 | ... | ... | 3 | 3.6 | ... | ... | 2 | 2.0 |
| Poltava | 3 | 1.2 | ... | ... | 1 | 1.2 | 1 | 2.0 | 1 | 1.0 |
| Outside the Pale | 16 | 6.5 | 1 | 7.7 | 5 | 6.0 | 2 | 4.1 | 8 | 7.9 |
| Courland | 8 | 3.2 | ... | ... | 4 | 4.8 | ... | ... | 4 | 4.0 |
| Livonia | 8 | 3.2 | 1 | 7.7 | 1 | 1.2 | 2 | 4.1 | 4 | 4.0 |
| TOTAL | 246 | 100.0 | 13 | 100.0 | 83 | 100.0 | 49 | 100.0 | 101 | 100.0 |
| Russia n.s. | 284 | | 3 | | 5 | | 22 | | 254 | |

n.s.—nonspecified

[a]When the federal government assumed responsibility for naturalization at the end of 1906, a new form was used which no longer listed province. Few of the smaller towns listed thereafter could be identified, and most of the identifiable places were in Lithuania. Therefore, the proportion of Lithuanian-born immigrants who filed declarations between 1907 and 1917 was probably lower than indicated.

*Note:* Percentages are rounded off to nearest 0.1 of 1%.

### · TABLE 15 ·

BIRTHPLACES OF IDENTIFIABLE ATLANTA JEWS, 1896

| Birthplace | *All Jews* No. | *All Jews* % | *Males Ages 18 & Over* No. | *Males Ages 18 & Over* % |
|---|---|---|---|---|
| Austria-Hungary | 58 | 3.9 | 34 | 7.3 |
| Germany | 189 | 12.8 | 104 | 22.4 |
| Great Britain and Ireland | 12 | .8 | 5 | 1.1 |
| Russia | 317 | 21.5 | 144 | 31.0 |
| United States | 876 | 59.4 | 167 | 36.0 |
| Europe n.s. and misc. | 22 | 1.5 | 10 | 2.2 |
| Other | 1 | .1 | ... | ... |
| TOTAL | 1,475 | 100.0 | 464 | 100.0 |
| Unknown | 26 | 1.7 | 23 | 4.7 |

n.s.—nonspecified

*Note:* Percentages are rounded off to nearest 0.1 of 1%. The 58 Austro-Hungarians include 3 Austrians, 8 Bohemians, 20 Galicians, and 27 Hungarians.

### · TABLE 16 ·

PARENTAGE OF IDENTIFIABLE ATLANTA JEWS, 1896

| Parentage | *All Jews* No. | *All Jews* % | *Males Ages 18 & Over* No. | *Males Ages 18 & Over* % |
|---|---|---|---|---|
| Austro-Hungarian | 91 | 7.4 | 35 | 8.8 |
| German | 305 | 24.8 | 153 | 38.5 |
| American | 66 | 5.4 | 7 | 1.8 |
| Russian | 487 | 39.5 | 152 | 38.3 |
| Mixed foreign or other | 82 | 6.7 | 20 | 5.0 |
| Mixed native and foreign | 201 | 16.3 | 30 | 7.6 |
| TOTAL | 1,232 | 100.0 | 397 | 100.0 |
| Unknown | 269 | 18.0 | 90 | 18.5 |

*Note:* Percentages are rounded off to nearest 0.1 of 1%.

Nearly all of the foreign parents referred to in the last two categories were German and Austro-Hungarian.

· TABLE 17 ·

AGE AND SEX OF IDENTIFIABLE ATLANTA JEWS, 1896

| Age | *Males* No. | *Males* % | *Females* No. | *Females* % | *Total* No. | *Total* % |
|---|---|---|---|---|---|---|
| ***All Jews*** | | | | | | |
| 0–9 | 190 | 25.0 | 171 | 25.1 | 361 | 25.1 |
| 10–19 | 170 | 22.4 | 171 | 25.1 | 341 | 23.7 |
| 20–29 | 124 | 16.3 | 141 | 20.7 | 265 | 18.4 |
| 30–39 | 127 | 16.7 | 95 | 14.0 | 222 | 15.4 |
| 40–49 | 64 | 8.4 | 63 | 9.3 | 127 | 8.8 |
| 50–59 | 51 | 6.7 | 29 | 4.3 | 80 | 5.6 |
| 60–69 | 31 | 4.1 | 7 | 1.0 | 38 | 2.6 |
| 70–89 | 3 | .4 | 3 | .4 | 6 | .4 |
| TOTAL | 760 | 52.7 | 680 | 47.3 | 1440 | 100.0 |
| Unknown | | | | | 61 | 4.0 |
| Mean Age 23.0 | | | | | | |
| Sex Ratio 111 | | | | | | |
| ***Russians*** | | | | | | |
| 0–9 | 14 | 8.4 | 19 | 13.9 | 33 | 10.9 |
| 10–19 | 24 | 14.5 | 31 | 22.6 | 55 | 18.2 |
| 20–29 | 40 | 24.1 | 41 | 29.9 | 81 | 26.7 |
| 30–39 | 60 | 36.1 | 32 | 23.4 | 92 | 30.4 |
| 40–49 | 17 | 10.2 | 9 | 6.6 | 26 | 8.6 |
| 50–59 | 8 | 4.8 | 4 | 2.9 | 12 | 4.0 |
| 60–69 | 1 | .6 | . . . | . . . | 1 | .3 |
| 70–89 | 2 | 1.2 | 1 | .7 | 3 | 1.0 |
| TOTAL | 166 | 54.8 | 137 | 45.2 | 303 | 100.0 |
| Unknown | | | | | 14 | 4.4 |
| Sex Ratio 121 | | | | | | |
| ***Germans*** | | | | | | |
| 0–9 | 5 | 4.3 | 6 | 8.7 | 11 | 5.9 |
| 10–19 | 9 | 7.8 | 8 | 11.6 | 17 | 9.2 |
| 20–29 | 9 | 7.8 | 4 | 5.8 | 13 | 7.0 |
| 30–39 | 12 | 10.3 | 14 | 20.3 | 26 | 14.1 |
| 40–49 | 26 | 22.4 | 16 | 23.2 | 42 | 22.7 |
| 50–59 | 30 | 25.9 | 16 | 23.2 | 46 | 24.9 |
| 60–69 | 24 | 20.7 | 3 | 4.3 | 27 | 14.6 |
| 70–89 | 1 | .9 | 2 | 2.9 | 3 | 1.6 |
| TOTAL | 116 | 62.7 | 69 | 37.3 | 185 | 100.0 |
| Unknown | | | | | 4 | 2.1 |
| Sex Ratio 168 | | | | | | |

· **TABLE 17**—*Continued* ·

| *Age* | *Males* No. | *Males* % | *Females* No. | *Females* % | *Total* No. | *Total* % |
|---|---|---|---|---|---|---|
| ***Austro-Hungarians*** | | | | | | |
| 0–9 | 3 | 7.5 | 3 | 17.6 | 6 | 10.5 |
| 10–19 | 6 | 15.0 | . . . | . . . | 6 | 10.5 |
| 20–29 | 5 | 12.5 | 5 | 29.4 | 10 | 17.5 |
| 30–39 | 10 | 25.0 | 5 | 29.4 | 15 | 26.3 |
| 40–49 | 7 | 17.5 | 2 | 11.8 | 9 | 15.8 |
| 50–59 | 6 | 15.0 | 2 | 11.8 | 8 | 14.0 |
| 60–69 | 3 | 7.5 | . . . | . . . | 3 | 5.3 |
| 70–89 | . . . | . . . | . . . | . . . | . . . | . . . |
| TOTAL | 40 | 70.2 | 17 | 29.8 | 57 | 100.0 |
| Unknown | | | | | 1 | 1.7 |
| Sex Ratio 235 | | | | | | |
| ***Americans*** | | | | | | |
| 0–9 | 166 | 39.4 | 142 | 32.3 | 308 | 35.8 |
| 10–19 | 130 | 30.9 | 128 | 29.2 | 258 | 30.0 |
| 20–29 | 69 | 16.4 | 89 | 20.3 | 158 | 18.4 |
| 30–39 | 40 | 9.5 | 40 | 9.1 | 80 | 9.3 |
| 40–49 | 10 | 2.4 | 33 | 7.5 | 43 | 5.0 |
| 50–59 | 5 | 1.2 | 6 | 1.4 | 11 | 1.3 |
| 60–69 | 1 | .2 | . . . | . . . | 1 | .1 |
| 70–89 | . . . | . . . | . . . | . . . | . . . | . . . |
| TOTAL | 421 | 49.0 | 438 | 51.0 | 859 | 100.0 |
| Unknown | | | | | 17 | 1.9 |
| Sex Ratio 96 | | | | | | |

*Note:* Percentages are rounded off to nearest 0.1 of 1%.

**· TABLE 18 ·**

MARITAL STATUS OF IDENTIFIABLE MALE ATLANTA JEWS (AGES 18 AND OVER) IN 1896 BY BIRTHPLACE

| | *All* | | *Russia* | | *Germany* | | *Aust.-Hung.* | | *USA* | |
|---|---|---|---|---|---|---|---|---|---|---|
| *Status* | *No.* | *%* | *No.* | *%* | *No.* | *%* | *No.* | *%* | *No.* | *%* |
| Married | 248 | 58.8 | 85 | 78.7 | 77 | 76.2 | 20 | 62.5 | 53 | 33.3 |
| Single | 150 | 35.5 | 19 | 17.6 | 16 | 15.8 | 9 | 28.1 | 104 | 65.4 |
| Widowed/divorced | 24 | 5.7 | 4 | 3.7 | 8 | 7.9 | 3 | 9.4 | 2 | 1.3 |
| TOTAL | 422 | 100.0 | 108 | 100.0 | 101 | 100.0 | 32 | 100.0 | 159 | 100.0 |
| Unknown | 65 | 13.3 | 34 | 23.9 | 2 | 2 | 0 | | 0 | |

*Note:* Percentages are rounded off to nearest 0.1 of 1%.

**· TABLE 19 ·**

NATIVE- AND FOREIGN-BORN ATLANTANS OF RUSSIAN PARENTAGE, 1890–1910

| *Year* | *Born in Russia* | *Native-born with 2 Russian parents* | *Native-born with 1 Russian parent* |
|---|---|---|---|
| 1890 | 126 | 38 | 17 |
| 1900 | 493 | 857 | 33 |
| 1910 | 1,283 | n.a. | n.a. |

n.a.—not available

*Note:* Percentages are rounded off to nearest 0.1 of 1%. In 1910 there were 998 native-born persons with one or two Russian-born parents.

## · TABLE 20 ·

EMPLOYED MALE ATLANTA JEWS (AGES 18 AND OVER) IN 1896 BY BIRTHPLACE AND INDUSTRIAL GROUP; EMPLOYED MALE ATLANTANS IN 1900 BY INDUSTRIAL GROUP

| | *All Jews* | | *Russia* | | *Germany* | | *Aust-Hung.* | | *USA.* | | *All Atlantans* | |
|---|---|---|---|---|---|---|---|---|---|---|---|---|
| *Industry* | *No.* | *%* | *No.* | *%* | *No.* | *%* | *No.* | *%* | *No.* | *%* | *No.* | *%* |
| Agriculture | ... | ... | ... | ... | ... | ... | ... | ... | ... | ... | ... | 1.3 |
| Clerical | 25 | 6.1 | ... | ... | 3 | 3.4 | 3 | 10.3 | 16 | 11.3 | ... | 9.7 |
| Domestic and personal service | 9 | 2.2 | 2 | 1.6 | 1 | 1.1 | ... | ... | 3 | 2.1 | ... | 20.7 |
| Manufacturing and the mechanical arts | 60 | 14.7 | 22 | 18.0 | 14 | 16.1 | 3 | 10.3 | 17 | 12.1 | ... | 27.9 |
| Professional service | 21 | 5.1 | 1 | .8 | 2 | 2.3 | 1 | 3.4 | 17 | 12.1 | ... | 6.0 |
| Public service | 2 | .5 | 1 | .8 | ... | ... | 1 | 3.4 | ... | ... | ... | .7 |
| Trade | 289 | 71.0 | 96 | 78.7 | 67 | 77.0 | 21 | 72.4 | 87 | 61.7 | ... | 17.6 |
| Transportation | 2 | .5 | ... | ... | ... | ... | ... | ... | 1 | .7 | ... | 16.0 |
| TOTAL | 408 | 100.0 | 122 | 100.0 | 87 | 100.0 | 29 | 100.0 | 141 | 100.0 | 25,871 | 100.0 |
| Unknown | 56 | 13.1 | 20 | 14.1 | 16 | 15.5 | 5 | 14.7 | 11 | 7.2 | | |

*Note:* Percentages are rounded off to nearest 0.1 of 1%. Figures in 1900 for Trade, Transportation, and the service categories were derived through interpolation.

· **TABLE 21** ·

DISTRIBUTION BY OCCUPATION AND BIRTHPLACE OF EMPLOYED, IDENTIFIABLE ATLANTA JEWISH MALES (AGES 18 AND OVER), 1896

| *Occupation* | *All Jews* No. | % | *Russia* No. | % | *Germany* No. | % | *Aust-Hung.* No. | % | *USA.* No. | % |
|---|---|---|---|---|---|---|---|---|---|---|
| *Professional* | 20 | 4.9 | 1 | .8 | 1 | 1.2 | 1 | 3.4 | 17 | 12.1 |
| Clergyman | 2 | .5 | 1 | .8 | ... | ... | ... | ... | 1 | .7 |
| Dentist | 1 | .2 | ... | ... | ... | ... | ... | ... | 1 | .7 |
| Editor/reporter | 3 | .7 | ... | ... | ... | ... | ... | ... | 3 | 2.1 |
| Lawyer | 11 | 2.7 | ... | ... | 1 | 1.2 | ... | ... | 10 | 7.1 |
| Physician | 3 | .7 | ... | ... | ... | ... | 1 | 3.4 | 2 | 1.4 |
| *Proprietor-Manager-Official* | 198 | 48.5 | 61 | 50.0 | 51 | 58.6 | 16 | 55.2 | 56 | 40.0 |
| Manufacturing | | | | | | | | | | |
| Agricultural implements | 2 | .5 | ... | ... | 1 | 1.2 | ... | ... | 1 | .7 |
| Bags | 1 | .2 | ... | ... | 1 | 1.2 | ... | ... | ... | ... |
| Bakery | 1 | .2 | ... | ... | 1 | 1.2 | ... | ... | ... | ... |
| Building supplies | 1 | .2 | ... | ... | ... | ... | ... | ... | 1 | .7 |
| Beer and liquor | 3 | .7 | ... | ... | 2 | 2.3 | 1 | 3.4 | ... | ... |
| Candy | 1 | .2 | ... | ... | ... | ... | 1 | 3.4 | ... | ... |
| Cotton mill | 3 | .7 | ... | ... | 1 | 1.2 | ... | ... | 1 | .7 |
| Furniture | 6 | 1.5 | ... | ... | 2 | 2.3 | ... | ... | 4 | 2.8 |
| Hats and bonnets | 2 | .5 | 1 | .8 | 1 | 1.2 | ... | ... | ... | ... |
| Jewelry | 1 | .2 | 1 | .8 | ... | ... | ... | ... | ... | ... |
| Leather trunks | 1 | .2 | ... | ... | ... | ... | ... | ... | 1 | .7 |
| Paper | 1 | .2 | ... | ... | ... | ... | ... | ... | ... | ... |
| Seed oil | 1 | .2 | ... | ... | 1 | 1.2 | ... | ... | ... | ... |
| n.s. | 2 | .5 | ... | ... | 2 | 2.3 | ... | ... | ... | ... |
| Wholesale | | | | | | | | | | |
| Beer, liquor, wine | 3 | .7 | ... | ... | ... | ... | ... | ... | 2 | 1.4 |
| Jewelry | 1 | .2 | ... | ... | ... | ... | ... | ... | 1 | .7 |
| Leather and hides | 5 | 1.2 | 1 | .8 | ... | ... | ... | ... | 3 | 2.1 |
| Millinery | 2 | .5 | ... | ... | 2 | 2.3 | ... | ... | ... | ... |
| Paper | 12 | 2.9 | ... | ... | 5 | 5.7 | 3 | 10.3 | 4 | 2.8 |
| Woodenware | 4 | 1.0 | ... | ... | ... | ... | ... | ... | 3 | 2.1 |
| Cloth and dry goods | 3 | .7 | ... | ... | 1 | 1.2 | 1 | 3.4 | ... | ... |
| Retail | | | | | | | | | | |
| Beer, wine, liquor | 2 | .5 | ... | ... | ... | ... | ... | ... | 1 | .7 |
| Cigars and tobacco | 5 | 1.2 | 1 | .8 | 1 | 1.2 | ... | ... | 3 | 2.1 |
| Clothing and dry goods | 46 | 11.3 | 28 | 23.0 | 10 | 11.4 | 1 | 3.4 | 3 | 2.1 |
| Crockery | 2 | .5 | 1 | .8 | ... | ... | ... | ... | 1 | .7 |
| Delicatessen | 1 | .2 | ... | ... | ... | ... | ... | ... | 1 | .7 |
| Department store | 3 | .7 | ... | ... | ... | ... | 3 | 10.3 | ... | ... |
| Fish and game | 1 | .2 | ... | ... | ... | ... | ... | ... | 1 | .7 |
| Fruit and Confectionery | 2 | .5 | 1 | .8 | 1 | .2 | ... | ... | ... | ... |
| Furniture | 3 | .7 | 2 | 1.6 | ... | ... | 1 | 3.4 | ... | ... |
| Groceries | 14 | 3.4 | 11 | 9.0 | 2 | 2.3 | 1 | 3.4 | ... | ... |
| Hardware | 1 | .2 | ... | ... | ... | ... | ... | ... | 1 | .7 |
| Jewelry | 1 | .2 | ... | ... | ... | ... | ... | ... | ... | ... |
| Junk | 2 | .5 | 1 | .8 | ... | ... | ... | ... | ... | ... |
| Millinery | 1 | .2 | ... | ... | ... | ... | ... | ... | 1 | .7 |
| Paper | 3 | .7 | ... | ... | 2 | 2.3 | ... | ... | 1 | .7 |
| Pharmacy | 3 | .7 | ... | ... | 1 | 1.2 | ... | ... | 1 | .7 |
| Shoes | 13 | 3.2 | 7 | 5.7 | 2 | 2.3 | ... | ... | 3 | 2.1 |
| n.s. and misc. | 6 | 1.5 | 2 | 1.6 | 2 | 2.3 | ... | ... | 3 | 2.1 |
| Auctioneer | 1 | .2 | ... | ... | 1 | 1.2 | ... | ... | ... | ... |
| Cotton broker | 1 | .2 | ... | ... | 1 | 1.2 | ... | ... | ... | ... |
| Insurance agency | 5 | 1.2 | ... | ... | 2 | 2.3 | 1 | 3.4 | 2 | 1.4 |
| Manager, store or factory | 3 | .7 | 1 | .8 | ... | ... | ... | ... | 2 | 1.4 |
| Orphanage, superintendent | 1 | .2 | ... | ... | 1 | 1.2 | ... | ... | ... | ... |
| Pawnbroker | 5 | 1.2 | 2 | 1.6 | ... | ... | ... | ... | 3 | 2.1 |
| Prescriptionist | 4 | 1.0 | 1 | .8 | 3 | 3.4 | ... | ... | ... | ... |
| Printer | 4 | 1.0 | ... | ... | ... | ... | ... | ... | 3 | 2.1 |
| Real estate agency | 3 | .7 | ... | ... | 1 | 1.2 | ... | ... | 2 | 1.4 |
| Restaurant | 1 | .2 | ... | ... | ... | ... | ... | ... | ... | ... |

· **TABLE 21**—*Continued* ·

| Occupation | *All Jews* No. | % | *Russia* No. | % | *Germany* No. | % | *Aust-Hung.* No. | % | *USA.* No. | % |
|---|---|---|---|---|---|---|---|---|---|---|
| Saloon | 2 | .5 | ... | ... | ... | ... | ... | ... | ... | ... |
| Steam laundry | 2 | .5 | ... | ... | 1 | 1.2 | ... | ... | 1 | .7 |
| Travel office | 1 | .2 | ... | ... | ... | ... | ... | ... | ... | ... |
| *White-collar workers* | 134 | 32.8 | 21 | 17.2 | 30 | 34.4 | 9 | 31.0 | 62 | 44.3 |
| Agent n.s. | 1 | .2 | ... | ... | ... | ... | ... | ... | 1 | .7 |
| Auctioneer | 1 | .2 | ... | ... | ... | ... | ... | ... | ... | ... |
| Bookkeeper | 16 | 3.9 | ... | ... | 1 | 1.2 | 2 | 6.9 | 11 | 7.8 |
| Cashier | 2 | .5 | ... | ... | ... | ... | ... | ... | 1 | .7 |
| Clerk, bank | 1 | .2 | ... | ... | 1 | 1.2 | ... | ... | ... | ... |
| Clerk, law | 1 | .2 | ... | ... | ... | ... | ... | ... | 1 | 1.4 |
| Clerk, store | 69 | 16.9 | 20 | 16.4 | 12 | 13.8 | 3 | 10.3 | 28 | 20.0 |
| Collector | 1 | .2 | ... | ... | 1 | 1.2 | ... | ... | ... | ... |
| Commercial traveler | 23 | 5.6 | ... | ... | 9 | 10.3 | 2 | 6.9 | 10 | 7.1 |
| Floorwalker | 1 | .2 | ... | ... | ... | ... | ... | ... | 1 | .7 |
| Insurance agent | 9 | 2.2 | ... | ... | 4 | 4.6 | 1 | 3.4 | 4 | 2.8 |
| Salesman | 5 | 1.2 | 1 | .8 | 2 | 2.3 | ... | ... | 2 | 1.4 |
| Stenographer | 3 | .7 | ... | ... | ... | ... | 1 | 3.4 | 2 | 1.4 |
| Telephone operator | 1 | .2 | ... | ... | ... | ... | ... | ... | 1 | .7 |
| *Self-employed artisan* | 15 | 3.7 | 12 | 9.8 | 2 | 2.3 | ... | ... | ... | ... |
| Shoemaker | 4 | 1.0 | 3 | 2.5 | 1 | 1.2 | ... | ... | ... | ... |
| Tailor | 10 | 2.5 | 9 | 7.4 | ... | ... | ... | ... | ... | ... |
| Watchmaker | 1 | .2 | ... | ... | 1 | 1.2 | ... | ... | ... | ... |
| *Skilled worker* | 16 | 3.9 | 9 | 7.4 | 1 | 1.2 | 1 | 3.4 | 4 | 2.9 |
| Foreman | 3 | .7 | ... | ... | 1 | 1.2 | ... | ... | 1 | .7 |
| Locksmith | 1 | .2 | 1 | .8 | ... | ... | ... | ... | ... | ... |
| Market inspector | 1 | .2 | ... | ... | ... | ... | 1 | 3.4 | ... | ... |
| Plumber | 1 | .2 | ... | ... | ... | ... | ... | ... | 1 | .7 |
| Policeman | 1 | .2 | 1 | .8 | ... | ... | ... | ... | ... | ... |
| Printer | 2 | .5 | ... | ... | ... | ... | ... | ... | 2 | 1.4 |
| Shochet | 1 | .2 | 1 | .8 | ... | ... | ... | ... | ... | ... |
| Tailor | 6 | 1.4 | 6 | 4.9 | ... | ... | ... | ... | ... | ... |
| *Peddler* | 18 | 4.4 | 16 | 13.1 | 1 | 1.2 | 1 | 3.4 | ... | ... |
| *Semiskilled worker* | 5 | 1.2 | 2 | 1.6 | 1 | 1.2 | ... | ... | 1 | .7 |
| Brewer | 1 | .2 | ... | ... | ... | ... | ... | ... | 1 | .7 |
| Cloth factory worker | 1 | .2 | ... | ... | ... | ... | ... | ... | ... | ... |
| Farm implement worker | 1 | .2 | ... | ... | 1 | 1.2 | ... | ... | ... | ... |
| Railroad worker | 1 | .2 | 1 | .8 | ... | ... | ... | ... | ... | ... |
| Umbrella repairer | 1 | .2 | 1 | .8 | ... | ... | ... | ... | ... | ... |
| *Unskilled* | 2 | .5 | ... | ... | ... | ... | ... | ... | ... | ... |
| Carpet layer | 1 | .2 | ... | ... | ... | ... | ... | ... | ... | ... |
| Drayman | 1 | .2 | ... | ... | ... | ... | ... | ... | ... | ... |
| TOTAL | 408 | 100.0 | 122 | 100.0 | 87 | 100.0 | 29 | 100.0 | 140 | 100.0 |
| Unknown | 56 | 13.7 | 20 | 14.1 | 16 | 15.5 | 5 | 14.7 | 12 | 7.9 |

n.s.—nonspecified.

*Note:* Percentages are rounded off to nearest 0.1 of 1%. Nearly all of the American-born were of non-Russian parentage.

**· TABLE 22 ·**

EMPLOYED RUSSIAN JEWISH MALES IN ATLANTA (AGES 18 AND OVER) AND RUSSIAN MALES IN FIFTEEN MAJOR CITIES BY INDUSTRIAL GROUP

| *Industry* | *Atlanta, 1896* % | *15 Cities, 1900* % |
|---|---|---|
| Agriculture and extractive industries | . . . | .5 |
| Clerical | . . . | 6.8 |
| Domestic and personal service | 1.6 | 7.0 |
| Manufacturing and the mechanical arts | 18.0 | 57.1 |
| Professional service | .8 | 2.9 |
| Public service | .8 | .4 |
| Trade | 78.7 | 23.3 |
| Transportation | . . . | 2.1 |
| TOTAL % | 100.0 | 100.0 |
| No. | 122 | 720,052 |

*Note:* Percentages are rounded off to nearest 0.1 of 1%. The 15 cities were Baltimore, Boston, Buffalo, Chicago, Cincinnati, Cleveland, Detroit, Milwaukee, New Orleans, New York, Philadelphia, Pittsburgh, San Francisco, St. Louis, and the District of Columbia. Not all the Russians in the 15 cities were Jews. However, there is a very high correlation between the distribution of Yiddish-speaking immigrants in 1910 and of Russians in 1900. Poland was listed separately.

**· TABLE 23 ·**

RESIDENTIAL PATTERNS OF IDENTIFIABLE ATLANTA JEWS: 1870, 1880, 1896, AND 1911

| | *1870* | | *1880* | | *1896* | | *1911* | |
|---|---|---|---|---|---|---|---|---|
| *Neighborhood* | *No.* | *%* | *No.* | *%* | *No.* | *%* | *No.* | *%* |
| A | 71 | 25.4 | 37 | 6.5 | 5 | .3 | 1 | .2 |
| B | 96 | 34.4 | 280 | 49.4 | 215 | 14.4 | 8 | 1.6 |
| C | 5 | 1.8 | 25 | 4.4 | 62 | 4.2 | 36 | 7.4 |
| D | 45 | 16.1 | 135 | 23.8 | 601 | 40.3 | 211 | 43.5 |
| E | . . . | . . . | . . . | . . . | 24 | 1.6 | 88 | 18.1 |
| F | . . . | . . . | . . . | . . . | 418 | 28.0 | 41 | 8.5 |
| G | 62 | 22.2 | 90 | 15.9 | 167 | 11.2 | 100 | 20.6 |
| TOTAL | 279 | 100.0 | 567 | 100.0 | 1,492 | 100.0 | 485 | 100.0 |
| Unknown | 5 | 1.8 | 3 | .5 | 9 | .6 | 13 | 2.6 |

*Note:* Percentages are rounded off to nearest 0.1 of 1%. The data for 1911 include only those males ages 18 and over in 1896 who were still present 15 years later, and all Russians not present in 1896 but present in 1911 who filed naturalization papers in Atlanta between 1897 and 1917.

## · TABLE 24 ·

RESIDENTIAL PATTERNS OF IDENTIFIABLE ATLANTA JEWS BY PARENTAGE, 1896 AND 1911

| | *1896* | | | | | | *1911* | | | | | |
|---|---|---|---|---|---|---|---|---|---|---|---|---|
| *Neigh-* | *All* | | *"German"* | | *Russian* | | *All* | | *"German"* | | *Russian* | |
| *borhood* | *No.* | *%* | *No.* | *%* | *No.* | *%* | *No.* | *%* | *No.* | *%* | *No.* | *%* |
| A | 5 | .3 | 1 | .1 | 1 | .2 | 1 | .2 | ... | ... | 1 | .3 |
| B | 215 | 14.4 | 187 | 25.2 | 4 | .8 | 8 | 1.6 | 5 | 3.8 | 3 | 1.0 |
| C | 62 | 4.2 | 16 | 2.2 | 43 | 8.9 | 36 | 7.4 | 2 | 1.5 | 34 | 11.1 |
| D | 601 | 40.3 | 401 | 54.0 | 11 | 2.3 | 211 | 43.5 | 91 | 68.9 | 86 | 28.1 |
| E | 24 | 1.6 | 3 | .4 | 20 | 4.1 | 88 | 18.1 | 3 | 2.3 | 84 | 27.5 |
| F | 418 | 28.0 | 36 | 4.8 | 369 | 76.4 | 41 | 8.5 | ... | ... | 41 | 13.4 |
| G | 167 | 11.2 | 99 | 13.3 | 35 | 7.2 | 100 | 20.6 | 31 | 23.4 | 57 | 18.6 |
| TOTAL | 1,492 | 100.0 | 743 | 100.0 | 483 | 100.0 | 485 | 100.0 | 132 | 100.0 | 306 | 100.0 |
| Unknown | 9 | .6 | 2 | .3 | 4 | .8 | 13 | 2.6 | 0 | | 47 | 13.3 |

*Note:* Percentages are rounded off to nearest 0.1 of 1%. "German" parentage includes persons of German, Austro-Hungarian, native, mixed foreign, and mixed native and foreign (i.e., all except those of Russian stock). The data for 1911 include only those males age 18 and over in 1896 who were still present 15 years later, and all Russians not present in 1896 but present in 1911 who filed naturalization papers in Atlanta between 1896 and 1917.

**· TABLE 25 ·**

PERSISTENCE IN ATLANTA OF IDENTIFIABLE JEWISH MALES (AGES 18 AND OVER) IN 1870, 1880, AND 1896

| *Enumeration* | *Uncorrected for Death* *No.* | *%* | *Corrected for Death* *%* |
|---|---|---|---|
| ***1870*** | | | |
| Present 1870 | 110 | 100.0 | 100.0 |
| died 1870–80 | 3 | 2.7 | . . . |
| moved 1870–80 | 45 | 41.0 | 42.1 |
| Present 1880 | 62 | 56.4 | 57.9 |
| died 1880–90 | 10 | . . . | . . . |
| moved 1880–90 | 9 | . . . | . . . |
| Present 1890 | 42 | 38.2 | 43.3 |
| died 1890–1900 | 6 | . . . | . . . |
| moved 1890–1900 | 2 | . . . | . . . |
| Present 1900 | 36 | 32.7 | 39.6 |
| moved or died 1900–11 | 11 | . . . | . . . |
| Present 1911 | 25 | 22.7 | n.a. |
| ***1880*** | | | |
| Present 1880 | 160 | 100.0 | 100.0 |
| died 1880–90 | 13 | 8.1 | . . . |
| moved 1880–90 | 56 | 35.0 | 38.1 |
| Present 1890 | 91 | 56.9 | 61.9 |
| died 1890–1900 | 14 | . . . | . . . |
| moved 1890–1900 | 9 | . . . | . . . |
| Present 1900 | 67 | 41.9 | 50.4 |
| died or moved 1900–11 | 10 | . . . | . . . |
| Present 1911 | 42 | 26.3 | n.a. |
| ***1896*** | | | |
| Present 1896 | 483 | 100.0 | n.a. |
| died or moved 1896–1911 | 222 | 46.0 | n.a. |
| Present 1911 | 261 | 54.0 | n.a. |

n.a.—not available

*Note:* Percentages are rounded off to nearest 0.1 of 1%. Although 110 adult Jewish males were present in 1870, 160 in 1880, and 483 in 1896, data on occupational status, wealth, and ownership of realty were not available for a few cases. This accounts for the slightly smaller size of the cohorts in some of the tables which follow.

## · TABLE 26 ·

PERSISTENCE IN ATLANTA OF IDENTIFIABLE JEWISH MALES (AGES 18 AND OVER) IN 1870, 1880, AND 1896 BY INITIAL OCCUPATIONAL STATUS

| | *Professional* | | | *Proprietor-Manager-Official* | | | *White-collar* | | | *Manual* | | |
|---|---|---|---|---|---|---|---|---|---|---|---|---|
| *Enumeration* | *No.* | *%* | *%CFD*[a] | *No.* | *%* | *%CFD* | *No.* | *%* | *%CFD* | *No.* | *%* | *%CFD* |
| ***1870*** | | | | | | | | | | | | |
| Present 1870 | 3 | 100.0 | 100.0 | 71 | 100.0 | 100.0 | 32 | 100.0 | 100.0 | 1 | 100.0 | 100.0 |
| died 1870–80 | ... | ... | ... | 2 | 2.8 | ... | 1 | 3.1 | ... | ... | ... | ... |
| moved 1870–80 | 2 | 66.6 | 66.6 | 21 | 29.6 | 30.4 | 23 | 71.9 | 74.2 | ... | ... | ... |
| Present 1880 | 1 | 33.3 | 33.3 | 48 | 67.6 | 69.6 | 8 | 25.0 | 25.8 | 1 | 100.0 | 100.0 |
| died 1880–90 | ... | ... | ... | 8 | ... | ... | 1 | ... | ... | ... | ... | ... |
| moved 1880–90 | ... | ... | ... | 8 | ... | ... | ... | ... | ... | ... | ... | ... |
| Present 1890 | 1 | 33.3 | 33.3 | 32 | 45.1 | 52.5 | 7 | 21.9 | 23.3 | 1 | 100.0 | 100.0 |
| died 1890–1900 | ... | ... | ... | 3 | ... | ... | 2 | ... | ... | ... | ... | ... |
| moved 1890–1900 | ... | ... | ... | 2 | ... | ... | ... | ... | ... | ... | ... | ... |
| Present 1900 | 1 | 33.3 | 33.3 | 26 | 36.6 | 44.8 | 6 | 18.8 | 21.4 | 1 | 100.0 | 100.0 |
| died or moved 1900–11 | 1 | ... | ... | 5 | ... | ... | 4 | ... | ... | 1 | 100.0 | 100.0 |
| Present 1911 | ... | ... | n.a. | 21 | 29.6 | n.a. | 2 | 6.6 | n.a. | ... | ... | ... |
| ***1880*** | | | | | | | | | | | | |
| Present 1880 | 5 | 100.0 | 100.0 | 90 | 100.0 | 100.0 | 45 | 100.0 | 100.0 | 9 | 100.0 | 100.0 |
| died 1880–90 | ... | ... | ... | 8 | 8.8 | ... | ... | ... | ... | 2 | 22.2 | ... |
| moved 1880–90 | 3 | 60.0 | 60.0 | 23 | 25.6 | 28.0 | 21 | 46.7 | 46.7 | 1 | 11.1 | 14.3 |
| Present 1890 | 2 | 40.0 | 40.0 | 59 | 65.6 | 72.0 | 24 | 53.3 | 53.3 | 6 | 66.7 | 85.7 |
| died 1890–1900 | ... | ... | ... | 8 | ... | ... | 3 | ... | ... | 2 | ... | ... |
| moved 1890–1900 | ... | ... | ... | 2 | ... | ... | 7 | ... | ... | 1 | ... | ... |
| Present 1900 | 3 | 60.0 | 60.0 | 49 | 54.4 | 66.2 | 13 | 28.9 | 31.0 | 3 | 33.3 | 60.0 |
| died or moved 1900–11 | 2 | ... | ... | 20 | ... | ... | 8 | ... | ... | 1 | ... | ... |
| Present 1911 | 1 | 20.0 | n.a. | 29 | 32.2 | n.a. | 9 | 20.0 | n.a. | 2 | 22.2 | n.a. |

***1896***[b]

| | *Professional* | | *Proprietor-Manager-Official* | | *White-collar* | | *Self-employed Artisans* | |
|---|---|---|---|---|---|---|---|---|
| Present 1896 | 20 | 100.0 | 198 | 100.0 | 134 | 100.0 | 15 | 100.0 |
| died or moved 1896–1911 | 6 | 30.0 | 79 | 39.9 | 59 | 44.0 | 7 | 46.7 |
| Present 1911 | 14 | 70.0 | 119 | 60.1 | 75 | 56.0 | 8 | 53.3 |

| | *Skilled* | | *Peddler* | | *Semiskilled, Unskilled* | |
|---|---|---|---|---|---|---|
| | *No.* | *%* | *No.* | *%* | *No.* | *%* |
| Present 1896 | 16 | 100.0 | 18 | 100.0 | 7 | 100.0 |
| died or moved 1896–1911 | 7 | 43.8 | 7 | 38.9 | 5 | 71.5 |
| Present 1911 | 9 | 56.2 | 11 | 61.1 | 2 | 28.6 |

n.a.—not available

[a] % Corrected for Death

[b] 1896 enumeration figures were not CFD.

*Note:* Percentages are rounded off to nearest 0.1 of 1%.

· TABLE 27 ·

PERSISTENCE IN ATLANTA OF IDENTIFIABLE JEWISH, NATIVE-BORN AND FOREIGN-BORN WHITE MALES: 1870 AND 1880

| Enumeration | *Jewish* *Ages 18+* No. | % | *Ages 18–29* No. | % | *Native-born Whites* *Ages 16+* No. | % | *Ages 20–29* No. | % | *Foreign-born White* *Ages 16+* No. | % | *Ages 20–29* No. | % |
|---|---|---|---|---|---|---|---|---|---|---|---|---|
| | | | | | | | *1870* | | | | | |
| Present 1870 | 110 | 100 | 50 | 100 | 258 | 100 | 924 | 100 | 208 | 100 | 105 | 100 |
| Present 1880 | 62 | 56 | 28 | 56 | 116 | 45 | 434 | 47 | 83 | 40 | 54 | 51 |
| Present 1890 | 42 | 38 | 24 | 48 | n.a. | n.a. | 323 | 35 | n.a. | n.a. | 36 | 34 |
| Present 1896 | 40 | 36 | 19 | 38 | 62 | 24 | n.a. | n.a. | 37 | 18 | n.a. | n.a. |
| Present 1900 | 36 | 33 | 19 | 38 | n.a. | n.a. | 231 | 25 | n.a | n.a. | 27 | 26 |
| Present 1910 (1911 for Jews) | 25 | 23 | 15 | 30 | n.a. | n.a. | 148 | 16 | n.a. | n.a. | 16 | 15 |
| | | | | | | | *1880* | | | | | |
| Present 1880 | 160 | 100 | 47 | 100 | n.a. | n.a. | 1882 | 100 | n.a. | n.a. | 128 | 100 |
| Present 1890 | 92 | 57 | 20 | 43 | n.a. | n.a. | 809 | 43 | n.a. | n.a. | 41 | 32 |
| Present 1900 | 67 | 42 | 15 | 32 | n.a. | n.a. | 546 | 29 | n.a. | n.a. | 23 | 18 |
| Present 1910 (1911 for Jews) | 42 | 26 | 11 | 23 | n.a. | n.a. | 414 | 22 | n.a. | n.a. | 17 | 13 |

n.a.—not available

*Note:* Percentages are rounded off to nearest 0.1 of 1%. None of the figures has been corrected for death.

· TABLE 28 ·

PERSISTENCE IN ATLANTA OF IDENTIFIABLE JEWISH, NATIVE-BORN AND FOREIGN-BORN WHITE MALE PROPRIETORS AND WHITE-COLLAR WORKERS: 1870 AND 1880

| | *Jewish* | | | | *Native-born Whites* | | | | *Foreign-born White* | | | |
|---|---|---|---|---|---|---|---|---|---|---|---|---|
| | *Ages 18+* | | *Ages 20–29* | | *Ages 16+* | | *Ages 20–29* | | *Ages 16+* | | *Ages 20–29* | |
| | *No.* | *%* | *No.* | *%* | *No.* | *%* | *No.* | *%* | *No.* | *%* | *No.* | *%* |
| ***1870 Sample*** | | | | | | | | | | | | |
| | | | | | ***Proprietors-Managers-Officials*** | | | | | | | |
| Present 1870 | 71 | 100 | 25 | 100 | 57 | 100 | 136 | 100 | 71 | 100 | 25 | 100 |
| Present 1880 | 48 | 68 | 16 | 64 | 36 | 64 | 78 | 57 | 31 | 43 | 14 | 56 |
| Present 1890 | 32 | 45 | 14 | 56 | n.a. | n.a. | 65 | 48 | n.a. | n.a. | 11 | 44 |
| Present 1896 | 31 | 44 | n.a. | n.a. | 18 | 32 | n.a. | n.a. | 17 | 24 | n.a. | n.a. |
| Present 1900 | 26 | 37 | 12 | 48 | n.a. | n.a. | 45 | 33 | n.a. | n.a. | 8 | 32 |
| Present 1910 (1911 for Jews) | 21 | 30 | 11 | 44 | n.a. | n.a. | 33 | 24 | n.a. | n.a. | 4 | 16 |
| | | | | | ***White-collar Workers*** | | | | | | | |
| Present 1870 | 32 | 100 | 18 | 100 | 56 | 100 | 257 | 100 | 25 | 100 | 28 | 100 |
| Present 1880 | 8 | 25 | 7 | 39 | 32 | 57 | 120 | 47 | 10 | 40 | 18 | 64 |
| Present 1890 | 7 | 22 | 7 | 39 | n.a. | n.a. | 95 | 37 | n.a. | n.a. | 14 | 50 |
| Present 1896 | 6 | 19 | n.a. | n.a. | 16 | 29 | n.a. | n.a. | 5 | 20 | n.a. | n.a. |
| Present 1900 | 6 | 19 | 5 | 28 | n.a. | n.a. | 69 | 27 | n.a. | n.a. | 11 | 39 |
| Present 1910 (1911 for Jews) | 2 | 7 | 1 | 6 | n.a. | n.a. | 46 | 18 | n.a. | n.a. | 8 | 29 |
| ***1880 Sample*** | | | | | | | | | | | | |
| | | | | | ***Proprietors-Managers-Officials*** | | | | | | | |
| Present 1880 | 90 | 100 | 15 | 100 | n.a. | n.a. | 235 | 100 | n.a. | n.a. | 27 | 100 |
| Present 1890 | 59 | 66 | 7 | 47 | n.a. | n.a. | 113 | 48 | n.a. | n.a. | 13 | 48 |
| Present 1900 | 49 | 54 | 7 | 47 | n.a. | n.a. | 78 | 33 | n.a. | n.a. | 8 | 30 |
| Present 1910 (1911 for Jews) | 29 | 32 | 5 | 33 | n.a. | n.a. | 61 | 26 | n.a. | n.a. | 6 | 22 |

n.a.—not available

*Note:* Percentages are rounded off to nearest 0.1 of 1%.

· TABLE 29 ·

OCCUPATIONAL MOBILITY OF IDENTIFIABLE JEWISH MALES IN 1870 TRACED TO 1880, 1890, 1900 AND 1911

| *Occupational Status 1870* | *No.* | *%* | *PPMO* | *White-collar* | *Self-empl. Art.* | *Skilled* | *Semi-skilled* | *Unskilled* |
|---|---|---|---|---|---|---|---|---|
| | | | *Occupational Status in 1880* | | | | | |
| PPMO | 48 | 84 | 83 | 11 | ... | ... | 4 | 2 |
| White-collar | 8 | 14 | 75 | 25 | ... | ... | ... | ... |
| Self-employed artisan | 1 | 2 | 100 | ... | ... | ... | ... | ... |
| Total No. | 57 | | 47 | 7 | ... | ... | 2 | 1 |
| Total % | ... | 100 | 82 | 12 | ... | ... | 4 | 2 |
| | | | *Occupational Status in 1890* | | | | | |
| PPMO | 31 | 82 | 77 | 13 | 7 | ... | 3 | ... |
| White-collar | 6 | 16 | 67 | 33 | ... | ... | ... | ... |
| Self-employed artisan | 1 | 2 | 100 | ... | ... | ... | ... | ... |
| Total No. | 38 | | 29 | 6 | 2 | ... | 1 | ... |
| Total % | ... | 100 | 76 | 16 | 5 | ... | 3 | ... |
| | | | *Occupational Status in 1900* | | | | | |
| PPMO | 22 | 79 | 64 | 32 | 5 | ... | ... | ... |
| White-collar | 5 | 21 | 60 | 40 | ... | ... | ... | ... |
| Total No. | 27 | | 17 | 9 | 1 | ... | ... | ... |
| Total % | ... | 100 | 63 | 33 | 4 | ... | ... | ... |
| | | | *Occupational Status in 1911* | | | | | |
| PPMO | 16 | 89 | 88 | 12 | ... | ... | ... | ... |
| White-collar | 2 | 11 | 50 | 50 | ... | ... | ... | ... |
| Total No. | 18 | | 15 | 3 | ... | ... | ... | ... |
| Total % | ... | 100 | 83 | 17 | ... | ... | ... | ... |

PPMO—Professional-Proprietor-Manager-Official

*Note:* Percentages are rounded off to nearest 0.1 of 1%.

· **TABLE 30** ·

OCCUPATIONAL MOBILITY OF IDENTIFIABLE JEWISH MALES IN 1880, TRACED TO 1890, 1900, AND 1911

| *Occupational Status 1880* | *No.* | *%* | *PPMO* | *White-Collar* | *Self-empl. Art.* | *Skilled* | *Semi skilled* | *Unskilled* |
|---|---|---|---|---|---|---|---|---|
| | | | ***Occupational Status in 1890*** | | | | | |
| PPMO | 54 | 68 | 87 | 7 | 4 | . . . | 2 | . . . |
| White-collar | 21 | 26 | 52 | 48 | . . . | . . . | . . . | . . . |
| Skilled | 3 | 4 | . . . | 33 | 33 | 33 | . . . | . . . |
| Semiskilled | 1 | 1 | . . . | 100 | . . . | . . . | . . . | . . . |
| Unskilled | 1 | 1 | . . . | . . . | . . . | . . . | . . . | 100 |
| Total No. | 80 | | 58 | 16 | 3 | 1 | 1 | 1 |
| Total % | . . . | 100 | 73 | 20 | 4 | 1 | 1 | 1 |
| | | | ***Occupational Status in 1900*** | | | | | |
| PPMO | 39 | 74 | 64 | 33 | 3 | . . . | . . . | . . . |
| White-collar | 12 | 23 | 42 | 58 | . . . | . . . | . . . | . . . |
| Skilled | 1 | 2 | . . . | . . . | . . . | 100 | . . . | . . . |
| Semiskilled | 1 | 2 | 100 | . . . | . . . | . . . | . . . | . . . |
| Total No. | 53 | | 31 | 20 | 1 | 1 | . . . | . . . |
| Total % | . . . | 100 | 58 | 38 | 2 | 2 | . . . | . . . |
| | | | ***Occupational Status in 1911*** | | | | | |
| PPMO | 16 | 89 | 88 | 12 | . . . | . . . | . . . | . . . |
| White-collar | 2 | 11 | 50 | 50 | . . . | . . . | . . . | . . . |
| Total No. | 18 | | 15 | 13 | . . . | . . . | . . . | . . . |
| Total % | . . . | 100 | 83 | 17 | . . . | . . . | . . . | . . . |

PPMO—Professional-Proprietor-Manager-Official

*Note:* Percentages are rounded off to nearest 0.1 of 1%.

## · TABLE 31 ·

### OCCUPATIONAL MOBILITY OF IDENTIFIABLE JEWISH MALES IN 1896, TRACED TO 1911

| | | | *Occupational Status 1911 (%)* | | | | | |
|---|---|---|---|---|---|---|---|---|
| *Occupational Status 1896* | *%* | *No.* | *PPMO* | *White-collar* | *Self-empl. Art.* | *Skilled* | *Peddler* | *Semi-skilled* |
| PPMO | 57 | 119 | 91 | 7 | 2 | ... | ... | ... |
| White-collar | 30 | 62 | 63 | 34 | 2 | ... | ... | 1 |
| Self-employed artisan | 3 | 7 | ... | ... | 71 | 29 | ... | ... |
| Skilled | 4 | 9 | 33 | ... | ... | 56 | 1 | ... |
| Peddler | 4 | 9 | 33 | 56 | ... | ... | 1 | ... |
| Semiskilled | 1 | 1 | 100 | ... | ... | ... | ... | ... |
| Unskilled | 1 | 1 | ... | 100 | ... | ... | ... | ... |
| Total No. | | 208 | 155 | 35 | 8 | 7 | 2 | 1 |
| Total % | 100 | ... | 74 | 17 | 4 | 3 | 1 | 1 |

PPMO—Professional-Proprietor-Manager-Official

*Note:* Percentages are rounded off to nearest 0.1 of 1%.

## · TABLE 32 ·

### OCCUPATIONAL MOBILITY OF IDENTIFIABLE JEWISH MALES IN 1896, TRACED TO 1911 BY BIRTHPLACE

| | | | *Occupational Status 1911 (%)* | | | | |
|---|---|---|---|---|---|---|---|
| *Occupational Status 1896* | *No.* | *%* | *PPMO* | *White-collar* | *Self-empl. Art.* | *Skilled* | *Peddler or Semiskilled* |
| ***Russians*** | | | | | | | |
| PPMO | 32 | 51 | 84 | 10 | 6 | ... | ... |
| White-collar | 8 | 13 | 50 | 38 | 12 | ... | ... |
| Self-employed artisan | 6 | 10 | ... | ... | 67 | 33 | ... |
| Skilled | 6 | 16 | 33 | ... | ... | 50 | 17 |
| Peddler | 9 | 14 | 33 | 56 | ... | ... | 11 |
| Semiskilled | 1 | 2 | 100 | ... | ... | ... | ... |
| Total No. | 62 | | 37 | 11 | 7 | 5 | 2 |
| Total % | ... | 100 | 60 | 18 | 11 | 8 | 3 |
| ***Non-Russians*** | | | | | | | |
| PPMO | 85 | 60 | 95 | 5 | ... | ... | ... |
| White-collar | 52 | 37 | 65 | 33 | ... | ... | 2 |
| Self-employed artisan | 1 | 1 | ... | ... | 100 | ... | ... |
| Skilled | 3 | 2 | 33 | ... | ... | 67 | ... |
| Total No. | 141 | | 116 | 21 | 1 | 2 | 1 |
| Total % | ... | 100 | 82 | 15 | 1 | 2 | 1 |

PPMO—Professional-Proprietor-Manager-Official.

*Note:* Percentages are rounded off to nearest 0.1 of 1%.

· TABLE 33 ·

CHANGES IN WEALTH OF IDENTIFIABLE JEWISH MALES IN 1870, TRACED TO 1880, 1890, AND 1900

| *Wealth in 1870* | | | *Wealth in 1880 (in %)* | | | | | |
|---|---|---|---|---|---|---|---|---|
| | *No.* | *%* | *$0–500* | *$600–3,000* | *$3,100–10,000* | *$10,100–20,000* | *$20,100–30,000* | *$30,100 +* |
| $0 – 500 | 21 | 51 | 38 | 14 | 43 | ... | 5 | ... |
| $600 – 3,000 | 8 | 19 | 50 | 38 | 12 | ... | ... | ... |
| $3,100 –10,000 | 8 | 19 | ... | 12 | 50 | 25 | 12 | ... |
| $10,100–20,000 | 4 | 10 | ... | ... | 50 | 50 | ... | ... |
| Total No. | 41 | | 12 | 7 | 16 | 4 | 2 | ... |
| Total % | ... | 100 | 29 | 17 | 39 | 10 | 5 | ... |
| | | | *Wealth in 1890* | | | | | |
| $0 – 500 | 12 | 50 | 8 | 17 | 42 | 17 | ... | 17 |
| $600 – 3,000 | 3 | 12 | 33 | 33 | 33 | ... | ... | ... |
| $3,100 –10,000 | 6 | 25 | ... | 17 | 33 | 50 | ... | ... |
| $10,100–20,000 | 3 | 12 | 33 | 33 | 33 | ... | ... | ... |
| Total No. | 24 | | 3 | 4 | 9 | 6 | ... | 2 |
| Total % | ... | 100 | 12 | 17 | 37 | 25 | ... | 8 |
| | | | *Wealth in 1900* | | | | | |
| $0 – 500 | 11 | 50 | 46 | ... | 36 | 18 | ... | ... |
| $600 – 3,000 | 3 | 14 | ... | 33 | 67 | ... | ... | ... |
| $3,100 –10,000 | 5 | 23 | ... | 20 | 20 | 40 | ... | 20 |
| $10,100–20,000 | 3 | 14 | 33 | 33 | ... | ... | 33 | ... |
| Total No. | 22 | | 6 | 3 | 7 | 4 | 1 | 1 |
| Total % | ... | 100 | 27 | 14 | 32 | 18 | 4 | 4 |

*Note:* Percentages are rounded off to nearest 0.1 of 1%. Wealth is rounded off to nearest $100.

### · TABLE 34 ·

CHANGES IN WEALTH OF IDENTIFIABLE JEWISH MALES IN 1880, TRACED TO 1890 AND 1900

| *Wealth in 1880* | *%* | *No.* | *$0–500* | *$600–3,000* | *$3,100–10,000* | *$10,100–20,000* | *$20,100–30,000* | *$30,100+* |
|---|---|---|---|---|---|---|---|---|
| | | | *(in %) Wealth in 1890* | | | | | |
| $0 – 500 | 49 | 41 | 46 | 24 | 20 | 7 | 2 | ... |
| $600 – 3,000 | 13 | 11 | 9 | 55 | 36 | ... | ... | ... |
| $3,100 –10,000 | 25 | 21 | 5 | 14 | 38 | 19 | 14 | 10 |
| $10,100–20,000 | 11 | 9 | 22 | 22 | 11 | 22 | 11 | 11 |
| $20,100–30,000 | 2 | 2 | ... | ... | ... | 50 | ... | 50 |
| Total No. | | 84 | 23 | 21 | 21 | 10 | 5 | 4 |
| Total % | 100 | ... | 27 | 25 | 25 | 12 | 6 | 5 |
| | | | *Wealth in 1900* | | | | | |
| $0 – 500 | 47 | 26 | 61 | 12 | 19 | 4 | 4 | ... |
| $600 – 3,000 | 13 | 7 | 43 | ... | 57 | ... | ... | ... |
| $3,100 –10,000 | 24 | 13 | 23 | 16 | 23 | 23 | 15 | ... |
| $10,100–20,000 | 13 | 7 | 29 | 14 | ... | 29 | ... | 29 |
| $20,100–30,000 | 4 | 2 | ... | ... | ... | 50 | 50 | ... |
| Total No. | ... | 55 | 24 | 6 | 12 | 7 | 4 | 2 |
| Total % | 100 | ... | 44 | 11 | 22 | 13 | 7 | 3 |

*Note:* Percentages are rounded off to nearest 0.1 of 1%. Wealth is rounded off to nearest $100.

### · TABLE 35 ·

CHANGES IN WEALTH OF IDENTIFIABLE RUSSIAN JEWISH MALES IN 1896, TRACED TO 1911

| *Wealth in 1896* | *No.* | *%* | *Wealth in 1911* $0 –50 | *$100 –500* | *$600 –1,000* | *$1,100 –3,000* | *$3,100 –5,000* | *$5,100 –10,000* | *$10,100 –20,000* | *$20,100 –30,000* | *$30,1 +* |
|---|---|---|---|---|---|---|---|---|---|---|---|
| $0 – 50 | 53 | 67 | 45 | 15 | 4 | 15 | 9 | 7 | 2 | 2 | .. |
| $100 – 500 | 18 | 23 | 17 | 11 | ... | 33 | 6 | 22 | 11 | ... | .. |
| $600 – 1,000 | 5 | 6 | 20 | ... | ... | ... | 60 | 20 | ... | ... | .. |
| $1,100 – 3,000 | 1 | 1 | 100 | ... | ... | ... | ... | ... | ... | ... | .. |
| $10,100–20,000 | 1 | 1 | ... | ... | ... | ... | ... | ... | 100 | ... | .. |
| $20,100–30,000 | 1 | 1 | ... | ... | ... | ... | ... | ... | ... | ... | 10 |
| Total No. | 79 | | 29 | 10 | 2 | 14 | 9 | 9 | 4 | 1 | |
| Total % | ... | 100 | 37 | 13 | 3 | 18 | 11 | 11 | 5 | 1 | |

*Note:* Percentages are rounded off to nearest 0.1 of 1%. Wealth is rounded off to nearest $1

· **TABLE 36** ·

CAREER MOBILITY OF YOUNG JEWISH AND GENTILE MALES IN POUGHKEEPSIE AND BOSTON, COMPARED WITH INITIAL 18- TO 29-YEAR-OLD ATLANTA JEWS

| | *Jews* | *Catholics* | *Protestants* |
|---|---|---|---|
| ***Poughkeepsie Germans 1850–1880*** | | | |
| Begin white-collar | 55% | 15% | 17% |
| End white-collar | 90% | 35% | 37% |
| No. | 29 | 113 | 238 |
| ***Bostonians 1860–1879 Birth Cohort*** | | | |
| Begin white-collar | 73% | 41% | 65% |
| End white-collar | 84% | 43% | 64% |
| No. | 26 | 297 | 340 |
| ***Bostonians 1880–1889 Birth Cohort*** | | | |
| Begin white-collar | 43% | 32% | 41% |
| End white-collar | 60% | 44% | 50% |
| No. | 37 | 203 | 151 |

*ATLANTA JEWS*

| | *1870 Sample* | *1880 Sample* | *1896 Sample* |
|---|---|---|---|
| Begin white-collar | 100% | 93% | 88% |
| End white-collar | 100% | 100% | 90% |
| No. | 48 | 42 | 135 |

· TABLE 37 ·

OCCUPATIONAL MOBILITY OF NEW YORK JEWISH HOUSEHOLD HEADS IN 1880, 1892, AND 1905, TRACED FOR TEN YEARS

| *Original Occupational Status* | % | *High White-collar* % | *Low White-collar* % | *Skilled* % | *Semi-skilled* % | *Unskilled* % |
|---|---|---|---|---|---|---|
| | | *Occupational Status After 10 Years* | | | | |
| High white-collar | 11.0 | 90.0 | 10.0 | . . . | . . . | . . . |
| Low white-collar | 35.4 | 9.2 | 81.6 | 5.9 | 1.6 | 1.6 |
| Skilled | 40.9 | 6.9 | 32.7 | 55.3 | 3.7 | 1.4 |
| Semiskilled | 11.5 | 9.8 | 27.9 | 27.9 | 31.1 | 3.3 |
| Unskilled | 1.0 | . . . | . . . | 60.0 | 20.0 | 20.0 |
| Total No. | 531 | 92 | 248 | 151 | 31 | 9 |
| Total % | 100.0 | 17.0 | 46.7 | 28.4 | 5.8 | 1.7 |

*Note:* Percentages are rounded off to nearest 0.1 of 1%. High white-collar includes professionals and major proprietors, managers and officials. Low white-collar includes clerks, salesmen, semiprofessionals, peddlers and petty proprietors, and managers and officials.

· **TABLE 38** ·

SIMPLIFIED OCCUPATIONAL MOBILITY IN ATLANTA OF INITIAL PPMOS AND WHITE-COLLAR WORKERS (AGES 20–29) IN 1870

| *Occupational Status 1870* | *Native-born Whites* *No.* | *Up* | *Stable (in %)* | *Down* | *Immigrants* *No.* | *Up* | *Stable (in %)* | *Down* | *Jews* *No.* | *Up* | *Stable (in %)* | *Down* |
|---|---|---|---|---|---|---|---|---|---|---|---|---|
| | | | | | | ***In 1880*** | | | | | | |
| PPMO | 99 | n.a. | 69 | 31 | 14 | n.a. | 79 | 21 | 16 | n.a. | 88 | 12 |
| White-collar | 119 | 40 | 46 | 13 | 18 | 50 | 33 | 17 | 7 | 71 | 29 | . . . |
| Total % | 100 | 22 | 56 | 22 | 100 | 28 | 53 | 19 | 100 | 22 | 70 | 9 |
| Total No. | 218 | 48 | 123 | 47 | 32 | 9 | 17 | 6 | 23 | 5 | 16 | 2 |
| | | | | | | ***In 1890*** | | | | | | |
| PPMO | 81 | n.a. | 75 | 25 | 11 | n.a. | 73 | 27 | 14 | n.a. | 79 | 21 |
| White-collar | 92 | 57 | 29 | 14 | 14 | 50 | 33 | 17 | 6 | 67 | 33 | . . . |
| Total % | 100 | 30 | 51 | 19 | 100 | 28 | 52 | 20 | 100 | 25 | 65 | 15 |
| Total No. | 173 | 52 | 88 | 33 | 25 | 7 | 13 | 5 | 20 | 4 | 13 | 3 |
| | | | | | | ***In 1900*** | | | | | | |
| PPMO | 56 | n.a. | 75 | 25 | 8 | n.a. | 50 | 50 | 12 | n.a. | 75 | 25 |
| White-collar | 65 | 55 | 28 | 17 | 10 | 70 | 30 | . . . | 5 | 60 | 40 | . . . |
| Total % | 100 | 30 | 50 | 20 | 100 | 39 | 39 | 22 | 100 | 18 | 64 | 18 |
| Total No. | 121 | 36 | 60 | 25 | 18 | 7 | 7 | 4 | 17 | 3 | 11 | 3 |
| | | | | | | ***In 1910 (1911)*** | | | | | | |
| PPMO | 37 | n.a. | 78 | 22 | 4 | n.a. | 50 | 50 | 10 | n.a. | 80 | 20 |
| White-collar | 43 | 63 | 28 | 9 | 6 | 67 | 33 | . . . | 1 | 100 | . . . | . . . |
| Total % | 100 | 34 | 51 | 15 | 100 | 40 | 40 | 20 | 100 | 9 | 73 | 18 |
| Total No. | 80 | 27 | 41 | 12 | 10 | 4 | 4 | 2 | 11 | 1 | 8 | 2 |

n.a.—not available

PPMO—Professional-Proprietor-Manager-Official

*Note:* Percentages are rounded off to nearest 0.1 of 1%. As there were no Jewish blue-collar workers age 20 to 29 who remained, the comparison was restricted accordingly.

## · TABLE 39 ·

SIMPLIFIED OCCUPATIONAL MOBILITY IN ATLANTA OF INITIAL PPMOS, WHITE-COLLAR AND SKILLED WORKERS (AGES 20–29) IN 1880

| *Occupational Status 1880* | *Native-born Whites* *No.* | *Up* | *Stable (in %)* | *Down* | *Immigrants* *No.* | *Up* | *Stable (in %)* | *Down* | *Jews* *No.* | *Up* | *Stable (in %)* | *Down* |
|---|---|---|---|---|---|---|---|---|---|---|---|---|
| | | | | | | ***In 1890*** | | | | | | |
| PPMO | 154 | n.a. | 75 | 25 | 13 | n.a. | 69 | 31 | 4 | n.a. | 100 | . . . |
| White-collar | 264 | 41 | 50 | 8 | 13 | 31 | 62 | 7 | 5 | 40 | 60 | . . . |
| Skilled | 189 | 20 | 75 | 5 | 5 | 40 | 60 | . . . | 2 | 50 | 50 | . . . |
| Total % | 100 | 24 | 64 | 12 | 100 | 19 | 65 | 16 | 100 | 38 | 62 | . . . |
| Total No. | 607 | 146 | 391 | 70 | 31 | 6 | 20 | 5 | 11 | 3 | 8 | . . . |
| | | | | | | ***In 1900*** | | | | | | |
| PPMO | 108 | n.a. | 73 | 27 | 9 | n.a. | 78 | 22 | 5 | n.a. | 100 | . . . |
| White-collar | 188 | 43 | 47 | 10 | 7 | 57 | 43 | . . . | 3 | 67 | 33 | . . . |
| Skilled | 127 | 28 | 65 | 7 | 3 | 67 | 33 | . . . | 1 | . . . | 100 | . . . |
| Total % | 100 | 28 | 59 | 13 | 100 | 32 | 58 | 10 | 100 | 22 | 78 | . . . |
| Total No. | 423 | 117 | 250 | 56 | 19 | 6 | 11 | 2 | 9 | 2 | 7 | . . . |
| | | | | | | ***In 1910 (1911)*** | | | | | | |
| PPMO | 76 | n.a. | 67 | 33 | 7 | n.a. | 100 | . . . | 6 | n.a. | 100 | . . . |
| White-collar | 139 | 50 | 40 | 10 | 5 | 40 | 40 | 20 | 2 | 50 | 50 | . . . |
| Skilled | 90 | 24 | 70 | 6 | 2 | 50 | 50 | . . . | 1 | . . . | 100 | . . . |
| Total % | 100 | 30 | 55 | 15 | 100 | 21 | 71 | 7 | 100 | 11 | 89 | . . . |
| Total No. | 305 | 91 | 169 | 45 | 14 | 3 | 10 | 1 | 9 | 1 | 8 | . . . |

n.a.—not available

PPMO—Professional-Proprietor-Manager-Official.

*Note:* Percentages are rounded off to nearest 0.1 of 1%. As there were no semiskilled or unskilled Jews age 20 to 29 who remained, the comparison was restricted accordingly.

# *Selected Bibliography*

An interpretive history of Atlanta is yet to be published, and most of the existing studies border on boosterism. Though discursive and antiquarian, Franklin M. Garrett, *Atlanta and Environs* (Athens, Ga., 1969), is a useful year-by-year chronicle, especially because of its thorough documentation, detailed index, and frequent mention of prominent Jews. Of less value are Wallace P. Reed, *Reed's History of Atlanta* (Syracuse, N. Y., 1889); Thomas H. Martin, *Atlanta and Its Builders* (Atlanta, 1902); and the Georgia Writers' Project, *Atlanta: A City of the Modern South* (New York, 1942). Several well-researched doctoral dissertations focus on Atlanta's early development, the best being James M. Russell, "Atlanta, Gate City of the South, 1847 to 1885" (Princeton University, 1971) and Grigsby H. Wotton, "New City of the South: Atlanta, 1843–1873" (Johns Hopkins University, 1973). Unfortunately, only fragmentary work has been done on the period after 1885. Richard J. Hopkins's dissertation, "Patterns of Persistence and Occupational Mobility in a Southern City: Atlanta, 1870–1920" (Emory University, 1972), provides both the methodology which I utilized to examine Jewish mobility patterns and the data with which my findings are compared.

Several earlier studies of Atlanta Jewry laid the foundation for the present work. [David Marx], "History of the Jews of Atlanta," *Reform Advocate* (November 4, 1911), contains valuable—if somewhat hagiographic—biographical sketches of sixty of the German community's founders and leading personalities. Solomon Sutker's sociology dissertation, "The Jews of Atlanta: Their Structure and Leadership Patterns" (University of North Carolina, 1952), is a sophisticated analysis of the community circa 1950. Harry Golden, *A Little Girl Is Dead* (Cleveland, 1965), and Leonard Dinnerstein, *The Leo Frank Case* (New York, 1968), are perceptive treatments of the event which marks the terminal point of this study, but neither accords more than cursory attention to the development of the Jewish community. Janice O. Rothschild, *As But a Day: The First Hundred Years, 1867–1967* (Atlanta, 1968), is a useful but undocumented history of the Hebrew Benevolent Congregation based largely upon congregational records. Rothschild's book and her superficial "Pre-1867 Atlanta Jewry," *American Jewish Historical Quarterly* 62 (March 1973), would both have benefited from an examination of the available periodical literature. Arnold Shankman, "Atlanta Jewry: 1900–1930," *American Jewish Archives* (November 1973), is based largely upon secondary sources and is of poor quality.

The most valuable source for the study of an American Jewish community is the local press. Every issue of the *Atlanta Constitution* from 1868 to 1915 was examined as were shorter runs of twelve other local periodicals of a general character. Despite the community's small size, local journalists accorded considerable attention to Jewish doings and personalities, especially during the autumn holiday season. In addition, eight Jewish periodicals were published in Atlanta between 1877 and 1915. However, except for the *Jewish South* (1877–1879), the *Jewish Sentiment* (1896–1901) and the *American Jewish Review* (1913–1916), only scattered issues have survived. Several northern Jewish newspapers which carried news from Atlanta were also consulted.

The second most important source are public records. Census schedules, tax digests, naturalization records, death certificates, interment records, and petitions for incorporation contain a wealth of data on the characteristics of Atlanta's Jews. City directories, guidebooks, and promotional tracts provide additional insights, especially regarding residential and occupational patterns.

Institutional records reflect the evolution of Jewish associational activity. Except for a few gaps, the minutes and ledgers of the Hebrew Benevolent Congregation are available from 1869 to 1915, and document the changing religious orientation of the German community. Unfortunately, Congregation Ahavath Achim's minutes are extant only for the years 1890 to 1895, and the early records of Atlanta's other Russian and Levantine congregations are even more fragmentary. The records of the Hebrew Orphans' Home are preserved in their entirety but contain little usable information. Much more valuable are the minutes of the Federation of Jewish Charities and the Jewish Educational Alliance. Scattered fraternal lodge records are also available.

Among the papers of national Jewish organizations, those of the Industrial Removal Office are the most important. This collection contains detailed information on all immigrants sent to Atlanta between 1901 and 1915, follow-up reports on their progress, and correspondence between the national office and the local affiliate.

Only a few written reminiscences and collections of personal papers could be located, the most valuable of which were the E. B. M. Browne, Leo M. Frank, and David Marx papers, and the memoirs of David Davis, Rabbi Tobias Geffen, and Charles Greenberg. Thirteen longtime members of the Jewish community were also interviewed.

A list of all the sources consulted would include many of only tangential relevance. To provide some indication of the study's scope, the bibliography which follows is confined primarily to material on Atlanta, her Jewish community, and southern Jewry.

## PRIMARY SOURCES

### *A. Manuscripts*

#### PUBLIC DOCUMENTS

Atlanta. City Cemetery Interment Records, 1853–1973. Office of the Sexton, Oakland Cemetery.

———. City Census of 1896. Woodruff Library, Emory University.

———. City Council Minutes, 1860–1863. Atlanta Historical Society.

———. Board of Health. Death Certificates, 1887–1911. Fulton County Bureau of Statistics.

Fulton County. Superior Court. Declarations of Intention and Petitions for Naturalization, 1878–1906. Office of the Clerk.

———. Superior Court. Petitions for Incorporation.

Beth Hamedresh Hagadol Anshe Sfard. #4647.
Concordia Association. Minute Book E, p. 309.
Congregation Ahavath Achim, #7358.
Congregation Beth Israel. Charterbook V, p. 478.
Congregation B'nai Abraham. #41 F. T. 1890.
Congregregation Chevra Kadisha. Charterbook II, p. 658.
Free Kindergarten and Social Settlement. #2143.
Harmony Club. #109.
Hebrew Association of Atlanta. #427.
Hungarian Benevolent Association. #3660.
Jewish Educational Alliance. #3077.
Jewish Orphans' Asylum. #842.
Jewish Progressive Club. #4918.
Montefiore Relief Association. Charterbook II, p. 695.
Mutual Order B'nai Israel. #2798.
Oriental Hebrew Association Or Hahayim. #4615.
Oriental Hebrew Association Or V'Shalom. #5035.
Shearith Israel Congregation. Charterbook V, p. 166.
Standard Club. #1628.
Workman's Circle Branch 20. #5599.
Young Men's Hebrew Association. #1673.

———. Tax Digests. 1880, 1890, 1896, 1897, 1900, 1911. Georgia Department of Archives and History.

Georgia. General Assembly. Memorial of the Cotton Planters' Convention of Georgia to the General Assembly. n.d. Immigration File, Georgia Department of Archives and History.

———. General Assembly. Memorial of Joseph Elsas to the General Assembly of Georgia on the Subject of the Immigration of Foreign Laborers into this State, n.d. Immigration File, Georgia Department of Archives and History.

———. General Assembly. Petition of H. Wolfe et al., to Hon. John I. Hall, [1892]. Georgia Department of Archives and History.

———. General Assembly. Report of the Commissioner of Land and Immigration, Francis Fontaine, 1880. Immigration File, Georgia Department of Archives and History.

———. Report of the Commissioners of Immigration, Samuel Weil and George N. Lester, 1870. Immigration File, Georgia Department of Archives and History.

United States. Census Schedules, 1850. De Kalb County, Georgia. Free White Population and Slaves.

———. Census Schedules, 1860. Fulton County, Georgia. Free White Population and Slaves.

———. Census Schedules, 1870. Fulton County, Georgia. Population.

———. Census Schedules, 1880. Fulton County, Georgia. Population and Manufactures.

———. Circuit Court for the Northern District of Georgia. Declarations of Intention and Petitions for Naturalization, 1893–1917. Federal Records Center, East Point, Georgia.

### INSTITUTIONAL RECORDS

Ahavath Achim Congregation. Minutes, 1890–1895. Membership List, 1900. Ahavath Achim Archives.

Anshe Sfard Congregation. Ledgers, 1913–1928. In possession of H. Taratoot, Atlanta.

Baron de Hirsch Fund Papers. American Jewish Historical Society.

B'nai B'rith Atlanta Lodge No. 548. Membership List, 1903. Office of the District Grand Lodge, Atlanta.

B'nai B'rith Gate City Lodge No. 144. Question Book, 1870–1896. Atlanta Historical Society.

———. Ledgers, 1883–1890. Hebrew Benevolent Congregation Archives.

Council of Jewish Women, Atlanta Section. Scrapbook, 1895–1941. CJW, Atlanta.

Don't Worry Club. Minutes, 1911–1917. Atlanta Historical Society.

Federation of Jewish Charities. Minutes, 1912–1923. Atlanta Jewish Welfare Federation.

Free Sons of Israel Atlanta Lodge No. 85. Membership List, 1877–1883. Hebrew Benevolent Congregation Archives.

Hebrew Benevolent Congregation. Minutes, 1877–1915. Ledgers, 1869–1878, 1905–1915. Membership Lists, 1877, 1895, 1902. HBC Archives.

Hebrew Orphans' Home. Minutes and Records of Admission, 1889–1917. Jewish Family and Children's Bureau, Atlanta.
Industrial Removal Office Papers. American Jewish Historical Society.
Jewish Educational Alliance. Minutes, 1906–1915. Atlanta Jewish Welfare Federation.
Masonic Grand Lodge of Georgia. Subordinate Lodge Returns, 1878, 1899, 1913. Office of the Grand Lodge, Macon.

FAMILY AND PERSONAL PAPERS, MEMOIRS, CORRESPONDENCE, AND SCRAPBOOKS

Alexander Family Papers. In possession of Cecil Alexander, Atlanta.
Edward B. M. Browne Papers. American Jewish Historical Society.
———. American Jewish Archives.
David Burgheim Papers. American Jewish Archives.
Cohen, Arye Loeb. Account Book. American Jewish Archives.
Cohen, Levi. Receipts for Slaves. American Jewish Archives.
Natalie Cohen Collection. Atlanta Historical Society.
Leo M. Frank Papers. Atlanta Historical Society.
———. American Jewish Archives.
———. Brandeis University.
Lemuel P. Grant Papers. Atlanta Historical Society.
Geffen, Tobias. Memoir. In possession of Louis Geffen, Atlanta.
Greenberg, Charles. Memoir. In possession of Mrs. David Eisenberg, Atlanta.
Herzberg, Heyman. Diary. American Jewish Archives.
Joel, Josephine. Diary. In possession of Josephine Heyman, Atlanta.
Louis Marshall Papers. American Jewish Archives.
David Marx Papers. Hebrew Benevolent Congregation Archives.
———. American Jewish Archives.
Steinheimer, Florence. Scrapbook. In possession of Janet Cohen, Atlanta.

## B. *Published*

NEWSPAPERS AND PERIODICALS

*American Israelite* (Cincinnati). 1874–1900.
*American Jewish Review* (Atlanta). 1913–1916.
*Atlanta Constitution.* 1868–1915.
*Atlanta Daily Herald.* 1873–1875.
*Atlanta Daily Intelligencer.* 1858–1868.
*Atlanta Daily New Era.* 1867, 1871.
*Atlanta Daily News.* 1874.
*Atlanta Daily Sun.* 1871.
*Atlanta Georgian.* 1907, 1913.
*Atlanta Independent.* 1901–1915.
*Atlanta Journal.* 1882–1900, 1913–1915.

*Gate City Guardian* (Atlanta). 1861.
*Israelite* (Cincinnati). 1857–1873.
*Jeffersonian* (Thomson, Ga.). 1914–1915.
*Jewish Advance* (Chicago). 1878.
*Jewish Messenger* (New York). 1869, 1885.
*Jewish Outlook* (Atlanta). April 1913.
*Jewish Sentiment* (Atlanta). 1896–1901.
*Jewish South* (Atlanta). 1877–1879.
*Jewish Star* (Atlanta). November 1909.
*Jewish Tribune* (Atlanta). February 28, 1896.
*Maccabean* (New York). 1901–1915.
*Magnet* (Atlanta). 1894.
*New York Age.* 1905, 1908, 1914.
*New York Freeman.* 1886.
*Occident* (Philadelphia). 1852–1867.
*People's Party Paper* (Atlanta). 1892–1896.
*Scott's Monthly Magazine* (Atlanta). 1866–1867.
*Southern Confederacy* (Atlanta). 1861–1862.
*Southern Guide* (Atlanta). March 10, 1908.
*Sunny South* (Atlanta). 1880–1899.
*Voice of the Negro* (Atlanta). 1904–1907.
Newspaper Clippings:
Leo M. Frank Papers. American Jewish Archives.
Police and Crime Scrapbooks. Atlanta Historical Society.

PUBLIC DOCUMENTS

Edwards, Alba M. *Alphabetical Index of Occupations by Industrial and Social-Economic Groups, 1937.* Washington, D.C.: Government Printing Office, 1937.

U.S., Bureau of the Census. *Thirteenth Census of the United States: 1910. Population.*

———. *Fourteenth Census of the United States: 1920. Population.*

———. *Index to Occupations: Alphabetical and Classified.* Washington, D.C.: Government Printing Office, 1915.

U.S., Census Office. *Eighth Census of the United States: 1860. Population.*

———. *Ninth Census of the United States: 1870. Population.*

———. *Tenth Census of the United States: 1880. Population, Compendium, and Statistics of Cities.*

———. *Eleventh Census of the United States: 1890. Population and Compendium.*

———. *Twelfth Census of the United States: 1900. Population and Occupations.*

———. *Thirteenth Census of the United States: 1910. Population.*

U.S., Immigration Commission. *Reports.* Washington, D.C.: Government Printing Office, 1911. Vols. 34–35.

ANNUAL REPORTS, CONSTITUTIONS, AND PROCEEDINGS

B'nai B'rith District Grand Lodge No. 5. *Proceedings.* 1903–1904, 1906–1910. Richmond: H. T. Ezekiel, 1903–1904, 1906–1910.

———. *Proceedings.* 1911–1915. Savannah: M. S. and D. A. Byck Co., 1911–1915.

Federation of Jewish Charities. *Annual Report for 1914.*

Hungarian Benevolent Association. *By-Laws of the Hungarian Benevolent Association of Atlanta, Ga.* Atlanta: Gershon Printing Co., n.d.

Industrial Removal Office. *Annual Report.* 1901–1915.

Masonic Grand Lodge of Georgia. *Proceedings of the Most Worshipful Grand Lodge of Georgia at the Annual Communication for the Year 1860.* Macon: S. Rose and Co., 1860.

———. *Proceedings of the Grand Lodge of Georgia of F and A Masons at the Annual Communication . . . for the Year 1867.* Macon: Office of the Journal and Messenger, 1867.

———. *Proceedings of the Most Worshipful Grand Lodge of Georgia, of Free and Accepted Masons.* 1870 and 1874. Macon: J. W. Burke and Co., 1870 and 1874.

Piedmont Driving Club. *By-Laws and Rules of the Piedmont Club of Atlanta, Georgia.* Atlanta: Franklin Printing and Publishing Co., 1899.

———. *By-Laws and Rules of the Piedmont Driving Club.* Atlanta: Bennett Printing House, 1903.

Southern Baptist Convention. *Proceedings of the Eighteenth Meeting of the Southern Baptist Convention.* Louisville: Bradley and Gilbert, 1873.

———. *Proceedings of the Southern Baptist Convention . . . 1867.* Baltimore: John F. Weishampel, Jr., 1867.

———. *Proceedings of the Twenty-Seventh Annual Session of the Southern Baptist Convention.* Atlanta: Jas. P. Harrison and Co., 1882.

### DIRECTORIES, GUIDEBOOKS, PROMOTIONAL TRACTS, AND MAPS

Atlanta Chamber of Commerce. *Atlanta as the Southeast Center of Commerce and Finance.* Atlanta, 1914.

———. *Atlanta: The Metropolis of the Southeast.* Atlanta, 1913.

Atlanta City Council. *A Few Points in 1895 about Atlanta.* Atlanta, 1895.

*Atlanta City Directory, 1900–1902.* Atlanta: Maloney Directory Co., 1900–1902.

*Atlanta City Directory, 1903–1908.* Atlanta: Foote and Davis Co., and Joseph W. Hill, 1903–1908.

*Atlanta City Directory, 1910–1915.* Atlanta: Atlanta City Directory Co., 1909–1914.

*Atlanta, Georgia.* New York: Sanborn Map Co., 1886.

———. New York: Sanborn-Perris Map Co., 1892.

*Atlanta, Ga., City Directory, 1883.* Atlanta: Charles F. Weatherbe, 1883.

*Atlanta: Past, Present and Future.* Atlanta: Reilly and Thomas, 1883.

*Atlanta Society Blue Book, Elite Family Directory.* New York: Dau Publishing Co., 1901.

*Atlanta Society Blue Book of Selected Names.* New York: Dau Publishing Co., 1907.

*Atlanta Standard City Guide.* Atlanta: Franklin-Turner, 1907.

Barnwell, V. T., comp. *Barnwell's Atlanta City Directory and Strangers' Guide . . . 1867.* Atlanta: Intelligencer Book and Job Office, 1867.

Bullock, V. V. and Mrs. F. A. Saunders, comps. *Atlanta City Directory for 1897.* Atlanta: Franklin Printing and Publishing Co., 1897.

Campbell, John P. *Southern Business Directory and General Commercial Advertiser.* Charleston: Walker and James, 1854.

Clarke, E[dward] Y[oung]. *Atlanta Illustrated.* 3rd ed. Atlanta: Jas. P. Harrison and Co., 1881.

*Hanleiter's Atlanta City Directory, 1870–1871.* Atlanta: William R. Hanleiter, 1870–1871.

Hopkins, G. M. *City Atlas of Atlanta, Georgia.* Baltimore: Southern and Southwestern Surveying and Publishing Co., 1878.

*Insurance Maps of Atlanta Georgia, 1899.* New York: Sanborn-Perris Map Co., 1899.

*Insurance Maps of Atlanta Georgia, 1911.* 4 vols. New York: Sanborn Map Co., 1911.

Janes, Thomas P. *Georgia From the Immigrant Settler's Stand-Point.* Atlanta: Jas. P. Harrison and Co., 1879.

*Map of Atlanta.* New York: Phillips and Hart, 1886.

*Official Map of Greater Atlanta, 1910.* Atlanta: Joseph W. Hill, 1909.

Saunders, H. G., comp. *Atlanta City Directory for 1891.* Atlanta: R. L. Polk and Co., 1891.

———. *Atlanta City Directory for 1896.* Atlanta: Franklin Printing and Publishing Co., 1896.

Sherwood, Adiel. *A Gazetteer of Georgia Containing a Particular Description of the State. . . .,* 4th ed. Atlanta: J. Richards, 1860.

*Sholes' Directory of the City of Atlanta, 1880–1881.* Atlanta: A. E. Sholes, 1880–1881.

White, George. *Statistics of the State of Georgia.* Savannah: W. Thorpe Williams, 1849.

———. *Historical Collections of Georgia.* New York: Pudney and Russell, 1854.

*Williams' Atlanta Directory, City Guide and Business Mirror.* Atlanta: M. Lynch, 1859.

Wilson, John Stainback. *Atlanta As It Is.* New York: Little, Rennie and Co., 1871.

## OTHER PUBLISHED PRIMARY SOURCES

Alexander, Henry A. *Introductory Address of Henry A. Alexander of the Bar of Atlanta, Georgia at Benefit Concert Given for the Kishineff Relief Fund.* Atlanta: Franklin Printing and Publishing Co., [1903].

*American Jewish Year Book,* 1900–17. Philadelphia: Jewish Publication Society of America, 1899–1916.

Amster, Ludwig. "A Plea for the Improvement of the 'Russian Immigrant.'" *Magnet* 1 (January 1894): 56–61.

Andrews, Sidney. *The South Since the War.* Boston: Ticknor and Fields, 1866.

Baker, Ray Stannard. *Following the Color Line: An Account of Negro Citizenship in the American Democracy.* New York: Doubleday, Page and Co., 1908.

Board of Delegates of American Israelites and Union of American Hebrew Congregations. *Statistics of the Jews in the United States.* Philadelphia: Union of American Hebrew Congregations, 1880.

Browne, Edward B. M., comp. *Prayers of Israel.* 2nd ed. New York, 1885.

———, trans. *The Book Jashar: The Lost Book of the Bible.* New York: United States Publishing Co., 1876.

Campbell, George. *Black and White: The Outcome of a Visit to the United States.* London: Chatto and Windus, 1879.

Davis, David [Yampolsky]. *The Passing Years: Memories of Two Worlds.* Tel Aviv, Israel: New Life Press, 1974.

Dennett, John R. *The South As It Is, 1865–1866.* Reprint ed. New York: Viking Press, 1965.

DuBois, W. E. Burghardt, ed. *The Negro In Business.* Atlanta University Publication No. 4. Atlanta: Atlanta University Press, 1899.

Geffen, Tobias. *Glory of Joseph.* New York, 1942.

———. *Joseph's Heart.* St. Louis, 1924.

———. *Ray of Splendor.* St. Louis, 1934.

Gersoni, Henry, trans. *Mumn, and the Diary of a Superfluous Man,* by Ivan Turgenev. New York: Funk and Wagnalls, 1884.

———. *Sketches of Jewish Life and History.* New York: Hebrew Orphan Asylum Printing Establishment, 1873.

Gibson, Thomas. "The Anti-Negro Riots in Atlanta." *Harper's Weekly* 50 (October 13, 1906): 1457–1459.

Hyman, H. Joseph. "The Alliance and Its Activities." *American Jewish Review* 3 (May 1914): 3–4.

———. "The Jewish Educational Alliance." *Jewish Outlook* 1 (April 1913): 5–9.

———. "The New Tendency in Jewish Communal Life." *American Jewish Review* 4 (February 1915): 6–7.

———. "The Problem of Jewish Charities in the South." *American Jewish Review* 3 (April 1914): 10–11, 40.

Kennaway, John H. *On Sherman's Track; or, The South After The War.* London: Seeley, Jackson and Halliday, 1867.

King, Edward. *The Southern States of North America.* London: Blackie and Son, 1875.

Knight, Lucian Lamar. *Reminiscences of Famous Georgians.* Atlanta: Franklin Turner, 1907.

Kriegshaber, Victor H. "The Jewish Educational Alliance." *American Jewish Review* 3 (May 1914): 3.

Latham, Henry. *Black and White.* London: Macmillan and Co., 1867.

Reid, Whitelaw. *After the War: A Southern Tour, May 1, 1865 to May 1, 1866.* London: S. Law, Son and Marston, 1866.

Sala, George A. *America Revisited.* London: Vizetally and Co., 1885.

Trowbridge, J. T. *A Picture of the Desolated States and the Work of Restoration, 1865–1868.* Hartford: L. Stebbins, 1868.

White, William N. "Diary and Letters." Edited by William S. Irvine. *Atlanta Historical Bulletin* 2 (July 1937): 35–50.

### *C. Interviews*

David Davis (né Yampolsky), in Atlanta, August 9, 1973. Mr. Davis was born in Russia in 1884, has lived in Atlanta since 1905, and was a leading member of the Arbeiter Ring.

Samuel Eplan, in Atlanta, December 8, 1971. Mr. Eplan was born in Atlanta in 1896 and was an early member of the Progressive Club. His father, Leon Eplan, was one of the leaders of the Russian community.

Solomon J. Gold, in Atlanta, December 10, 1971. Mr. Gold was born in Russia in 1878, came to Atlanta in 1902, and was one of the founders of Congregation Shearith Israel.

H. C. Hamilton, by telephone, March 21, 1973. Professor Hamilton was born in Atlanta in 1899 and taught education at Morehouse College.

Josephine Heyman (née Joel), in Atlanta, February 21, 1973. Mrs. Heyman was born in Atlanta in 1901. Her family has long been associated with the affairs of the Temple community.

Sinclair Jacobs, in Atlanta, February 23, 1973. Mr. Jacobs was born in Atlanta in 1888. Like his father, Joseph Jacobs, he achieved prominence in the pharmacy business and belonged to the Temple, the Standard Club, and the Burns Club.

M. L. Kahn, by telephone, March 14, 1973. Mr. Kahn was born in Atlanta in 1884 and was an early member of Congregation Shearith Israel.

Simon Mendel, in Atlanta, February 8, 1973. Mr. Mendel was born in Atlanta in 1900. His father, Hyman Mendel, came to Atlanta from Russia in 1890 and founded the large wholesale establishment which bears his name.

Betsy Merlin (née Yampolsky), in Atlanta, March 9, 1973. Mrs. Merlin was born in Russia in 1893 and came to Atlanta in 1906. Her father and husband were leading members of the Arbeiter Ring.

Josephine Murphy (née Dibble), in Atlanta, March 23, 1973. Mrs. Murphy was born in South Carolina in 1888 and came to Atlanta in 1906 in order to attend Atlanta University. Her family has long been prominent in the Negro community.

Alfred Myers, in Atlanta, February 19, 1973. Mr. Myers was born in Cincinnati in 1880 and moved to Atlanta in 1901.

Ethel Myers (née Lieberman), in Atlanta, February 19, 1973. Mrs. Myers was born in Atlanta in 1878 and married Alfred Myers in 1904. Her father, Leon Lieberman, was a charter member of the Hebrew Benevolent Congregation.

Judah H. Notrica, in Atlanta, February 5, 1973. Mr. Notrica was born on Rhodes in 1893, came to Atlanta at the age of twenty, and is a charter member of Congregation Or Ve Shalom.

T. Schloffer, in Atlanta, March 16, 1973. Mr. Schloffer was born in the Ukraine in 1888, settled in Atlanta in 1910, and is a charter member of Congregation Anshe Sfard.

H. Taratoot, in Atlanta, March 11, 1973. Mr. Taratoot was born in Russia in 1885, came to Atlanta in 1910, and is a charter member of Congregation Anshe Sfard.

## SECONDARY SOURCES

### A. Published

Alexander, Henry A. *Notes on the Alexander Family of South Carolina and Georgia.* n.p., [1954].

Atherton, Lewis E. "Itinerant Merchandizing in the Antebellum South." *Bulletin of the Business Historical Society* 19 (April 1945): 35–59.

Avery, I. W. *History of the State of Georgia from 1850 to 1881.* New York: Brown and Derby, 1881.

Baker, Henry G. *Rich's of Atlanta.* Atlanta: School of Business Administration, University of Georgia, 1953.

Bender, Eugene I. "Reflections on Negro-Jewish Relationships: The Historical Factor." *Phylon* 30 (Spring 1969): 56–65.

Berman, Jeremiah J. "The Trend of Jewish Religious Observance in Mid-Nineteenth Century America." *Publications of the American Jewish Historical Society* 37 (1947): 31–53.

Bond, Horace Mann. "Negro Attitudes Toward Jews." *Jewish Social Studies* 27 (January 1965): 3–9.

Bricker, L[uther] O. "A Great American Tragedy." *Shane Quarterly* 4 (April 1943): 89–95.

Cash, W[ilber] J. *The Mind of the South.* New York: Alfred A. Knopf, 1941.

Clark, Thomas D. "The Post-Civil War Economy in the South." *American Jewish Historical Quarterly* 55 (June 1966): 424–33.

*Congregation Or Ve Shalom Dedication Book.* n.p., [1971].

Connolly, C. P. *The Truth About the Frank Case.* New York: Vail-Ballau Co., 1915.

Cooper, Walter G. *Official History of Fulton County.* Atlanta, 1934.

———. *The Story of Georgia.* 4 vols. New York: American Historical Society, 1938.

Coulter, E. Merton. *A History of the South.* Vol. 7, *The Confederate States of America, 1861–1865.* Baton Rouge: Louisiana State University Press, 1950.

———. *A History of the South.* Vol. 8, *The South During Reconstruction.* Baton Rouge: Louisiana State University Press, 1947.

Council of Jewish Women, Atlanta Section. *Twenty-Fifth Anniversary Book.* Atlanta, 1920.

Crowe, Charles. "Racial Massacre in Atlanta, September 22, 1906." *Journal of Negro History* 54 (April 1969): 150–73.

———. "Racial Violence and Social Reform—Origins of the Atlanta Riot of 1906." *Journal of Negro History* 53 (July 1968): 234–56.

Dinnerstein, Leonard. "A Neglected Aspect of Southern Jewish History." *American Jewish Historical Quarterly* 61 (September 1971): 52–60.

———. "Atlanta in the Progressive Era: A Dreyfus Case in Georgia." In *The Age of Industrialism in America,* edited by Frederick C. Jaher, pp. 127–59. New York: Free Press, 1968.

———. "A Note on Southern Attitudes Toward Jews." *Jewish Social Studies* 32 (January 1970): 43–49.

———. *The Leo Frank Case.* New York: Columbia University Press, 1968.

——— and Palsson, Mary D., eds. *Jews in the South.* Baton Rouge: Louisiana State University Press, 1973.

Duker, Abraham G. "An Evaluation of Achievement in American Jewish Local Historical Writing." *Publications of the American Jewish Historical Society* 49 (June 1960): 215–53.

*Encyclopaedia Judaica.* 16 vols. New York: Macmillian Co., 1971.

Evans, Eli N. *The Provincials: A Personal History of Jews in the South.* New York: Atheneum, 1973.

Fleming, Walter W. "Immigration to the Southern States." *Political Science Quarterly* 20 (June 1905): 276–97.

*Fortieth Anniversary Celebration of the Don't Worry Club.* N.p., [1951].

Garrett, Franklin M. *Atlanta and Environs: A Chronicle of Its People and Events.* 3 vols. Athens: University of Georgia Press, 1969.

Georgia Writers' Project. *Atlanta: A City of the Modern South.* American Guide Series. New York: Smith and Durrell, 1942.

Glanz, Rudolph. *Studies in Judaica Americana.* New York: Ktav Publishing Co., 1970.

Glazer, Nathan. *American Judaism.* Chicago History of American Civilization. Chicago: University of Chicago Press, 1957.

———. "The American Jew and the Attainment of Middle Class Rank: Some Trends and Explanations." In *The Jews: Social Patterns of an American Group,* edited by Marshall Sklare, pp. 138–46. New York: Free Press, 1958.

Golden, Harry. *A Little Girl Is Dead.* Cleveland: World Publishing Co., 1965.

———. *Forgotten Pioneer.* Cleveland: World Publishing Co., 1963.

Handlin, Oscar. "American Views of the Jew at the Opening of the Twentieth Century." *Publications of the American Jewish Historical Society* 40 (June 1951): 323–44.

Hero, Alfred O. *The Southerner and World Affairs.* Baton Rouge: Louisiana State University Press, 1965.

Hertzberg, Steven. "The Jewish Community of Atlanta from the End of the Civil War Until the Eve of the Frank Case." *American Jewish Historical Quarterly* 62 (March 1973): 250–85.

Higham, John. "American Anti-Semitism Historically Reconsidered." In *Jews in the Mind of America,* edited by Charles H. Stember et al., pp. 237–58. New York: Basic Books, 1966.

———. "Anti-Semitism in the Gilded Age: A Reinterpretation." *Mississippi Valley Historical Review* 43 (March 1957): 559–78.

———. "Social Discrimination Against Jews in America, 1830–1930." *Publications of the American Jewish Historical Society* 47 (September 1957): 1–33.

______. *Strangers in the Land: Patterns of American Nativism, 1860–1925.* New Brunswick, N.J.: Rutgers University Press, 1955.

Hopkins, Richard J. "Are Southern Cities Unique? Persistence as a Clue." *Mississippi Quarterly* 26 (Spring 1973): 121–41.

______. "Occupational and Geographic Mobility in Atlanta, 1870–1896." *Journal of Southern History* 34 (May 1968): 200–13.

______. "Status, Mobility and the Dimensions of Change in a Southern City: Atlanta: 1870–1910." In *Cities in American History,* edited by Kenneth T. Jackson and Stanley K. Schultz, pp. 216–31. New York: Alfred A. Knopf, 1972.

Korn, Bertram W. *American Jewry and the Civil War.* Philadelphia: Jewish Publication Society of America, 1951.

______. "Jews and Negro Slavery in the Old South, 1789–1865" *Publications of the American Jewish Historical Society* 50 (March 1961): 151–201.

Levy, Eugene. " 'Is the Jew a White Man?'—Press Reaction to the Leo Frank Case, 1913–1915." *Phylon* 35 (June 1974): 212–22.

Lowenberg, Bert J. "Efforts of the South to Encourage Immigration, 1865–1900." *South Atlantic Quarterly* 33 (October 1934): 363–85.

Martin, Thomas H. *Atlanta and Its Builders.* 2 vols. Atlanta: Century Memorial Publishing Co., 1902.

[Marx, David]. "History of the Jews of Atlanta." *Reform Advocate* (November 4, 1911): 9–72.

______. *A History of the Hebrew Benevolent Congregation of Atlanta Georgia.* N.p., 1917.

McDonald, T. C. *Free Masonry and Its Progress in Atlanta and Fulton County, Georgia.* Atlanta, 1925.

*Memoirs of Georgia.* 2 vols. Atlanta: Southern Historical Association, 1895.

Meyer, Isadore S. and Davis, Moshe, eds. *The Writing of American Jewish History.* New York: American Jewish Historical Society, 1957.

Northern, William J., ed. *Men of Mark in Georgia.* 6 vols. Atlanta: A. B. Caldwell, 1908–1910.

Philipson, David. *The Reform Movement in Judaism.* New York: Macmillan Co., 1931.

Phillips, Ulrich B. *A History of Transportation in the Eastern Cotton Belt to 1860.* New York: Columbia University Press, 1908.

*Pioneer Citizens' History of Atlanta, 1833–1902.* Atlanta: Pioneer Citizens' Society of Atlanta, 1902.

Pool, David de Sola. "The Levantine Jews in the United States." *American Jewish Year Book 14* (1913–14): 207–20.

Raphael, Marc Lee. "American Jewish Local Histories: Deficiencies and Possibilities." *CCAR Journal* 20 (Autumn 1973): 59–68.

Reed, Wallace P. *Reed's History of Atlanta.* Syracuse, N.Y.: D. Mason and Co., 1889.

Rockaway, Robert. "Ethnic Conflict in an Urban Environment: The German and Russian Jews in Detroit." *American Jewish Historical Quarterly* 60 (December 1970): 133–50.

Rothschild, Janice O. *As But a Day: The First Hundred Years, 1867–1967.* Atlanta: The Hebrew Benevolent Congregation, 1967.

———. "Pre-1867 Atlanta Jewry." *American Jewish Historical Quarterly* 62 (March 1973): 242–49.

Samuels, Charles and Louise. *Night Fell on Georgia.* New York: Dell Publishing Co., 1956.

Shankman, Arnold. "Atlanta Jewry: 1900–1930." *American Jewish Archives* 25 (November 1973): 131–55.

Southern Israelite. *One Hundred Years Accomplishments of Southern Jewry.* Atlanta: Southern Newspaper Enterprises, 1934.

Sutker, Solomon. "The Jewish Organizational Elite of Atlanta, Georgia" and "The Role of Social Clubs in the Atlanta Jewish Community." In *The Jews: Social Patterns of an American Group,* edited by Marshall Sklare, pp. 249–70. New York: Free Press, 1958.

Weisbord, Robert G., and Stein, Arthur. *Bittersweet Encounter: The Afro-American and the American Jew.* Westport, Conn.: Negro Universities Press, 1970.

Wirth, Louis. *The Ghetto.* Reprint. Chicago: University of Chicago Press, Phoenix Books, 1956.

Wischnitzer, Mark. *To Dwell in Safety: The Story of Jewish Immigration Since 1800.* Philadelphia: Jewish Publication Society of America, 1948.

Woodward, C. Vann. *A History of the South,* vol. 9. *Origins of the New South.* Baton Rouge: Louisiana State University Press, 1951.

## *B. Unpublished Monographs*

Adams, Bobby E. "Analysis of a Relationship: Jews and Southern Baptists." Th.D. dissertation, Southwestern Baptist Theological Seminary, 1969.

Amato, Albert. "Sephardim and the Seattle Sephardic Community." M.A. thesis, University of Washington, 1939.

Appel, John J. "Immigrant Historical Societies in the United States." Ph.D. dissertation, University of Pennsylvania, 1960.

Branch, Anne Lavina. "Atlanta and the American Settlement House Movement." M.A. thesis, Emory University, 1966.

Cameron, William. "Anti-Semitism and the Leo Frank Case." M.A. thesis, University of Cincinnati, 1965.

Cohen, Joseph. "History of the Congregation Or Ve Shalom, Atlanta, Georgia from Its Founding to February 28, 1954." Typescript article, American Jewish Archives.

Crimmins, Timothy J. "The Crystal Stair: A Study of the Effects of Class, Race, and Ethnicity on Secondary Education in Atlanta, 1872–1925." Ph.D. dissertation, Emory University, 1972.

Deaton, Thomas M. "Atlanta During the Progressive Era." Ph.D. dissertation, University of Georgia, 1969.

English, Carl Dean. "The Ethical Emphases of the Editors of Baptist Journals in the Southeastern Region of the United States, 1865–1915." Th.D. dissertation, Southern Baptist Theological Seminary, 1948.

Garafalo, Charles P. "Business Ideas in Atlanta, 1916–1935." Ph.D. dissertation, Emory University, 1972.

Hopkins, Richard J. "Patterns of Persistence and Occupational Mobility in a Southern City: Atlanta, 1870–1920." Ph.D. dissertation, Emory University, 1972.

Jones, Alton D. "Progressivism in Georgia, 1898–1918." Ph.D. dissertation, Emory University, 1963.

Korn, Bertram W. "American Jewish Local History: Retrospect and Prospect." Paper delivered at Conference on New Approaches to American Jewish Local History, Columbus, Ohio, October 13, 1974.

Lyon, Elizabeth A. M. "Business Buildings in Atlanta: A Study in Urban Growth and Form." Ph.D. dissertation, Emory University, 1971.

Mebane, Ann F. "Immigrant Patterns in Atlanta, 1880 and 1896." M.A. thesis, Emory University, 1967.

Moynihan, Kenneth J. "History as a Weapon for Social Advancement: Group History as Told by Jewish, Irish, and Black Americans, 1892–1950." Ph.D. dissertation, Clark University, 1973.

Price, Isabel B. "Black Response to Anti-Semitism: Negroes and Jews in New York, 1880 to World War II." Ph.D. dissertation, University of New Mexico, 1973.

Rabinowitz, Howard N. "The Search for Social Control: Race Relations in the Urban South, 1865–1890." Ph.D. dissertation, University of Chicago, 1973.

Racine, Philip N. "Atlanta's Schools: A History of the Public School System, 1869–1955." Ph.D. dissertation, Emory University, 1969.

Rainey, Glenn W. "The Race Riot of 1906 in Atlanta." M.A. thesis, Emory University, 1929.

Rockaway, Robert A. "From Americanization to Jewish Americanism: The Jews of Detroit, 1850–1914." Ph.D. dissertation, University of Michigan, 1970.

Russell, James M. "Atlanta, Gate City of the South, 1847 to 1885." Ph.D. dissertation, Princeton University, 1971.

Singer, Ralph B. "Confederate Atlanta." Ph.D. dissertation, Emory University, 1973.

Slade, Dorothy. "The Evolution of Negro Areas in the City of Atlanta." M.A. thesis, Atlanta University, 1946.

Stanley, Raymond W. "The Railroad Pattern of Atlanta." M.A. thesis, University of Chicago, 1947.

Sutker, Solomon. "The Jews of Atlanta: Their Structure and Leadership Patterns." Ph.D. dissertation, University of North Carolina, 1952.

Taylor, Arthur R. "From the Ashes: Atlanta During Reconstruction, 1865–1876." Ph.D. dissertation, Emory University, 1973.

Wotton, Grigsby H. "New City of the South: Atlanta, 1843–1873." Ph.D. dissertation, Johns Hopkins University, 1973.

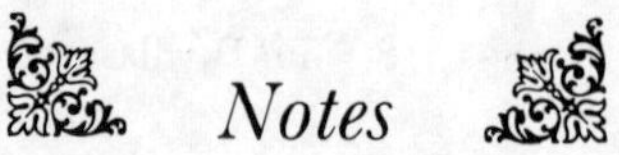

# Notes

## *Introduction*

1. Board of Delegates of American Israelites and the Union of American Hebrew Congregations, *Statistics of the Jews in the United States* (Philadelphia: Union of American Hebrew Congregations, 1880), p. 55; Ira Rosenwaike, "The Jewish Population of the United States as Estimated from the Census of 1820," *American Jewish Historical Quarterly* 53 (December 1963): 146–52 (hereafter cited as *AJHQ*). *American Jewish Year Book* 9 (1907–08): 433; 41 (1939–40): 184–86; and 70 (1968–69): 264–65 (hereafter cited as *AJYB*). Unless otherwise specified, references to the antebellum South are intended to include all fifteen states in which slavery was legal in 1861. For the postwar period, references to the South denote only the eleven former Confederate states plus Kentucky.

2. Eli N. Evans, *The Provincials: A Personal History of Jews in the South* (New York: Atheneum, 1973), p. vii.

3. Kenneth J. Moynihan, "History as a Weapon for Social Advancement: Group History as Told by Jewish, Irish, and Black Americans, 1892–1950" (Ph.D. dissertation, Clark University, 1973), pp. 1–15, 32, 47, 114–15; John J. Appel, "Immigrant Historical Societies in the United States" (Ph.D. dissertation, University of Pennsylvania, 1960), pp. 188–270.

4. Josef J. Barton, *Peasants and Strangers: Italians, Rumanians, and Slovaks in an American City, 1890–1950* (Cambridge: Harvard University Press, 1975); Kenneth L. Kusmer, *A Ghetto Takes Shape: Black Cleveland, 1870–1930* (Urbana: University of Illinois Press, 1976); Oscar Handlin, *Boston's Immigrants, 1790–1880* (Cambridge: Harvard University Press, 1941).

5. Notable exceptions are Moses Rischin, *The Promised City: New York's Jews, 1870–1914* (Cambridge: Harvard University Press, 1962); Arthur A. Goren, *New York Jews and the Quest for Community: The Kehillah Experiment, 1908–1922* (New York: Columbia University Press, 1970); and Irving Howe, *World of Our Fathers* (New York: Harcourt Brace Jovanovich, 1976). All three books are based largely upon narrative sources and focus on aspects of the East European Jewish experience in New York City.

6. For a critical discussion of local Jewish historiography, see Marc Lee Raphael, "American Jewish Local Histories: Deficiencies and Possibilities," *CCAR Journal* 20 (Autumn 1973): 59–68; idem, "Utilization of Public Local and Federal Sources for Reconstructing American Jewish Local History: The Jews of Columbus, Ohio," *AJHQ* 65 (September 1975): 10–35; and Bertram W. Korn, "American Jewish Local History: Retrospect and Prospect" (paper delivered at Conference on New Approaches to American Jewish Local History, Columbus, Ohio, October 13, 1974).

7. No effort will be made to summarize all of the literature on southern Jewry. For useful bibliographies see Leonard Dinnerstein and Mary D. Palsson, eds., *Jews in the South* (Baton Rouge: Louisiana State University Press, 1973), pp. 389–92; Evans, *The Provincials,* pp. 350–56; Alfred O. Hero, *The Southerner and World Affairs* (Baton Rouge: Louisiana State University Press, 1965), pp. 636–39.

8. Chief among these studies are Leon Hueher, "The Jews of Georgia from the Outbreak of the American Revolution Until the Close of the 18th Century," *Publication of the American Jewish Historical Society* 17 (1909): 89–108 (hereafter cited as *PAJHS*); Isador Blum, *The Jews of Baltimore* (Baltimore: Historical Review Publishing Co., 1910); Barnett A. Elzas, *The Jews of South Carolina from the Earliest Times to the Present Day* (Philadelphia: J. B. Lippincott Co., 1905); Herbert T. Ezekiel and Gaston Lichtenstein, *History of the Jews of Richmond from 1769 to 1917* (Richmond: H. T. Ezekiel, 1917); Leo Shpall, *The Jews of Louisiana* (New Orleans: Steeg Printing and Publishing Co., 1936).

9. The major historical works were Charles Reznikoff and Uriah Z. Engelman, *The Jews of Charleston: A History of an American Jewish Community* (Philadelphia: Jewish Publication Society of America, 1950); Fedora Frank, *Five Families and Eight Young Men: Nashville and Her Jewry, 1850–1861* (Nashville: Tennessee Book Co., 1962); Bertram W. Korn, *American Jewry and the Civil War* (Philadelphia: Jewish Publication Society of America, 1951); idem, "Jews and Negro Slavery in the Old South, 1789–1865," *PAJHS* 50 (March 1961): 151–201. Among the sociological and journalistic studies were Julian B. Feibelman, *A Social and Economic Study of the New Orleans Jewish Community* (Philadelphia: University of Pennsylvania, 1941); Benjamin Kaplan, *The Eternal Stranger: A Study of Jewish Life in the Small Community* (New York: Bookman Associates, 1957); Solomon Sutker, "The Jewish Organizational Elite of Atlanta, Georgia" and "The Role of Social Clubs in the Atlanta Jewish Community," both in Marshall Sklare, ed., *The Jews: Social Patterns of an American Group* (New York: Free Press, 1958), pp. 249–61, 262–70; Hero, *The Southerner and World Affairs,* pp. 474–503; Leonard Reissman, "The New Orleans Jewish Community," *Jewish Journal of Sociology* 4 (June 1962): 110–23; Theodore Lowi, "Southern Jews: Two Communities," *Jewish Journal of Sociology* 6 (July 1964): 103–17; Harry Golden, "Jew and Gentile in the New South: Segregation at Sundown," *Commentary* 20 (November 1955): 403–12.

10. Leonard Dinnerstein, *The Leo Frank Case* (New York: Columbia University Press, 1968), especially pp. 64–70; idem, "A Note on Southern Attitudes Toward Jews," *Jewish Social Studies* 32 (January 1970): 43–49; idem, "A Neglected Aspect of Southern Jewish History," *AJHQ* 61 (September 1971): 52–68; idem and Palsson, eds., *Jews in the South;* Mark H. Elovitz, *A Century of Jewish Life in Dixie: The Birmingham Experience* (University, Ala.: University of Alabama Press, 1974); Bertram W. Korn, *The Early Jews of New Orleans* (Waltham, Mass.: American Jewish Historical Society, 1969); idem, *The Jews of Mobile, Alabama, 1763–1841* (Cincinnati: Hebrew Union College Press, 1970); Isaac M. Fein, *The Making of an American Jewish Community: The History of Baltimore Jewry from 1773 to 1920* (Philadelphia: Jewish Publication Society, 1971)

11. *AJHQ* 62 (March 1973). The papers delivered at the Conference on the History of Southern Jewry (Richmond, October 24–25, 1976) will be published in a future issue of the *AJHQ.* Evans, *The Provincials;* Harry Golden, *Our Southern Landsman* (New York: G. P. Putnam's Sons, 1974); Ronald L. Bern, *The Legacy* (New York: Mason Charter, 1975); Richard Kluger, *Members of the Tribe* (New York: Doubleday and Co., 1977).

12. Jewish population statistics for this period tend to be unreliable. According to *AJYB* figures based upon local estimates, the Jewish population of Atlanta increased from 3,500 in 1907, to 10,000 in 1912 and remained stable through 1917. In contrast, Dallas Jewry increased from 4,000 to 6,000 to 8,000; Louisville's Jewish inhabitants increased from 8,000 to 10,000 before dropping back to 8,000; and New Orleans's remained stable at about 8,000. If these figures are correct, then Atlanta had the largest Jewish population in the South by 1915. However, published 1910

and 1920 census information on the mother tongue and parentage of Atlanta residents suggests that the 1912 and 1917 *AJYB* estimates are inflated by at least 3,000. Assuming this is so and that the figures for other cities are accurate, then Atlanta would have ranked either second or third. *AJYB 19* (1917–18): 412–13.

## *1 · The Pioneers*

1. Ulrich B. Phillips, *A History of Transportation in the Eastern Cotton Belt to 1860* (New York: Columbia University Press, 1908), pp 1–8, 109–16, 126–31; James M. Russell, "Atlanta, Gate City of the South, 1847 to 1885" (Ph.D. dissertation, Princeton University, 1971), pp. 9–18.

2. Phillips, *Transportation,* pp. 221–318; Russell, "Gate City," pp. 18–24; Raymond W. Stanley, "The Railroad Pattern of Atlanta" (M.A. thesis, University of Chicago, 1947), pp. 42–54, 82–85, 87; A. Hollis Edens, "The Founding of Atlanta," *Atlanta Historical Bulletin* 4 (July and October 1939): 203–31, 275–90 (thereafter cited as *AHB*).

3. Writers' Program of the Works Projects Administration in the State of Georgia, *Atlanta: A City of the Modern South,* American Guide Series (New York: Smith and Durrell, 1942), pp. 9–13; Phillips, *Transportation,* pp. 334, 335; Russell, "Gate City," pp. 23–25; Stanley, "Railroad Pattern," pp. 54–65.

4. WPA, *Atlanta,* p. 13; V. T. Barnwell, comp., *Barnwell's Atlanta City Directory and Stangers' Guide . . . 1867* (Atlanta: Intelligencer Book and Job Office, 1867), pp. 31, 57–61; Adiel Sherwood, *A Gazetteer of Georgia Containing a Particular Description of the State. . . .,* 4th ed. (Atlanta: J. Richards, 1860), p. 69; George White, *Statistics of the State of Georgia* (Savannah: W. Thorpe Williams, 1849), p. 205; idem, *Historical Collections of Georgia* (New York: Pudney and Russell, 1854), p. 421; *Thirteenth Census of the United States: 1910, Population,* vol. 1, tables 56, 57. The two Southern cities that had larger populations than Atlanta in 1910 were Louisville and New Orleans. Between 1850 and 1910 Atlanta rose from the eighty-ninth to the thirty-first largest city in the country.

5. Phillips, *Transportation,* pp. 390–92; Russell, "Gate City," pp. 31–49.

6. Russell, "Gate City," pp. 51, 56–66, 71–89; Wallace P. Reed, *Reed's History of Atlanta* (Syracuse, N.Y.: D. Mason and Co., 1889), pp. 55–56, 237.

7. Thomas H. Martin, *Atlanta and Its Builders,* 2 vols. (Atlanta: Century Memorial Publishing Co., 1902), 1:11–12; *Pioneer Citizens' History of Atlanta, 1833–1902* (n.p.: Pioneer Citizens' Society of Atlanta, 1902), p. 224; "Federal Census of Atlanta, De Kalb County," *AHB* 7 (January and April 1942): 16–82.

8. William N. White, "Diary and Letters," William S. Irvine, ed., *AHB* 2 (July 1937): 40–41; "Federal Census of Atlanta, De Kalb County," pp. 16–82; *Eighth Census of the United States: 1860, Population,* vol. 1, pp. 74–75.

9. Charles Reznikoff and Uriah Z. Engelman, *The Jews of Charleston: A History of an American Jewish Community* (Philadelphia: Jewish Publication Society of America, 1950), pp. 4–5; Malcolm Stern, "New Light on the Jewish Settlement of Savannah," *AJHQ* 52 (March 1963): 177; Ira Rosenwailke, "An Estimate of the Jewish Population of the United States in 1790," *PAJHS* 50 (September 1960): 27–28, 31–34.

10. Ira Rosenwaike, "The Jewish Population of the United States as Estimated from the Census of 1820," *AJHQ* 53 (December 1963): 146–47, 152. Bertram W. Korn considers Rosenwaike's estimates to be too low and suggests the figures of 3,000 in 1790 and 5,000 in 1820 as more appropriate. Korn, "Factors Bearing Upon the Survival of Judaism in the Ante-bellum Period," *PAJHS* 53 (June 1964): 342.

11. Oscar Handlin, *Adventure in Freedom: Three Hundred Years of Jewish Life in America* (New York: McGraw-Hill Book Co., 1954), pp. 46–47.

12. Rudolph Glanz, "The Immigration of German Jews up to 1880," in idem, *Studies in Judaica Americana* (New York: Ktav Publishing Co., 1970), pp. 89, 91–93; Mark Wischnitzer, *To Dwell in Safety: The Story of Jewish Immigration Since 1900* (Philadelphia: Jewish Publication Society of America, 1948), pp. 7, 21, 25; Howard M. Sachar, *The Course of Modern Jewish History* (New York: Dell Publishing Co., Delta Book, 1958), pp. 166–68. Despite the magnitude and special causes of Jewish emigration from Germany, no discussion of the phenomenon is made in Mack Walker's otherwise comprehensive *Germany and the Emigration 1816–1885* (Cambridge: Harvard University Press, 1964).

13. Handlin, *Adventure in Freedom,* pp. 47–48.

14. Nathan Glazer, *American Judaism,* Chicago History of American Civilization (Chicago: University of Chicago Press, 1957), pp. 23–24.

15. Maxwell Whiteman, "Notions, Drygoods, and Clothing: An Introduction to the Study of the Cincinnati Peddler," *Jewish Quarterly Review* 53 (April 1963): 306–21.

16. Lewis E. Atherton, "Itinerant Merchandizing in the Antebellum South," *Bulletin of the Business Historical Society* 29 (April 1945): 55–59; Rudolph Glanz, "Notes on Early Jewish Peddling in America," *Jewish Social Studies* 7 (April 1945): 128.

17. Atherton, "Itinerant Merchandizing," pp. 35–37.

18. In 1859 Rev. Isaac Leeser of Philadelphia, who had contacts in almost every Jewish community in the United States, estimated that there were somewhat under 150,000 American Jews and then made state-by-state estimates which totaled 115,-200. The Southern states were credited with 33,200 Jews as follows: Alabama, 2,000; Georgia, 2,500; Kentucky, 2,500; Louisiana, 8,000; Mississippi, Arkansas and Florida, 1,200; Maryland, 5,000; Missouri, 3,000; South Carolina, 3,000; Tennessee, 2,000; Texas, 1,000; Virginia, 2,000; North Carolina, 1,000. *Occident* (Philadelphia) 17 (July 6, 1859): 88, 89. Some of these estimates may have been high in the light of table 2.

19. The eight other cities with Jewish benevolent societies or cemeteries but not synagogues were Huntsville, Alabama; Alexandria, Donaldsonville, Baton Rouge, and Monroe, Louisiana; Wilmington, North Carolina; Galveston, Texas; and Alexandria, Virginia. *Encyclopaedia Judaica,* 2:506; 11:519; 12:154, 158, 1219; 15:1109, 1035; *American Jewish Year Book 9* (1907–08): 123–421 (hereafter cited as *AJYB*); Max J. Kohler, "The Board of Delegates of American Israelites, 1859–1878," *PAJHS* 29 (1925): 129–35.

20. [David Marx], "History of the Jews of Atlanta" *Reform Advocate,* November 4, 1911 (Special Edition), pp. 11–12.

21. Ibid., p. 12; Aaron Haas to David Marx, n.d. [1911], Jews of Atlanta File, Atlanta Historical Society.

22. Henry A. Alexander, *Notes on the Alexander Family of South Carolina and Georgia and Connections* (n.p., [1954]), pp. 7, 11, 18–30; *Pioneer Citizens' History,* pp. 354–55.

23. [Marx], "Jews of Atlanta," pp. 11, 13; *Pioneer Citizens' History,* pp. 355–56; U.S. Manuscript Census Schedules, De Kalb County, Georgia, 1850; Franklin M. Garrett, *Atlanta and Environs: A Chronicle of Its People and Events,* 3 vols. (Athens: University of Georgia Press, 1969), 1:355–56.

24. David Mayer to Feitel Mayer, October 11, 1839, typed translation in Correspondence File, American Jewish Archives, Cincinnati; Reed, *History of Atlanta,* p. 41; [Marx], "Jews of Atlanta," p. 14; *Pioneer Citizens' History,* pp. 346–47.

25. U.S. Manuscript Census Schedules, De Kalb County, Georgia, 1850; U.S. Census Enumeration Schedules, Fulton County, Georgia, 1860; *Eighth Census of the United States: 1860, Population,* vol. 1, pp. 74–75.

26. *Williams' Atlanta Directory, City Guide and Business Mirror* (Atlanta: M. Lynch, 1859), pp. 51–53, 93, 120, 148; John P. Campbell, *The Southern Business Directory and*

*General Commercial Advertiser* (Charleston: Steam Power Press of Walker and James, 1854), pp. 247, 255; Garrett, 1:295, 464; *Atlanta Daily Intelligencer,* June 1, 1860, p. 2; *Gate City Guardian,* February 12, 1861, p. 2.

27. Simon Frankfort to Lemuel P. Grant, February 27, 1854; and Adolph J. Brady to Grant, 12 July 1853, L. P. Grant Papers, Atlanta Historical Society; Russell, "Gate City," pp. 90–91; Reed, *History of Atlanta,* p. 49; Fulton County Tax Digest, 1862, Atlanta Historical Society.

28. To locate residences in 1850 and 1860, *Williams' [1859] Atlanta Directory* and the consecutive dwelling enumeration numbers in the 1850 and 1860 census schedules were utilized. Three of postwar Atlanta's most prominent citizens—Calvin Hunnicutt, J. W. Rucker, and John Silvey—clerked for Jewish firms and boarded with Jewish families in 1850.

29. U.S. Manuscript Census Schedules, De Kalb County, Georgia, 1850; U.S. Manuscript Census Enumeration Schedules, Fulton County, Georgia, 1860; White, "Diary and Letters," pp. 45, 47; Haas to Marx; Alexander, *Notes on the Alexander Family,* p. 33.

30. *Atlanta Examiner* quoted in *Israelite* (Cincinnati), September 21, 1855, p. 86. Soulé was not a Jew, and Belmont had severed all of his connections with Judaism years before.

31. Few of Hill's speeches from the 1857 campaign could be located, and none of these mentioned immigration, which was not an important issue. The reference in the text to Hill's early views was attributed to him thirty years later by journalist "Sarge" Plunkett who also noted that in the 1850s "a Jew in Georgia was not as good as er [*sic*] nigger, and you see where he is now." *Atlanta Constitution,* June 23, 1889, p. 3.

32. *Occident* 14 (March 1857): 580–81; Bertram W. Korn, "The Know-Nothing Movement and the Jews," in Korn, ed., *Eventful Years and Experiences: Studies in Nineteenth Century American Jewish History* (Cincinnati: American Jewish Archives, 1954), pp. 58–78; W. Darrell Overdyke, *The Know-Nothing Party in the South* (Baton Rouge: Louisiana State University Press, 1950); [Marx], "Jews of Atlanta," p. 13.

33. T. C. McDonald, *Free Masonry and Its Progress in Atlanta and Fulton County, Georgia* (Atlanta, 1925), pp. 34–35, 50–51; *Proceedings of the Most Worshipful Grand Lodge of Georgia at the Annual Communication for the Year 1860* (Macon, Georgia: S. Rose and Co., 1860), p. 181. Hardware merchant Solomon Solomon or watchmaker Solomon Solomonson was also a charter member of the lodge.

34. Reed, *History of Atlanta,* pp. 67, 281; *Atlanta Daily Intelligencer,* December 31, 1858, p. 2; July 9, 1860, p. 2; May 29, 1861, p. 3.

35. Bertram W. Korn, "Jews and Negro Slavery in the Old South, 1789–1865," *PAJHS* 50 (March 1961): 199–200. Although this is the best available treatment of the subject, most of Korn's sources either relate to the period before 1830 or involve Jews with deep southern roots. Korn does not consider possible changes in Jewish attitudes toward slavery during the nine decades under examination. Had manuscript census schedules been more extensively utilized, perhaps changing attitudinal patterns would have been evident.

36. U.S. Manuscript Census Schedules of Slaves, De Kalb County, Georgia, 1850; U.S. Manuscript Census Schedules of Slaves, Fulton County, Georgia, 1860; Fulton County Tax Digest, 1862; Levi Cohen's receipts for slaves dated February 29, 1862, August 1, 1863, and October 3, 1864, American Jewish Archives; *Atlanta Daily Intelligencer,* September 11, 1862, p. 2; September 28, 1862, p. 2; November 12, 1862, p. 4.

37. *Occident* 11 (August 1853): 276; 18 (February 23, 1860): 294.

38. Ibid., 10 (May 1852): 112; 12 (November 1854): 442; [Marx], "Jews of Atlanta," p. 17. During the 1850s the nearest synagogue and source of kosher food was in Augusta, 171 miles to the east.

39. *Occident* 14 (December 1856): 410; *Israelite,* November 14, 1862, p. 147; *American Israelite* (Cincinnati), March 21, 1889, p. 9. Marx was mistaken when he placed the year of the congregation's founding at 1867, which was actually the year of its incorporation and reorganization. This error is repeated in Janice Rothschild's recent history of the congregation. Marx, "Jews of Atlanta," p. 19; Janice O. Rothschild, *As But a Day: The First Hundred Years 1867–1967* (Atlanta: The Hebrew Benevolent Congregation, 1967), pp. 2–3. Atlanta City Council Minutes, December 7, 1860, at Atlanta Historical Society; *Atlanta Daily Intelligencer,* September 23, 1862, p. 3 and September 25, 1862, p. 3.

40. Reed, *History of Atlanta,* pp. 187–90; Russell, "Gate City," pp. 92–102.

41. Stephens Mitchell, "Atlanta, the Industrial Heart of the Confederacy," *AHB* 1 (May 1930): 20–27; Elizabeth Bowlby, "The Role of Atlanta During the War Between the States," *AHB* 5 (July 1940): 177–96; Garrett, *Atlanta and Environs,* 1:531–3.

42. V. T. Barnwell, comp., *Barnwell's Atlanta City Directory and Strangers' Guide . . . 1867,* p. 24; Haas to Marx; Richard B. Harwell, "Atlanta Publications During the Civil War," *AHB* 6 (July 1941): 168.

43. T. Conn Bryan, *Confederate Georgia* (Athens: University of Georgia Press, 1953), pp. 85–90, 138–46; Reed, *History of Atlanta,* pp. 187–88; Russell, "Gate City," pp. 95–103.

44. On the whole, American Jews responded positively to the call to arms and approximately 7,000 fought for the Union and 3,000 for the Confederacy. Although all-Jewish companies were raised in Chicago and Syracuse and in Macon and West Point, Georgia, nearly all Jews fought in largely non-Jewish units. Bertram W. Korn, *American Jewry and the Civil War* (Philadelphia: Jewish Publication Society of America, 1961), p. 119.

45. Reed, *History of Atlanta,* pp. 88, 99; Walter G. Cooper, *Official History of Fulton County* (Atlanta, 1934), pp. 890–900; [Marx], "Jews of Atlanta," pp. 14, 53; Garrett, *Atlanta and Environs,* 1:517; *Atlanta Daily Intelligencer,* April 2, 1862, p. 3; September 12, 1861, p. 2.

46. There was considerable disagreement over whether the term "resident" included unnaturalized inhabitants of the Confederacy who did not intend to remain permanently. In Georgia, however, the State Secession Convention adopted an ordinance which automatically naturalized all aliens who lived in the state and who did not, within three months after the passage of the act, declare before a court of law that they did not wish to become citizens. Ella Lonn, *Foreigners and the Confederacy* (Chapel Hill: University of North Carolina Press, 1940), pp. 386–97; Haas to Marx; [Marx], "Jews of Atlanta," pp. 15, 17. Also see *Atlanta Daily Intelligencer,* April 8, 1862, p. 2.

47. *Southern Confederacy* (Atlanta), January 31, 1864, p. 1.

48. Korn, *American Jewry and the Civil War,* pp. 175–88; E. Merton Coulter, *A History of the South, The Confederate States of America, 1861–1865,* vol. 7 (Baton Rouge: Louisiana State University Press, 1950), pp. 219–34.

49. Russell, "Gate City," pp. 104–15.

50. *Atlanta Daily Intelligencer,* October 7, 1862, p. 3.

51. "Diary of Heyman Herzberg," pp. 1–10, typescript copy, American Jewish Archives. Most of the memoir is printed in Jacob R. Marcus, *Memoirs of American Jews, 1775–1865,* 3 vols. (Philadelphia: Jewish Publication Society of America, 1955–56), 3:115–32.

52. *Southern Confederacy* (Atlanta), January 31, 1864, p. 1.

53. Quoted in Garrett, *Atlanta and Environs,* 1:535–36. David Mayer was one of the twenty grand jurors.

54. *Atlanta Daily Intelligencer,* October 7, 1862, p. 3.

55. Ibid.

56. Ibid., July 12, 1862, p. 2; Atlanta City Council Minutes, April 3, 1863.

57. For two versions of this possibly apocryphal incident see *Sunny South* (Atlanta), November 15, 1884, p. 5; and *Atlanta Constitution*, January 12, 1890, p. 16.

58. Garrett, *Atlanta and Environs*, 1:640–55.

59. Quoted in WPA, *Atlanta*, p. 23.

## 2 · *The Reborn City*

1. *Macon Daily Telegraph and Confederate*, December 12, 1864, p. 1; *Atlanta Daily Intelligencer*, December 20, 1864, p. 2.

2. James M. Russell, "Atlanta, Gate City of the South, 1847 to 1885" (Ph.D. dissertation, Princeton University, 1971), pp. 170, 185–86, 256–57, 332.

3. Ibid., pp. 164–65, 173–76; V. T. Barnwell, comp., *Barnwell's Atlanta City Directory and Strangers' Guide . . . 1867* (Atlanta: Intelligencer Book and Job Office, 1867), p. 31; William R. Hanleiter, comp., *Hanleiter's Atlanta City Directory for 1870* (Atlanta: William R. Hanleiter, 1870), pp. 23–24.

4. Sidney Andrews, *The South Since the War* (Boston: Ticknor and Fields, 1866), p. 341; J. T. Trowbridge, *A Picture of the Desolated States and the Work of Restoration 1865–68* (Hartford: L. Stebbins, 1868), pp. 454–55; John R. Dennett, *The South As It Is: 1865–1866* (reprint ed., New York: Viking Press, 1965), p. 268.

5. Whitelaw Reid, *After the War: A Southern Tour, May 1, 1865 to May 1, 1866* (London: S. Law, Son and Marston, 1866), pp. 355–56; Andrews, *The South Since the War*, pp. 340–41.

6. *Atlanta Daily New Era*, May 7, 1868, p. 3; *Atlanta Constitution*, March 2, 1879, p. 2; George Campbell, *White and Black: The Outcome of a Visit to the United States* (London: Chatto and Windus, 1879), p. 369; George A. Sala, *America Revisited* (London: Vizetelly and Co., 1885), p. 265.

7. Walter W. Fleming, "Immigration to the Southern States," *Political Science Quarterly* 20 (June 1905): 276–78; Rowland T. Berthoff, "Southern Attitudes Toward Immigration, 1865–1914," *Journal of Southern History* 17 (August 1951): 328–31; *Atlanta Constitution*, July 29, 1881, p. 3 and March 26, 1881, p. 2.

8. Weil was born in Germany in 1824 and came to America twenty-one years later, settling first in Pensacola, Florida and then in Canton, Georgia. After merchandising for several years, he entered the law firm of future governor Joseph E. Brown, served in the Confederate Army, and settled in Atlanta after the war. In his new home Weil cultivated a lucrative law practice, represented Fulton County in the Georgia House in 1886 and 1887, and served as president of the synagogue and other Jewish bodies. As immigration commissioner, he traveled for fourteen months through Germany and Bohemia. [David Marx], "History of the Jews of Atlanta" *Reform Advocate*, November 4, 1911 (Special Edition), pp. 56–57; Joseph Elsas, "A Memorial to the General Assembly of Georgia on the Subject of imigration [*sic*] of Foreign laborers into this State," 1866; John Thomas et al., "Memorial of the Cotton Planters' Convention of Georgia to the General Assembly," n.d.; Samuel Weil and George N. Lester, "Report of the Commissioners of Immigration," August 27, 1870; all three mss. in Immigration File, Georgia Department of Archives and History, Atlanta. Alan Conway, *The Reconstruction of Georgia* (Minneapolis: University of Minnesota Press, 1966), pp. 92–93, 112–14.

9. *Atlanta Constitution*, January 22, 1871, p. 3 and April 19, 1872, p. 2; Thomas P. Janes, *Georgia: From the Immigrant Settler's Stand-Point* (Atlanta: James P. Harrison and Co., 1879); idem, *A Manual of Georgia for the Use of Immigrants and Capitalists* (Atlanta: James P. Harrison and Co., 1878).

10. *Ninth Census of the United States: 1870, Population,* vol. 1, table 1; *Tenth Census of the United States: 1880, Population,* vol. 1, Population by Race, Sex and Nativity, table 5; *Thirteenth Census of the United States: 1910, Population,* vol. 2, Georgia, Composition and Characteristics of the Population, table 1.

11. Weil and Lester, "Report of the Commissioners of Immigration;" *Atlanta Constitution,* August 28, 1869, p. 2 and July 29, 1881, p. 3; Francis Fontaine, "Report of the Commissioner of Land and Immigration," (ms. 1880) in Immigration File, Georgia Department of Archives and History; Fleming, "Immigration," pp. 276–77; Berthoff, "Southern Attitudes Toward Immigration," pp. 328, 343; Thomas D. Clark, "The Post-Civil War Economy in the South," *American Jewish Historical Quarterly* 55 (June 1966): 430 (hereafter cited as *AJHQ*). An enthusiastic Democrat, Weil added that immigrants "do not fancy risking their liberty and material interests in States where the white man is disfranchised, and the recently emancipated slave is . . . put in power over white men." *Atlanta Constitution,* June 9, 1870, p. 1.

12. E. Merton Coulter, *A History of the South, The South During Reconstruction, 1865–1877,* vol. 8 (Baton Rouge: Louisiana State University Press, 1947), p. 202; Clark, "Post-Civil War Economy," p. 430.

13. Dennett, *The South as It Is,* pp. 1–2. Also see ibid., p. 66; and John H. Kennaway, *On Sherman's Track; or, The South After the War* (London: Seely, Jackson and Halliday, 1867), p. 88.

14. *American Jewish Year Book* (1907–08): 123–421 (hereafter cited as *AJYB*); *Encyclopaedia Judaica,* 6:1362, 7:429, 12:158 and 1219; Board of Delegates of American Israelites and Union of American Hebrew Congregations, *Statistics of the Jews in the United States* (Philadelphia: Union of American Hebrew Congregations, 1880). *Tenth Census of the United States: 1880, Population,* vol. 1, tables 6 and 8.

15. *Richmond Whig,* quoted in *Sandersonville Central Georgian,* November 7, 1866, p. 1.

16. *Atlanta Daily Herald,* May 25, 1875, p. 3.

17. *Scott's Monthly Magazine* (Atlanta) 2 (September 1865): 724.

18. *Atlanta Daily New Era,* January 3, 1867, p. 3; Franklin M. Garrett, *Atlanta and Environs: A Chronicle of Its People and Events,* 3 vols. (Athens: University of Georgia Press, 1969), 1:739–40; *Hanleiter's Atlanta City Directory for 1870,* p. 29. One postwar booster *cum* historian wrote: "The rude lessons of war revolutionized the ideas of our people. The new city, built upon the site of the old Atlanta, was largely built by new men with new ideas, new hopes and new ambitions. Honest differences of opinion were respected, diversified industries were encouraged, and geographical lines were ignored. Immigrants from all quarters were welcomed, and gradually all were fused together . . . all pulling together for the common good." Wallace P. Reed, *Reed's History of Atlanta* (Syracuse, N.Y.: D. Mason and Co., 1889), p. 19.

19. *Eighth Census of the United States: 1860, Population,* vol. 1, pp. 74–75; *Ninth Census of the United States: 1870, Population,* vol. 1, tables 3 and 7; *Tenth Census of the United States: 1880, Compendium,* table 33; *Thirteenth Census of the United States: 1910, Population,* vol. 1, Color of Race, Nativity, and Parentage, tables 46, 47; *Atlanta Constitution,* September 25, 1870, p. 2 and January 12, 1890, p. 1; *Jewish Encyclopaedia,* 2:273; Board of Delegates of American Israelites and Union of American Hebrew Congregations, *Statistics of the Jews in the United States;* Board of Delegates of American Israelites, *Population Survey Questionnaire,* 1872 (in B.D.A.I. papers, American Jewish Historical Society, Waltham, Mass.); Baron de Hirsch Fund, *U.S. Jewish Population Survey* (Paris, 1911).

20. In 1870 the *Atlanta Constitution* estimated that there were 400 to 500 Jews in the city. However, two years later local Jewish leaders informed the Board of Delegates of American Israelites that there were 58 Jewish families. If the average size of Jewish households in 1872 was the same as in 1880 (5.8), that would mean 336 persons. An estimate of 300–400 Jews in 1870 therefore seems appropriate. Another

Board of Delegates survey in 1878 indicated a Jewish population of 525. Making allowances for growth during the next two years, an 1880 estimate of 600 seems proper. A total of 284 Jews in 1870 and 570 in 1880 could be identified in either the federal census schedules or the city directories, from which data were obtained on their demographic, economic, and residential patterns. Because much of this and subsequent chapters will be devoted to the analysis of these data, the reader is directed to Appendix 1 for a discussion of the sources and techniques utilized to identify Jews and their characteristics.

21. Clark, "Post-Civil War Economy," p. 427, identifies the Jews who went South directly after the war as Alsatian. However, no Atlanta Jew listed in the 1870 or 1880 censuses declared Alsace as a birthplace, and only two declared France.

22. Henry G. Baker, *Rich's of Atlanta* (Atlanta: University of Georgia School of Business Education, 1953), pp. 5–9.

23. Most of the fifty-nine males whose whereabouts in 1861 could not positively be determined probably spent the war years in the North.

24. *Tenth Census of the United States: 1880, Social Statistics of Cities,* vol. 19, pt. 2, p. 157. There are no comparable data available for 1870.

25. Intermarriage did not necessarily entail estrangement from the Jewish community. Moses Frank, who married a wealthy English-born widow in 1866, joined the synagogue and several Jewish fraternal and cultural societies; other intermarried Jews, like Alex Steinheimer, had few if any formal ties to the community.

26. *Atlanta Constitution,* May 17, 1885, p. 11.

27. Although women constituted more than a third of Atlanta's work force in 1880, only one Jewish woman in 1870 and six in 1880 were gainfully employed. The seven included one boardinghouse keeper, a teacher in the synagogue school, a dry goods cashier, a fruit and confectionary stand owner, and three millinery clerks. Three of the women were married, four were single, and only two were members of households that possessed property valued at over three hundred dollars.

28. John Stainback Wilson, *Atlanta as It Is* (New York: Little, Rennie and Co., 1871), p. 85.

29. *Atlanta Constitution,* May 8, 1879, p. 6 and September 22, 1880, p. 1; Reed, *History of Atlanta,* p. 461; [Marx], "Jews of Atlanta," pp. 49, 51; U.S. Manuscript Census Schedules 1880, Manufactures, Fulton County, Georgia; Walter G. Cooper, *The Story of Georgia,* 4 vols. (New York: American Historical Society, 1938), 4:751–52.

30. U.S. Manuscript Census Schedules 1880, Manufactures, Fulton County, Georgia.

31. Ibid.

32. Barnett A. Elzas, *The Jews of South Carolina from the Earliest Times to the Present Day* (Philadelphia: J. B. Lippincott Co., 1905), pp. 199–202; I. W. Avery, *The History of the State of Georgia from 1850 to 1881* (New York: Brown and Derby, 1881), pp. 43, 324–29, 352, 359, 386–90, 524.

33. Tax assessment data must be interpreted with caution. There was a general tendency to undervalue assets (though the assessments were purportedly at full valuation), property owned outside of the city was not subject to taxation, corporate stock was not included under individual owners, business assets like merchandise were only sporadically listed among the holdings of proprietors, and circumvention of the tax laws could be accomplished without much difficulty. For a discussion of these problems and the manner in which they were handled, see Appendix 1, pp. 227–28.

34. The individuals and businesses in 1876 were: L. Cohen and Co. ($10,200); Elsas, May and Co. ($27,950); J. T. Eichberg ($15,250); Herman Franklin ($10,900); Friedman and Co. ($21,700); Mrs. Caroline Haas ($11,500); M. and J. Hirsch ($24,-

700); M. Menko and Bro. ($13,400); David Mayer ($16,800); and M. Wiseberg ($13,700). *Atlanta Constitution,* April 16, 1869, p. 1 and August 13, 1876, p. 1.

35. The manuscript schedules of the 1870 census from which these data were extracted failed to enumerate some Jews, while information on some others could not be obtained because of fading and illegibility.

36. The eight Jews and their property assessments were: Julius M. Alexander ($10,000), Levi Cohen ($18,000), Solomon Dewald ($15,000), Moses Frank ($15,-000), Morris Hirsch ($10,000), David Mayer ($15,000), Abram Rosenfeld ($11,500), and Morris Wiseberg ($13,000). All except Rosenfeld spent the war years in the South.

37. Fulton County Tax Digest for 1880, in Georgia Department of Archives and History, Atlanta.

38. Ibid.

39. Trowbridge, *A Picture of the Desolated States,* pp. 453–55.

40. The areas delineated in these and subsequent maps probably were not genuine neighborhoods in the sense that their inhabitants shared certain common characteristics. Indeed, beyond the material presented in this study, little work has been done on the city's residential patterns. I first plotted the location of Jewish residences in 1870, 1880, 1896, and 1911 and then drew lines largely based upon "natural" boundaries like the railroad tracks and major streets that would best illustrate the tendency of Jews to cluster. Although Jews comprised the majority of the population on certain blocks, they were never the largest group in any of the seven areas.

41. Russell, "Gate City," pp. 263–69.

42. Many white-collar workers also lived in the households of relatives who were proprietors.

43. G. M. Hopkins, *City Atlas of Atlanta, Georgia* (Baltimore: Southern and Southwestern Surveying and Publishing Co., 1878); *Atlanta Georgia* (New York: Sanborn Map Publishing Co., 1886); *Tenth Census of the United States: 1880, Population,* vol. 1, table 25.

44. Based on data kindly supplied by Dr. Richard Hopkins of Ohio State University.

45. *Occident* (Philadelphia), 25 (June 1867): 152–53.

46. *Occident* 25 (August 1867): 265; *Israelite* (Cincinnati), March 8, 1867, p. 6; Janice O. Rothschild, *As But a Day: The First Hundred Years 1867–1967* (Atlanta: The Hebrew Benevolent Congregation, 1967), pp. 4–6, 55–56; *Atlanta Constitution,* November 30, 1869, p. 3; January 4, 1871, p. 2; May 25, 1875, p. 3; September 1, 1877, p. 4.

47. Wilson, *Atlanta As It Is,* pp. 30–31; *Israelite,* June 7, 1870, p. 7; *Jewish South* (Atlanta), December 14, 1877, p. 4 and May 23, 1879, p. 1.

48. Wilson, *Atlanta As It Is,* pp. 32–33; E[dward] Y[oung] Clarke, *Atlanta Illustrated* (Atlanta: James P. Harrison and Co., 1881), pp. 56, 58; *Atlanta Constitution,* June 24, 1871, p. 3; *Jewish South,* June 28, 1878, p. 5; *The Christmas Present* (*Atlanta Constitution* supplement), December 9, 1869, p. 3.

49. *Atlanta Constitution,* April 11, 1877, p. 4; March 30, 1893, p. 8; October 12, 1901, p. 5; *Atlanta, Ga., City Directory 1883* (Atlanta: Charles F. Weatherbe, 1883), p. 183.

50. *American Israelite* (Cincinnati), November 6, 1874, p. 5; *The Christmas Present,* December 9, 1868, p. 3; Wilson, *Atlanta As It Is,* pp. 32–33; *Jewish South,* June 7, 1878, p. 5; *Atlanta Constitution,* March 4, 1874, p. 3.

51. Rudolph Glanz, "Jews in Relation to the Cultural Milieu of the Germans in America up to the Eighteen Eighties," in idem, ed., *Studies in Judaica Americana* (New York: Ktav Publishing House, 1970), pp. 229–30; idem, "The Rise of the Jewish Club in America," *Jewish Social Studies* 31 (April 1969): 86–87.

52. Clarke, *Atlanta Illustrated,* p. 59; *Atlanta Constitution,* September 23, 1869, p. 3; July 7, 1871, p. 3; April 12, 1877, p. 4; October 19, 1902, p. 2; April 19, 1872, p. 2; August 17, 1871, p. 3; September 16, 1890, p. 7.

53. *Atlanta Constitution,* October 18, 1871, p. 3; October 19, 1871, p. 1; November 9, 1871, p. 3; *Atlanta Daily New Era,* November 8, 1871, p. 4.

54. *Atlanta Constitution,* September 10, 1872, p. 1.

55. Marvin Lowenthal, *The Jews of Germany* (Philadelphia: Jewish Publication Society of America, 1936), pp. 260–63, 300–18; Glanz, "The Rise of the Jewish Social Club in America," p. 89.

## *3 · From Traditional to Classical Reform*

1. David Philipson, *The Reform Movement in Judaism* (New York: Macmillan Co., 1931), pp. 3–6; Nathan Glazer, *American Judaism,* Chicago History of American Civilization (Chicago: University of Chicago Press, 1957), pp. 25–27.

2. Glazer, *American Judaism,* pp. 27–31; Moshe Davis, *The Emergence of Conservative Judaism: The Historical School in 19th Century America* (Philadelphia: Jewish Publication Society of America, 1963), pp. 11–12.

3. Glazer, *American Judaism,* pp. 33–35; Davis, *Conservative Judaism,* pp. 7–9; W. Gunther Plaut, ed., *The Growth of Reform Judaism: American and European Sources until 1948* (New York: World Union of Progressive Judaism, 1965), p. xxi.

4. Davis, *Conservative Judaism,* pp. 13, 18–20, 340–42, 347–49; Jeremiah J. Berman, "The Trend of Jewish Religious Observance in Mid-Nineteenth Century America," *Publications of the American Jewish Historical Society* 37 (1947): pp. 31–32 (hereafter cited as *PAJHS*).

5. Berman, "Trend of Jewish Observance," pp. 47–53.

6. Glazer, *American Judaism,* pp. 36–42; Philipson, *The Reform Movement in Judaism,* pp. 329–81.

7. *Atlanta Constitution,* October 28, 1869, p. 1; October 5, 1870, p. 3; August 23, 1903, p. 3; *Occident* (Philadelphia) 25 (March 1868): 621. Silverberg had studied for the rabbinate in his native Warsaw and briefly filled a pulpit in Memphis before he acquired a fortune as a blockade runner during the Civil War and then established himself as a retail dry goods merchant in Atlanta.

8. Frank J. Adler, *Roots in a Moving Stream: The Centennial History of Congregation B'nai Jehudah of Kansas City, 1870–1970* (Kansas City, Mo.: The Temple, Congregation B'nai Jehudah, 1972), pp. 39–40; *Israelite* (Cincinnati), August 13, 1869, p. 8.

9. *Israelite,* November 19, 1869, p. 6; June 7, 1870, p. 7.

10. *Atlanta Constitution,* September 25, 1870, p. 2.

11. Among the communities in which Burgheim later served were Louisville, Kentucky; St. Paul, Minnesota; Kansas City, Missouri; Akron, Ohio; Syracuse, New York; Charleston, West Virginia; and Hartford, Connecticut. Adler, *Roots in a Moving Stream,* pp. 39–40; *Israelite,* October 13, 1871, p. 6.

12. Abraham I. Shindling, *West Virginia Jewry: Origins and History, 1850–1958,* 3 vols. (Philadelphia: Maurice Jacobs Press, 1963), 3:1469–70; *Atlanta Constitution,* July 15, 1873, p. 3 and January 4, 1872, p. 2; *Atlanta Daily Sun,* September 15, 1871, p. 4.

13. *Atlanta Constitution,* May 10, 1873, p. 4.

14. Ibid., June 3, 1873, p. 3; July 15, 1873, p. 3; June 10, 1875, p. 3.

15. Ibid., August 21, 1874, p. 3; September 12, 1874, p. 3.

16. *American Israelite* (Cincinnati), August 28, 1874, p. 5.

17. Bonnheim served as a rabbi in Columbus, Georgia; Columbus, Ohio; Wheeling, West Virginia; Las Vegas, Nevada; and Winnipeg, Manitoba. In 1882 he received a medical degree from the Columbus College of Medicine and during the next six years was superintendent of the Hebrew Hospital and Asylum in Baltimore. Shingling, *West Virginia Jewry,* 3:1469–70.

18. *Jewish Encyclopaedia,* 5:641; *Encyclopaedia Judaica,* 7:518–19; Henry Gersoni, *Sketches of Jewish Life and History* (New York: Hebrew Orphan Asylum Printing Establishment, 1873). Gersoni subsequently denied the charge of apostasy and discussed his early years in "A Leaf from My Own History," published in sixteen weekly installments in the *Jewish Advance* (Chicago), from January 2 to April 16, 1880.

19. *American Israelite,* December 1, 1876, p. 3.

20. Ibid., January 1, 1875, p. 5.

21. For samples of Gersoni's sermons see ibid., November 13, 1874, p. 6; December 25, 1874, p. 5; March 19, 1875, p. 5; June 4, 1875, p. 5; *Atlanta Constitution,* December 20, 1874, p. 1.

22. *American Israelite,* August 25, 1876, p. 5.

23. *Atlanta Constitution,* March 30, 1875, p. 1.

24. Ibid., May 25, 1875, p. 3. The lay leadership may have felt otherwise, for Gersoni wore his robes at the confirmation ceremony a month later. Ibid., June 10, 1875, p. 3.

25. *American Israelite,* October 15, 1875, p. 2.

26. Ibid., December 1, 1876, p. 3; *Atlanta Constitution,* July 29, 1876, p. 4.

27. Although the specifics of his departure are unknown, it is noteworthy that during his three-year editorship, the *Jewish Advance* never mentioned Atlanta, though news from smaller southern Jewish communities was carried. Gersoni may have been too radical for his Atlanta parishioners, for he favored the abolition of the bar mitzvah ceremony before the Hebrew Benevolent Congregation took that step. *Jewish Advance,* June 21, 1878, p. 4. Wise may have been responsible for resurrecting the apostasy charge for he had a falling out with Gersoni and then wrote: "Henry Gersoni has been made solely and exclusively by himself, for the man is ignorant of all that is called learning . . . [and] is malicious, wicked and disreputable. Like other Polanders, he learned some Talmud when he was young and to write Hebrew when he was older, to neglect and forget both in Christian boarding houses in St. Petersburg and London. What he knows now are reminiscences of former days when he was a Jew." Wise even alleged that Gersoni was the "cunning . . . masked agent of some church [sent] to undermine American Judaism. . . ." *American Israelite,* April 30, 1880, p. 4. Back in New York, Gersoni contributed to several periodicals and translated several of Turgenev's stories into English. *Encyclopaedia Judaica,* 7:518–19; Henry Gersoni, trans., *Mumn, and the Diary of a Superfluous Man,* by Ivan Turgenev (New York: Funk and Wagnalls, 1884).

28. Louis J. Swichkow and Lloyd P. Gartner, *History of the Jews of Milwaukee* (Philadelphia: Jewish Publication Society of America, 1963), p. 178; Janice O. Rothschild, *As But a Day: The First Hundred Years, 1867–1967* (Atlanta: The Hebrew Benevolent Congregation, 1967), pp. 11–12; Morris U. Schappes, ed., *A Documentary History of the Jews in the United States, 1654–1875* (New York: Citadel Press, 1950), p. 733; Edward Benjamin Morris Browne, trans., *The Book Jashar: The Lost Book of the Bible* (New York: United States Publishing Co., 1876).

29. Isaac Mayer Wise to Browne, March 28, 1873, in Browne Papers, American Jewish Archives, Cincinnati.

30. *Atlanta Constitution,* July 18, 1877, p. 4; *Jewish South* (Atlanta), October 14, 1877, p. 8.

31. The *Jewish South* was conceived "purely as a business venture" by the gentile publishing firm of J. H. and W. B. Seals. As editor, Browne billed the weekly as "The Largest and Cheapest Jewish Journal in the World, Independent and Fearless," and at one point claimed a readership of 15,000. The attractive eight-page format included local news items submitted by correspondents from throughout the Southeast, serialized novels, sermons, editorial and chess columns, domestic and international news of Jewish interest, and a feature entitled "The American Jewish Pulpit —Its Shame and Its Glory." Browne frequently embroiled himself in journalistic controversy, often at the expense of the paper's owners. Early in 1879 they sold their interest to a New Orleans firm which continued to publish the *Jewish South* (with Browne as editor) until 1881. *Jewish South,* October 14, 1877, p. 4; February 14, 1879, p. 4. Microfilm copies for the period October 1877 to December 1879 are available at the American Jewish Periodical Center, Cincinnati.

32. Isaac Mayer Wise was among those with whom Browne quarreled. See *American Israelite,* April 30, 1880, p. 4. On Browne's dismissal see idem, April 22, 1881, p. 334. His inflated sense of self-importance is revealed in a letter to his attorney: "Let the *Times* be sued for a *million* of dollars. You can make of me just as big a man as there is in the American pulpit, a prominent author orator Editor and Rabbi *without a stain* upon my character and known the country over." Browne to his attorney, March 23, 1881, Browne Papers, America Jewish Historical Society, Waltham, Mass.

33. In New York, Browne served and was subsequently dismissed from two Reform congregations. He became active in Republican politics and represented American Jewry at the funeral of Ulysses S. Grant. Because the burial occurred on Saturday, Browne refused to ride and accompanied the cortege on foot from the Battery to 123rd Street. He lived in Chicago during the nineties, served congregations in Columbus, Georgia, and Toledo, Ohio, and continued to lecture until his death in 1928. See memorabilia and clippings in Browne Papers, American Jewish Archives, Cincinnati.

34. *Atlanta Constitution,* July 16, 1887, p. 4.

35. *American Israelite,* July 15, 1887, p. 5.

36. Edward Benjamin Morris Browne, comp., *Prayers of Israel,* 2nd edition (New York, 1885), pp. 168–69; Hebrew Benevolent Congregation Minutes (hereafter cited as HBC), January 6, 1878; Rothschild, *As But a Day,* p. 19.

37. HBC Minutes, November 21, 1881 and January 27, 1886; *Souvenir Fortieth Anniversary Zion Congregation of West Chicago* (n.p., 1904). Jacobson remained in Natchez until 1896, was principal of the Englewood (Illinois) Hebrew Education Society from 1898 to 1900, and served as Rabbi of Zion Congregation of West Chicago from 1900 until shortly before his death in 1911.

38. *Who's Who in American Jewry,* 1926 (New York: Jewish Biographical Bureau, 1927), p. 493; *Atlanta Constitution,* January 12, 1890, p. 16; HBC Minutes, June 24, 1888.

39. The final vote was 27 for Reich and 37 for his successor, with 10 abstentions. A reporter noted that Reich "was greatly beloved by the children and poorer members of the church" and suggested that had the suffrage been broader (only 53 percent of the members—those who owned pews—could vote), the result might have been different. In his farewell sermon, Reich warned the congregation to beware of indifference which would lead to "spiritual gangrene"—a particularly apt metaphor since the rabbi had just received his M.D. from the Southern Medical College and was about to begin postgraduate work in dermatology in Berlin. Except for a seven-

year term as rabbi of an Augusta congregation, Reich practiced medicine until his death in 1942. HBC Minutes, January 6, 1895 and January 20, 1895; *Atlanta Constitution,* March 11, 1895, p. 5; April 16, 1895, p. 9; *Who's Who in American Jewry,* 1926, p. 493.

40. *Atlanta Constitution,* July 8, 1895, p. 4. The only Jews known to have violated the law were Orthodox immigrants from Russia, and the only Jewish protest against it was apparently made on their behalf. See idem, May 8, 1899, p. 5; *Jewish Sentiment* (Atlanta), May 5, 1899, p. 3.

41. *Jewish South,* April 26, 1878, p. 4.

42. Ibid., September 27, 1878, p. 5.

43. *Atlanta Constitution,* October 1, 1886, p. 5; *Jewish Messenger* (New York), December 11, 1885, p. 10. See also *American Israelite,* August 28, 1874, p. 5.

44. *Occident* 10 (May 1852), p. 112; Berman, "Trend of Jewish Observance," p. 36; Aaron Haas to David Marx, n.d. [1911], Jews of Atlanta file, Atlanta Historical Society; *American Israelite,* August 28, 1874, p. 5.

45. *Jewish South,* March 22, 1878, p. 4.

46. Only fifteen to twenty families sent their poultry to the *shohet* to be slaughtered. Circumcision was another Jewish rite whose prophylactic value came to be highly regarded, and in 1885 Rabbi Jacobson operated on twice as many Christian as Jewish infants. *Atlanta Constitution,* December 13, 1885, p. 20; *Jewish Messenger,* December 25, 1885, p. 5.

47. *Atlanta Constitution,* March 30, 1893, p. 8; February 13, 1895, p. 5; *Jewish Sentiment,* November 26, 1897; December 10, 1897, p. 5; March 30, 1900, p. 3. Frank J. Cohen came to Atlanta from Arkansas in 1881, married one of Morris Wiseberg's daughters, entered the paper and printing business, and published the first issue of the *Jewish Sentiment* late in 1895. The paper was similar in format to Browne's *Jewish South,* boasted a regional circulation of 4,600, and had dozens of local correspondents. Publication was discontinued in August 1901. Cohen briefly moved to Texas where he edited the *Southwestern Jewish Sentiment,* then returned to Atlanta in 1904, held various jobs and died in 1918. Bound volumes of the *Jewish Sentiment* for the period November 1897 to August 1901 are at the Jewish Division of the New York Public Library.

48. Synagogue members also tended to be older, married, wealthier, and holders of higher status occupations than nonmembers. While 66 percent of the employed Jewish males ages 18 and over in 1870 and 50 percent of those in 1896 were proprietors, managers, and officials, persons with these occupations respectively accounted for 92 and 67 percent of the membership. Although 49 percent of the males in 1870 and 59 percent of those in 1896 were married, the respective proportion of married members was 63 and 78 percent. Only 18 percent of the males in 1870 owned realty and 36 percent possessed taxable assets of $600 or more, but among synagogue members the proportion was 29 and 56 percent. Similarly, while only 31 percent of the males in 1870 ages 18–29 were members, 62 percent of those ages 30 and over belonged. Data on the age and wealth of the 1896 members were not collected.

49. [David Marx], "Jews of Atlanta" *Reform Advocate,* November 4, 1911 (Special Edition), pp. 12, 23, 27, 45.

50. Only 285 persons were listed as Russian-born in the severely flawed 1896 city census, but by checking the census data against the naturalization records, 317 Jews could be so identified. The figures for 1890 and 1900 are for Russians, not necessarily Jews—but in fact, more than 90 percent of Russian-born Atlantans were Jewish. In all three years there were also a few Yiddish-speaking Jews from Galicia and Hungary, but the size of this group can not be precisely determined. *Eleventh*

*Census of the United States: 1890, Population,* vol. 1, pt. 1, tables 53, 56, 59; *Fourteenth Census of the United States: 1920, Population,* vol. 2, Country of Birth, table 15, and Country of Origin, table 9.

51. Plaut, *Growth of Reform Judaism,* pp. xxi, xxii. The complex relationship between Atlanta's German and Russian Jews will be treated in a subsequent chapter.

52. Rothschild, *As But a Day,* pp. 45–46. The *Journal* observed that many of the members desired an American-born rabbi. *Atlanta Journal,* March 11, 1895, p. 5.

53. *Atlanta Constitution,* September 9, 1896, p. 7; October 6, 1897, p. 7; Rothschild, *As But a Day,* p. 46. On the bar mitzvah controversy, see HBC Minutes, June 1, 1897; February 22, 1898; May 3, 1898; July 3, 1898; January 1, 1899.

54. *Jewish Sentiment,* April 27, 1900, p. 19. HBC Minutes, November 14, 1904 and January 4, 1905; Uriah Zevi Engelman, "Jewish Statistics in the U.S. Census of Religious Bodies (1850–1936)," *Jewish Social Studies* 9 (1947): 142.

55. Rothschild, *As But a Day,* p. 56; *HBC Minutes, January 6, 1909; November 28, 1902, p. 12; November 21, 1904, p. 7. Cordial but informal interfaith contacts had existed since the 1870s. Atlanta Constitution,* January 4, 1871, p. 2; October 9, 1878, p. 4; *Jewish South,* April 18, 1879, p. 1. The three congregations and their dates of founding were Ahavath Achim (1887), Shearith Israel (1902), and Beth Israel (1905). The development of these congregations will be treated in the next chapter.

56. Rothschild, *As But a Day,* p. 50.

57. Marx's activities are recorded in his Day Book, a typescript copy of which is in his papers at the Temple.

58. The Temple's new members were not recent arrivals in the city but rather persons who had previously not desired to affiliate themselves with a congregation.

59. HBC Minutes, January 6, 1909; January 14, 1913; Rothschild, *As But a Day,* pp. 64–65.

## *4 · The New Immigrants*

1. Samuel Joseph, *Jewish Immigration to the United States from 1881 to 1910* (New York, 1914), pp. 27–52; Howard M. Sachar, *The Course of Modern Jewish History* (New York: Dell Publishing Company, Delta Books, 1958), pp. 188–98.

2. Joseph, *Jewish Immigration,* pp. 56–60; Sachar, *Modern Jewish History,* pp. 78–96, 181–88. Because, as will be demonstrated shortly, relatively few of the East Europeans who came to Atlanta were from Galicia or Rumania, a discussion of anti-Jewish disabilities and other incentives to emigration from these lands has not been included. Interested readers are referred to Joseph, *Jewish Immigration,* pp. 69–80; Raphael Mahler, "The Economic Background of Jewish Emigration from Galicia to the United States," *Yivo Annual of Jewish Social Science* 7 (1952): 255–67; Joseph Kissman, "The Immigration of Rumanian Jews Up to 1914," *Yivo Annual of Jewish Social Science* 2–3 (1947–48): 160–79.

3. Joseph, *Jewish Immigration,* pp. 60–68; Sachar, *Modern Jewish History,* pp. 240–60.

4. Joseph, *Jewish Immigration,* pp. 117–51.

5. Sachar, *Modern Jewish History,* p. 309. For a more comprehensive treatment of the complex manner in which the established community perceived the immigrants, see Esther Panitz, "The Polarity of American Jewish Attitude Toward Immigration (1870–1891)," *American Jewish Historical Quarterly* 53 (December 1963): 99–130 (hereafter cited as *AJHQ*); idem, "In Defense of the Jewish Immigrant (1891–1924)," *AJHQ* 55 (September 1965): 57–97; Zosa Szajkowski, "The Attitude of American Jews to East European Jewish Immigration (1891–1893)," *Publication of the American*

*Jewish Historical Society* 40 (March 1951): 221–80 (hereafter cited as *PAJHS*); Moses Rischin, *The Promised City: New York's Jews 1870–1914* (Cambridge: Harvard University Press, 1962), pp. 93–111.

6. Gilbert Osofsky, "The Hebrew Emigrant Aid Society of the United States (1881–1883)," *PAJHS* 49 (March 1960): 173–87; Szajkowski, "Attitude of American Jews," p. 272; *Atlanta Constitution,* March 5, 1882, p. 7.

7. The proportion of Jews among the total immigration from Russia to the United States was 63 percent during the decade 1881–1890, 55 percent during the decade 1891–1900, and 44 percent for the years 1901–1910, or 48 percent for the entire thirty-year period. However, an examination of the Atlanta Census for 1896 and naturalization papers filed by approximately 750 Russian-born Atlantans between 1883 and 1917 uncovered fewer than two dozen adult males who could not be positively identified as Jews. Furthermore, while 2,281 Atlantans in 1910 were of Russian parentage (both native- and foreign-born), Russian, Polish, and Lithuanian were the mother tongues of only 247 Atlantans, whereas Yiddish and Hebrew were the mother tongues of 2,118. Since some of the Polish-speaking Atlantans were natives of Germany or Austria-Hungary and some of those who indicated Russian as their mother tongue were Jews, the proportion of Jews among the city's Russian population may be placed at over 85 percent in 1910 and perhaps as high as 95 percent before 1900. Joseph, *Jewish Immigration,* p. 102; *Eleventh Census of the United States: 1890, Population,* vol. 1, pt. 1, tables 53, 56, 59; *Thirteenth Census of the United States: 1910, Population,* vol. 1, Mother Tongue of Foreign White Stock, table 24.

8. *Constitution of the Jewish Alliance of America and Abstract of the Proceedings of the First Convention* (Philadelphia: Billstein and Son, 1891), pp. 7–9, 29–40; *Atlanta Constitution,* December 27, 1891, p. 4 and October 9, 1891, p. 4; Petition of H. Wolfe et al. to Hon. John I. Hall, Chairman of the Finance Committee, Georgia House of Representatives, n.d. [1892?], in Georgia Department of Archives and History, Atlanta.

9. *Industrial Removal Office Annual Report,* 1904–15 (New York, 1904–15); IRO Record of Removals, 1901–1922, ms. in IRO Collection, American Jewish Historical Society, Waltham, Mass. The distribution of removals to Atlanta was as follows: 1901 (5), 1902 (16), 1903 (29), 1904 (31), 1905 (61), 1906 (49), 1907 (77), 1908 (64), 1909 (47), 1910 (35), 1911 (32), 1912 (110), 1913 (66), 1914 (29), 1915 (3). The activities of the Removal Office dropped sharply after the outbreak of World War I. *Thirteenth Census of the United States: 1910, Population,* vol. 1, Mother Tongue of Foreign White Stock, table 24; *Fourteenth Census of United States: 1920, Population,* vol. 2, Mother Tongue of Foreign White Stock, table 13 and n.5 p. 973. The 1920 census reported 2073 persons who listed Yiddish and Hebrew and 1379 who indicated Russian as their mother tongue. However, nearly all who declared Russian were actually Yiddish-speaking Jews. Most of the increase during the decade 1910–1920 occurred during the four years before the war.

10. *Atlanta Ga., City Directory, 1883* (Atlanta: Charles F. Weatherbe, 1883); *Atlanta City Directory, 1912* (Atlanta: Atlanta City Directory Co., 1911).

11. Atlanta Census of 1896, microfilm in Woodruff Library, Emory University; Fulton County Superior Court, Declarations of Intention (1878–1906) and Petitions for Naturalization (1883–1906), in Office of the Clerk, Fulton County Superior Court; U.S. Circuit Court for the Northern District of Georgia, Declarations of Intention and Petitions for Naturalization (1893–1917), in Federal Records Center, East Point, Georgia (hereafter cited as Jewish Naturalization Data); IRO Record of Removals.

12. Jewish Naturalization Data.

13. David Davis [Yampolsky], *The Passing Years: Memories of Two Worlds* (Tel Aviv, Israel: New Life Press, 1974), p. 176.

14. John Higham, *Strangers in the Land: Patterns of American Nativism 1860–1925* (New Brunswick, N.J.: Rutgers University Press, 1955), pp. 90–91, 168–69; *Atlanta Constitution,* August 20, 1906, p. 6; November 14, 1905, p. 3; October 9, 1894, p. 4.

15. Jewish Naturalization Data; IRO Record of Removals.

16. Jewish Naturalization Data; IRO Record of Removals; *Atlanta Constitution,* April 13, 1895, p. 5.

17. Joseph, *Jewish Immigration,* pp. 187–88; IRO Record of Removals; IRO follow-up reports for the years 1904–1912.

18. IRO Record of Removals.

19. *Atlanta Constitution,* February 17, 1882, p. 4; March 1, 1882, p. 4; Also see idem, December 1, 1881, p. 4; February 19, 1882, p. 4; February 22, 1882, p. 4.

20. Ibid., March 5, 1882, p. 7; July 16, 1882, p. 9.

21. The term is used to characterize the growing proportion of Southern and Eastern Europeans who landed on American shores in the four decades after 1880.

22. Ibid., February 20, 1884, p. 5; April 11, 1885, p. 4; June 29, 1886, p. 4; July 11, 1887, p. 4; May 6, 1891, p. 4. The tiny but prosperous colony of northern Italians was affronted by the blanket condemnation of the Italian people, and the *Constitution* (June 6, 1891, p. 22) issued a clarification: "They [the local Italians] are all of the better class, none from southern Italy whence emigrate the inferior and the lowest sorts."

23. *Atlanta Constitution,* January 17, 1893, p. 4; July 4, 1893, p. 4. See also the newspaper's criticism of the Atlanta anti-immigrant position articulated in Josiah Strong's *Our Country.* Ibid., September 6, 1887, p. 4.

24. Ibid., December 9, 1895, p. 4; February 8, 1896, p. 7; May 24, 1896, p. 14; January 1, 1897, p. 4; Higham, *Strangers in the Land,* pp. 169–71; *Atlanta Journal,* December 23, 1906, p. 8; December 30, 1906, p. 6.

25. *Atlanta Constitution,* July 17, 1904, p. 4; July 26, 1907, p. 7; House Committee on Immigration and Naturalization, 61 Congress, *Hearings* (January 25, 1910), p. 92.

26. *Atlanta Constitution,* July 16, 1904, p. 8; August 2, 1904, p. 3; June 1, 1906, p. 6; October 26, 1906, p. 2; February 4, 1907, p. 5; August 4, 1907, p. 7; February 21, 1907, p. 8.

27. *Thirteenth Census of the United States: 1910, Population,* vol. 1, Country of Birth of the Foreign-Born Population, tables 18 and 26. The Russians were the largest foreign-born group in both the city and the state. *Atlanta Constitution,* February 14, 1892, p. 4; November 6, 1892, p. 22; September 16, 1899, p. 4; September 6, 1905, p. 4. For just a few of many editorials which condemned anti-Semitism in Russia and the U.S. see ibid., March 24, 1888, p. 6; August 14, 1890, p. 4; June 12, 1891, p. 4; May 2, 1892, p. 5; May 23, 1903, p. 6.

28. *Atlanta Constitution,* February 20, 1907, p. 3. Interestingly, the invocation at the opening session of the convention was delivered by a Macon rabbi.

29. Ibid., September 14, 1902, p. 3; July 21, 1903, p. 6.

30. See Mark Zborowski and Elizabeth Herzog, *Life Is with People* (New York: International Universities Press, 1952); Arthur A. Goren, *New York Jews and the Quest for Community: The Kehillah Experiment, 1908*–1922 (New York: Columbia University Press, 1970).

31. *Atlanta Constitution,* October 8, 1886, p. 7; October 19, 1886, p. 9. Relations between the Germans and Russians will be treated at length in the next chapter.

32. Ibid., September 26, 1898, p. 5; August 9, 1900, p. 8; December 20, 1903, p. 10. The Baron de Hirsch Fund, established by the wealthy Franco-Jewish philanthropist, contributed five hundred dollars to the construction fund. The residential structure of the Jewish community will be examined in the next chapter.

33. Ibid., September 26, 1898, p. 5; December 10, 1903, p. 10; May 16, 1903, p. 3; Congregation Ahavath Achim Minutes, September 21, 1890, and October 5, 1890, at Congregation Ahavath Achim; *One Hundred Years Accomplishments of Southern*

*Jewry* (Atlanta: Southern Israelite, Southern Newspaper Enterprises, 1934), p. 42; *American Jewish Review* (Atlanta), March, 1914, p. 39 and June 1914, p. 23 (hereafter cited as *AJR*).

34. *Atlanta Constitution,* November 6, 1892, p. 22 October 12, 1903, p. 10; Ahavath Achim Minutes, November 5, 1893, *Jewish Sentiment* (Atlanta), February 11, 1898, p. 3; *AJR,* May, 1914, p. 6; May 1915, p. 4; June, 1914, p. 23; Thomas H. Martin, *Atlanta and Its Builders,* 2 vols. (Atlanta: Century Memorial Publishing Co., 1902), 2:569.

35. *Atlanta Constitution,* December 13, 1885, p. 8 and November 6, 1892, p. 22; Ahavath Achim Minutes, May 22, 1892 and June 17, 1894.

36. Ahavath Achim Minutes, February 21, 1891 and December 18, 1892; *Atlanta Constitution,* May 13, 1896, p. 9; Hebrew Benevolent Congregation Minutes, June 28, 1891 (hereafter cited as HBC).

37. *Atlanta Constitution,* December 27, 1891, p. 4 and May 13, 1896, p. 9; Ahavath Achim Minutes, February 8, 1891; October 24, 1892; July 16, 1893; August 27, 1893; Zborowski and Herzog, *Life Is with People,* p. 213; Montefiore Relief Association Petition for Incorporation, Fulton County Superior Court Charter Book 2, p. 695, at Fulton County Superior Court House. A Ladies' Charity Society was also organized during the nineties.

38. Ahavath Achim Minutes, August 10, 1890; August 24, 1890; February 21, 1891; April 5, 1891; February 17, 1895.

39. Ibid., April 10, 1892; August 6, 1893; May 3, 1891; May 17, 1891; May 24, 1891.

40. Ibid., January 1, 1893; August 6, 1893; August 20, 1893; *Atlanta Constitution,* October 6, 1897, p. 7; May 13, 1896, p. 9; September 6, 1897, p. 7; B'nai Israel Petition for Incorporation, Fulton County Superior Court Charter Box #41 Fall Term 1890; Chevra Kaddisha Petition for Incorporation, Fulton County Superior Court Charter Book 2, p. 658; Jewish Naturalization Data. Of 23 Ahavath Achim members between August 1890 and August 1893 whose birthplaces are identifiable, 6 came from Kovno, 4 from Kherson, 3 each from Grodno and Vilna, 2 each from Minsk and Kiev, and 1 each from Courland, Lomza, and Warsaw.

41. Joshua Trachtenberg, *Consider the Years: The Story of the Jewish Community of Easton, 1752–1942* (Easton, Pa.: Centennial Committee of Temple Brith Shalom, 1944), pp. 195–96.

42. Dubrovsky, "I. J. Schwartz's *Kentucky,*" p. 244. Schwartz settled in Lexington, Kentucky, in 1918 and published his epic poem seven years later. Tobias Geffen, Autobiographical Memoir (mimeo, n.d. [1941?], p. 13, in possession of Louis Geffen, Atlanta. B. Wildauer to D. Bessler, May 30, 1905, in IRO Atlanta correspondence file. My understanding of this matter was enhanced by conversations in Atlanta with David Davis (August 9, 1973), Solomon J. Gold (December 8, 1971), and T. Schloffer (March 16, 1973), all of whom had been born in Russia and came to Atlanta between 1902 and 1910. Several Russians tried to evade the closing law, and at least one, M. Cohen, who ran a fruit stand on Decatur Street, was arrested three Sundays in a row. *Atlanta Constitution,* May 8, 1899, p. 7.

43. Interviews in Atlanta with S. J. Gold, M. L. Kahn (March 14, 1973), and Louis Geffen (December 9, 1971). Gold was a charter member of Shearith Israel; Kahn was born in Atlanta in 1894, and his father was a charter member; and Geffen was born in Atlanta, the son of Rabbi Tobias Geffen. *Southern Israelite* (Atlanta), July 20, 1945, p. 20; Solomon Sutker, "The Jews of Atlanta: Their Structure and Leadership Patterns" (Ph.D. dissertation, University of North Carolina, 1952), p. 123; Ahavath Achim Minutes, May 20, 1894.

44. *Southern Israelite,* July 20, 1945, p. 20; December 14, 1929, p. 5; *Atlanta Constitution,* October 13, 1907, p. 4C; September 7, 1907, p. 7; Shearith Israel Petition for Incorporation, Charter Book 5, p. 116; *Who's Who in American Jewry,* 1926

(New York: Jewish Biographical Bureau, 1927), pp. 191–92; *Encyclopaedia Judaica,* 7:536; Geffen, Autobiographical Memoir, pp. 1–33.

45. Beth Israel Petition for Incorporation, Charter Book 5, p. 478; Geffen Memoir, p. 11; Interview with Leon Eplan in Atlanta, December 8, 1971. Eplan was born in Atlanta in 1896, the son of Leon Eplan who was among the founders of both Ahavath Achim and Beth Israel.

46. *Atlanta Constitution,* July 10, 1907, p. 1; *Atlanta Journal,* July 7, 1907, p. 1.

47. [David Marx], "History of the Jews of Atlanta" *Reform Advocate,* November 4, 1911 (Special Edition), pp. 47, 49; *Southern Guide* (Atlanta), March 10, 1908; *AJR,* October, 1915, p. 16; *Atlanta Constitution,* October 1, 1913, p. 7; September 20, 1914, p. 4B; J. D. Braverman to H. Wolfe, December 1, 1912 and D. Bressler to P. Fligner, December 11, 1912, both in IRO correspondence file; *American Jewish Year Book* 21 (1919–20): 357; Eplan Interview.

48. Zborowski and Herzog, *Life Is with People,* pp. 166–88.

49. Anshe Sfard Petition for Incorporation, #4647, C–98; *Atlanta Constitution,* September 29, 1913, p. 12; November 23, 1913, p. 7D; November 24, 1913, p. 10; Interviews in Atlanta with H. Taratoot (March 11, 1973) and T. Schloffer (March 16, 1973), both founding members of Anshe Sfard.

50. David de Sola Pool "The Levantine Jews in the United States," *American Jewish Year Book* (1913–14): 207–20; Albert Amato, "Sephardim and the Seattle Sephardic Community (M.A. thesis, University of Washington, 1939), pp. 45–54.

51. Mair Jose Benardete, *Hispanic Culture and Character of the Sephardic Jews* (New York: Hispanic Institute in the United States, 1953 [1952]), pp. 121–23, 138–39; Pool, "Levantine Jews," pp. 207–12.

52. Oriental Hebrew Association Or Ve Shalom Petition for Incorporation, #4615. This document listed sixty-nine Sephardim, perhaps the entire adult male population. Their birthplaces, marital status, and emigration patterns were disclosed in their naturalization papers, the IRO Record of Removals, and especially through a conversation with Judah H. Notrica (February 5, 1973), who was born in Rhodes in 1893, came to Atlanta in 1913, and was a founding member of the congregation.

53. Isaac N. Habif, "Or Ve Shalom the Sephardic Congregation of Atlanta," *The American Sephardi* 2 (1969): 77–78; Or Hahayim Petition for Incorporation, # 4615; Benardete, *Hispanic Character,* p. 145; Notrica Interview.

## *5 · The Divided Community*

1. Atlanta Chamber of Commerce, *Atlanta: The Metropolis of the Southeast* (Atlanta, 1913); idem, *Atlanta as the Southeastern Center of Commerce and Finance* (Atlanta, 1914), pp. 9, 13, 21; *Tenth Census of the United States: 1880, Social Statistics of Cities,* vol. 19, pt. 2, pp. 157–62; Elizabeth A. M. Lyon, "Business Buildings in Atlanta: A Study in Urban Growth and Form" (Ph.D. dissertation, Emory University, 1971), pp. 483–90.

2. *Thirteenth Census of the United States: 1910, Population,* vol. 1, Color and Race, Nativity or Parentage, table 46. The manuscript schedules of the 1896 local, rather than the 1900 federal, census were used because the latter were not opened to scholars until after this research was completed.

3. *Twelfth Census of the United States: 1900, Population,* vol. 2, pt. 2, Ages, table 9.

4. Ibid., vol. 1, pt. 1, Sex, General Nativity and Color, table 24; Ann F. Mebane, "Immigrant Patterns in Atlanta, 1880 and 1896" (M.A. thesis, Emory University, 1967), p. 78; Samuel Joseph, *Jewish Immigration to the United States from 1881 to 1910* (New York, 1914), p. 130.

5. *Twelfth Census of the United States: 1900, Population,* vol. 1, pt. 1, Foreign Parentage, table 60, and Conjugal Condition, table 31. The 1896 census did not indicate marital status. Therefore, I based my judgments on data in earlier censuses and upon the age and sex distribution within the households. The large number of Russians who could not be classified is a consequence of the census's failure to enumerate many Russians listed in the city directory and the tendency of married Russian males to settle in Atlanta prior to the arrival of their families.

6. As in 1880, women constituted more than a third of Atlanta's work force, yet only a handful of Jewish women were gainfully employed. A dozen—all single, native-born, and in their twenties—taught in the public schools, and a few others were stenographers, milliners, postal clerks, and telephone operators. Two Russian widows operated stores on Decatur Street. Significantly, the ratio of employed males to employed females in 1900 was 22:1 for persons of Russian parentage, 3.6:1 for native whites of native parentage, and 1.7:1 for the city as a whole. *Twelfth Census of the United States: 1900, Special Report, Occupations,* table 23.

7. Both Haases were also active in the development of real estate. *Atlanta Constitution,* March 12, 1893, p. 3; May 7, 1893, p. 10.

8. John R. Hornady, *Atlanta: Yesterday, Today and Tomorrow* (Atlanta: American Cities Book Club, 1922), pp. 306–08; Sinclair Jacobs, "Joseph Jacobs," *Southern Israelite* (Atlanta), July 1, 1955, pp. 35–37; Joseph Jacobs, "How I Won and Lost an Interest in Coca-Cola," *Drug Topics* 45 (July 1929): 189–90, 220, 222, 227.

9. David Davis [Yampolsky], *The Passing Years: Memories of Two Worlds,* (Tel Aviv, Israel: New Life Press, 1974), pp. 148–57.

10. The six Russians with property assessed at over $1,000 were Jacob M. Friend ($1,800), Asher L. Feurstenberg ($2,500), Louis Gordon ($2,900), Aaron Landsberger ($3,300), Judah W. Hirshfeld ($13,700), and Morris Wiseberg ($20,700). Tax assessment data were not examined for non-Russians in 1896, but in 1880 54 percent of adult Jewish males (only one of whom was Russian-born) had property assessed at over $50 and 42 percent were worth over $1,000. Fulton County Tax Digest for 1896, in Georgia Department of Archives and History, Atlanta.

11. Nathan Goldberg, *Occupational Patterns of American Jewry* (New York: Jewish Teachers' Seminary and People's University, 1947), pp. 9–11; United States Immigration Commission, *Reports,* 38 vols. (Washington, D.C.: Government Printing Office, 1911), 26:217, 309, 397, 475, 569, 653, 733.

12. Oriental Hebrew Association Or Ve Shalom Petition for Incorporation, #4615, Fulton County Superior Court; *Atlanta City Directory, 1915* (Atlanta: Atlanta City Directory Co., 1914). Fifty-nine of the sixty-nine names listed on the petition could be found in the directory.

13. *Insurance Maps of Atlanta Georgia, 1899* (New York: Sanborn-Perris Map Co., 1899); *Atlanta Constitution,* February 8, 1882, p. 7.

14. Louis Wirth, *The Ghetto* (Chicago: University of Chicago Press, Phoenix Books, 1956), pp. 19, 20, 202.

15. *Insurance Maps of Atlanta Georgia, 1899; Atlanta Constitution,* January 22, 1905, p. 4.

16. *Twelfth Census of the United States: 1900, Population,* vol. 2, pt. 2, table 89. There were an average of 5.3 Jews in Temple-affiliated households, but these dwellings were larger than the Russians'. Ludwig Amster, "A Plea for the Improvement of the Sanitary Conditions of the 'Russian Immigrants,'" *Magnet* (Atlanta) 1 (January 1894): 57; E. B. Latham and H. R. Baylor, comps., *Atlas of Atlanta Georgia* (n.p., 1893).

17. Because the typed results of the 1896 Atlanta Census are arranged alphabetically within each ward, no attempt was made to determine the precise composition of the district.

18. Oriental Hebrew Association Or Ve Shalom Petition for Incorporation, #4615, Fulton County Superior Court; *Atlanta City Directory, 1915* (Atlanta: Atlanta City Directory Co., 1914); Ann Ellis, "A History of the Greek Community in Atlanta, 1900–1920" (unpublished paper, Georgia State University, 1970), pp. 8, 10, 17.

19. Hebrew Benevolent Congregation Minutes, January 14, 1913, at the Temple, Atlanta (hereafter cited as HBC).

20. *Jewish Tribune* (Atlanta), February 28, 1896, p. 7; Harmony Club Petition for Incorporation, #109 Superior Court of Fulton County; *Atlanta Journal,* March 3, 1905, p. 5; [David Marx], "History of the Jews of Atlanta" Reform Advocate, November 4, 1911 (Special Edition), p. 71; *Atlanta Constitution,* January 22, 1910, p. 7 and November 26, 1911, p. 3A; *American Jewish Review* (Atlanta), December, 1913, p. 12.

21. *Jewish South* (Atlanta), December 14, 1877, p. 4; August 8, 1879, p. 5; August 22, 1879, p. 5; September 12, 1879, p. 9; *Atlanta Constitution,* April 23, 1889, p. 9; April 30, 1882, p. 9; January 10, 1898, p. 5; *Jewish Tribune,* February 28, 1896, p. 1; Hebrew Association Petition for Incorporation, #429; *Jewish Sentiment* (Atlanta), January 26, 1897, p. 12; April 8, 1898, p. 13. The *Jewish Tribune* made its debut in November 1895 and survived for about two years. Its motto was "Judaism-Americanism-Liberalism," and a Xerox copy of the sole extant issue is on file in the Atlanta Historical Society.

22. *Atlanta Constitution,* January 17, 1898, p. 4; *Jewish Sentiment,* December 3, 1897, p. 12; *American Jewish Review,* December 1913, p. 12 and March 1914, p. 14; Council of Jewish Women, Atlanta Section, *Twenty-Fifth Anniversary Book* (Atlanta, 1920), pp. 1–17.

23. *Jewish Sentiment,* April 29, 1898, p. 14 and October 6, 1899, p. 15; *Atlanta Constitution,* October 18, 1905, p. 2; February 21, 1880, p. 4; December 26, 1891, p. 7; Meta Leinkoff Memory Book, 1899–1905, in the Natalie Cohen Collection, Atlanta Historical Society.

24. *Southern Israelite* (Atlanta), July 20, 1945, p. 14.

25. *Atlanta Constitution,* March 29, 1889, p. 3; October 26, 1886, p. 9; December 7, 1893, p. 23; January 11, 1914, pp. 4F and 10F; *American Israelite* (Cincinnati), March 21, 1889, p. 5 and March 4, 1889, p. 4; *American Jewish Review,* March 1914; *Atlanta Journal,* March 30, 1896, p. 4; Hebrew Orphans' Home Records of Admission, 1889–1921, in the office of Jewish Children's Service, Atlanta. The location of the Home in Atlanta incidentally made the Gate City the logical place for the annual grand lodge conventions. As a result, such prominent Jews as Simon Wolf were frequent visitors, and provided members of the host community direct contact with the main currents of American Jewish life.

26. John Higham, "Social Discrimination Against Jews in America, 1830–1930," *Publications of the American Jewish Historical Society* 47 (September 1957): 9–11 (hereafter cited as *PAJHQ*); Rudolph Glanz, "The Rise of the Jewish Club in America," *Jewish Social Studies* 31 (April 1969): 89.

27. HBC Membership List for 1895; HBC Ledger for 1911; HBC Minutes for 1896 and January 6, 1909.

28. I. O. B'nai B'rith Gate City Lodge Applications, 1882–1896, in Jewish Collection of Atlanta Historical Society; Gate City Lodge Ledger Book, 1883–1890, in Temple Archives; I. O. B'nai B'rith Atlanta Lodge Membership List, 1903, in office of District Grand Lodge No. 5; IOBBDGL No. 5, *Proceedings* (Richmond: H. T. Ezekiel, 1906 and 1910), 1906, p. 16 and 1910, p. 30; *Atlanta Constitution,* December 23, 1907, p. 4; *American Jewish Review,* October 1913, pp. 17–18; June 1914, p. 23; September 1914, p. 38; November 1915, p. 18; Mutual Order B'nai Israel Petition for Incorporation, #2793.

29. Davis, *The Passing Years,* pp. 152–53, 181–86; *American Jewish Review,* May 1914, p. 8 and May 1915, p. 13. My understanding of the Ring's early development

was enhanced by interviews in Atlanta with charter members David Davis (August 9, 1973) and Betsy (Mrs. M. J.) Merlin (March 9, 1973).

30. *By-Laws of the Hungarian Benevolent Association of Atlanta, Georgia* (n.p., n.d. [1911?]), p. 12.

31. Young Men's Hebrew Association Petition for Incorporation, 1673 A 172; *Atlanta Constitution,* February 13, 1904, p. 2 and June 28, 1905, p. 10; *American Jewish Review,* January 1914, p. 17; Davis, *The Passing Years,* p. 176.

32. *Southern Guide* (Atlanta), March 10, 1908. Microfilm copies of this sole extant issue are available at the American Jewish Periodical Center in Cincinnati, the American Jewish Historical Society in Waltham, Mass., and the Atlanta Historical Society. *Jewish Star,* undated fragment [November 1909], in possession of author. Wortsman to Bressler, November 12, 1909; Bressler to Wortsman, November 23, 1909, in Atlanta Correspondence File, IRO Papers, American Jewish Historical Society. *Ayer's American Newspaper Annual and Directory* (Philadelphia: N. W. Ayer and Son, 1912), p. 134. In 1922 Wortsman established the Yiddish language *California Jewish Voice* in Los Angeles. Max Vorspan and Lloyd P. Gartner, *History of the Jews of Los Angeles* (San Marino, California: Huntington Library, 1970), p. 141.

33. At times when there was no local Jewish publication, the *Atlanta Constitution* and the *Sunny South* (Atlanta) had special weekly columns devoted to Jewish news. For example, see *Atlanta Constitution,* December 10, 1911, p. 7F.

34. *American Jewish Review,* April 1914, pp. 18–19; March 1915, p. 13; January 1916, pp. 1–17; *Jewish Outlook* (Atlanta), March 1913, pp. 6–8; Don't Worry Club, Minutes, 1911–1917, at Atlanta Historical Society; Interview in Atlanta with Sam Eplan, December 8, 1971. Eplan was born in Atlanta in 1896 and was a founding member of the Don't Worry Club and the Osceola Club and a former president of the Progressive Club.

35. *Atlanta Constitution,* March 5, 1882, p. 7; *Jewish Sentiment,* December 11, 1898, p. 3; Levi Cohen et al., Petition to Hon. John J. Hall (n.d. [1892]), at Georgia Department of Archives and History. The 1891 law was probably directed against the Russians. Previously, only patent medicine and jewelry peddlers had been taxed. However, shopkeepers viewed the immigrant dry goods peddlers as unfair competition and used their influence with legislative representatives to protect their interests.

36. Benjamin Rabinowitz, "The Young Men's Hebrew Associations (1854–1913)," *PAJHS* 37 (1947): 251; *Atlanta Constitution,* December 29, 1890, p. 7; February 18, 1891, p. 2; May 16, 1903, p. 3; May 20, 1903, p. 7; May 21, 1903, p. 8; May 22, 1903, p. 1; May 24, 1903, p. 2; June 5, 1903, p. 4; November 13, 1905, p. 5; November 14, 1905, p. 6; Henry A. Alexander, *Introductory Address . . . At the Concert Given for the Kishineff Relief Fund* (Atlanta: Franklin Printing and Publishing Co., 1903), pp. 5–6; Federation of Jewish Charities, Minutes, February 28, 1912; Jewish Educational Alliance Minutes, August 7, 1912.

37. *Atlanta Constitution,* February 12, 1904, p. 5; February 13, 1904, p. 4; February 15, 1904, p. 2; February 19, 1904, p. 4; HBC Minutes, November 28, 1905.

38. *Atlanta Constitution,* December 27, 1891, p. 4; February, 15, 1894, p. 2; HBC Minutes, January 4, 1892; January 31, 1895; September 30, 1883; September 29, 1889; October 25, 1904; November 21, 1910; *American Israelite,* September 30, 1897, p. 5; March 21, 1889, p. 9.

39. *Atlanta Constitution,* April 24, 1869, p. 4; January 12, 1890, p. 16; September 14, 1913, p. 4F.

40. Amster, "A Plea for Improvement," pp. 56–57.

41. *Atlanta Constitution,* May 11, 1896, p. 7.

42. Ibid.

43. Ibid., May 13, 1896, p. 9.

44. Ibid., May 12, 1896, p. 10; June 5, 1896, p. 9; June 13, 1896, p. 5.

45. Arthur Hertzberg, ed., *The Zionist Idea* (Garden City, N.Y.: Doubleday and Herzl Press, 1959), pp. 14–100.

46. A. Loeb Cohen, Account Book, November 12, 1867, microfilm at American Jewish Archives, Cincinnati; Salo W. and Jeanette M. Baron, "Palestinian Messengers to America, 1849–79: A Record of Four Voyages," *Jewish Social Studies* 5 (July 1943): pp. 244–45; *American Israelite,* January 28, 1876, p. 5; *Atlanta Constitution,* November 1, 1871, p. 3; July 29, 1876, p. 4; Edward Benjamin Morris Browne, comp., *Prayers of Israel,* 2nd edition (New York, 1885), p. 169.

47. *Jewish Sentiment,* February 11, 1898, p. 14; *Maccabean* (New York), April 1904, p. 200 and April 1905, p. 168; *American Jewish Review,* March 1914, pp. 21–27; June 1914, p. 24; September 1914, p. 25; Jewish Educational Alliance, Minutes, January 1, 1914.

48. Naomi W. Cohen, "The Reaction of Reform Judaism in America to Political Zionism (1897–1922)," *PAJHS* 40 (June 1951): 361–62; *Jewish Sentiment,* June 8, 1900, p. 19.

49. Janice O. Rothschild, *As But a Day: The First Hundred Years, 1867–1967,* (Atlanta: The Hebrew Benevolent Congregation, 1967), pp. 64, 90, 100; HBC Minutes, January 14, 1914; *Atlanta Georgian,* March 30, 1907, p. 13.

50. HBC Minutes, January 14, 1914.

51. *Atlanta Constitution,* July 9, 1868, p. 2; March 6, 1891, p. 4; August 20, 1899, p. 15; September 16, 1913, p. 6.

52. *American Jewish Year Book,* (1907–08): 152; Montefiore Relief Association Petition for Incorporation, Charter Book 2, #695.

53. Federation of Jewish Charities Minutes, January 12, 1912; January 16, 1912 (hereafter cited as FJC).

54. FJC *Annual Report for 1914* (n.p., n.d. [1915]), p. 5; H. Joseph Hyman, "The Problem of Jewish Charities in the South," *American Jewish Review,* April 1914, p. 11.

55. FJC *Report for 1914,* pp. 6–9.

56. *Atlanta Constitution,* September 19, 1913, p. 4; U.S. Immigration Commission, *Reports,* 34:4, 35:9.

57. *Atlanta Constitution,* February 4, 1906, p. 2; February 5, 1906, p. 5; February 6, 1906, p. 6; March 5, 1906, p. 3; November 21, 1910, p. 3; March 26, 1911, p. 15M; Jewish Educational Alliance Petition for Incorporation, #3077; Jewish Educational Alliance Minutes, October 24, 1906, at Atlanta Jewish Welfare Federation.

58. FJC *Annual Report for 1914,* pp. 7–8; H. Joseph Hyman, "The Jewish Educational Alliance," *Jewish Outlook* 1 (April 1913): 5–11; *American Jewish Review,* May 1914; May 1915, p. 4.

59. H. Joseph Hyman, "The New Tendency in Jewish Communal Work," *American Jewish Review,* February 1915, p. 6; idem, "The Alliance and Its Activities," *American Jewish Review,* May 1914, pp. 3–4.

60. *Atlanta Constitution,* January 2, 1898, p. 5; Jewish Educational Alliance Minutes, pp. 56, 100.

61. *American Jewish Review,* May 1914, p. 16; June 1914, p. 12; November 1915, p. 5; Victor H. Kriegshaber, "The Jewish Educational Alliance," *American Jewish Review,* May 1914, p. 3. A graduate of the University of Chicago Law School, Hershkowitz had published the *Oklahoma Jewish Review* for a year before moving to Atlanta in September 1913. The first issue of the *American Jewish Review* appeared later that year and continued every month until 1917 when Hershkowitz moved to Buffalo.

## 6 · *Making It: Parameters of Geographic Persistence and Economic Mobility*

1. Beginning with Stephan Thernstrom, *Poverty and Progress: Social Mobility in a Nineteenth-Century City* (Cambridge: Harvard University Press, 1964), the study of mobility has become quite popular. Among recent studies are idem, *The Other Bostonians: Poverty and Progress in the American Metropolis, 1880–1970* (Cambridge: Harvard University Press, 1973); Howard P. Chudacoff, *Mobile Americans: Residential and Social Mobility in Omaha, 1880–1920* (New York: Oxford University Press, 1972); Clyde Griffen, "Making It in America: Social Mobility in Mid-Nineteenth Century Poughkeepsie," *New York History* 51 (October 1970): 479–99; Dean R. Esslinger, *Immigrants and the City: Ethnicity and Mobility in a Nineteenth-Century Midwestern Community* (Port Washington, N.Y.: Kennikat, 1975); and Peter R. Knights, *The Plain People of Boston, 1830–1860: A Study in City Growth,* Urban Life in America Series (New York: Oxford University Press, 1971).

2. For tabular depiction of the relationship between persistence and property ownership, see Steven Hertzberg, "The Jews of Atlanta, 1865–1915" (Ph.D. dissertation, University of Chicago), pp. 207–08.

3. See ibid., pp. 209–11 for tabular depiction of the influence of age and marital status on persistence.

4. Thernstrom, "Urbanization, Migration and Social Mobility in Late Nineteenth Century America," in Barton J. Bernstein, ed., *Towards a New Past: Dissenting Essays in American History* (New York: Pantheon Books, 1968), pp. 167–68.

5. See Hertzberg, "The Jews of Atlanta," p. 212, for tabular depiction of this relationship.

6. Thernstrom and Peter R. Knights, "Men In Motion: Some Speculations About Urban Population Mobility in Nineteenth Century America," *Journal of Interdisciplinary History* 1 (Autumn 1970): 9–10.

7. Ibid., pp. 17–18; Chudacoff, *Mobile Americans,* pp. 40–41; Thomas Kessner, *The Golden Door: Italian and Jewish Immigrant Mobility in New York City, 1880–1915,* Urban Life in America Series (New York: Oxford University Press, 1977), p. 142.

8. Richard J. Hopkins, "Occupational and Geographic Mobility in Atlanta, 1870–1896," *Journal of Southern History* 34 (May 1968): 202–03; idem, "Patterns of Persistence and Occupational Mobility in a Southern City: Atlanta, 1870–1920" (Ph.D. dissertation, Emory University, 1972), p. 54. Both the native-born white and immigrant cohorts included a proportional representation of Jews. Could these somehow have been excluded from the samples, the difference between Jewish and general mobility patterns would have been even more marked. To insure comparability with Hopkins's figures, mine have been left uncorrected for death.

9. Hopkins, "Occupational and Geographic Mobility in Atlanta," pp. 202–03; idem, "Patterns of Persistence and Occupational Mobility," p. 59.

10. *Jewish South* (Atlanta), February 28, 1879, p. 5.

11. This shift usually, but not necessarily, entailed a decline in income, economic security, and social status. But especially after the growth of elaborate corporate bureaucracies during the 1890s, some proprietors who became white-collar workers may have actually improved their condition.

12. For a tabular depiction, see Hertzberg, "The Jews of Atlanta," p. 227.

13. See ibid., p. 228 for a tabular depiction of this relationship.

14. See ibid., pp. 236 and 238 for a tabular depiction of this relationship.

15. For a further discussion of the methodological problems of similar studies, see ibid., pp. 238–39.

16. Griffen, "Making It in America," p. 491; Thernstrom, *The Other Bostonians,* pp. 149–51.

17. Thomas Kessner, "The Golden Door: Immigrant Mobility in New York City, 1880–1915" (Ph.D. dissertation, Columbia University, 1975), p. 185.

18. Comparable data are not available for other age groups. For tabular representation, see Hertzberg, "The Jews of Atlanta," p. 242.

19. Hopkins, "Patterns of Persistence and Occupational Mobility," pp. 107–10.

20. Miriam K. Slater, "My Son the Doctor: Aspects of Mobility Among American Jews," *American Sociological Review* 34 (June 1969): 369.

21. Nathan Hurvitz, "Sources of Motivation and Achievement of American Jews," *Jewish Social Studies* 23 (October 1961): 217–34.

22. Nathan Glazer, "The American Jew and the Attainment of Middle Class Rank: Some Trends and Explanations," in Marshall Sklare, ed., *The Jews: Social Patterns of an American Group* (New York: Free Press, 1958), pp. 138–46.

## 7 · *Citizen and Symbol*

1. *Atlanta Constitution,* October 10, 1902, p. 6. For similar appraisals of Jewish involvement in local affairs, see idem, September 25, 1870, p. 2; January 4, 1871, p. 2; September 14, 1882, p. 8; February 12, 1886, p. 4; January 12, 1890, p. 16; May 7, 1893, p. 10; September 29, 1897, p. 4; February 13, 1901, p. 4; September 16, 1913, p. 6; March 31, 1914, p. 4; *Atlanta Daily Herald,* May 25, 1875, p. 3.

2. *Atlanta Constitution,* June 24, 1868, p. 2; July 5, 1868, p. 2; July 24, 1868, p. 3; July 23, 1868, p. 2; October 31, 1868, p. 2; November 3, 1868, p. 1. For a Republican attempt to court the Jewish vote, see *Atlanta Daily New Era,* June 30, 1868, p. 2. Grant's Order No. 11 is discussed at length in Bertram W. Korn, *American Jewry and the Civil War* (Philadelphia: Jewish Publication Society of America, 1951), pp. 121–55.

3. *Daily New Era,* November 10, 1870, p. 3; *Atlanta Constitution,* October 19, 1871, p. 1; August 17, 1872, p. 3; August 24, 1872, p. 3; October 2, 1872, p. 2.

4. *Atlanta Constitution,* October 28, 1873, p. 3; October 11, 1874, p. 3; December 8, 1887, p. 5; December 6, 1888, p. 5. Besides Weil, at least four other Jews served in the Georgia Legislature during the seventies and eighties: Raphael J. Moses, Adolph Brandt, Lewis Arnheim, and Charles Wessolowsky.

5. Ibid., January 10, 1889, p. 7; November 10, 1897, p. 7; April 11, 1897, p. 14; November 28, 1909, p. 6C.

6. Ibid., November 1, 1893, p. 5; November 15, 1892, p. 5; October 4, 1894, p. 5; January 7, 1896, p. 4; November 3, 1897, p. 4; October 6, 1899, p. 1; February 20, 1900, p. 1; October 6, 1904, p. 1; August 8, 1907, pp. 1–2; September 26, 1908, p. 3; *Jewish Sentiment* (Atlanta), August 10, 1900. p. 3; September 28, 1900, p. 4; August 31, 1900, p. 3; September 7, 1900, p. 3; September 16, 1915, p. 3.

7. *Atlanta Constitution,* July 24, 1908, p. 3; September 20, 1908, p. 6A; September 25, 1908, p. 1; November 14, 1908, pp. 1, 5; November 29, 1908, p. 5D. Interestingly, while leaders of the established Jewish community rallied to Maddox's standard, their Russian counterparts supported Woodward. Ibid., November 21, 1908, pp. 1–2.

8. Ibid., June 6, 1908, p. 1; August 24, 1910, p. 1. Two Jews held appointive positions during the first two decades of the twentieth century: Joseph Fuld as deputy city clerk and Alex Dittler as deputy clerk of the superior court and recorder of deeds. Ibid., August 30, 1902, p. 7; May 9, 1915, p. 5M.

9. Candidates for the Democratic primary were generally chosen either at ward caucuses or at meetings composed of delegates from each ward. Because of their tendency to cluster residentially, Jews were sometimes disproportionately repre-

sented at the caucuses. However, the primary and general elections themselves were held on an at-large basis which meant that a Jewish aspirant for council required considerable support from Gentiles outside his own ward. The electoral process and the fact that the major Jewish residential concentrations were incidentally bisected by ward boundaries had their origin in the attempt to prevent the election of black councilmen.

10. *Atlanta Constitution,* June 5, 1896, p. 6; Fulton County Superior Court and the U.S. District Court for the Northern District of Georgia, Declarations of Intention and Petitions for Naturalization, 1883–1917.

11. Hebrew Benevolent Congregation Minutes, January 14, 1914 (hereafter cited as HBC); *American Jewish Review* (Atlanta), May 1914, p. 14; September 1914, pp. 24, 36; Declarations of Intention and Petitions for Naturalization, 1883–1914.

12. Rufus B. Spain, *At East in Zion: A Social History of Southern Baptists 1865–1900* (Nashville: Vanderbilt University Press, 1967), p. 190; Carl Dean English, "The Ethical Emphases of the Editors of Baptist Journals in the Southeastern Region of the United States 1865–1915" (Th.D. dissertation, Southern Baptist Theological Seminary, 1948), pp. 20–25, 60.

13. *Atlanta Constitution,* November 20, 1885, p. 4; November 24, 1885, p. 7; November 26, 1885, p. 1; December 8, 1887, p. 5; October 23, 1888, p. 4.

14. *Jewish Messenger* (New York), December 11, 1885, p. 10; *Atlanta Constitution,* July 14, 1895, p. 5; *Jewish Sentiment,* November 24, 1899, p. 3; June 21, 1901, p. 4.

15. *Atlanta Constitution,* March 16, 1904, p. 4; August 25, 1906, p. 1; September 22, 1906, p. 2; August 8, 1907, pp. 1–2; Thomas Gibson, "The Anti-Negro Riots in Atlanta," *Harper's Weekly* 50 (October 13, 1906): 1458; J. N. T. Cawhern, *State Prohibition Souvenir of Georgia's Victory* [1908], in Anti-Semitism File, American Jewish Historical Society. The indirect involvement of Jewish saloonkeepers is noted in Ray Stannard Baker, *Following the Color Line* (New York: Doubleday, Page and Co., 1908), pp. 34–35. Modern scholarship has placed the blame elsewhere. See Charles Crowe, "Racial Violence and Social Reform—Origins of the Atlanta Race Riot of 1906," *Journal of Negro History* 53 (July 1968): 234–56.

16. The historiography of Populist anti-Semitism is extensive and oriented almost entirely toward the midwestern Populists. For a discussion of the literature, see Walter T. K. Nugent, *The Tolerant Populists: Kansas Populism and Nativism* (Chicago: University of Chicago Press, 1963), pp. 3–32, 231–35.

17. *People's Party Paper* (Atlanta), February 25, 1892, p. 6; October 5, 1894, p. 7; October 2, 1896, p. 2; October 18, 1895, pp. 5–6; October 25, 1895, p. 4.

18. *Atlanta Journal,* June 2, 1896, p. 1; June 21, 1896, p. 5; June 5, 1896, p. 3. The *Atlanta Constitution* reported (though perhaps not accurately) that the East European Jews were solidly behind free silver. Ibid., June 5, 1896, p. 9.

19. *Atlanta Constitution,* February 3, 1895, p. 13; July 19, 1896, p. 14; *Atlanta Journal,* June 29, 1896, p. 4.

20. *American Israelite* (Cincinnati), November 6, 1874, p. 4; *Atlanta Constitution,* September 11, 1880, p. 4; June 7, 1896, p. 19; Timothy J. Crimmins, "The Crystal Stair: A Study of the Effects of Class, Race and Ethnicity on Secondary Education in Atlanta, 1872–1925" (Ph.D. dissertation, Emory University, 1972), pp. 91–97.

21. *Jewish South* (Atlanta), April 19, 1878, p. 5; Thomas H. Martin, *Atlanta and Its Builders,* 2 vols. (Atlanta: Century Memorial Publishing Co., 1902), 2:276–79, 297–98; *American Israelite,* March 21, 1889, p. 9.

22. *Atlanta Constitution,* May 3, 1890, p. 4; May 6, 1890, p. 5; September 21, 1897, p. 7; January 6, 1903, p. 7. A decade before Mayer's death, Levi Cohen and Aaron Haas were asked to serve but declined. *Jewish South,* December 12, 1879, p. 5.

23. *Atlanta Constitution,* April 12, 1899, pp. 1–2; April 18, 1899, p. 7; May 5, 1899, p. 7; December 1, 1902, p. 5; HBC Minutes, March 28, 1899; January 14, 1914; *Atlanta City Directory* (Atlanta: Atlanta City Directory Co., 1913, 1915), 1913, p. 425; 1915, p. 911.

24. *Atlanta Constitution,* March 31, 1914, p. 4. For similar statements see ibid., February 5, 1893, p. 3; March 6, 1891, p. 4; March 26, 1911, p. 4.

25. V. T. Barnwell, Comp., *Barnwell's Atlanta City Directory and Strangers' Guide . . . 1867* (Atlanta: Intelligencer Book and Job Office, 1867), pp. 58–61; Wallace P. Reed, *Reed's History of Atlanta,* (Syracuse, N. Y.: D. Mason and Co., 1889), p. 283; *Jewish South,* August 24, 1878, p. 5; September 6, 1878, p. 8; September 13, 1878, p. 4; *Atlanta Constitution,* January 4, 1871, p. 2; February 5, 1881, p. 3; *Jewish Messenger,* December 25, 1885, p. 5.

26. *Atlanta Constitution,* December 15, 1892, p. 6; October 22, 1893, p. 3; October 3, 1894, p. 9; June 25, 1898, p. 11; July 6, 1898, p. 9.

27. Ibid., June 3, 1903, p. 1; June 4, 1903, p. 1; March 31, 1903, p. 1; April 29, 1907, p. 4; January 29, 1909, p. 3; HBC Minutes, September 25, 1900; Council of Jewish Women, Atlanta Section, *Twenty-Fifth Anniversary Book,* pp. 15–17.

28. *Atlanta Constitution,* April 17, 1911, p. 7; September 14, 1914, p. 4; May 1, 1913, p. 6; June 19, 1915, p. 6; January 11, 1914, p. 4F; June 16, 1914, p. 1; December 5, 1915, p. 9A; Anne Lavina Branch, "Atlanta and the American Settlement House Movement" (M.A. thesis, Emory University, 1966), p. 55.

29. *Atlanta Constitution,* March 6, 1891, p. 4; September 9, 1914, p. 7.

30. While Jews constituted less than 4 percent of Atlanta's population in 1911, they contributed nearly half of the charity funds raised in the city. This proves, said H. Joseph Hyman, that Jews are not "only after the dividends," as one critic had charged. Ibid., September 13, 1913, p. 4.

31. Ibid., December 12, 1892, p. 4; March 12, 1905, p. 5.

32. Ibid., April 17, 1911, p. 7; April 24, 1911, pp. 2, 5.

33. Charles W. Ferguson, *Fifty Million Brothers: A Panorama of American Lodges and Clubs* (New York: Farrar and Rinehart, Inc., 1937), pp. 12–13; Oscar Handlin, *The Dimensions of Liberty* (Cambridge: Harvard University Press, Belknap Press, 1961), pp. 97–98, 117; Arthur M. Schlesinger, Sr., "Biography of a Nation of Joiners," *American Historical Review* 50 (October 1944): 15; Rowland T. Berthoff, *An Unsettled People: Social Order and Disorder in American History* (New York: Harper and Row, 1971), pp. 272–74.

34. *Atlanta Constitution,* October 29, 1872, p. 3; July 6, 1873, p. 8; May 25, 1899, p. 2; January 25, 1903, p. 2; [David Marx], "History of the Jews of Atlanta" *Reform Advocate,* November 4, 1911 (Special Edition), pp. 57, 63.

35. *Atlanta Constitution,* May 16, 1888, p. 7; May 17, 1888, p. 8; *One Hundred Years Accomplishments of Southern Jewry,* (Atlanta: Southern Israelite, Southern Newspaper Enterprises, 1934), pp. 35, 70.

36. *Proceedings of the Most Worshipful Grand Lodge of Georgia* (Macon, Ga: various publishers), 1860, p. 181; 1867, pp. 174, 106; 1870, pp. 135–36, 160–61, 236; 1874, pp. 109–10, 187. Subordinate Lodge Returns to the Grand Lodge of Georgia, 1878, 1899, 1913. The above materials are in the archives of the Grand Lodge of Georgia, Macon, Georgia. *Israelite* (Cincinnati), August 3, 1855, p. 28; T. C. McDonald, *Free Masonry and Its Progress in Atlanta and Fulton County, Georgia* (Atlanta, 1925), pp. 28, 34–35, 50–51, 50–59. Interestingly, of the fourteen Jews who held the office of Grand Master of Masons in the U.S. between 1865 and 1913, seven were from the South and the remainder from the West and Midwest, Meyerhardt's term in office was the longest. Herbert Friedenberg, "A List of Jews Who Were Grand Masters of Masons in Various States of This Country," *Publication of the American Jewish Historical Society,* 19 (1910): 95–100 (hereafter cited as *PAJHS*); idem, "Additional List of Jewish Grand Masters," *PAJHS* 22 (1914): 182.

37. A. E. Sholes, comp., *Sholes' Directory of the City of Atlanta for 1877* (Atlanta: A. E. Sholes, 1877), p. 38; *Atlanta Constitution,* April 9, 1901, p. 9; *Dau's Atlanta Blue Book, 1907* (New York: Dau Publishing Co., 1907); Franklin M. Garrett, *Atlanta and Environs: A Chronicle of Its People and Events,* 3 vols. (Athens: University of Georgia Press, 1969), 2:341–42, 547, 685.

38. E[dward Y[oung] Clarke, *Atlanta Illustrated* (Atlanta: James P. Harrison and Co., 1881), p. 129; George Campell, *White and Black: The Outcome of a Visit to the United States* (London: Chatto and Windus, 1879), p. 369; *Atlanta Constitution,* June 26, 1877, p. 1; March 2, 1879, p. 2; September 11, 1875, p. 8; Edward King, *The Southern States of North America* (London: Blackie and Son, 1875), p. 350; Henry Latham, *Black and White* (London: Macmillan and Co., 1867), p. 130.

39. John Higham, "Social Discrimination Against Jews in America, 1830–1930" *PAJHS,* (September 1957): 8–14.

40. Garrett, *Atlanta and Environs,* 2: 60–61, 136–45; *Atlanta Constitution,* July 3, 1892, p. 5; Piedmont Driving Club, *By-Laws and Rules of the Piedmont Driving Club* (Atlanta: Franklin Printing and Publishing Co., 1899); idem, *By-Laws and Rules of the Piedmont Driving Club* (Atlanta: Bennett Printing House, 1903); *Dau's Atlanta Blue Book, 1907.* Massell, whose Russian grandparents had settled in Atlanta prior to 1900, declined to join and ended the eight-decade-long tradition whereby every Mayor of Atlanta had belonged to the club. Eli N. Evans, *The Provincials: A Personal History of Jews in the South* (New York: Atheneum, 1973), p. 285.

41. Higham suggests that social exclusion touched Jews in the South and West less than those elsewhere. While a definitive judgment must await additional local and regional studies, the findings for Atlanta tend to confirm his hypothesis. "Social Discrimination," pp. 23–26.

42. W[ilber] J. Cash, *The Mind of the South* (New York: Alfred A. Knopf, 1941), pp. 333–34; Benjamin Kendrick, "The Study of the New South," *North Carolina Historical Review* 3 (January 1926): 11.

43. *Atlanta Constitution,* September 25, 1870, p. 2; September 24, 1871, p. 3; October 9, 1878, p. 4; September 23, 1881, p. 7; *Atlanta Daily New Era,* November 25, 1871, p. 4; *American Israelite,* July 10, 1885, p. 4. See also *Atlanta Constitution,* October 5, 1870, p. 3; January 4, 1871, p. 4; September 18, 1877, p. 4; and *Atlanta Daily Sun,* September 15, 1871, p. 4.

44. *Atlanta Constitution,* September 25, 1870, p. 2; January 4, 1871, p. 2; April 3, 1877, p. 4; October 9, 1878, p. 4; October 1, 1886, p. 5; *Jewish South,* April 18, 1879, p. 1; May 16, 1879, p. 1. A further sign of amity was the frequent presence of local and state dignitaries at Jewish cornerstone-layings, dedications, funerals, fairs, and bazaars. Georgia's two senators, Atlanta's mayor and congressman, and prominent civic leaders participated in the Temple service which commemorated the one hundredth birthday of Sir Moses Montefiore. Strangely, the choir sang "Nearer My God to Thee." *Atlanta Constitution,* October 24, 1884, p. 5.

45. *Atlanta Constitution,* September 18, 1896, p. 7; October 2, 1894, p. 8; October 13, 1907, p. 5C; May 18, 1903, p. 5.

46. Bobby E. Adams, "Analysis of a Relationship: Jews and Southern Baptists" (Th.D. dissertation, Southwestern Baptist Theological Seminary, 1969), p. 98.

47. *Atlanta Daily Intelligencer,* January 13, 1860, p. 2; January 25, 1860, p. 3; *Proceedings of the Southern Baptist Convention . . . 1867* (Baltimore: John F. Weishampel, Jr., 1867), p. 19; *Proceedings of the Eighteenth Meeting of the Southern Baptist Convention* (Louisville: Bradley and Gilbert, 1873), pp. 19–20, 35–36; *Proceedings of the Twenty-Seventh Annual Session of the Southern Baptist Convention* (Atlanta: Jas. P. Harrison, 1882), p. 16; *Atlanta Constitution,* May 24, 1873, p. 3; June 6, 1874, p. 4; July 19, 1897, p. 6. Like most other American "rabbis" in the early seventies, Jaeger had never received ordination. For more on his background, see *Israelite,* July 12, 1872, p. 8; Abraham Jaeger, *Mind and Heart in Religion or, Judaism and Christianity* (Chicago: Goodspeed's Publishing House, 1873), pp. 2, 14–16.

48. *Atlanta Constitution,* August 3, 1902, p. 4; December 5, 1904, p. 5; June 19, 1905, p. 6; February 5, 1905, p. 4; April 20, 1911, p. 7; April 24, 1911, p. 2; June 2, 1912, p. 13M; *Atlanta City Directory* (Atlanta: Atlanta City Directory Co., 1913–16), 1913, p. 485; 1914, pp. 1002, 1084; 1915, p. 235; 1916, p. 1044.

49. HBC Minutes, January 14, 1914; Jewish Educational Alliance Minutes, August 7, 1912; June 2, 1913; Rabbi Marx's Record of Conversions, 1898–1944, in Marx Papers, The Temple.

50. Higham, "Social Discrimination," pp. 4–5; Oscar Handlin, "American Views of the Jew at the Opening of the Twentieth Century," *PAJHS* 40 (June 1951): 331–34, 342–44.

51. *Atlanta Daily Herald,* May 25, 1875, p. 3; *Atlanta Constitution,* September 19, 1879, p. 4; February 12, 1886, p. 4; May 7, 1893, p. 10; September 29, 1897, p. 4.

52. *Atlanta Constitution,* July 14, 1876, p. 2; August 28, 1879, p. 2; April 10, 1886, p. 7.

53. Ibid., January 22, 1906, p. 4; January 7, 1912, p. 7B.

54. *Jewish Sentiment,* November 26, 1897, p. 1; September 8, 1899, p. 3; Lucian Lamar Knight, *Reminiscences of Famous Georgians,* 2 vols. (Atlanta: Franklin Turner, 1907), 1:512; Gibson, "Anti-Negro Riots," p. 1458.

55. *Atlanta Constitution,* January 24, 1878, p. 4; May 18, 1888, p. 7; July 23, 1891, p. 3; January 24, 1896, p. 10; April 1, 1898, p. 10; July 7, 1899, p. 5; August 5, 1899, p. 6; May 8, 1899, p. 7.

56. Ibid., June 1, 1902, p. 12; April 12, 1914, p. 8A; January 16, 1907, p. 7; March 12, 1909, p. 1; August 26, 1915, p. 8.

57. Ibid., January 16, 1907, p. 7; September 16, 1913, p. 6.

58. *Atlanta Georgian,* May 28, 1913, p. 3.

59. *Jewish Sentiment,* February 4, 1898, p. 3; October 5, 1900, p. 3.

60. Marx protested to the warden, but receiving no satisfaction, communicated with Simon Wolf, who successfully intervened with the U.S. Attorney General and the Superintendent of Prisons. Myer Cohen to David Marx, September 23, 1914, in Marx Papers, the Temple.

62. *Atlanta Constitution,* May 19, 1876, p. 2; September 25, 1904, p. 8; April 21, 1912, p. 2F; May 4, 1913, p. 3G; March 8, 1914, p. 12B; February 3, 1913, p. 7; January 1, 1915, p. 14.

63. *Proceedings of B'nai B'rith District Grand Lodge No. 5, 1910* (Richmond: Herbert T. Ezekiel, 1910), p. 38; HBC Minutes, January 14, 1914; *Jewish Outlook* (Atlanta), April 1913, p. 23.

64. *Atlanta Constitution,* September 25, 1870, p. 2.

## *8 · Jews and Blacks*

1. Notable exceptions to this neglect are Bertram W. Korn, "Jews and Negro Slavery in the Old South, 1789–1865," *Publication of the American Jewish Historical Society* 50 (March 1961): 151–201 (hereafter cited as *PAJHS*); Philip S. Foner, "Jewish-Black Relations in the Opening Years of the Twentieth Century," *Phylon* 36 (December 1975): 359–67; Hasia R. Diner, *In the Almost Promised Land: Jewish Leaders and Blacks, 1915–1935* (Westport, Conn.: Greenwood Press, 1977); and Arnold Shankman, "Friend or Foe: Southern Afro-Americans View the Jew, 1880–1935" (paper delivered at Conference on the History of Southern Jewry, Richmond, Va., October 25, 1976).

2. David Marx, "History of the Jews of Atlanta" *Reform Advocate,* November 4,

1911 (Special Edition), p. 17; U.S. Census Slave Schedules, De Kalb County, Georgia, 1850; Ira Rosenwailke, "The Jewish Population of the United States as Estimated from the Census of 1820," *American Jewish Historical Quarterly* 53 (December 1963): 147 (hereafter cited as *AJHQ*); Levi Cohen's receipts for slaves dated February 29, 1862, August 1, 1863, and October 3, 1864, American Jewish Archives; *Atlanta Daily Intelligencer,* September 28, 1862, p. 2; November 12, 1862, p. 4.

3. Thomas D. Clark, "The Post-Civil War Economy in the South," *AJHQ* 55 (June 1966): 430; E. Merton Coulter, *A History of the South, The South During Reconstruction, 1865–1877,* vol. 8, (Baton Rouge: Louisiana State University Press, 1947), p. 202; Eli N. Evans, *The Provincials: A Personal History of Jews in the South* (New York: Atheneum, 1973), p. 312.

4. *Atlanta Independent,* October 22, 1910, p. 3; November 1, 1913, p. 8; *Atlanta Constitution,* May 4, 1898.

5. Charles Greenberg, Unpublished Autobiography, [1942], pp. 38–41, in possession of Mrs. David Eisenberg, Atlanta.

6. David Davis [Yampolsky], *The Passing Years: Memories of Two Worlds* (Tel Aviv, Israel: New Life Press, 1974), pp. 32–38, 84; Greenberg, Autobiography, pp. 43–45; Harry Golden, *Forgotten Pioneer* (Cleveland: World Publishing Co., 1963), pp. 68–73.

7. Greenberg, Autobiography, pp. 51–53. Jewish grocers were common in Negro neighborhoods throughout the South. See Howard N. Rabinowitz, "The Search for Social Control: Race Relations in the Urban South, 1865–1890" (Ph.D. dissertation, University of Chicago, 1973), pp. 69, 95–97.

8. W. O. Murphy, "The Negro Grocer"; and Hattie G. Escridge, "The Need for Negro Merchants," both in W. E. Burghardt DuBois, ed., *The Negro in Business,* Atlanta University Publications No. 4 (Atlanta: Atlanta University Press, 1899), pp. 61, 64–65.

9. Dubrovsky, "I. J. Schwartz's *Kentucky,*" pp. 249–50.

10. *Atlanta Constitution,* January 22, 1906, p. 4.

11. Ibid., September 9, 1896, p. 7; November 5, 1897, p. 5; October 4, 1906, p. 3; November 4, 1906, p. 1; *Atlanta Independent,* November 12, 1904, p. 5; Thomas Gibson, "The Anti-Negro Riots in Atlanta," *Harper's Weekly* 50, (October 13, 1906): p. 1457–58.

12. Interviews in Atlanta with Solomon J. Gold, December 19, 1971; David Davis, August 9, 1973; H. Taratoot, March 11, 1973; H. C. Hamilton, March 21, 1973; Mrs. Homer Nash, March 20, 1973; and Mrs. Josephine D. Murphy, March 23, 1973.

13. *Atlanta Constitution,* July 31, 1900, p. 12.

14. Ibid., April 4, 1898, p. 10; July 26, 1902, p. 9. Greenblatt was acquitted of the charge of murder.

15. Ibid., October 18, 1903, p. 5; July 29, 1907, p. 3; March 1, 1908, p. 1; March 24, 1908, p. 9. The Jewish community offered a $300 reward for the apprehension of Hirsowitz's killers, at least one of whom was later caught.

16. Ibid., March 23, 1912, pp. 1, 12; March 30, 1912, p. 1; The *Constitution* initiated a campaign which netted over $2000 (mostly from other Jews) for Morris's family.

17. Ibid., January 17, 1900, p. 10; February 15, 1912, p. 11; January 3, 1915, p. 1.

18. Interviews with Davis, Gold, and Taratoot; Greenberg, Autobiography, pp. 47, 53–60; Davis, *The Passing Years,* pp. 45–47, 57; Milton Himmelfarb, "Negroes, Jews and Muzhiks," *Commentary* 42 (October 1966): 83–86.

19. Horace Mann Bond, "Negro Attitudes Toward Jews," *Jewish Social Studies* 27

(January 1965): 3–4; Interview in Atlanta with Samuel Eplan, December 8, 1971; Charles Rubin, *The Log of Rubin The Sailor* (New York: International Publishers, 1973), p. 15.

20. *Jewish Sentiment* (Atlanta), June 5, 1896, p. 7; October 28, 1898, p. 3; November 18, 1898, p. 3; August 11, 1899, p. 3; March 26, 1899, p. 4; August 3, 1900, p. 3.

21. *Atlanta Constitution,* June 19, 1910, p. 3; October 10, 1906, p. 8; Janice O. Rothschild, *As But a Day: The First Hundred Years, 1867–1967* (Atlanta: The Hebrew Benevolent Congregation), p. 50.

22. Hebrew Benevolent Congregation Minutes, October 14, 1901 (hereafter cited as HBC); W. E. B. Du Bois, "The Opening of the Library," *Atlanta* 54 (April 3, 1902): 809–10.

22. Thomas Tally, *Negro Folk Rhymes* (New York: Macmillan, 1922), pp. 314–15; Harold Courlander, *Negro Folk Music USA* (New York: Columbia University Press, 1963), pp. 41–58; E[dward] A. McIlhenny, comp., *Befo' de War Spirituals* (Boston: Christopher Publishing House, 1933), pp. 44, 59, 77–78, 236; *Atlanta Constitution,* November 22, 1903, p. 8.

23. McIlhenny, *Befo' de War Spirituals,* pp. 38–39, 126; Richard Wright, *Black Boy: A Record of Childhood and Youth* (New York: Harper and Bros., 1945), pp. 53–54; *Atlanta Constitution,* March 23, 1875, p. 4; Bond, "Negro Attitudes Toward Jews," pp. 3–4.

24. Arnold Shankman, "Brothers Across the Sea: Afro-Americans and the Persecution of Russian Jews, 1881–1917," *Jewish Social Studies* 37 (1975): 114–21.

25. *Voice of the Negro* (Atlanta) 2 (October 1905): 675; 3 (July 1906): 546–47; *Atlanta Independent,* December 10, 1910, p. 4.

26. Louis R. Harlan, ed., *The Papers of Booker T. Washington,* vol. 3 (Urbana, Ill.: University of Illinois Press, 1974), pp. 584–85; *Voice of the Negro* 2 (September 1905): 594–96; *Atlanta Independent,* March 23, 1907, p. 4; June 19, 1909, p. 4.

27. *Atlanta Independent,* February 7, 1914, p. 4; July 12, 1913, p. 4; June 6, 1912, p. 4; *Voice of the Negro* 3 (January 1906): 20.

28. Robert L. Brafton, "The End of Immigration to the Cotton Fields," *Mississippi Valley Historical Quarterly* 50 (March 1964): 610; Arthur T. Abernethy, *The Jew A Negro: Being a Study of Jewish Ancestry from an Impartial Standpoint* (Moravia Falls, N.C.: Dixie Publishing Co., 1910); Harlan, *Washington Papers,* 3:408–12.

29. August Meier, *Negro Thought in America, 1880–1915* (Ann Arbor: University of Michigan Press, 1963), pp. 56–57, 100–118; Booker T. Washington, *The Future of the American Negro* (Boston: Small, Maynard and Co., 1902), pp. 182–83; idem, *Putting the Most into Life* (New York: Thomas Y. Crowell Co., 1906), p. 33; Harlan, *Washington Papers,* 3:408–409; Robert Factor, *The Black Response to America: Men, Ideals and Organization from Frederick Douglass to the NAACP* (Reading, Mass.: Addison-Wesley Publishing Co., 1970), p. 190; *New York Age,* July 2, 1914, p. 4; May 18, 1905, p. 2.

30. *Atlanta Independent,* February 7, 1914, p. 4; April 16, 1910, p. 4; June 12, 1915, p. 4; July 12, 1913, p. 4; September 20, 1913, p. 4; January 3, 1914, p. 4.

31. Meier, *Negro Thought,* pp. 190–206; *Crisis* 9 (October 1915): 235.

32. *Voice of the Negro* 1 (October 1904): 551–52; 3 (September 1906): 623–25; 3 (January 1906): 20.

33. *Atlanta Independent,* December 7, 1912, p. 4; Alfred O. Hero, *The Southerner and World Affairs* (Baton Rouge: Louisiana State University Press, 1965), p. 499.

34. *Atlanta Independent,* June 6, 1912, p. 4.

## 9 · The Leo Frank Case

1. Leonard Dinnerstein, *The Leo Frank Case* (New York: Columbia University Press, 1968), pp. vii–ix.

2. Harry Golden, *A Little Girl Is Dead* (Cleveland: World Publishing Co., 1965) pp. 7–8.

3. Ibid., pp. 10–12.

4. Leonard Dinnerstein, "Atlanta in the Progressive Era: A Dreyfus Affair in Georgia," in Frederick C. Jaher, ed., *The Age of Industrialism in America* (New York: Free Press, 1968), pp. 128–32.

5. Ibid., pp. 132–38.

6. Dinnerstein, *Leo Frank Case,* pp. 9–16, 34; Golden, *A Little Girl Is Dead,* p. 30.

7. Dinnerstein, *Leo Frank Case,* pp. 16–20, 28–32, 57–59, 84–87. Golden calls the solicitor-general an anti-Semite and suggests that his prejudice against Jews influenced his handling of the case. This is untrue. Regardless of his unscrupulous tactics and failure to condemn anti-Semitism, there is no evidence that Dorsey harbored any personal enmity toward Jews. Dorsey lectured at the Jewish Educational Alliance in early 1912, and when he ran for the solicitorship later that year, he received the endorsement of twelve Jewish attorneys. One of the partners in his law firm, Arthur Heyman, was also an active member of the Hebrew Benevolent Congregation. *A Little Girl Is Dead,* p. 179; *Atlanta Constitution,* March 20, 1912, p. 5; August 20, 1911, p. 11.

8. Dinnerstein, *Leo Frank Case,* pp. 36–54.

9. Ibid., pp. 55–56, 60; Dinnerstein, "Atlanta in the Progressive Era," p. 145; Golden, *A Little Girl Is Dead,* p. 227; C. P. Connolly, *The Truth About the Frank Case* (New York: Vail-Ballau, 1915), pp. 19–20.

10. *Macon Daily Telegraph,* August 27, 1913; and *Southern Ruralist* (Atlanta), undated clipping, both in Leo Frank Papers, American Jewish Archives in Cincinnati.

11. Dinnerstein, *Leo Frank Case,* pp. 77–91, 107–13.

12. Ibid., pp. 74–76, 90–93.

13. Ibid., p. 33; Golden, *A Little Girl Is Dead,* p. 183; L[uther] O. Bricker, "A Great American Tragedy," *Shane Quarterly* 4 (April 1943): 90.

14. *Atlanta Constitution,* May 31, 1913, p. 1; Golden, *A Little Girl Is Dead,* p. 183; Louis Marshall to Henry Cohen, December 9, 1914, Louis Marshall Papers, American Jewish Archives (The Louis Marshall Papers are quoted with the permission of James Marshall); Eugene Levy, " 'Is the Jew a White Man?'—Press Reaction to the Leo Frank Case, 1913–1915," *Phylon* 35 (June 1974): 212–22.

15. *Atlanta Independent,* March 21, 1914, p. 4; April 4, 1914, p. 4; *Atlanta Georgian,* August 7, 1913, p. 3.

16. Dinnerstein, *Leo Frank Case,* pp. 94–99; *Jeffersonian* (Thomson, Ga.), March 19, 1914, pp. 1, 8; December 3, 1914, pp. 8–9; *Atlanta Constitution,* January 3, 1915, p. 3.

17. Dinnerstein, *Leo Frank Case,* pp. 113–20; *Jeffersonian,* June 10, 1915, p. 3.

18. Dinnerstein, *Leo Frank Case,* pp. 122–29.

19. Ibid., pp. 129–35; *Jeffersonian,* July 22, 1915, pp. 2, 12; *American* (New Orleans), June 22, 1915, p. 1; June 24, 1915, p. 1.

20. Dinnerstein, *Leo Frank Case,* pp. 139–47.

21. Golden, *A Little Girl Is Dead,* p. 227.

22. *Atlanta Georgian,* April 30, 1913, p. 3; May 2, 1913, p. 1; *Atlanta Constitution,*

May 31, 1913, p. 1; August 16, 1913, p. 2; January 3, 1915, p. 3; Affidavits of Isaac J. Hazan and Morano Benbenisty, *State of Georgia* v. *Leo M. Frank.*

23. *American Jewish Review* (Atlanta), June 1914, p. 12; Interviews in Atlanta with David Davis (August 9, 1973), Sinclair Jacobs (February 23, 1973), Betsy Merlin (March 9, 1973), and Mr. and Mrs. Alfred Myers (February 19, 1973); Golden, *A Little Girl Is Dead,* p. 227; *Atlanta Constitution,* January 3, 1915, p. 3.

24. *American Jewish Review,* October 1913, pp. 2–4; March 1914, p. 18; May 1914, pp. 16–17; May 1915, p. 14.

25. Ibid., May 1914, p. 14; *Atlanta Constitution,* December 29, 1914, p. 3.

26. *American Jewish Review,* May 1914, p. 14.

27. FJC Minutes, October 31, 1915.

28. Golden, *A Little Girl Is Dead,* pp. 275–76. I asked Golden about his sources for this claim and was told that the information was garnered from interviews with survivors. Harry Golden to Steven Hertzberg, November 5, 1972. None of those I interviewed agreed with his description and David Davis, who read Golden's account, explicitly notes the exaggeration. Davis [Yampalsky], *The Passing Years: Memories of Two Worlds,* (Tel Aviv, Israel: New Life Press, 1974), p. 204; Josephine Joel, Diary, August 2, 1915, in possession of Josephine Heyman of Atlanta; *Philadelphia Public Ledger,* quoted in *Atlanta Constitution,* June 25, 1915, p. 8.

29. *Philadelphia Public Ledger,* quoted in *Atlanta Constitution,* June 25, 1915, p. 8; *American* (New Orleans), June 24, 1915, p. 1; *Jewish Tribune* (Portland, Ore.), quoted in *American Jewish Review,* January 1916, p. 5.

30. Both Loewus and Williamson received the Democratic endorsement because each indicated that he would run if the other was nominated. *Atlanta Constitution,* November 30, 1915, p. 14; December 1, 1915, pp. 3, 6–7; December 2, 1915, p. 1; *American Jewish Review,* December 1915, p. 4.

31. *New York Times,* December 6, 1915, p. 8; *Atlanta Constitution,* December 9, 1915, p. 6.

32. Pierre Van Paassen, *To Number Our Days* (New York: Charles Scribner's Sons), pp. 237–38; Dinnerstein, *Leo Frank Case,* pp. 158, 220; Golden, *A Little Girl Is Dead,* pp. 256–57.

33. Dinnerstein, *Leo Frank Case,* pp. 149–50, 156–60.

## *Appendix 1*

1. Hebrew Benevolent Congregation, Minutes, 1877–1915; Ledgers, 1869–1874, 1905–1908; and Membership Lists, 1878, 1895, and 1902, at the Temple, Atlanta. B'nai B'rith Gate City Lodge Question Book, 1870–1896, at Atlanta Historical Society; typed summary of Free Sons of Israel applications, 1877–1883, at the Temple.

2. U.S. Manuscript Census Schedules, Fulton County, Georgia, 1870 and 1880; William R. Hanleiter, comp., *Hanleiter's Atlanta City Directory for 1871* (Atlanta: William R. Hanleiter, 1871); A. E. Sholes, comp., *Sholes' Directory for the City of Atlanta for 1881* (Atlanta: A. E. Sholes, 1881). The directory canvass generally occurred during the autumn prior to the year of publication.

3. Atlanta Census of 1896, at Woodruff Library of Emory University; V. V. Bullock and F. A. Saunders, comps., *Atlanta City Directory for 1897* (Atlanta: Franklin Printing and Publishing Co., 1897); Congregation Ahavath Achim, Minutes, 1890–1895, and Membership List, 1900, at Congregation Ahavath Achim, Atlanta. While 2,281 Atlantans in 1910 were of Russian parentage (both native and foreign-born), Russian, Polish, and Lithuanian were the mother tongues of only 247, whereas

Yiddish and Hebrew were the mother tongues of 2,118 Atlantans. Since some of the Polish-speaking residents were natives of Germany and Austria-Hungary, and some of those who indicated Russian as their mother tongue were actually Jews, the proportion of Jews among the city's Russian population may be placed at over 85 percent in 1910 and perhaps as high as 95 percent before 1900. The 1896 census schedules and the naturalization papers filed by approximately 750 Russian-born Atlantans between 1883 and 1917 indicated fewer than two dozen adult Russian males who could not reasonably be identified as Jews. Judgments were based upon name, address, occupation, and—in the case of the naturalization records—signature (often in Yiddish) and sponsors (usually leaders of the Jewish community). Fulton County Superior Court, Declarations of Intention, 1878–1906, and Petitions for Naturalization, 1883–1906, in Office of the Clerk, Fulton County Courthouse; U.S. District Court for the Northern District of Georgia, Declarations of Intention and Petitions for Naturalization, 1893–1917, in Federal Records Center, East Point, Georgia.

4. Board of Delegates of American Israelites Questionnaire [1872], in BDAI Papers, American Jewish Historical Society, Waltham, Mass.; Board of Delegates of American Israelites and Union of American Hebrew Congregations, *Statistics of the Jews in the United States* (Philadelphia: Union of American Hebrew Congregations, 1880), p. 24; Cyrus Adler, "Atlanta," *Jewish Encyclopaedia* (New York and London: Funk and Wagnalls, 1901–06), 2:273. The 1872 estimate of 336 was derived by multiplying 58 families (1872 questionnaire) by an 1870 average of 5.8 Jews per household.

5. H. G. Saunders, comp., *Atlanta City Directory for 1891* (Atlanta: R. L. Polk and Co., 1891); *Atlanta City Directory for 1901* (Atlanta: Maloney Directory Co., 1901); *Atlanta City Directory, 1912* (Atlanta: Atlanta City Directory Co., 1911).

6. Oakland Cemetery Interment Records, 1853–1970, in Sexton's Office, Oakland Cemetery; Atlanta Board of Health, Death Certificates, 1887–1911, at Fulton County Bureau of Statistics. Members of the 1870 and 1880 cohorts were traced to 1900 and only the Russians in the 1896 enumeration were traced to 1911. By the twentieth century, the city directories indicated deaths and departures from the city.

7. Fulton County Tax Digests for 1880, 1890, 1896, 1900, and 1911, in Georgia Department of Archives and History, Atlanta. The 1870 digest could not be located.

8. For a fuller discussion of the problems entailed in working with this material, see Timothy J. Crimmins, "The Crystal Stair: A Study of the Effects of Class, Race and Ethnicity on Secondary Education in Atlanta, 1872–1925" (Ph.D. dissertation, Emory University, 1972), pp. 49–52.

9. For an introduction to the quantitative methodology employed here see Edward Shorter, *The Historian and the Computer: A Practical Guide* (Englewood Cliffs, N.J.: Prentice-Hall, 1971); Charles M. Dollar and Richard J. Jensen, *Historian's Guide to Statistics: Quantitative Analysis and Historical Research* (New York: Holt, Rinehart and Winston, 1971); Roderick Floud, *An Introduction to Quantitative Methods for Historians* (Princeton, N.J.: Princeton University Press, 1973).

10. Norman H. Nie, Dale H. Bent, and C. Hadlai Hull, *Statistical Package for the Social Sciences* (New York: McGraw-Hill Book Co., 1970).

11. Richard J. Hopkins, "Patterns of Persistence and Occupational Mobility in a Southern City: Atlanta, 1870–1920" (Ph.D. dissertation, Emory University, 1972), pp. 24–48.

12. Alba M. Edwards, *Alphabetical Index of Occupations by Industrial and Social-Economic Groups, 1937* (Washington, D.C.: Government Printing Office, 1937); U.S., Bureau of the Census, *Index to Occupations: Alphabetical and Classified* (Washington, D.C.: Government Printing Office, 1915). The occupational codes in the latter index were keyed to industrial classifications.

# Index

REFERENCES.

1 State House
2 City Hall
3 Medical College
4 Governors Mansion
5 Kimball House
6 U S Barracks
7 Gas Works
8 Union Depot
9 1st Baptist
10 2d Baptist

A Oglethorpe College
B Freedmans College
C Storrs Col School
D Summer Hill Col School
E W&A Rr Freight H. Office
F Georgia
G Macon
H West Point

BIRD'S-EYE VIEW OF ATLANTA, 1871